BEYOND
GLORY

W9-BNN-460

BEYOND
Medal of Honor Heroes

EXTRAORDINARY STORIES OF COURAGE

FROM WORLD WAR II TO VIETNAM

GLORY

in Their Own Words

LARRY SMITH

W. W. NORTON & COMPANY

New York · London

Copyright © 2003 by Larry Smith

All rights reserved
Printed in the United States of America
First published as a Norton paperback 2004

For information about permission to reproduce sections from this
book, write to Permissions, W. W. Norton & Company, Inc.,
500 Fifth Avenue, New York, NY 10110

Manufacturing by the Haddon Craftsmen, Inc.
Book design by Charlotte Staub
Production manager: Julia Druskin

Library of Congress Cataloguing-in-Publication Data

Smith, Larry
  Beyond glory : Medal of Honor heroes in their own words :
extraordinary stories of courage from World War II to Vietnam /
Larry Smith.
        p. cm.
  ISBN 0-393-05134-X (hardcover)
  1. Medal of Honor—Biography. 2. United States—Armed
Forces—Biography. 3. United States—Biography. 4. Oral history.
I. Title.
  UB433.S65 2003
  355'.0092'273—dc21   2003002214

ISBN 0-393-32562-8 pbk.

W. W. Norton & Company, Inc.
500 Fifth Avenue, New York, N.Y. 10110
www.wwnorton.com

W. W. Norton & Company Ltd.
Castle House, 75/76 Wells Street, London W1T 3QT

1 2 3 4 5 6 7 8 9 0

FOR
The Blonde Bombshell,
and Stacey, Jennifer,
and Stephen

CHARACTER ISOLATED BY A DEED

TO ENGROSS THE PRESENT AND DOMINATE MEMORY.

—W. B. Yeats,
"The Circus Animals' Desertion"

CONTENTS

INTRODUCTION

General H. Norman Schwarzkopf

U.S. Army, Retired

THE EXACT WORDS from the citation of a Medal of Honor recipient state: "For conspicuous gallantry and intrepidity, at the risk of life above and beyond the call of duty." Those last words are particularly meaningful: "above and beyond the call of duty."

Duty. Robert E. Lee used that word in explaining why he had to leave the Union Army and go into the Confederate Army. He said, "Duty is the sublimest word of them all." Lee was a graduate of the United States Military Academy at West Point, the institution I also attended. Its motto is "Duty, Honor, Country."

Over the years I've met many people who were heroes, and the interesting thing I've found about every single one of them, bar none, was that they did not think of themselves as heroes.

They would say things like "I couldn't leave my buddy out there. I couldn't do that." Or, someone would say, "Those bastards were shooting at us, and I was going to shoot back before one of my men got hurt." Or, "Shucks, sir, it was my duty."

They say beauty is in the eye of the beholder. Well, valor is also in the eye of the beholder. Not one of the people who hold the Medal of Honor said at the time he took action, "Well, I think I'm getting ready to carry out a heroic act." Absolutely not.

In the minds of every single one of them at that time was something like "Gosh, I've got to do it, because it's my duty to my country." Not even that. Rather, "It's my duty to my outfit." And not even that. "It's my duty to my buddy on my right, or my buddy on my left." That's what it was all about, as the stories in this volume will show. That's truly what it was all about.

And somebody else—the recipients probably don't even know to this day who—saw them do it. And said, "There's a hero." And truly the recipients of this great award, I am sure, even to this day would say, "Gosh, it was just my duty. It was just my job. It was just my buddy. It was just my outfit. I had to do it." And that's what makes them heroes in my mind.

The men who tell their stories in this book—indeed, all the recipients of the Medal of Honor—embody the sense of duty in its deepest form.

We thank them for doing their duty in serving their country.

PREFACE

THE UNITED STATES BEGAN its existence with virtually no decorations for military valor. The Founding Fathers distrusted the trappings of aristocracy and monarchy, given the kind of class system that had existed under the British. In 1792, however, George Washington created something called the Badge of Military Merit, shaped like a heart in purple cloth, but it was seldom awarded.

Indeed, it wasn't until the Civil War that Congress felt the need for additional recognition. An Iowa senator introduced a bill in December of 1861 "to promote the efficiency of the navy," authorizing among other things the award of a "medal of honor" to soldiers and sailors who displayed gallantry in action. President Abraham Lincoln signed the measure into law on December 21, 1861.

The Navy came up with the first medal; the Army followed soon after. The original award was intended for enlisted personnel and noncoms but then was extended to include officers. The first medals were awarded to six Union soldiers who tried to hijack a Confederate locomotive in 1862. By the time the war ended, 1,520 medals had been awarded. A typical award was to a soldier who captured an enemy flag on the battlefield. Lincoln also offered the medal to all those of a Union regiment, the 27th Maine Infantry, who were willing to reenlist. Because of a clerical error, all eight hundred men in the regiment were awarded the medal. These medals came to be revoked, as were those awarded to twenty-nine

officers and enlisted men who traveled with Lincoln's remains to
Illinois, as well as a medal that had been held by William F. Cody,
also known as Buffalo Bill, an Army scout. These actions were
taken in 1917 by a military commission that altogether rescinded
about a thousand medals. The only woman ever to receive the
medal, a Civil War doctor named Mary Walker, also saw her award
revoked, although it ultimately was reinstated in a measure signed
by Jimmy Carter in 1977.

Following the Civil War, 423 medals were awarded to soldiers,
many of them blacks, fighting Indians on the western frontier. Up
until the Spanish American War in 1898, the Navy had given 128
medals to sailors and marines, often for the rescue of someone who
had fallen overboard and who was in danger of drowning. It was so
freely given because it was the only medal we had.

Finally, during World War I, the Army created several new decorations to recognize varying degrees of accomplishment. Just
below the Medal of Honor came the Distinguished Service Cross
and then the Silver Star. In turn, the Navy created the Navy Cross
and the Silver Star. In 1932, Washington's Badge of Military Merit
was revived as the Purple Heart, awarded to those wounded or
killed in action.

The principal criteria for receiving the Medal of Honor have to do
with displaying "intrepidity" at the risk of life "above and beyond"
the call of duty in military action. The deed must be conspicuous,
with incontestable proof of performance. Despite these qualifica-
tions, the Congress in the 1920s awarded Medals of Honor to the
Arctic explorer Richard Byrd and the aviator Charles Lindbergh.

During and after World War I, the services awarded 123 Medals
of Honor, 32 to men killed in action. The most famous recipient was
Alvin York, the Tennessee Army sergeant who, unbelievably, killed
25 enemy, knocked out 35 machine-gun positions, and captured
132 prisoners in one day, October 8, 1918, just a month before
Armistice Day.

It was not until World War II that the Medal achieved the stature
it holds today. This was primarily because standards became more

stringent, review boards more demanding. Out of 13 million men serving in the war, only 433 received the Medal, and more than half of them were killed in action. In the Korean conflict, there were only 37 survivors out of 131 Medals awarded. And in Vietnam, 188 survived out of 238.

Although the correct name for the decoration is Medal of Honor, its surviving recipients are loosely banded in a group called the Congressional Medal of Honor Society. The word *Congressional* is employed to distinguish the Medal from any other of a similar name. The group was officially created by President Dwight D. Eisenhower on August 5, 1958. Its aim is to protect the Medal and the recipients from exploitation, preserve its dignity, help members in need, and foster patriotism and stimulate young people to be good citizens.

Since the Medal was established, it has been awarded to 82 African-Americans, 41 Hispanic-Americans, 32 Asian-Americans, 16 representatives of the Jewish faith, and 3,269 others.

Those who hold the Medal of Honor do not like to be called "winners." They feel that the actions for which they have been recognized have nothing to do with anything that might be interpreted as a contest. Therefore they are "recipients" to whom the Medal has been "awarded."

I became interested in writing this book when I interviewed nine Medal recipients—two veterans of World War II, three recognized for actions in the Korean conflict, and four from the Vietnam War— for an article that appeared in *Parade* magazine on July 2, 2000. I wanted to find out how they thought the Fourth of July should be observed.

I was impressed by the response to the article but, more than that, I was moved by the stories these men told. They were fascinating, but I couldn't begin to get the color and texture of those stories into the confines of a magazine article. Yet it was clear they would make an extraordinary book, even though my own background was quite different. I never served in the military, I took my children to Wash-

ington to protest against the Vietnam War, and I never in my life had
any illusions about the destructiveness and the carnage—and the
waste—of combat. But, as I listened to these men tell in their own
words what it was like, time and again I found myself choking up at
the sacrifice in their actions and the power of their words. I wanted
to know these guys. There wasn't much out there in print that truly
revealed who they were, what they were like. Too often the language
was toned down, the grammar was cleaned up, and the whole truth
of what took place was not told. These changes muted, I thought, the
reality of what these men had gone through. They were salty in their
speech, they were funny, they were bawdy, and many of them swore
like the troopers they were. So, I have kept their words as they spoke
them, brutally harsh though they are at times. War is not a pretty subject, and these are not Sunday school teachers. I felt that I understood them, and I felt that if I could get to them I could preserve their
stories for current and future generations.

Heroism and valor, as General Schwarzkopf points out, are
descriptives shaped in the eye of the beholder of such action. The
recipients of the Medal inhabit a realm beyond glory. As Nicky
Bacon says, they have humility and a certain nobleness. They never
sought recognition, yet it came to them, often inexplicably in set-
tings where men all around them were being slaughtered. Yet these
men survived.

What they witnessed was not in the least bit pretty: Mitchell
Paige and his machine-gun platoon on Guadalcanal, standing off a
regiment of screaming Japanese all night long; Vernon Baker and
his men at Castle Aghinolfi in Italy, calling for artillery against the
Germans, the artillerymen refusing to fire because they did not
believe a black outfit could have advanced that far behind enemy
lines; Jay Vargas, surrounded by the enemy in Vietnam, ordering his
men, in one of the book's most visceral sections, to throw enemy
bodies out of the graves in a cemetery in order to find shelter from
devastating shrapnel and gunfire. These things really happened;
they were not created by Hollywood in an age when so many things
feel hyped or manufactured.

Ours is an age in need of and in search of heroes. These men are the heart and soul of what distinguishes this country. Their stories underscore the meaning of genuine sacrifice. They remind us of our capacity to preserve our heritage and a world in which democracy can prevail. Freedom is not an abstraction for these men. As they are fond of saying, freedom isn't free.

The theme of this book turns on the sense of duty and service of these men to whom death in battle is an old familiar, men who have watched good friends die, men who have sent other men to their deaths because of their understanding of the need to serve their country.

A frequently asked question is: What do the recipients have in common? The answer is: beyond exceptional courage, not much. Many of those in the following pages grope for answers, but it would be hard to find a more disparate group of characters. They come from all walks of life, all our nationalities, varying income levels, different levels of education. The one quality I saw in them was this: They tend to be the type of men who look outward, who think of someone else before they think of themselves. Hence you get the answer: "I was only doing my duty."

For example, Joe Foss of Scottsdale, Arizona, was a star performer in the so-called Cactus Air Force that was instrumental in the survival of the American forces on the ground at Guadalcanal early in World War II. A Marine pilot, he became known as America's Ace of Aces after he shot down twenty-six enemy aircraft in a few months. He was on the cover of *Life* magazine, became a confidant of the famous, served two terms as governor of South Dakota, eventually became the first commissioner of the American Football League, and helped inspire the creation of the Super Bowl. He turned up on the cover of *Time* magazine in 1990 as president of the National Rifle Association.

More than one recipient has observed that many Americans do not know what the Medal of Honor is. Shaped as a five-pointed star suspended from a light blue ribbon, it got Foss in trouble at the Phoenix airport in February of 2002 as he was trying to board a plane for a flight to the U.S. Military Academy at West Point, where he was to give a talk. Security personnel made him remove his boots and tie and belt and hat three different times because they thought the Medal, with its five points, might pose as a weapon of some kind. "I wasn't upset for me," Foss, eighty-six at the time, said afterward. "I was upset for the Medal of Honor, that they just didn't know what it even was. It represents all of the guys who lost their lives— the guys who never came back. Everyone who put their lives on the line for their country. You're supposed to know what the Medal of Honor is." Foss died January 1, 2003.

Not all the recipients share the same feelings. For example, Charles Angelo Liteky, an Army chaplain, who was awarded the Medal for action in Vietnam on December 6, 1967, when he stood in the face of hostile fire to rescue more than twenty men, renounced his Medal July 29, 1986, in protest against United States policies in Central America. Liteky, whose personal story is not part of the book, left his Medal of Honor along with a letter to President Reagan in a brown paper bag at the base of the Wall, the Vietnam Memorial. (The Medal was picked up by the National Park Service and is now at the National Museum of American History in Washington.) He left the Army in 1971 and retired from the priesthood in 1975.

He became an active protester against the School of the Americas at Fort Benning, Georgia, which trains Latin American military officers. Litekey and other foes of the school charged that many of its graduates were responsible for massacres of peasants and human rights workers in Central and South America.

In June of 2000, when he was sixty-nine years old, Liteky was sentenced to two consecutive six-month terms in Lompoc Prison, California, and fined $10,000 for trespassing illegally in his protests at Benning. "I consider it an honor to be going to prison as a result of an act of conscience in response to a moral imperative that impelled and obligated me to speak for voices silenced by graduates of the School of the Americas," Liteky, who now lives in San Francisco, said at the time, "We're doing acts of civil disobedience in the tradition of our democracy."

Following the attacks at the World Trade Center and at the Pentagon on September 11, 2001, Liteky wrote President George W. Bush: "If there is an enemy here, it's violence. We need to protest and boycott violence because we eat, drink and sleep it in our country; we are entertained by it. If we don't stop, we're just going to join in an unending cycle of violence, like an escalator that keeps going up and up and up." Liteky described himself subsequently as "a nonviolent revolutionary."

Yet Liteky's actions have not incurred only derision or scorn. Paul Bucha, a West Pointer and past president of the Medal of Honor Society, who also holds the Medal (see chapter 13), said he respected the courage of Liteky's views. "It's difficult to be an iconoclast," Bucha said. "It's much easier to go along. Men like Liteky are people who should force us to pause and think. They should not be ostracized and criticized. They are entitled to their views, and perhaps if we listened, we'd be better off."

In July of 2002, when President Bush awarded a Medal of Honor posthumously to Special Forces Captain Humbert Roque (Rocky) Versace, a Vietnam prisoner of war executed by the enemy in 1965, the total number of recipients stood at 3,440. With 19 double recipients recorded, the total number of Medals awarded is 3,459, according to the Medal of Honor Society, whose stated goal is to cease to exist since that will mean there have been no more wars.

In September of 2002, the number of living recipients stood at 142. They are living history. They are dying off. Their stories are compelling. Here are 24 of them, in their own words.

—Larry Smith
Norwalk, Connecticut
November 2002

ACKNOWLEDGMENTS

IN AN ENTERPRISE such as this, the author is little more than the point man heading a patrol into unknown territory. Without the support of the platoon behind him, his chances of reaching his objective and making it back safely would be slight indeed. So it is with deep and abiding gratitude that I thank Walter Anderson, whose original idea turned out to be the inspiration for this book; Lee Kravitz and Lamar Graham, for keen advice and encouragement; my amazing wife, Dorothea, who kept the project on track; Dotson Rader, who kept bugging me; Marilyn vos Savant; Sara Brzowsky; Fran Carpentier; Nancy Crowley; Patti Vento; Michael O'Shea; Annemarie Palmer; Lyric Wallwork Winik and her husband, Jay; Miriam Lorentzen; Paul Maier, for shelter in Seattle; Jud Randall, an old pal; Carole Smith Strasser; Robert Garmendiz and Esteban Haigler, two computer geniuses; and the incomparable Lou Leventhal. Jack Scovil is an agent nonpareil, and Bob Weil at Norton is my kind of guy. And these stories could not have been told without the support of the Congressional Medal of Honor Society and Victoria Leslie, as well as strong support and direction from the Medal recipients Harvey Barnum, Paul Bucha, and Nicky Bacon. Bless them all.

And finally, a very special thanks to Eddie Adams, who donated his genius to this book and these men.

Part One

WORLD WAR II

THE "GOOD" WAR
World War II

Although World War II had commenced in Europe on September 1, 1939, when Germany invaded Poland, the war began for the United States when the Japanese, allies of the Third Reich, attacked Pearl Harbor on December 7, 1941. The Navy's John Finn, whose actions led to his being the first man to receive the Medal of Honor in that war, was there that day, at Kaneohe Bay, across the island of Oahu from Pearl. Daniel Inouye, then a student, was also on Pearl Harbor that morning, and Finn and Inouye are two of the six men whose stories are recounted in this section.

The United States' first major engagement with the Japanese on the ground occurred eight months after Pearl Harbor, when American forces invaded the island of Guadalcanal in the Solomons on August 7, 1942. The months-long battle was critical because the Solomons were the gateway to Australia and Guadalcanal was the site of an important landing strip called Henderson Field. Here the Marine Mitchell Paige led his machine-gun platoon in standing off a regiment of Japanese.

In the European Theater of action, the United States finally struck against Hitler and Germany on November 8, 1942, in North Africa, taking part in Allied landings in Algeria and French Morocco, followed by the invasion of Sicily on July 19, 1943. Walter Ehlers and his brother Roland took part in these campaigns and then shifted around to England to train for the invasion of Normandy. Lew Millett, the deserter, fought in Africa, Sicily, and major battles on the Italian mainland, before going on to teach bayonet fighting in Korea in 1950.

The battle for Italy was intense, and it lasted from September 3, 1943, to April 19, 1945, when the Germans finally surrendered the country. Key outfits in the campaign were Daniel Inouye's 442d Regimental Combat Team, the Go-For-Broke Nisei, and the Army's all-black 92d Division, which included a young lieutenant from Cheyenne, Wyoming, named Vernon Baker, who saw the dictator Benito Mussolini hanging by his heels in a public square on April 28, 1945, after Mussolini was slain by partisans.

Ten months after the first landing in Italy came the invasion of Normandy, where Ehlers and his brother landed early on D-Day, June 6, 1944. It was in the hedgerows of Normandy where Ehlers took part in the actions that led to his being awarded the Medal of Honor. Allied troops pushed eastward from there, fighting across France, Belgium, and into Germany, which finally surrendered on May 7, 1945.

The fighting had continued simultaneously all this time in the Pacific, and it was February 23, 1945, on the island of Iwo Jima, when Lieutenant Bill Barber and his men looked up and saw the American flag being raised atop Mount Suribachi. The bloody battle for Okinawa, where the noncombatant Desmond Doss saved the lives of so many soldiers, started two months afterward.

The Japanese did not capitulate until August 14, 1945, after atom bombs had been dropped on Hiroshima (August 6) and on Nagasaki (August 9).

ONE

Mitchell Paige

Marine Corps Machine Gunner
Guadalcanal, August–February 1942

*"You know, a lot of the Japanese could speak English, and,
when their assault on us began, this guy started screaming, 'Blood for the
emperor! Blood for the emperor!' And Stansberry, he was throwing
hand grenades and yelling back, 'Blood for Eleanor! Blood for
Eleanor!' [Eleanor Roosevelt, the wife of the president.]
Bad as it was, I couldn't help but laugh."*

Photo by Eddie Adams

Mitchell Paige, at eighty-four, at
his home in Palm Desert, California,
October 2002.

Mitchell Paige, third from left, received the Medal of Honor in Mount Martha, Victoria,
Australia, several months after the action on Guadalcanal, along with Major General A. A.
Vandegrift, far left, commander of the First Marine Division; Colonel Mike Edson, second
from left, and Sergeant John Basilone, who was to die during the invasion of Iwo Jima,
February 19, 1945.

IN FRONT OF a World War II museum in Eldred, Pennsylvania, ninety miles south of Buffalo, New York, stands a seven-foot statue of Platoon Sergeant Paige, cradling a 30-caliber machine gun, ready to fire. Paige, a persnickety lifelong collector, had just sent off a truckload of memorabilia to the museum the day I arrived at his home on the edge of a golf course in Palm Desert, California, and he was bushed. He had been so ill earlier in the year that he and his wife had said good-bye to each other.

When he decided, in July of 1936, to join the Marine Corps after graduating from high school in McKeesport in western Pennsylvania, young Mitch Paige walked to the recruiting station in Baltimore, a distance of almost two hundred miles. It was the middle of the Depression and there were few cars, but he did get a couple of rides with farmers for short distances. The rest of the way he walked, sleeping along the road at night.

"My mother packed a big old sack of food for me, sandwiches and apples and all that stuff, and I had a few dollars," Paige said. "There was hardly any traffic at all. And do you know the rascals sent me home because my birthday wasn't until the thirty-first of August? So I had to turn around and walk home. Then I walked back again a second time. I got there on the thirtieth, and they weighed me in and the doctor checked me and everything, and he says, 'Well, you're too light. You got to get a little weight on you.' So they made me eat bananas. They bought the bananas for me. I ate I don't know how many bananas, and drank I don't know how many gallons of water, but they kept weighing me as I was eating and drinking until I got up to one hundred and twenty. I was six feet tall then; now I'm five-ten. I can't figure it out. They say when you go past eighty, you go this way."

He started out in H Company, 2d Battalion, 5th Marines, did a tour of the Caribbean, went through the Panama Canal, and survived an explosion aboard ship when a five-inch gun blew up during gunnery practice. "I was still a new Marine, a boot. You were a boot for a long time in those days because we only had seventeen thousand

Marines and you had to wait until somebody died to get promoted. They were moving Marines all over the world in those days."

He put in for duty in China after seeing a notice on a bulletin board. The transfer was granted. "We got sent to Hawaii and, boy, I was really enjoying things because I'd never been away from McKeesport. I liked to just go off by myself because all the guys wanted to do was go ashore and get drunk and get tattooed and everything. I said, 'Hey, I like to see things and do things,' so I'd just have fun by myself. There was no way I'd get a tattoo because the D.I. says, If any of you guys get tattooed, I'll kill ya. You couldn't help but love the drill instructors, but they were the meanest, toughest, orneriest characters who ever lived."

Paige was stationed in China from 1937 well into 1940, when he came home on a thirty-day leave and then got sent to Cuba. "On February first, nineteen forty-one, we formed the First Marine Division. Last year we had our sixtieth anniversary."

After the war began at the end of 1941, Paige, now a sergeant in command of a machine-gun platoon, was sent to Guadalcanal in the Solomon Islands not far off the coast of Australia. United States forces had captured a key airstrip, which came to be called Henderson Field. While the Japanese held virtually everything else in the Solomons, possession of the airstrip was critical, and they fought ferociously to get it back.

"The jungles in Guadalcanal were worse than New Britain. It rained for days and days, weeks. It was a treacherous place: You're fighting snakes and swamps. My legs were all bandaged up from leeches when I came out.

"My machine-gun platoon probably killed more Japanese than any machine-gun platoon in the history of the Marine Corps, including World War I. I'd wager my life on it. How can I say that? Well, we killed over a thousand on October twenty-sixth, in one night, and we killed over five hundred a week later at a place called Koli Point, when the Japanese landed up there. My platoon was always out of our perimeter fighting the Japanese because I had fast-firing machine guns."

Paige explained: "I had fast-firing guns because, in Cuba, I stepped up the rate of fire from five hundred and fifty to thirteen hundred rounds a minute on my machine guns by drilling holes through the bolts and using a stronger driving spring, taking the back plate apart and using a triple-spring system. Captain Michael Mahoney, my company commander in Cuba, had all the machine guns in our company in my tent. We did this because I was literally destroying government property by drilling holes through the bolts and testing things." They were .30 caliber machine guns of World War I vintage.

"We kept to the premise that, when you fired a thousand yards, for instance, at a twenty-inch bull's-eye and you have your forty-two-pound machine gun set up on a fifty-one-pound tripod with a twenty-two-pound belt of ammunition sitting right there with sandbags all over it, when you pull the trigger, the machine gun goes like this: See, my finger's moving upward, but that's moving right now about four mils, that's twelve feet, and there's no man in the world that's twelve feet tall. So I told the captain, 'Well, if we fire fast enough, it'll be steady, and once we get on a target, you just pull the trigger, and that way we'll get more rounds into the target, whether it's the enemy or a paper bull's-eye.' So we developed that. And I named it myself the Mahoney System, for Captain Mahoney. He was killed at Guadalcanal.

"Everybody knew we had these guns, so when Chesty Puller* took his whole battalion and Colonel Herman H. Hanneken, the greatest jungle fighter who ever lived, took his whole battalion, my platoon was sent out ahead to find a high hill to give overhead fire as they went down through the canyons and everywhere else. We got orders that the Japanese were attacking Puller's outfit down at Henderson Field along the river. Our scouts had followed them and knew exactly where they were coming: One regiment was going to hit at the airfield and the other was going to hit from the west.

"See, our little perimeter ran around Henderson Field. That was

*Lewis Burwell "Chesty" Puller greatly distinguished himself as a Marine Corps officer and leader in World War II and at the Chosin Reservoir during the Korean conflict.

the prize. Both General MacArthur and Admiral Nimitz stated that the most valuable piece of real estate in all the Pacific Theater was Henderson Field. The reason it was so significant was that the Japanese had decided this was it. It was now or never. They had their whole fleet there. We could see it sailing back and forth in the channel, in the daytime, and they would throw those fourteen-inch rounds at us. You heard them go boom boom boom and pretty soon there'd be a whistle like a freight train through the air, and when they hit they were red hot, like a piece of charcoal. And we had enemy planes overhead all the time.

"And that Cactus Air Force of ours, bless them all, boy, I'll tell you they were really something. ['Cactus' was the code name for Guadalcanal.] I really admired those guys. We still have three living: Joe Foss, Bob Galer, and Jeffrey LeBlanc. Foss didn't come until late September. [Foss was to receive the Medal of Honor for shooting down twenty-six enemy aircraft, and other action. He died at eighty-seven on January 1, 2003.] The greatest fighter pilot in the history of the Marine Corps, I think, has to be Marion Carl. He got two Navy Crosses. And the reason I say that is because he was the only one that got the cream of the crop of the Japanese Air Force at Midway Island in June of forty-two, before we seized Guadalcanal. The Cactus Air Force fought off the Japanese from the air, making it possible for us to hold the island.

"Anyhow, we found ourselves in October fighting for this little island ninety miles long and thirty miles wide. The airstrip was all that mattered to us, and the Japanese controlled everything else. Water, air, everything. Major Odell Conoley, the commander of George Company who was with his men down over the crest of the hill, told me during the day, 'Just remember,' he says, 'I'm back over the hill, and you gotta hold this line. You have to hold this line. Otherwise they'll break through and go to the airport. And they got their ships out there, and they'll knock the dickens out of us. They'll isolate the division out here that was stretched all through the boonies to the jungle.' A little line around the airfield, that's all we had. And they'd have wiped out the whole First Marine Division."

Was he scared?

"I never gave it a thought. I was awarded the Medal of Honor for action on October twenty-sixth but really it was October twenty-fourth, twenty-fifth, and twenty-sixth. Here we were in enemy territory. We could be observed. The Japanese knew this terrain because right behind us was a straight shot right down to the beach road and they could come right in where their ships were sailing back and forth. It was dark, pitch-dark, and I had to pat the ground to find places for my machine guns. It was a little saddle, and Easy Company was supposed to be to my right flank and Fox Company that I was protecting would be to my left. They realized that if the enemy came, they would come up our way because they knew the terrain. It was the only way through. They would rush this little spot because they could see us from Mount Austen.

"We had four heavy machine guns and four light guns. The heavies had the fast firing. They didn't know we had fast-firing machine guns or anything. They could see a small group of people, our thirty-three machine gunners, that's all. I had forty-eight guys in my platoon when I started, but on October twenty-six, I had thirty-three, and thirty-three men held off a regiment.

"I strung a wire out in front of the line. I always carried a bag of burned C-ration cans, and I'd tie 'em on this line as a trip wire, put an empty cartridge in each can. I said, 'We cannot fire; we have to wait until they're right on top of us because, if we open fire too soon, they'll go back through the kunai grass into the jungle and call in artillery to knock us off this hill.' They had tried to do this during the night, but they weren't hitting us. It was raining when we got there and so dark you couldn't see anything.

"Anyhow, I got my machine guns in position for when they attacked. I knew the Japanese just loved to run a bayonet through you. I saw this in China on the streets of Shanghai. They just loved to impale you on a bayonet, and then shoot you. I don't know why. Mind you, these guys had already defeated the Americans in the Philippines and knocked everybody off all over the Far East. And they were big—these guys that we faced were two-hundred-pounders. They came right up to the edge of the jungle. They had little lights, and the guys thought they were fireflies. This one says, in a whispery voice, 'Mitch, Mitch, there's fireflies right down there.' I said, 'They're not fireflies. Those are squad leaders getting their men into position.' We whispered back and forth. Our guys were hardly breathing. You could hardly hear anybody. But I knew they were getting ready for the attack and, when the attack came, they came with fixed bayonets.

"And when they hit my line, they were like fifteen feet away, and my guns opened up. I couldn't describe it. Three guys were killed in Fox Company right behind me, you see, because they fired right through us, and those guys got up and ran. The company commander said, 'Run for your life!' That's why they never wrote the story of the battle.

"That's why they tried to hide it all those years, because they said it would kill the Marine Corps. Well, the captain was transferred to Tulagi. They got him out of there because somebody said, you know how the grapevine is, somebody said Sergeant Paige is going to shoot him on sight. But I never said anything like that. I did pick up a Springfield rifle and fired in the air. I said, 'Hold the line!' But all they had to do was go a few feet to get down over the hill, which many of them did, but they took off so fast they ran through Major Odell Conoley's position, and he grabbed the captain and sent him under arms to the regiment, arrested him, literally.

"It was unfortunate. I thought years later about what I would have done if I was back there. You know you can't shoot because you'd kill your own men in front of you. The noises, the screaming, the hollering, guys getting bayoneted and clobbered, and losing their limbs. Everybody in the platoon got it."

How did Paige survive? "God. God, and His guardian angel. It couldn't be anything else. The platoon was completely overrun at one point. I had to swing a gun around to fire at Conoley's position at one point, but he was a hundred yards down the hill. He telephoned in to the regiment to Major Sims and said that the Japanese had Paige's guns because the bullets were going over his head.

But that was me, firing at the enemy between him and me. Half my platoon died that night. The rest of them were wounded. We just fought them hand to hand all night long, with bayonets, pistols, clubs. Gaston, one of my men, killed one with his leg. The guy was whacking him with a Samurai sword. It was unbelievable. There's no way in the world I could tell the story, and I didn't. I didn't say anything to anybody."

Paige resumed: "Conoley and his men helped write my citation, apparently. But none of them could join our defense. When the Japanese overran me, there were just so many of them, and it was pitch-dark. Actually, I would literally, absolutely, positively run into them, and they didn't know whether I was Japanese or anybody else. They were just hollering, 'Banzai! Banzai! Banzai!' And all that and the screaming and hollering and flashes were all over the place, because mortars were landing all around us. That was Captain Lou Ditta; he was firing his mortars right in front of my position. I started with a pistol but that didn't last very long. In the pitch dark you see flashes, just for a second, and you can see this thing happening, you can see it's a man there. These Japanese ran their bayonets through one of our guys, and literally picked him up and threw him over their heads.

"I tell you the screaming and the hollering you couldn't describe, no way in the world could I describe the sound. You know, a lot of the Japanese could speak English, and, when their assault on us began, this guy started screaming, 'Blood for the emperor! Blood for the emperor!' And Stansberry, he was throwing hand grenades and yelling back, 'Blood for Eleanor! Blood for Eleanor!' Bad as it was, I couldn't help but laugh. He and I were just like brothers.

"There was this big Japanese, and, for some reason or other—it had to be God's will, had to be Providence—when I turned around, I'd already fired my revolver at this guy and dropped it because it was empty. I didn't have time to look for another, so I just dropped it. Now I only have a K-Bar, this knife. I had it in my belt, and for some reason I pulled that out and stuck my hand out and it was stiff and that Japanese bayonet went right through there, through my hand, and he went off balance. I didn't know what I was doing, I just automatically did that [gestures in a wide swing], trying to ward this thing off, and the K-Bar lodged in his neck. And then Gaston, who was warding off this other guy with the Samurai sword, he got pretty well whacked in his leg. But he was about two hundred and fifteen pounds, a powerful young guy, and he got that Japanese and just literally broke his neck, kicked him and killed him.

"A lot of this stuff I had to find out later on by questioning different people. But I ran back and forth, and when a gun wasn't firing, I'd fire the gun, and I guess the Japanese thought we had a lot more men than we did because I kept all the guns going. I'd just be running back and forth, and people were bringing ammo up. We had more casualties with guys bringing ammo up because they had to run across this flat area. I don't know how many casualties Fox Company and George Company had.

"At one point I ran back to the rear. I knew they had a machine gun there but they couldn't fire it, so I told them to pick up the gun, and I got the trail leg and we ran back to the line and way over to where Gaston was. Now, all these men are gone, they're all off the line, I'd been there for about two hours, by myself, running around. I didn't know this, but the riflemen knew this, because when men were pulled back they'd ask how many men have you got left up there? Just Platoon Sergeant Paige, that's all."

Why didn't some of the people with guns from the rifle company come up and support him? "That's what I always wanted to find out, all my lifetime."

It would be incorrect to say Paige fought off the entire attacking force by himself because a lot of his men were killing them too before they were killed or injured. And there were the mortars. Paige interjected, "That's why when the general gave me the Medal, I said, 'This belongs to thirty-three men, too.' And to this day I always talk this way."

Was a name given to the action? "No. They tried every way in the world to squelch that thing. They had little pieces of paper they sent out and said there was a skirmish somewhere but they couldn't find it. Yet they had thousands of dead Japanese, somebody told me. I didn't count, our men were pulling them by their legs down and all you had to do was take 'em off my little ridge and let 'em go and they'd slide right down the bank, because we lost a can of peaches there, and it went right down to the bottom, you know, it was that steep. Conoley said it was twenty-five hundred attacked my platoon. He said twenty-five hundred to three thousand. And he got a Navy Cross out of it.

"It was America's first and last major ground battle of the Pacific War," Paige said. "The Japanese never had a major attack after that. As one attack, see? They had fifteen hundred or even two thousand Japanese attack at Okinawa, and at Iwo Jima, but ours was considered two thousand five hundred to three thousand. But they don't write it. They left Guadalcanal out of my citation altogether in the rewrite. I never saw the first citation, nobody ever came up and questioned me or investigated me or anything. They had it written up at regiment before I even knew what was going on.

"When I went back to get that machine gun, it was right before daylight. It was still dark, the darkest time of the night is right before daylight. That was when I realized there was no more shooting around me. I was falling all over these guys, you know, stepping on them and everything else. I knew there had to be some commanding officer down the hill. And so I yelled at our guys down over our hill—I don't know why I did it, but I did—I said, 'I want all you guys to have fixed bayonets and when you see me disappear over the hill to the left, I want you to come charging after me with fixed bayonets.'

"And, sure as heck, as I started down they popped up out of the kunai grass, it was about this high, and the Japanese just came up, and I fired just one burst. They were so shocked they didn't know what was going on. They figured they were all Japanese up there because all these guys had gone up during the night. So I just had a burst, and this guy had a revolver in his hand. He had field glasses when I first saw him, and he immediately dropped them and pulled out his revolver and started firing at me. But I was bouncing, and I heard these pings. Two of 'em hit my helmet but he missed me otherwise.

"And just as I got to him, two feet from him, he threw his revolver down and reached for his Samurai sword. He got it out about this far, and I fired one burst. It just went right down like this, through his face, his shoulder and down here, hit the sword, just grazed the scabbard, put a dent in the sword. To make a long story short, it was a very famous sword. They had an interpreter in division headquarters, a Japanese, and they found out the sword was made in sixteen thirty-one. They said, 'My God, this was made by the master sword maker Muneshige in 1661, and they had a big story about it. So General Vandegrift [the commanding general of the First Marine Division] kept it." But eventually Paige got it back, after a reporter wrote a story about the incident.

In addition to being bayoneted in the hand, Paige said, "I got shot right through the pistol belt; I got a scar right here on my left side. In 1957, when I was in recruiting, I had this thing bothering me so I went to the sick bay and they took a piece of steel about the size of the end of my little finger out. I always felt something, you know, but it didn't bother me that much. I thought it was from my pack rubbing or something. But with my bayoneted finger, I didn't want the corpsman to report it; I was really scared to death that somebody would send me back to sick bay, and I'd lose my platoon. So the corpsman just lashed it up and promised me he would not make a report on it. And Captain Ditta was there. I said, 'Captain, you got to help me.' As a result you'll never see anything about it except in the original handwritten citation. Conoley or Ditta, one or the other, wrote, 'Wounded.' And then I pleaded with them not to put me in sick bay. As for the bullet wound, the corpsman looked at it and it was coagulating and he says, 'Good, let's let it alone.' But everybody wanted my pistol belt because it had a hole here and it had a hole there. It went right through, just like my helmet when the Japanese officer was shooting at me with the revolver as I was bouncing down the hill with the machine gun."

Paige took the sword and the revolver, which he gave to one of

his guys for a souvenir. "Then right before we went to Koli Point
an intelligence officer came. I had stacks of things I had taken off
what I thought were leaders: overlays, maps, plans, and all kinds of
stuff. They said enlisted men were not allowed to have swords. We
could get court-martialed if we had a camera. Can you imagine?
Yet, in the Army everybody carried a camera. I laugh about all these
things nowadays."

Paige's outfit left Guadalcanal for Australia near the end of January 1943. In Melbourne on May 21, "Deathless Paige," as they
now were calling him, received the Medal of Honor from General
Alexander A. Vandegrift, who himself was awarded the Medal for
action on Guadalcanal even though, as Paige said, "He never fired
a shot."

Paige was now a second lieutenant. Vandegrift wanted him to
stay two more years in the Pacific, which he did, serving on New
Britain and elsewhere. He had recurrences of malaria. "But I gave
the corpsmen instructions: I'll lay on the ground until I get over this
siege, and I did, many times. My men would watch me sweat and
shake, put blankets on me. It'd be one hundred degrees and I'd be
freezing to death, and my eyes would hurt, like a knife going into
my eyeballs and my spine. Those were my only symptoms.

"I came home and went on a bond tour, and had a bout of
malaria and they looked at my record and found I had one hundred
and eighteen recurrences over almost three years. So they shipped
me off to Oregon to a research hospital in the mountains behind
Klamath Falls. The Army had captured Rommel's medical train in
North Africa and, lo and behold, they had a medicine. The German
doctors were pretty sharp, and our doctors claimed the Germans
had the best medicine in the world for malaria. So they rushed it to
the States, and I became a guinea pig for SN7618. Today it's called
Chloraquil. I guinea-pigged that."

Paige eventually rose to the rank of colonel, and he was headed
for Yugoslavia following intensive study of Serbo-Croatian at the
Army Language School in Monterey, California, in 1958, when he

had a major heart attack. That meant a desk job, so he took the alternative, which was to retire, on July 1, 1964.

He became involved in research and development of miniature rockets and rocket weapon systems with a company in San Ramon, California. "King Hussein sent a man over. He wanted me to train his army in rocketry. And Prince somebody from Abu Dhabi sent an Arab who wined me and dined me. All these sheikhs are cousins, and they all have their individual armies. They all wanted me to equip their army and train them in rocketry." But his wife didn't want him to go. "I said, no way. I can't move to Abu Dhabi. I'm not moving. I've been roaming around long enough."

So he stayed close to home, becoming among other things the liaison officer from the Congressional Medal of Honor Society to the FBI, working to expose impostors claiming to hold the Medal. He said he had exposed more than five hundred such poseurs.

In 1975, at the vigorous encouragement of the actor Lee Marvin, Paige wrote his own story, *A Marine Named Mitch*, and in 2002 he was proud to see it on the current commandant's list of recommended reading for all Marines.

Paige met his first wife, Jan, in 1945. She died in 1977, after a critical illness. He met his second wife, Marilyn, on a trip for Marine veterans to Guadalcanal, Fiji, Tahiti, Australia, and New Zealand around that time. Marilyn lived near Palm Springs; he was in San Francisco. After Jan died, he and Marilyn got together. They married in 1981. Marilyn had four children from a previous marriage; he had two. They were quite pleased with fourteen grandchildren and five great-grandchildren.

Three years ago, Hasbro Toys told the Paiges they were going to make a GI doll of each service of a Medal of Honor man, and wanted to use Mitch Paige as the model. But Paige demurred. "I told them I'm no doll, and I'm not going to be a doll for anybody and besides that, I'm a Marine." But Marilyn insisted, "You got to do it," she told him. "Because it's not a doll. It's an action figure. And our kids today need some heroes besides movie stars and rock stars and people like that. They need some true historical figures, and they'll get the story of World War II." So he agreed, and the doll was made. Paige said Hasbro was supposed to have made a contribution to the Medal of Honor Society.

The Medal, of course, played a big role in his life. "It does in everybody's," he said. "Every recipient has got to be different because, you take a guy from a coal mine or steel mill or the farm, and he's awarded the Medal of Honor, his life changes immediately."

What do recipients have in common? "We're loyal Americans, Number One. Most of them are dependable. You can depend on them for anything. I think there's a feeling of unity in the society that no other group in the country has because you know that people expect a lot of things from you, and you'll make a concerted effort to abide by that, and honor it. And I always mention the fact that this doesn't belong to me. It belongs to thirty-three other guys, too. And then I can tell the story about that. I don't know how else to tell it because, after all, they were there and fought with me, but they didn't get anything but Purple Hearts. And half of them died. The last thing I ever thought about was a medal."

Editor's note: Mitchell Paige died in La Quinta, California, on November 15, 2003, at the age of eighty-five, of congestive heart failure. Services were held November 23 at Riverside National Cemetery, known as the Arlington of the Pacific, in Riverside, California. More than 1,000 people attended. "He was laid to rest with the greatest of honors," his wife, Marilyn, reported. "The Marine Corps Band was there, and they had a flyover. I suggested they call it a celebration, because he's with his precious Lord, and no longer suffering."

TWO

Walter D. Ehlers

Staff Sergeant, U.S. Army
The Battle for Normandy
June 10, 1944

*"Man, I'll tell you, until the first bullet is fired when you're
going into an assault, you have all kinds of things going on in your
stomach. You think you're going to throw up or something.
But once the first bullet's shot, all that stuff goes away."*

Walter Ehlers, eighty-three, at his home in
Buena Park, California, September 2002.

Walter Ehlers, left, and his brother Roland, four years older, stand with their mother,
Marie Magdalen, at their grandfather's farm while home on a thirty-day Thanksgiving
leave in Junction City, Kansas, in 1941. Walter was to lead a squad unscathed up and over
the sands of Omaha Beach, while Roland, known as Bud, would be killed two hours later,
in the second wave of the invasion, on June 6, 1944, when a German .88 hit his landing
craft. A third brother, Claus, served in the Pacific. Marie Ehlers lived to be ninety-six.

WALTER EHLERS had just settled back into an easy chair in the study of his modest home one morning in January of 2001 in Buena Park, California, and had begun to talk about the Normandy invasion when the phone rang. It was a colonel from the First Infantry Division, calling from Chicago. "No, nope. I have a good doctor," Ehlers told the colonel. "He takes care of me." Ehlers, eighty years old at the time, got off the phone, leaned back, and laughed. "He's calling to make sure I was still alive; somebody thought I had died or something. That was my division. It was the first they called me in a long time."

Staff Sergeant Ehlers and his squad of twelve green troopers rode to shore just about dead center of Omaha Beach in a Higgins assault boat at 8 A.M. on June 6, 1944, not long after the first wave of attacking Americans had been decimated. "I came in ahead of the second wave; the second wave came in on the LCIs, the Landing Craft Infantry, and the 18th Infantry was all on them. My brother came in the second wave. He was in K Company. I was in L Company, and I was on a headquarters ship because L Company had more people than they needed. They wanted more people on the beach immediately, and so my squad and I were taken off the ship onto a Higgins boat. We landed out there in the water and waded into shore amongst all the guys on the beach. We went around and up through them, and got up to the last row of wire. We had to have it blown." Crossing the beach through that hail of deadly fire, not one of them got so much as a scratch.

"The first wave suffered fifty percent casualties. The assault boats carried thirty people at the most. There was twelve in my squad and some other people. That's why I hit the beach an hour and a half or two hours ahead of my company, about eight or eight-thirty A.M. We circled around till we got more troops on other assault boats.

"They don't talk about it, but they put us on the assault boats because they wanted more people on the beach immediately because they were pinned down. I was what they called the 'Intermittent.'

"The whole attack took in sixty miles of beach. You never saw so many airplanes in the sky at one time. It was unbelievable. We saw ducks sinking in the water. Bombs had landed behind the lines, but they didn't land on Omaha Beach. There were no shell holes on the beach. It was mined all the way down to the edge. When our LCIs came in, a lot of them were knocked completely out of the water. If you've ever seen the opening of the movie *Saving Private Ryan*, well, the scene that you saw there in real life was about sixty times worse than the scene in the movie. It was just a mass of people; you couldn't believe it. Some companies were completely wiped out. When we headed in, we hit a sandbar before we got to the beach part. So the ramp goes down in the front, and we go out into water that's over the heads of the short guys. It went over the head of my second-in-command, I forget his name, but I had to drag him along." Ehlers, who was six feet one, and weighed 165 pounds, paused to laugh. "I got him so his feet touched the sand, and he could get his head above water, and we waded in.

"There were guys laying on the beach, bodies, guys hanging onto beach obstacles, and there were bullets coming around overhead. And the guys wanted to dig in on the beach, and they were trying to dig in, and I said, 'Come on, you got to go! We can't stop here. We got to keep going!'

"No one even got wounded running up the beach. There was a lot of firing going on and there was more people coming in, and I guess the Germans were distracted or something by the other elements. I was leading the squad. I always led my squad, I always had them follow me. Of course, I had all new men. They didn't know anything about fighting in combat. So we came through that, right in the middle of the beach. There was a pillbox in a valley over here on the side and then there was one right in front, and we came just to the left of that pillbox. I went through a lot of the guys who were pinned down or already killed on the beach.

"And there happened to be a beachmaster up there, and I said, 'Where do we go from here?' And he said, 'Just follow that passage made by guys that already cleared the mines, because if you go to the right or the left, you'll be in a minefield.' So I went straight up the pass. When I got up there, the last row of wire hadn't even been blown yet. We had two torpedo men, who were laying in a kind of defiladed area. Every time they moved, they'd be fired on by the Germans up in the trenches. So I said, 'We'll fire up into the trenches,' and we fired up there while they tried to move, and one of the guys got killed as soon as he stood up. But the other guy got the torpedo under the wire, and then he blew it, and we said, '*Adiós*,' and went up into the trenches. He used a bangalore, ten or twelve feet long, and blew the wire apart. We charged up a hill and then into the trench.

"The pillbox was over to our right, laying devastating fire. We saw a guy assaulting it. He was going to put a satchel charge into the pillbox breach, but he got killed by the Germans in the trenches before he got there. We captured a bunch of Germans in the trenches, and then we went and got the pillbox from behind. We took it out with rifles. We just attacked it and captured all the guys who were in there. There were no doors on it, and what few were there surrendered. A lot of them had already escaped. We sent four prisoners back down the beach.

"They had machine guns, and that's where they had the big 88 mm guns. Those pillboxes were eight and ten feet thick in some places. They're still intact. They made a house out of the one we assaulted. I don't know how many of us were killed that day, but there was a heck of a lot of them. [Two thousand American soldiers died in the landing on June 6.]

"Then we started going inland. My objective for D-Day was to go into Trevieres on a reconnaissance patrol, and we got into a fight right after we captured the pillbox. Then we went on in. Next day was when I first met up with the rest of the company. We didn't get to Trevieres for about two days.

"My brother Roland, we called him Bud, was killed on the second wave, with K Company. His whole squad was caught when the ramp went down. They all got wounded or killed. He was on the way down the ramp when he got hit; that's what I heard from other people in the squad. But he was apparently very seriously wounded, and he died on the beach that day. My mother got a telegram that he was wounded, and then she got another telegram later that he was killed in action, and it was on the same day.

"They just told me that he was missing in action, and I didn't find out until July the fourteenth that he was dead. His company commander came over and told me. That was a devastating moment in my life. We were very close." Roland Bud Ehlers, four years older than Walter, was buried on the beach. His body was brought home around 1948, and interred in the cemetery in Manhattan, Kansas, where the Ehlers family lived.

A third brother, Claus, fought in Pacific for three years as a machine gunner with the 24th Infantry Division. "His outfit saw more combat time than most Marine divisions over there. He fought on several different islands: New Guinea, Leyte, and in the Philippines. Claus has some real horror stories. He would never talk about it for a long time until he and I got talking about it once, but he would never talk about his role. There's only four of his friends from his old company who still get together. Most of them were killed. You stay in the war three years, you're lucky if you got any left that came in with you."

Walter joined the Army in November of 1940, a full year before Pearl Harbor. "I was born and raised in the state of Kansas. I was a farm boy, and nowadays I keep hearing people say, 'Well, a lot of farm boys got the Medal of Honor.' I don't know if that's true or not, but I do know a lot of city boys who got the Medal of Honor. The first thing I experienced was that to join the Army in Kansas under the age of twenty-one you had to have your parents' signature. When I confronted my mother and dad, my dad said he would sign, but my mother said, 'Son, I will sign on one condition: If you promise to be a Christian soldier.' She said that with tears in her eyes. I promised her that I would do my best. I carried that faith throughout my military career. It helped all the way through."

Walter was nineteen, and part of the reason he went was because Bud was going in. They enlisted at Fort Riley, Kansas, and were sent to Monterey, California. The United States military was so short of weaponry that the brothers trained with sticks. "When I first went into the military service, you had to be tough: If you hadn't been in jail, you never got promoted." The brothers were stationed at Fort Lewis, Washington, when Pearl Harbor was bombed. That action may have saved Walter's neck, because he and some friends were at 8,000 feet on Mt. Rainier, about to try skiing for the first time. "I looked down this mountain and said, 'How in the world are we going to get down on this pair of skis?' And then they announced on the radio that Pearl Harbor had been bombed, and all troops should return to their units immediately. So we took off our skis and went back down the mountain. I had no idea where we were going, and to this day I look back and say that's probably the first day of my life that was saved because of the Army. We were way up there."

By November of 1942 the Ehlers brothers were on their way to North Africa. They landed north of Casablanca on the Atlantic side, in French Morocco, with the 3d Infantry Division. "I saw my first man killed in my life landing on the beach. It was quite a trauma. I had been so seasick; you can't imagine how seasick a person can get. We were out on this Higgins boat that had a rounded front end; you had to jump over the side. I figured if one of those shells would just knock my head off, I'd be out of my misery. But as soon as I landed, the seasickness went away. When the shells are landing all around, you forget all about being sick. Later, in January of forty-three, we were the honor guard for President Roosevelt and the Casablanca Conference. Our company was standing on both sides of the street when Roosevelt was coming down in a car, and he says, 'These are mighty fine-looking troops. They'd make good replacements for the First Infantry Division.' That division had been badly mauled not long before.

"So we got transferred out immediately. Our first fight was at El Guettar, the biggest battle we fought. It went on for a whole day. The Germans kept trying to break through the lines. I was in the mortar section of our rifle company, and we had used up all our ammunition, so I was up on the front lines with the riflemen. I had a carbine because I was a mortar squad leader, and carried base plates and things like that. We were right up there shooting the Germans as they assaulted. They attacked us about three times that day. They just kept bringing troops up, and we kept killing them. There was over two hundred Germans killed on that hill that day. Our company was the first company in World War II to win a Presidential Unit Citation." Walter narrowly escaped injury when a forward observer called in the wrong coordinates, and the company was shelled by American artillery. "I gave up my carbine after that hill, and carried an M-1. That's what I got my Medal of Honor with." While the M-1 was relatively heavy, weighing about ten pounds, its bullet, a .30-06, had great stopping power. The rifle itself was extremely reliable. It fired an eight-shot clip.

Bud and Walter took part in the invasion of Sicily, landing at Gala, and fought the entire campaign with General George S. Patton. Bud was wounded. After Sicily, their outfit was put on a ship and sent around to England to start training for Normandy. "My brother Bud joined us later, probably around March. He was in the same company with me but when we got back to England the company commander called us in and said they had to separate us because they got an order . . . You know when the Sullivan brothers all got killed at the same time? They transferred me out of K Company to L.

"My new squad was supposed to be what they called the Goof-Off Squad, because they were guys who couldn't make muster all the time. They were just sloppy. And so I had to train them. The brass told us if we didn't pass inspection, we wouldn't get to go on leave. And so I told them, 'If we don't get to go on leave, there's going to be a heck of a lot of trouble going on here.' So they bore down, and we passed our first inspection, and the camp commander said it was the first time they ever passed. We had a guitarist, an accordion player, a violinist, and a boxer. Anyway, I got all the goldbrickers and musicians squared away so we could go on leave and, after that, they followed me everywhere I went.

"When we got a pass for the first time, we learned how much the

English had suffered. You never saw such devastation. Whole blocks of cities in rubble. We had a buzz bomb attack and went to a bomb shelter, sitting there, hearing the bombs overhead. We were just amazed. We were all scared stiff. When the raid was over, the people just went right on about their business. They had been doing this for three years.

"I got my Medal of Honor on the tenth of June in the hedgerows of Normandy in Goville. We landed on the sixth, seventh, and eighth, and we were fighting inland. On the morning of the ninth we were making an assault. Actually I had taken out a patrol the night before, and we had captured some Germans who had come through our lines. They didn't even know we were out there. We followed them and then one of their guys got wounded and dropped this satchel, and we found maps for their second and third line of defense. So the next few days we were following these defenses and hitting them on the ends. It was all hedgerows. They can vary, depending on how old they are, and some of those in Normandy were very old. They had dirt, and the trees had grown up on both sides of the mound. It was pretty good cover. We mostly attacked during the day; we'd start very early in the morning before they'd get up for breakfast.

"We'd go out by platoon, but my squad was leading. The platoon on our left got fired on, and we were out in this field. I said, 'Well, we can't be out here.' So we rushed forward to our hedgerow, which luckily didn't have any Germans on it. But they were firing from the other one. So we went down and started up the other one, and that's where we came in contact with a German patrol, and I killed all four of them. They were on the other side of the hedgerow, one of those thick hedgerows with a little path down between the trees. I got up into the middle of it, and here was this patrol coming down, so I shot them. Because I didn't have time to argue with them or capture them, which would have given away our position. Their machine gun was right up there in the corner of the hedgerow firing on our troops that were coming across the other field. There's square fields of hedgerows there.

"I attacked the machine gun and got it. There was three men on the gun. It was a .30 caliber. Then I followed up the hedgerow about a hundred yards and they had another line of defense, and there was another machine gun covering the field. I took the first machine gun out with my rifle. You didn't throw grenades because you didn't want to give away your position. Fortunately, they weren't trained enough apparently to know the difference between their fire and our fire, and that was to my advantage. So there was another machine-gun nest I came upon. There were four guys, firing across a field, and I took it out.

"Behind the second machine gun were three 80 mm German mortars. The shrubs on top of the hedgerow were smooth, and I was down below, and I had just knocked out this machine-gun nest and I heard something over there. So I ran up the bank, and here's all these Germans down there in these three mortar positions. So I started firing on them, and my squad came up and they started firing too. The Germans were just flabbergasted, and they started running. Well, we didn't want them to get away so we started shooting, and we killed most of them. There was about twelve or fifteen of them. They were horrified to see a man up there shooting point-blank, so they started running. They didn't even throw up their hands. They just started running, so we had to shoot them. We weren't going to fight them again.

"Then we went on down the hedgerow, and they had a backup down there, another machine-gun nest, and I knocked it out. So I took out three machine-gun nests and a mortar section in one morning's work.

"The next day we were on the assault again, and we got into what they call an unintended position. This time we decided we didn't want to get caught out in the middle of the field, but unbeknownst to us, their troops were across the field and down the hedgerow and across both hedgerows in front of us, sort of like a U shape, and they were going on the attack. Our company commander saw the predicament our squad was in, and he told us to withdraw. So I stood up and fired in a semicircle with my automatic rifleman to keep them pinned down while the rest of the squad withdrew. As soon as they withdrew he got hit, and I got hit as I was knocking out a machine gun they were putting into position down in the corner of the hedgerow.

"My rifleman was down, so I went and carried him back. He was shot in the back. I was hit in the back, too. The bullet went in my side, hit a rib, and went right out through the back of my pack." The medics were attending to the rifleman, putting him in the ambulance, when Ehlers suggested they take a look at him, as well. "So they turned me around and saw this hole in my trench shovel. After the bullet hit my rib it went into my pack, hit a bar of soap, which turned it straight through the back of the shovel. It went through the edge of my mother's picture. I still have the picture. They dressed my wound, and I refused to be medevacked at the time. That was crazy, but you know I was just out there doing my job." Ehlers says this quietly, as if he's talking about a trip to the store.

"But I didn't have to carry my pack anymore, because I had this big patch covering the hole where it went in and went out. I wore that patch for a long time—until I got wounded again. But I went right back into action. I don't know what they put in there. You know, when you first get wounded, it doesn't hurt. It hurts later. I just put my pack in the Jeep, and then I had my M-1 and my bandolier of ammunition around my shoulder. The bandolier held eight or ten clips, of eight shells each.

"We were the farthest troops inland. We held our ground there for two or three weeks, and they finally took us off the front lines. So we went back and got our showers and some clean clothes, and then they said Patton wanted the First Division to be with him when he made the breakthrough at St.-Lô. So we were only out of combat for two days. After the breakthrough, I got wounded again, in July. It was a bomb fragment and it went in very close to my testicles. We were where that Falaise Gap is, after St.-Lô. It was at night, and this airplane came over while we were on an advance march. I was laying in a gateway, and the squad was out in ditches on both sides of the road.

"I went up in the air when the bomb hit, and came down. It killed eight men in our platoon. A bunch of us were wounded." Ehlers was taken to a hospital in Cherbourg. The surgeon gave him a shot but didn't freeze the injured area deep enough. "I thought the guy was going to pull my gut out when he went after that piece of shrapnel. It went in my thigh and lodged up near my hipbone. He had one of these tweezers, a pointed probe like a scissors in reverse. It was about eight inches long, and I thought, 'My God, where's he going with that?' He pulled out a bunch of chewed-up meat with the piece of shrapnel. He would back off, then go in again, and he finally came out with it. First time he got hold of the shrapnel he had a piece of muscle with it, I told him I'd never let him operate on me again. He said that was the first piece of shrapnel he'd ever taken out of a GI. I said, 'I thought so.' He said, 'Can I keep it for a souvenir?' I said, 'Yes, you can, but don't ever do it again.'"

Ehlers and his squad fought on, across France, and into Germany. "We were out in the forest, and we were shelled during the night, the last part of October 1944, and I got a piece of shrapnel through this leg here and pieces in both shoulders. A big piece was sticking out of my leg, so I had to be medevacked to Paris, and I was in the hospital there and I couldn't walk. The nurse came down and told me they were going to send me to the MP ward because I wasn't walking, and they thought I was faking. I said you get that doctor in here. Tell him I want to see him right now. And he came in and I said, 'There's something the matter with the back of my leg because I cannot walk. Every time I try to step on it, it feels like my leg is being cut in two.' Well, another piece had gone in ahead of the piece that they had taken out. It was lodged on this tendon right here, my Achilles tendon, about halfway through it. I'd go to the bathroom, and I'd come into a heavy sweat before I could make it back to the bed."

Ehlers finally got that taken care of. He was on his way back to the front in December of 1944 when he read in the *Stars and Stripes*, the military newspaper, that he had been awarded the Medal of Honor. "I was on the train, and another fellow says, 'I'm reading here where your brother got the Medal of Honor.' I said, 'Yes, I'm reading that too.' But I didn't tell him it was me he was reading about because I had not got the Medal yet. I got off the train, and I was headed for the CP, the Command Post, when a colonel called me by my last name. I was in my fatigue uniform, and I didn't know any colonels. But this colonel knew me. He said, 'Sergeant Ehlers, what are you doing here?' I said, 'Well, sir, I'm reporting back to duty.' He says, 'Well, you're supposed to be back in the States getting the Medal of Honor from President Roosevelt.' And I said, 'Yes sir, I read about it in *Stars and Stripes.*'

"A couple of days later they had me come to a press conference, and I'm just standing there. Then the general told the people that he wanted to introduce me to them and what I did in Normandy and so forth. Me? The Medal of Honor? It was quite a sensation to the press corps there to meet a Medal of Honor guy. I didn't look like anything, a young kid with a helmet, no stripes, never decorated before. Major General Clarence R. Huebner promoted me after he introduced me to the press as having received the Medal of Honor—which I still hadn't received yet. He introduced me as Lieutenant Ehlers. After the press conference, we were coming out of there, he had his arm around my shoulder, and he said, 'Sergeant Ehlers, I'm going to promote you to second lieutenant.' I said, 'Well, sir, I don't think I qualify.' He said, 'You qualify.' I said, 'Yes, sir.'

"I had medals, but they were never presented because we were always in combat. So when I got my Medal of Honor, why, they found out that I had gotten the Silver Star in Germany, and then I got bronze stars in Africa and Sicily, and then I got a bronze star for D-Day for that action I did there, taking out that pillbox. Also the British Military Medal.

"I got the Silver Star in Germany before getting wounded for the fourth time. I got the Purple Heart three times. I could have had it four."

Once the German counterattack known as the Battle of the Bulge began, somebody came during the night and told him, "Lieutenant Ehlers, we have to get you out of here to get your Medal of

Honor before you get killed." Ehlers laughs. "I said, 'That's all right with me.' So they sent me back to Paris, and that's how I got it, from General John C. H. Lee. You know, he was the rear-echelon commander. We used to call him 'Jesus Christ Himself' because he was very strict about rear-echelon troops wearing proper uniform when they were back in Paris, and things like that. And I arrived in Paris in fatigues because I didn't own a uniform. They had to make one up for me. I was twenty-three when I got the Medal."

Finally, the sergeant, now Lieutenant Ehlers, went on thirty-day leave. He flew to Washington, D.C., took another plane to Topeka, and then a smaller plane to Manhattan, Kansas, where his parents and a few people came to meet him. "I read the newspaper the next day. It said two hundred people were out there to meet me. I said, 'Man, where were they?' I only saw about fifteen or twenty. I got there December fourteenth, 1944." When his leave was up, he took a train to New York and told a taxi driver he wanted to go to Fort Totten. "My gosh, it was the first time I'd ever been in a city that big."

He took the *Queen Elizabeth* back to England, and from there went on to France and Belgium. He was shot once again, accidentally, by a soldier who had broken down his M-1 and was trying to get a jammed cartridge out of the barrel. "The bolt slipped out of his hand, fired the gun, and the slug went through the sergeant's leg, and into my leg, clear up to my hip. It's still there." The bullet has shifted once or twice since then but never really bothered him. He went to the hospital once more, then rejoined the outfit, except now he was in C Company. "I couldn't stay with my own company because of being an officer. When Germany surrendered, we were in Czechoslovakia."

Over four years of combat, did Ehlers ever think about the odds against him for survival? "I was concerned about it, but I never thought about getting killed. I didn't concentrate on that because you drive yourself nuts if you do that. I was more concerned about what I had to do until this war was over. I was scared when I went in. Man, I'll tell you, until the first bullet is fired when you're going into an assault, until that first bullet's fired, you have all kinds of things going on in your stomach. You think you're going to throw up or something. But once the first bullet's shot, all that stuff goes away. Now you got other things to worry about."

At Omaha Beach, he adds, "We came in right through the thick of it. A lot of guys didn't go through, and I just happened to be one of the lucky few. I don't know, I never thought about death. I was always worried about my men," he laughs, "and what was going on around me."

He got out in October of 1945. "I was in the Army five years and ten days." Discharged at Fort Leavenworth, he went home to Manhattan, Kansas, and went to work for the Veterans' Administration in January. Then he contracted scarlatina, was quarantined for three weeks, quit his job, and took some courses at Kansas State. "They had eight hundred students in a class, and I couldn't even get a word in edgewise. My first test I got back I got a B-plus, and the next one I said I'm going to get an A. So I worked real hard on it, and I got an F, so I said, 'These people don't know what they're doing,' so I quit. I decided I wanted to see more of the country. I wasn't ready to be tied down yet, after I'd spent most of my time in military service out in the field. I never slept in a bed in Europe, except when I got to England. It was always a sleeping bag or in a trench, something like that."

Ehlers hooked up with an Army buddy, and they went east, to North Carolina, Washington, D.C., and Maryland, then went home for a time, and eventually moved on to California in a light blue 1941 Dodge. "When we got to L.A. I didn't find a job right away, and I never wanted to draw an unemployment check. Since I'd worked at the Veterans', I went up there and asked if they'd hire me back, and they said sure they would. So I hired on as a GF-7, which is not too bad of a grade when you don't have an education. I worked for them for thirty years. I retired in February of 1980 and then worked for the Disabled American Veterans for another eight years, and then I retired again."

He had met his wife-to-be, a girl named Dorothy, from Long Beach, on the ice rink at Paramount, where he was a skating guard, in 1953. They got married in March of 1955 and had three chldren. "They're all doing good. I got eleven grandchildren. It's fun."

In the early 1950s, Ehlers also met the director John Ford, who had filmed the Normandy invasion, at a meeting of the Motion Picture Chapter of the Purple Heart Organization. Walter was a handsome man, and Ford went on to cast him as a cadet in the film *The Long Gray Line*, starring Tyrone Power and Maureen O'Hara. Ehlers went on location at West Point for six weeks, for which he was paid $250 a week. "It was the most money I ever made in my life." Although he appeared in several scenes, he had only one line to speak.

What other bearing did the Medal have in the years to come? "It probably changed my life, no doubt about it. But then, like I tell most people, I live life one day at a time, and what happens, happens. And that just happened to be a part of it. I didn't do any great big planning about my career—except I never wanted to be unemployed.

"When I came home, I never used the Medal at any time, except when I went to the inaugurations of the Presidents. They always invite the Medal of Honor recipients. I went to about every inauguration from Truman to now. I went to the one for Bush, but I didn't go to Clinton's because I wasn't a Clinton man. In 1994, on the fiftieth anniversary of the invasion, I went to France and gave the main address at Omaha. There was a French liberation ceremony on the beach that day, and I come marching in with the troops, and then they marched me up. There was a microphone out in the middle of the field, and of course I had a general escorting me."

Walter chortles at the memory. "It was pretty nice. And I'm standing out here in the middle of this field and I'm giving the address that day for the First Division; they had another guy, from the 29th Division, I think it was, but I gave the first speech. I got tremendous applause and accolades. Anyway, Clinton was in the audience that day, and I talked to him down on the beach."

Here are some of the words Walter Ehlers spoke on the beach at Normandy that day, June 6, 1994:

Good morning. What a peaceful, pleasant place this is today. How different it is from fifty years ago when many of you and thousands of our comrades approached this shore.

What was it like on D-Day? That is the question most asked of veterans who were here then. We will surely all agree that it was the longest day of our lives.

We prepared for D-Day in England. I was not new to battle, having survived the North Africa and Sicily invasions where my brother and I had fought side by side. Still, I remember my amazement when we came into the Southhampton area prior to our embarkation. Rows and rows of tanks, artillery guns, trucks, Jeeps, armored personnel carriers, and warehouses of logistical supplies lined England's lush fields. The harbors were so filled with boats that we could have walked their length stepping from craft to craft. I suddenly appreciated the United States' support of the war effort. We were the men on the front line, but the hard work of our mothers and fathers, sisters and brothers still at home made this tremendous military operation possible. We came on our feet, but we brought their hearts—and prayers—with us.

A final battalion briefing readied us for the invasion. My brother and I had been assigned to different companies, and as the briefing ended we waved to each other. We would make the landing from separate ships.

Two days later, when the ship I was on pulled out, we certainly were not alone. There were ships in front of us and to each side of us for as far as the eye could see. By the time we were partway across, the ships behind us seemed not to end. We looked skyward where planes from horizon to horizon headed toward Europe.

When we got near the beaches, battleships and cruisers were firing toward shore. We could hear bombs exploding in the distance. There was such firepower from the ships and planes that we didn't expect much resistance on the beach. I believe a lot of us wondered how anyone on shore could survive the onslaught of that massive firepower.

My platoon boarded an assault craft to approach the beach. Luckily for us, the Germans were concentrating their firepower on the larger landing crafts. When we hit a sandbar, the ramp went down and, as soon as we left the boat, we were in water up to our armpits; for the shorter personnel it was deeper. We waded and scrambled toward shore.

We found men pinned down on the beach, many wounded or killed and many terrified, all surrounded by ruined and swamped landing craft. The dead and wounded soldiers, the wreckage, the ability of the enemy to cause so much damage, made us realize that this war—with its noise of mines detonating, airplanes' continuous roar, mortar and artillery shells bursting on the beach, rifle and machine-gun fire ripping holes in the sand and splashing in the water—this war was far from over.

However, D-Day turned the tide. Sadly, it was the end of the war for a great many brave men who died here that day. But it was also the beginning of the end of the war for Hitler.

The world changed on June 6, 1944, the day the good guys took charge again. It did not mean peace, but it marked the stand for freedom that would continue through the Korean War, the Vietnam conflict, the fall of the Berlin Wall, and the Allied containment of Iraq. The spirit of D-Day carried Allied momentum across the hedgerows of France, through the Ardennes and the Battle of the Bulge, and toward Berlin; it put new hope into the battle-weary troops in the Pacific.

While we braved these then-fortified beaches to beat back Hitler and to liberate Europe, to stop his massacres and to rescue his prisoners, we fought for much more than that. We fought to preserve what our forefathers had died for. We picked up our guns to protect our faith, to preserve our liberty.

Our purpose went well beyond aiding our allies as they faced the German blitz. It was to save our way of life, for our parents and siblings at home, for our children, and the children we hoped to have, and for their children.

It has been a way of life that was worth fighting for. We have enjoyed the longest period of world peace in modern history. We relish new spectrums of religious, racial, and political tolerance. We are free of the tyrannies of the likes of Hitler.

We must not forget, however, what this freedom cost. We earned that security with our sweat and our blood, some of us with our lives. Much of it was earned right here in Normandy. Many of those who enjoy freedom know little of its price.

This anniversary must be not only a remembrance, but a new beginning. Many of us still live with D-Day but never talk about it.

We need to talk about it, not for ourselves, but for those who weren't here; not to the media but to the heirs of our accomplishments, those we did it for. Our children and grandchildren and great-grandchildren must know the price of freedom. I pray that the price we paid on this beach will never be mortgaged, that my grandsons and granddaughters will never face the terror and horror that we faced here. But they must know that without freedom, there is no life, and that the things most worth living for may sometimes demand dying for.

Today, fifty years later, the beaches are quiet. We come back to mourn our losses, and to celebrate our success. Our presence here commemorates our and our comrades' lives, and it validates the sacrifices we all made on D-Day.

What was it like on D-Day?

That wave in Southhampton, England, was the last time I saw my brother. He died here, on Omaha Beach. That we can be here today proves that it was not in vain.

THREE

Daniel Inouye

442d Regimental Combat Team
Italy and France
April 21, 1945

*"My father just looked straight ahead, and I looked
straight ahead, and then he cleared his throat and said:
'America has been good to us. It has given me two jobs.
It has given you and your sisters and your brothers education.
We all love this country. Whatever you do, do not dishonor
your country. Remember: Never dishonor your family.
And if you must give your life, do so with honor.'
"I knew exactly what he meant. I said, 'Yes, sir. Good-bye.'"*

This "official" photograph of the senator from Hawaii was taken in 1993, when he was sixty-nine. Inouye and eighteen other members of the all-Japanese 442d had received Distinguished Service Crosses that were upgraded to Medals of Honor in ceremonies at the White House on June 21, 2000. By then, he had served nearly seven consecutive terms in the U.S. Senate.

Twenty-year-old Lieutenant Daniel Inouye of the 442d Regimental Combat Team stands with his favorite weapon, the .45 caliber Thompson submachine gun, on a roadway in Italy in spring 1945. While the Thompson was notorious for its inaccuracy over any significant distance, Inouye liked it because, he said, it was loud, and it had stopping power.

THE 442D REGIMENT, with spaces for 4,500 men, ended up engag-
ing 12,000 Japanese-Americans because of the turnover from death
and injury in combat. The combat soldiers in the 442d received, along
with seven Presidential Unit Citations, 19,000 decorations, including
9,400 Purple Hearts and 53 Distinguished Service Crosses, 19 of
which were upgraded to Medals of Honor fifty-five years later. Based
on size and length of service, the 442d was the most highly decorated
unit in the history of the American Army. Daniel Inouye, who has
been a U.S. senator from Hawaii for forty years, talked about his com-
bat service during an interview in his Washington office.

Inouye was a seventeen-year-old Honolulu high-school student
whose family was getting ready to go to church the morning the
Japanese bombed Pearl Harbor. The radio said the attack was
under way and that this was not a test. Inouye was allowed to go
outside with his father. They stood next to their home and watched
puffs of antiaircraft smoke. They saw smudge from a great fire and
the dive-bombers zooming up, flashing the red ball of the empire,
the rising sun, on the underside of their wings. Inouye was called
down to the Red Cross station where he had been teaching first aid.
There were so many injuries to treat that he did not return home
for five days.

Japanese-Americans in Hawaii, like the Inouyes, were thun-
derstruck because, as he later wrote in his autobiography, *Jour-
ney to Washington*, they had worked so hard. They had wanted
so desperately to be accepted, to be good Americans. Now, in a
few cataclysmic minutes, it was all undone. ". . . My people were
only a generation removed from the land that had spawned the
bombers and sent them to drop death on Hawaii." As he pedaled
along to the aid station, he looked up in the sky and screamed,
"You dirty Japs!"

Inouye's grandfather, Asakichi, traveled from Yokoyama, a village in the mountains of southern Japan, to Kauai, Hawaii, in 1899
to work in the sugar plantations in order to pay a $400 fine that had
been assessed to his father after a fire destroyed his own and two

neighboring homes. Asakichi signed a five-year contract for $10 a month, very good money. He took his wife, Moyo, and his only son, Hyotoro, who was to become Daniel's father. However, it took thirty years to pay off the debt. In that time, Daniel's father grew up and married Kame Imanaga, an orphan girl living in the home of a Methodist minister. They found a place to live on Queen Emma Street in the Japanese ghetto in Honolulu. A year later, September 7, 1924, their son Daniel was born. Had it not been for the house burning down in Yokoyama, Asakichi's grandson might very well have ended up in the Japanese army.

After Pearl Harbor, the Hawaiian Nisei, which simply means second-generation Japanese-American, were widely considered to be spies for Japan. They and the Japanese-Americans on the mainland were classified 4-C, which meant enemy alien. The guilt among Japanese-Americans was overwhelming. The National Guard units were disbanded, and weapons held by Japanese-Americans in ROTC and the Territorial Guard were confiscated. The following September, in 1942, Daniel Inouye graduated from high school and enrolled in the University of Hawaii, in pre-med.

"I considered myself a good American, patriotic like any other young man of my age," Inouye recalled. "I was a senior then. And then I was told that we were to be designated 4-C: enemy alien. It's either 1-A or 4-F or 4-C: Enemy alien—that's us. And that meant we could not be drafted. Our neighbors and friends were sensitive, and they understood, but I wanted, like thousands of my fellow Japanese-Americans, to demonstrate that we were just as good. So somebody started a petition movement, and I joined up and signed petitions to the President of the United States to give us an opportunity. And I remember the petition because it did not specify that. We said, 'We'll do anything you want us to do. Fight? You want us to do ditch digging? Labor battalion? We'll do anything you want.' Then, around January of forty-three, we got word that the President of the United States had issued an executive order establishing a twelve-hundred-man battalion, the 100th, made up mostly of men who had been drafted before December seventh of forty-one.

Within a few months, the 442d Regimental Combat Team, consisting of four battalions, was formed."

In the issuance of his presidential order, Inouye recalled, Franklin Roosevelt "used a phrase that meant a lot to the men of the regiment: 'Americanism is not and has never been a matter of race or color. Americanism is a matter of mind and heart.' I think it's an exact quote. And that's how we signed up."

The 100th was subsequently shipped to Wisconsin for basic training. Shortly afterward, the 442d was formed and sent to Camp Shelby in Hattiesburg, Mississippi. The 100th went overseas. "So they took part in the battles of Salerno, Anzio, Monte Cassino, and we joined up with them just about in time for Rome and the Arno campaign. They were in action about six months before we got there."

Because he was a pre-med student and employed at the medical aid station in Honolulu, young Daniel was left off the first roll call for those who had volunteered. Discovering the reason, he promptly quit the aid station and left the university and was called up shortly thereafter. "There were sixty-four of us who were in pre-med that I know of at the University of Hawaii. Sixty-four of us volunteered. And of that number not one became a doctor. They all got killed or injured."

The father, Hyotoro, accompanied the son, Daniel, on his way to the military pickup point: "He and I were in a streetcar. He took part of the day off. This was during wartime, so it was martial law, and under martial law men and women who were employed had to be at their jobs unless they were ill or if they got a written permit to be off. And so he got permission to take the morning off so he could accompany me to the place where you get on a truck.

"We rode the streetcar to that point just before we came to the stop. If you can imagine, from the time we left home, he never said a word. He was not a talkative fella. My father just looked straight ahead, and I looked straight ahead, and then he cleared his throat and said: 'America has been good to us. It has given me two jobs. It has given you and your sisters and your brothers education. We all love this country. Whatever you do, do not dishonor your country. Remember: Never dishonor your family. And if you must give your life, do so with honor.'

"I knew exactly what he meant. I said, 'Yes, sir. Good-bye.' "

The 442d consisted not only of Nisei from Hawaii but also mainland Japanese who had volunteered from internment (or concentration) camps that had been established in the United States. There were ten major camps, Inouye said, and a number of smaller ones, including one on Hawaii that the Nisei didn't know about. Altogether, 120,000 Japanese-Americans were interned. There was no anger or resentment on the part of the men from the camps, Inouye said. "Not really. In fact, those fellas who were in these camps never spoke about that. In fact, we didn't know about it, until there came a point in our training when somehow the mainland fellas and the fellas from Hawaii just couldn't get along.

"It sounds strange, but they couldn't get along. Well, we were darker of complexion, we were out in the tropics, our English was pidgin, their English was much finer. They were a bit more polite than us plantation boys. And we were rougher. So it got to a point where the senior officers of the regiment felt something had to be done. And I remember these social hours and discussion groups— if you can imagine GIs sitting down in a discussion group. Finally each company got an invitation. My company got it from Rohwer, Arkansas.

"I just assumed that this was a community in which there were Japanese-American families, and they wanted us to have a weekend of festivity and edible food. And so we thought it's gonna be a real treat to see Japanese-American girls—we hadn't seen one for ages—it seemed like that. Ten of us in our company got invited to go there, and we were all in this convoy of trucks. When we saw what we saw, we realized that these fellas from the mainland had come from these camps. It was a stunning revelation. To think that these men had volunteered from these concentration camps— that's what they were called by the American government.

"There have been times when I have asked myself the question

'Would I have volunteered under those circumstances?' The easy answer is 'Oh yes, yes.' That's the patriotic answer. But, honestly, I don't know. You know, it's not easy to have your own country put you in a camp of that nature, and then suggest that you volunteer and fight while your sister and your brother and your families are living in these barracks until the end of the war.

"So right away all hard feelings were forgotten, and we became one unit—a combat team. The 100th was there for a few months. So we overlapped. A lot of our men who were in the regiment were sent ahead of the combat team to serve as replacements in the 100th because the casualties were high there. So I would say the equivalent of about a battalion left Shelby. And all of us volunteered. We wanted to go ahead, but they handpicked a few and they went—because the regulations said the only replacements we can get have to be Japanese-Americans. So we could not go to the replacement depot and get you [a non-Japanese-American], for example, unless you were an officer."

Asked why the 442d went on to fight with such distinction, Inouye replied, "Well, we sailed overseas from Newport News in Virginia. That's where we assembled and got on a huge convoy of about three hundred ships to go across the Atlantic to Gibraltar. Not just us, you know, cargo and all. It took us twenty-two days to get to Naples. Ordinarily it might take about six, seven days. We'd go in circles all over the place. I noticed that on the last night, the night we were approaching the Italian peninsula, most of the men were not playing cards. Most of the men were on the deck. Those who were in the bunks were not sleeping, you could tell that. And they were looking out. So when we landed, and when I got my squad together—I was assistant squad leader then—I said, 'Could I ask a personal question?' They said, 'Sure, go ahead.'

" 'What were you fellas thinking about on that last night?' And every one of them—that's twelve of us, so eleven of them—gave me an answer which was very similar. It ran something like 'Well, I hope I don't bring shame to the family. I hope I don't become a coward. I hope like hell I do all right.' Which meant the same thing, that I hope I don't bring dishonor to the family. I think that was the unwritten spirit that somehow was kept with us throughout." Feeling they had something to prove "was part of honor. Oh yes. Because, if we did not succeed, then the ones who would really suffer were not us. It would be the little brothers and sisters and the parents back home. But we knew very well that, if we succeeded, their lives would be better."

The 442d consisted of three battalions of about 1,200 men each and an artillery battalion as well. It had an engineer company, an antiaircraft company, and an antitank company. It even had a band. "We were established as an autonomous organization that could be shipped out anywhere they wanted. And after about four months in combat, I believe the Army decided that we would be assault troops. So, wherever we went, we knew that something was gonna break open."

Casualties came fast. "In my outfit it was understood that the platoon leader would lead, instead of sending the scouts out. You were the first scout. As a result, the casualty rates among platoon leaders were extremely high. One day I'm assistant squad leader, next thing you know I'm a squad leader, and on the third battle I was a platoon guide; fourth battle I was a platoon sergeant. Bing bing bing. I was a platoon leader while I was still a sergeant, for several months. I was surprised when I was commissioned to second lieutenant. The whole division casualty rate was high. We ended up with twelve thousand men; we started out with forty-five hundred. The combat team received nineteen thousand decorations, ninety-four hundred Purple Hearts and twenty Medals of Honor."

They entered combat in the Rome-Arno campaign in late June 1943. Inouye's best friend, Jen Hatsu Chinen, was killed in their second battle. Inouye was to live on through six major campaigns. "I was in almost constant action for about eleven months. My first injury was on Thanksgiving Day. I remember very well. It was a foolish injury. I was considered by some as being a rather astute patrol leader. Patrol leaders are supposed to follow certain combat rules. One is never return on the same route that you took going out, because the enemy might have seen you going out and they might lay some traps, assuming that you might come back on the same trail. This was Thanksgiving Day, and I was a bit young and a little hungry, and I figured, if I didn't get back in time with my patrol, all the goodies would be consumed by the others and we'd be left out. Well, sure enough, when I started heading back to home base by the route we went out on, I felt a wire right across my leg and I knew I tripped a wire. Well, it was a grenade, and fortunately it just put some shrapnel in my thigh and that's about it. You don't forget that."

Another incident made a deep impression. Inouye and his platoon were out one day during the Italian campaign, approaching what they thought was an empty farmhouse when a machine gun opened fire from inside and killed his lead scout. "That was a moment I could never forget," he said. "This machine gun was on the second-floor window firing at us and killed one of my best friends. I fired a bazooka right through the window and that silenced the machine gun, so I rushed up to the second floor to make certain the gun was out of commission. There were three Germans there. Two were dead, one was still alive. And his legs were injured, so he couldn't move.

"He had his hands up and he said, 'Kamerad.' It was just a term they all used. And I had my rifle. I didn't have my tommy gun then. I was just a sergeant then, see. I had an M-1. I was just pointing it at him like this, then all of a sudden, and I couldn't understand German, he just stuck his hand into his jacket, inner pocket. My first reaction was, he's going for his holster, his pistol, and so I swung up my rifle and hit his face with the butt. I smashed his head actually. And his hand came flying out and flying out together with his hand was a batch of photographs, family photographs of him, his wife, his daughter. Oh my God, it made me sick. It was at that point I really began to realize that the men I killed were either a husband, a father,—a brother, a cousin, an uncle—or a son. It was a human being.

"Up until then, he was just quote enemy unquote. But, after that, killing became personalized: You were killing someone's loved one.

I may not love him, but there must have been a small group that loved him. In this case, by that one lack of communication, I created a widow and an orphan. That's a terrible feeling. When I saw the chaplain, I said, 'Gee, I don't know how long I can keep this up?' He says, 'Well, we have a mission, it's an ugly mission and the sooner you finish it, the better. And in the process, unfortunately, they'll either try to kill you or you'll have to kill them. It's either that, or you get out.' " Inouye could not do that. That would be dishonor. "No way. No way."

After fighting north of Rome along the Arno, the 442d was pulled out and sent to France, where it took part in an extraordinary episode that was to become known as the Rescue of the Lost Battalion. The operation happened in France in the fall of 1944 in the Vosges Mountains. Members of the 1st Battalion of the 141st Infantry of the Texas National Guard had been trapped and surrounded by the Germans for several days.

"In terms of distance, they were, I'd say, a good mile and a half away, through woods and mountains. This Texas battalion had been moving forward fast and, oftentimes when you're moving fast, you don't realize that this may be a trap. And, sure enough, they moved fast, and they got surrounded by several German units. We found out later it was about the equivalent of a division. That's a big number. So, as one would expect, our division commander sent a battalion after them, then another one, and they all were pushed back. So we were somewhere out on the flanks doing our business, and he put out a call, brought us to his sector and, he says, 'I want you to rescue them.'

"It must have been embarrassing for them, because Texans have a reputation." Before the Nisei went in, Inouye said, "We made it a point, all of us, to take a pack of cigarettes, some candy, chewing gum, chocolates, food, not for us but for them because we assumed they were starving, you know? They had been there for about a week. You know, my God, you feel for them. We used to see these aircraft flying around. We didn't know that they were dropping food and all the goodies. In fact, they were even dropping sandbags filled with sand, you know? But you couldn't know that, with all the trees around the place. You could just hear the engines. So when we finally got up there, they gave *us* candy, and they gave us cigarettes."

On the fifth day of the rescue effort, Inouye received his battle-field commission. "I didn't seek that. The company commander never discussed it with me. On the last push on the fifth day, which was November fifth or thereabouts. I was instructed by the mes-senger who came crawling up: 'The captain wants to see you.' So I went down to see the captain. I said, 'Sir, what's up?' He gave me an envelope and said the adjutant wants to see you. He said, 'There's the Jeep, take that.'

"I didn't have the good sense to ask what this was all about. I was afraid that this was a court-martial or something. Then, when I got there, the regimental sergeant saluted me. We were friends, he was a former police officer, and I said, 'Who are you saluting?' Because I didn't see anyone around. 'You!' 'Me? What for?' 'You're an offi-cer.' So I laughed. I said, 'Yeah, that's good.' I said, 'What's up?' 'Haven't you opened the envelope?' I said, 'No.' So I opened it up. It was my commission. I had to see the adjutant to take the oath.

"Because of my promotion, I missed the last battle. When I came back, there were thirteen left in the platoon. When I left, it was about thirty-two. About half the platoon was killed. In the battle of the Lost Battalion, the regiment suffered eight hundred casualties. Of that number, a little over three hundred were killed. That's a pretty heavy casualty list. To save fewer than two hundred Texans.

"But I remember about a week later, when everything was set-tled. That battle was over, the Germans were taken in custody, and we were so busted up that they had to pull us back. We had a cou-ple of days of free time, so we'd go to the French saloons, and there'd be a lot of Texans around the place and we walked in to get a beer or something. All of a sudden, they would all stand up, move to the side. And we walk in, What's going on here? We sit down and the rest of the evening was free. But I think they were a little embarrassed. Also very grateful.

"It was a terrible thing to even suggest this, but many of us in the regiment felt that this was the definitive battle, that we were expendable. That's why we were called up to save them. But we felt that, if we did well, then the curse would be taken away once and for all. And so, you can sense this in the men: When you go into a battle and they put on the bayonet, you know they mean business. So we meant business. When you put on a bayonet, that's do or die. Our motto was: Go for Broke, which is, I suppose, a slang phrase that young gamblers used to use back in Hawaii. Go for Broke means All the Way. This was a Shoot the Works battle. That means you put on the bayonet. You're going to get them no matter what the cost. Absolutely. The cost was heavy."

Five months later, in April 1945, the 442d was back in Italy, operating near San Terenzo, taking part in an attack on a defended ridge. On April 21, his company commander put him in for another promotion.

"I was young and, keep in mind, you got the macho spirit, I suppose. I carried a Thompson submachine gun. Not because it was accurate—the Thompson is about as inaccurate a weapon as you can find. But it's got a loud noise, oh, ho ho. If you're on the other side and you hear all this—*Brrraahhhh!*—you know, it will scare the bejeebers out of you. And if it does hit, you know you've been hit. It's a .45 caliber slug. I recall hitting a German once in his ankle and his foot blew off, shoe and all. That's how powerful it is. I carried it for stopping power. I also had a sidearm plus a bag of grenades."

Inouye carried two silver dollars in his shirt pocket. He considered them good-luck charms because they had stopped a bullet during fighting in France. On the night of April 20, 1945, they disappeared. The next day E Company was ordered to assault a high ridge called Colle Musatello. Inouye's platoon was on the left flank. The other two platoons were ordered to make a frontal attack. They were pinned down, but Inouye's platoon proceeded in textbook fashion, took out an observation post, and reached to the main line of resistance well ahead of the other two platoons. They were within forty yards of the German bunkers, confronting a crossfire from three enemy machine guns.

Inouye drew a grenade, stood up to throw it, and was shot. "I used a lot of grenades, because I found them so effective. Unlike German grenades, American grenades were very dependable. One thing about Germans during that time, as soon as they pulled the pin, they threw the grenade—so you could avoid it. Or kick it away. In our case, we were so confident that the grenade was perfectly timed to five seconds, so that you could pull the pin, snap the lever and count, One, two, three and toss it so that, when it hits the ground, it explodes.

"I remember being shot in my abdomen, first, on the right side. The bullet came out in the middle of my back, and it felt like someone had slugged me. There was no intense pain or anything like that. I fell backwards and then I kept on going until my messenger right in the back of me, the fellow who carries the radio, said, 'By the way, you're bleeding.' So I stuck my hand there and, sure enough, it was warm and moist. I took out my hand. It was all bloody but, since it wasn't bleeding profusely and I had no pain to speak of, I just kept on going. In my bag I still had a half a dozen grenades. I carried a bag, sort of like a schoolbag."

He threw a grenade at the nearest bunker and killed the shell-shocked Germans as they stood up. He took out a second emplacement with two more grenades. He worked his way up the flank of the third, preparing to throw again. As he pulled the pin and drew back his arm, a German soldier stood up waist high and fired a rifle grenade from ten yards away. The grenade practically tore his arm off.

"I don't really recall what happened after my right elbow was hit by this rifle grenade. I saw the fellow pointing it at me and I felt the blast and I recall going for my grenade, prying it out of my right hand and throwing it with my left. My arm was dangling by a couple of shreds, so when I lifted it up, it was hanging like that. Just shredded. So I knew it was gone. First I was looking all over for the grenade, I thought it fell. And then I looked at my hand and I said,

'Oh, my Lord. It's there.' I had pulled the pin, and my hand was back ready to toss it, so I knew it was armed. The fingers somehow froze over the grenade, so I just had to pry it out. When I pulled it out, the lever snapped open and I knew had five seconds, so I flipped it into the German's face as he was trying to reload. And it hit the target. From that point on, until I found myself at the bottom of the hill, I really don't recall.

"When I received my Distinguished Service Cross, I must tell you that I couldn't believe it. I said, 'What's this for?' They said, 'It's for all you did there.' And when I read the citation, that's when I got in touch with some of my former platoon members, and I said, 'What really happened? I must know.' They told me that, after I threw my grenade, I picked up my tommy gun with my left hand— keep in mind that my stump is bleeding now—and I just charged up to the third gun, and I knocked that one out. I was going for the next one and I got hit in the leg, and I rolled down the hill, and that's when I woke up, I guess. And when my platoon members told me that, I said, 'No, it can't be. It can't be. You'd have to be insane to do all that.' I think it's all part of the training where you do things almost automatically. It's a sense of duty. That's what they told me, and the company commander who was also observing from the backside, he said, 'I couldn't believe what I saw, because you were a crazy man.' "

How could he control the notoriously erratic Thompson with his left hand only? "Well, I was just squeezing the trigger. It's a strange thing about human beings: You have extraordinary strength when you need it. Like men and women have been known to lift up like four hundred pounds to lift a car so that someone can get out. Strange things happen."

Inouye was shot in the shinbone of his right leg while going for a fourth emplacement. "It just tripped me, and I went tumbling downhill with a bloody arm flapping around. Then I got to my senses, and I put on a tourniquet. I just took out my handkerchief and wrapped it around the arm, and the medic came in a few seconds. At that point I just leaned against a tree. They wanted to evacuate me right away, and I said, 'No, let's wait until the men are placed in their positions.' I called my sergeant and I said, 'Now put so and so there, and so and so here,' because it's elementary that after an attack, when you accomplish a mission, the odds are that there will be a counterattack. So you got to prepare yourself for that. I wanted to get them ready to defend the ridge from a counterattack before I left.

"My arm was not taken off right away. I assumed they would take it off that night. But the doctor said, 'We are not taking it off at this moment. Your arm is dead.' And my fingers were all black. Dried. So I said, 'Why are you keeping it, then? This is like a mummy.' He said, 'Well, you've got gangrene, pal, and if we're going to operate on you, we'll wait until we are able to stop the gangrene.' They were giving me gallons of penicillin to stop the progress. Once they felt they stopped it, then they cut above the infected area.

"One thing that I'll never forget. When I was wounded, the hospital was actually in the all-black 92d Division sector, and I don't know whether it was customary or regulations but, each time they gave me a transfusion, they showed me the bottle. And the bottle had the name, rank, serial number, and unit of the donor. Every one was 92d Division. I had seventeen transfusions. The blood of black men. I was told later on I could have turned it down, but I said, 'Thank God blood was available. Otherwise I'd be dead.' I had lost lot of blood, moving around like a damn fool.

"They took my arm off just above the elbow. The hospital was in Leghorn or Livorno, Italy. I was there about a month. The day after my surgery, I'm groggy and the nurse comes by and says, 'Welcome back.' I had been sleeping I don't know how many hours. And she inquired, 'What can I do for you?' She expected me to say, 'May I have a glass of water?' or something. I say, 'Can I get a cigarette?' I want a smoke. Because I hadn't had a smoke for days now. At that time it was Camels and Chesterfields. Luckies were hard to get. And so she looked at me and said, 'Cigarettes are no good, you know.' I said, 'But I need a smoke.'

"So she said, 'Just a moment.' She went away, and she came back with a new pack. She tossed it right here, on my chest. And I had never opened a pack of cigarettes one-handed. She walked away. I wanted to tell her, 'Hey hey hey, open this for me,' but she just walked away. And I had no idea how to open this, so I was using my teeth, smashed the pack, finally got a cigarette out, all mashed up. I'm fuming with anger now. Finally she came back. She said, 'Good smoke?' 'I need a light.' 'Oh, I'm sorry.' So she goes out again. I think she was purposely letting me fume. Came back with a book of matches, the kind you open up, and she put it right here, tossed it right on my chest again and walked away.

"I was ready to call her all kinds of names, but she was a lady, a little older. So here I'm trying to light this, I don't know what to do. Finally she came back. She said, 'Let me have the match.' I got the match, she folded the match, closed the matchbook, snap. She said, 'I'll do it again.' Snap. 'You try it.' Hey, it works.

"Then she looked at me and she says, 'You know, I won't be around the rest of your life. I'm not going to be here to feed you for the rest of your life. I'm not gonna be around to light your cigarettes for the rest of your life. You'll have to learn how to put your shoes on, dress yourself, take a bath, light your cigarettes, and feed yourself. You better start now.' Yes, ma'am!

"We have started on Day One. Oh, I was in love with her. She became the most beautiful thing on earth. She put me right on track. She told me how to be a man. She told me to be independent, that you are not a cripple. In other words, don't feel sorry for yourself. No self-pity. Oh, it's good to know these things. And so that afternoon I remember I said, 'Nurse?' 'Yep?' 'May I have two pencils? Unused pencils?' She says, 'May I ask, what for?' I said, 'Where I come from at a formal dinner you have a fork, and possibly a knife and a spoon. Usually I use chopsticks and, if I don't know how to use chopsticks when I get home, I'll starve.' And I said, 'I don't want to do that.' She laughed and laughed, then she called the ward boy over. 'You know what a chopstick is?' 'Yeah, that kind of stuff you use in chop suey houses.' 'Yep, make two of them up.' She was from Eagle Pass, Texas. I never knew her name.

It was always Nurse. She was a lieutenant, first lieutenant. I've looked for her, but I never found her. She was gone.

"I had chopsticks overseas. I carried them all the way to Atlantic City, so when I got to Atlantic City I got a real pair of chopsticks."

By coincidence, Inouye was promoted to first lieutenant the day he was wounded. "I was scheduled to leave the European Theater sometime in May and report to the United States Military Academy at West Point about June and begin what they called the summer orientation program. My last battle was April twenty-first of nineteen forty-five, and I was supposed to leave a few weeks later." He was in the hospital for twenty months. "Otherwise I would have been in the Class of forty-nine, and I would have been just in time for Korea and, if I got through that, I'd be ready for Vietnam and, if I got through that, God knows what else."

Daniel Inouye came home a captain minus one arm on his discharge May 27, 1947. Along with the Distinguished Service Cross, he held a Bronze Star, Purple Heart with cluster, and twelve other medals and citations. His Distinguished Service Cross, awarded for the action in which he lost his arm, was upgraded to the Medal of Honor at the White House on June 21, 2000. President Clinton approved the Army's recommendation to upgrade twenty-one Distinguished Service Crosses awarded to Asian-Americans in World War II to Medals of Honor.

In 1950, he graduated from the University of Hawaii with a degree in economics and government. In 1952 he graduated from George Washington University Law School, and in 1959 became Hawaii's first United States congressman when he was elected to the House of Representatives. He was elected to the Senate in 1962 and has served for more than forty years. He wed Margaret Shinobu Awamura on June 12, 1948. They have a son, Daniel Jr.

An official apology for the government's wrongdoing was issued to Japanese-Americans by President Ronald Reagan in 1988. He also approved $20,000 in reparations for each internee.

FOUR

John William Finn

Chief Ordnance Man
Naval Air Station, Kaneohe Bay
December 7, 1941

*"I said to Sully, 'It's the real McCoy!
It's the God damn Japs!'"*

Photo by Eddie Adams

John Finn, at ninety-three, was
the oldest living recipient of the
Medal of Honor when this photo
was taken at his ranch in Southern California in the fall of 2002.

John Finn was thirty-two years old and had been in
the Navy fifteen years when Pearl Harbor and the
Naval Station at Kaneohe Bay, twelve miles away,
came under attack on December 7, 1941. Since the
Kaneohe Station was hit minutes before the attack
on Pearl began, it is arguable that his actions that
day made his the first Medal of Honor action of
World War II.

53

JOHN FINN was ninety-two years old when I went to visit him at his ninety-three-acre ranch out in the Southern California scrub, seventy miles from San Diego. He was annoyed that day because the nurse who had been looking in on him since his wife died a few years previously refused to date him. The nurse, Dorie, who called herself Sunshine, also declined to call him anything other than "Mr. Finn." But Finn was not just some randy old coot. For a man of his age, he displayed extraordinary vigor and agility. And he loved to talk. Rambling all over the landscape of his life, he went on nonstop for several hours.

The path that led John Finn to lifelong recognition and honor among his peers started out bumpy at best. He was born in Compton Lynwood, Los Angeles, which he never liked, on July 23, 1909. "It took me two years to get out of the eighth grade. I hated arithmetic; I just hated it. And that's the reason why, when I got to be an officer, I didn't stay in the Navy. I was the dumbest shit lieutenant, I hardly knew the multiplication tables. Oh God, I hated it, and I wouldn't study it. I was a tough old boy, fourteen years old, five feet five, one hundred twenty-five pounds. I said, 'Dad, I'm gonna quit school. There's no use of me laying around here sponging off you.' And, by God, I quit. I got a job and worked for three years."

About that time, he decided to join the Navy. "I was still sixteen when I got up there. I was a kid. I thought, 'Oh shit, a few weeks don't make any difference.' But when I got to the recruiting station, naturally the first thing they asked was, 'How old are you? When were you born?' They didn't tell me I wasn't old enough; I guess maybe they needed recruits. So they gave me an exam, gave me the physical. The recruiter said, 'How are your teeth?' I said, 'I got pretty good teeth.' I did have beautiful teeth. 'Good, son, come with me.' Then I got my first bawling out. This guy—a medical officer, he had a white coat on, no insignia—sat me down in a chair. I shoved the chair up: 'Put that chair back! If I want you to move that chair, I'll tell you to move it!' So I put the chair back. Then it was, 'Okay, all right, son. You take these papers home, get your mother and father to sign them, and come back in about two weeks. And bring your mother and father with you.'

"I came back on the twenty-ninth of July, 1926. I was now seventeen. My mother went with me. My dad was a plumber—he said he didn't have to be there. He was busy plumbing houses. Well, my God, they treated her like she was a queen, got her a cup of coffee and set her down in a chair. It was wonderful.

"Now came this tough-looking sailor. I knew he was a sailor even though he was in civilian clothes: 'Son,' he said, 'Are you sure you want to join the Navy?' 'Oh, yeah.' 'Do you know you're going to have to scrub all your own clothes?' Didn't affect me a bit, I used to help my mother do the laundry—if she could catch me. 'Do you realize if you're in the Navy you've got to stand a lot of watches? You don't get to sleep all night all the time. Do you understand that?' 'Yeah, I knew there was such a thing, but I didn't know anything about it.' A couple of 'em looked at me. I was so God damn young-looking. I looked like I was about twelve years old. I didn't shave for two years after I got in the Navy. I never had any whiskers.

"One thing worried me: They gave me a little brochure, a little leaflet, that had some pictures of boot camp, some guys lashing hammocks, and then a few statements. It said, 'The Navy food is plain but wholesome.' Boy, that worried me. I thought 'plain and wholesome' meant I was going to eat boiled rice and boiled potatoes with no salt on 'em three meals a day for four years, and I didn't like rice or potatoes, either one. I wanted to join the Navy. I thought, God, how can I stand that, three meals a day, for four years? And then, when I got to boot camp, oh my god, I loved the Navy."

Finn went on to relate how he and a few other recruits were taken to boot camp in San Diego, told to hurry up and wait, and finally got marched inside to the mess hall. "This old cook says, 'All right, fellas, go over to that rack there and getcha one of those trays and pass right by the steam tables, and take all you want. And if you need seconds, come back and get more.' Now, I'd been worried about that, because I didn't like either one of those things, potatoes or rice, and here we had sliced roast beef! And of course it had

gravy. There was lettuce and tomato salad. This was in July, and I
think they had slices of watermelon or corn on the cob. Man, I just
couldn't believe that food! Some guy there complained about the
God damned Navy slop, but, shit, I never had such good food in
my life as I got in the Navy. I thought I died and went to heaven. I
kept thinking, God damn rice and boiled potatoes."

Finn met his wife-to-be, Alice Diltf, in San Diego in 1932. "I met
her right after we come back from China. I had a whole bellyful of
little Chinese girls, and I come back, and I saw that beautiful
blonde there, and I said, 'I've gotta do something about this.'"

He was palling around with some friends on motorcycles and
Alice showed up with an old shipmate, Joe Bauer. "He said, 'This
is Alice.' And I looked at that girl. God damn! She was attractive!
Joe had only just met Alice at a dance the night before." They went
to visit a friend of Alice's who had been hurt in an accident and she
stayed inside so long that eventually Bauer left, so Alice ended up
with John Finn.

"When she come out, she looked all around, and said, 'Where's
Joe?' So I went over to her, I said, 'Alice, I'll take you anywhere you
want to go, but I got to tell you I haven't ridden this bike very long
and maybe you'd better go with Bobby or Slim.' She said, 'I'd like
to go with you.' So we took off and rode around. We got to Pacific
Beach, and about that time it was getting a little chilly. Alice just
had on a little sweater and a tam-o'-shanter and a pair of slacks. I
remember saying, 'Look, I'm glad you came with me. Do you feel
nervous?' She said, 'No, it seems to me you know how to ride a
bike.' I had a BMW motorcycle I'd brought from China.

"Then I felt a little tremor on the back of the bike: What's that?
Well, that girl was now standing up on that pack rack on the bike;
she had the tips of her fingers on my shoulders and she was standing up. I'm thinking, 'Jesus Christ, she's got a lot of guts. This beautiful blonde is the last girl in the world you'd think would be playing
tricks on a motorcycle.' We drove along there, not going fast,
twenty or twenty-five miles an hour. She was muscular and strong
and graceful and everything.

"We got married a year later, in 1933. Everybody was dirt poor. A lot of people didn't have enough to eat. It was terrible." Finn was making ninety-two dollars a month, but a lot of it was going to help support his sister, who was getting a divorce.

After they were married, they eventually were transferred to Hawaii. The BMW was long gone, and the new pride in John's life, after his blonde wife, was a black 1938 Ford sedan, which he had brought with him to Oahu. He was stationed at the Naval Station at Kaneohe Bay, twelve miles across the island from Pearl Harbor.

On December 7, 1941, at 7:55 A.M., the Japanese hit the Kaneohe Station, five minutes before they attacked Pearl Harbor.

"Those God damn Japs, I should have hated 'em. Those bastards screwed up my nooky on a Sunday morning," Finn recalled fondly. "I only was a mile from the hangar, and I was after love with my beautiful wife. When they came early that's honest to God what I was doing. Everybody said later they come and awakened me. The only people asleep were the bastards in Washington who didn't advise the admiral as to what was coming off. But hell, my hard-on awakened me that morning.

"About the time I saw a plane flash by my window, I'm laying flat, and my wife had jumped out of bed. It was just a few steps to the window, and she could look out and see that Hawaiialoh Hill, and she said, 'Oh, John, it's beautiful!' And I'm lookin' at her beautiful little ass, and I said, 'It sure is!'

"You gotta understand I'd been in the Navy for fifteen years, and I'd participated in all kinds of war games. I heard the planes flying. The thing was, they were not flying the pattern. You don't have a God damn air station with people flying in all kinds of crazy directions. I didn't know where they were. I just heard 'em. Then, all of a sudden, I heard these damn machine guns. Who the hell's firing machine guns? I'm a chief ordnance man. If one squad was going to do some ordnance-type work, it was just natural they'd come and talk to me. I heard the God damn guns. All of sudden I thought, 'Hey, what the hell's happening? It's Sunday.'

"And why are the guns firing so slow? I rationalized. 'They must have a gun they couldn't fix.' They're down at the machine-gun range, and why is it firing so slow? 'Oh, it's a .50 caliber and some stupid bastard has got the oil buffer wrong.' But they were Jap planes, and they were Jap machine guns. They had an old machine gun that was a good copy of British Vickers. It was a slow firing gun, a .30 caliber. A 7.7 mm, they called it. The Jap planes, the Zeroes, had two 7.7 mm machine guns, synchronized guns shooting through the prop. And out on both wings, port and starboard, they had real primitive 20 mm cannons, real slow. I don't think all this even took a minute to figure out. Another plane flashed by the window. I said to Alice, 'Hey, there's carrier planes.' I thought they were from our carriers; that we were having a mock attack. Well, about that time something hit me. My old gut just wadded up to a big damn ball of wax. I was stark naked, and I heard a real sharp feminine rap on my door. I heard that rapid knock, and I lost my hard-on. My gut had turned to a little lead ball. I knew something was wrong.

"I grabbed my dungaree pants and pulled them on and got decent as I run down and opened my door. Here stood Lou Sullivan, Eddie Sullivan's wife. He was the next senior ordnance man to me in my squadron. And old Eddie was a beer drinker. He had a pot gut, and he was home laying in bed. Anyway, I said, 'What the hell's up, Lou?' She said, 'They want you down at the hangar right away.' Then she turned and run. I found out later two men had come through the place in a pickup, one guy driving and the other yelling: 'All hands down to the hangar!'

"I just turned around, went upstairs, grabbed my shirt, put on my hat and my socks. I always hated to go without socks. I put my shoes on and I'm walking now, but I'm hurrying. My thirty-eight Ford was parked in a little area close by, and I got in and started backing up. Here come old Sully. He kinda waddled; he had a pot belly, and he was not a runner. I could run like a deer, even when I was an old man. He come out there, and he had his brand-new chief's hat on, and he was buttoning up his shirt. I always gave him a ride to the hangars. He didn't have a car. He was the squadron parachute man. That was his billet.

"Sully didn't say a word. He had a cigarette dangling from his lip, and he was still buttoning his shirt. I backed up and went out of there, and the station speed limit was twenty miles an hour. I got on the road that went around the base of the hill, and I got around, and I heard a plane come roaring in from astern of me. As I glanced up, the guy made a wing-over, and I saw that big old red meatball, the rising sun insignia, on the underside of the wing. It was the dirtiest looking red I ever saw, looked like they'd mixed their fuckin' lead paint with mud, just an old nasty horrible dirty red color. Well, I threw it into second, and it was a wonder I didn't run over every sailor in the air station.

"I said to Sully, 'It's the real McCoy! It's the God damn Japs!'

"Down to the hangar I went. I had to scream around the corner, throw on my brakes, and skid my wheels. I parked in the regular parking area because I didn't have sense enough to drive down to the hangar. We were not allowed to, you see. I jumped out of the car before it stopped and ran like a deer over there.

"It wasn't 8 A.M. yet, because Kaneohe was hit at least five to ten minutes before Pearl." As a naval air station, the base was home to three squadrons, each with twelve big twin-engine PBY-4 float planes that were used for reconnaissance and patrol. Finn's squadron, BP 14, had sent up three PBYs earlier that morning. The Japanese were in the process of reducing every plane left on the field to a rubble of smoke and melted aluminum. The hangars were quite large, twenty-five yards wide and twenty yards deep.

"When I got near to my armory, the first thing I saw was a whole bunch of bomb-handling trucks, or carts, and each one of those bastards had two to three five hundred-pound TNT depth charges on it. Inside the hangar, I run in there, and I saw those things and, man, it hit me. I thought, 'Jesus Christ.' I was not familiar with that fuse on a depth charge. It's not aviation. It's a very safe explosive, but I am not aware at that time, and suppose a Jap bullet hit that thing? There's enough charges there to blow that hangar all to hell if they'd gone off. On a depth charge, they call it an ash can, the Goddamn case is not much thicker than a common trash can. A .30

caliber, any bullet, could go through that thin tin and I thought, 'My God, if that went off, there'd be hell to pay.'

"Then I heard machine guns. I hadn't got out there yet. I ran right through my armory, and there was two or four guys strolling along, looking around. They didn't have any guns. There was no mount for the God damn guns, that's what made me so mad. Here's the God damn Japs swarming all over us, and no gun mounts." Each PBY had two .50 caliber and two .30 caliber machine guns but, incredibly, there was nothing in the way of antiaircraft weaponry on the base. As chief petty officer and an aviation ordnance or weapons and munitions man, Finn had urged his superiors a month before to let him build some mounts for the machine guns, for land-based shooting, and they had failed to respond.

"Meantime, I got right near the door, and I heard these machine guns going off outside the door that led out of my armory. I peeked my head out the door. I wasn't going to run and get killed by one of our own guns. I run right to the door and out to the edge of the parking area." Second Class Radioman Robert J. Peterson was firing a .30 caliber machine gun on a makeshift mount from outside the door that went into the hangar. "When I run out there, I passed through the guns, and on my right hand was big Bucky Walters, one of my Indian boys from Oklahoma, J. E. Walters, and he was firing a .50 caliber gun. Bucky was an ornery bastard when he got drunk but he was a good man, and I loved his ass. When I ran out there, I said, 'Pete, move your God damn gun out! You're gonna kill Bucky!'

"And he said, 'We cain't, Chief! They's a firing at us!' "

Finn took the gun from the radioman. "Out to the left there was a Jap making a big circle out over the bay, and he was coming down, lining right up alongside of that hangar, and he sprinkled some bullets along there. There was a lot less strafing than everybody thought [later] because they'd go in circles; they'd come around, make a strafing run right down the ramp, shooting the PBYs and setting 'em on fire. There might have been nine or ten planes out there at any one time. They were making big circles out of sight behind the hangar. Finally, when the battle was half over, what I did was grab that .30—a .30 caliber gun was quite light—and, oh my god, did they fire fast, and the tripod mount was just three pieces of pipe. It was a little old makeshift stand that was only set up to get your gunners around dummy belts of ammunition and teach 'em to charge the gun, to clear stoppages. I picked the whole thing up and drug it twenty yards out toward the runway out so I could see over the hangars, and I fired that gun from then on. There was ammo in the gun, belts of ammo in a tin box. You'd charge it once, you're ready to shoot." Finn charged the gun, cocking it, in effect, and began to look for targets.

"I fired at the Japs for the next two hours and a half. All I did was shoot at every one I could. You don't knock 'em down out of the air. That plane is doing close to two hundred knots, just a flick, and he's gone. You might not get fifteen or twenty seconds—that's a long blast. I kept firing till the last Jap left, but I did lots of things in between. There were lulls. I said to Sully when he showed up, 'Get those God damn things, the bomb-handling carts, out of here!' And he said a stupid thing: 'Where shall I take 'em?' I said, 'Take 'em out and disperse 'em in the brush. Whatever you do, don't put them all in one place.' And immediately I went back out and fired some machine gun again. Next time, I come back, there were those God damn things all in the corner. They hadn't been moved. Well, I made up my mind I was gonna kill Sullivan. I thought he lost his nerve and ran out and hid someplace, because there was one or two cases where guys hid in the bushes.

"Well, what happened, he had gone off to find the squadron truck. He was doin' exactly what I told him. I didn't have to shoot him. And you could never find that fuckin' truck. Always somebody's got it off somewhere else. He finally traced the truck and come back to the hangar with it, but now he needed the tractor to get the squadron door open. It was a brand-new hangar, and you needed the tractor or all three hundred men in the squadron to open that door." Sullivan finally located the tractor, got the doors open, and towed the bomb-handling carts to a safer spot well away from the hangar.

"When a plane comes diving right in, and when he's diving in at you, if his guns work and if he ain't half asleep or doped up, he's strafing you, see? All you can do is aim right at the nose of a strafing plane as it's coming in. My idea was to aim into that propeller area of that engine. I know I hit some, but I never, ever said I shot one down. Guys said, 'Ah hell, I know you shot one, you shot down a half a dozen planes!' Well, that's a buncha bullshit. The whole air station that whole two and a half hours was credited with shooting down three airplanes, and I never ever talked to anybody. Hey. Where were those other two? See, one airplane [which Finn was credited with shooting down] actually crash-landed right on the base, and the pilot, Fusata Iida of the Japanese Imperial Navy, was killed. We got his body, had almost a complete Zero plane shot down, and, to the best of my knowledge we never had any engineering officer with enough sense to go over there and check that plane and say, 'Get the hell out of there,' and immediately order a Marine sentry or somebody with a gun to keep everybody away. Later they pulled the wreckage of that plane out and slapped it right at the north end of the U.S. Naval Air Station machine shop. In the meantime all the souvenir hunters came and started tearing at that thing. There evidently wasn't enough fuckin' brains in all the engineering officers on that base to think, 'Hey, this is a valuable thing: Preserve it, get these fuckin' souvenir scavengers out of here.' "

As he stood out on the runway firing his .30 caliber, Finn was peppered by pieces of shrapnel as the diving enemy planes strafed the concrete runways with 20 mm cannon. "I actually counted. I got shot in the left arm and shot in the left foot, broke the bone. I had shrapnel blows in my chest and belly and right elbow and right thumb. Some were just scratches. My scalp got cut, and everybody thought I was dying: Oh, Christ, the old chief had the top of his head knocked off! I didn't even know. As far as I know, I never got hit by a single complete bullet, but I had four or five things that were serious. I had twenty-eight, twenty-nine holes in me that were bleeding. I was walking around on one heel. I was barefooted on that coral dust. My left arm didn't work. It was just a big ball hanging down."

He also narrowly escaped a bomb blast. "There were several times I left that gun, when I couldn't see a plane anywhere. I'd run back in my armory, kick somebody in the ass, fix the .50 caliber when it got jammed, and get back to the .30. I saw these planes coming, five bombers way up there, and I had a hundred-round belt in the .30 caliber. I got on 'em, and this was one time when I let a whole hundred-round belt go because I was absolutely walking the gun along with the plane. I was letting the gun cover, right ahead, leading the planes and I was actually leading 'em.

"They're the only friggin' planes I absolutely know I hit with the machine gun because I was concentrating on the lead plane of a five-plane group, two on each side. Each belt had a ball, an armor-piercing slug, and a tracer, in sequence. I saw three, possibly four or five, of my tracers hit those airplane propellers. I saw my tracer bullets go up there, and hit that prop and the propeller slung 'em off in an arc. And I know if the tracers hit the plane, there were two other armor-piercing slugs in the belt. So, for every tracer that hit, there could have been one or two of the other cartridges hitting the plane too.

"All of a sudden, the planes changed their course to their own right hand. The other planes followed the leader, and when he dropped his bombs, they dropped theirs. I had just a great pile of ammo, more ammo than I could ever shoot. I grabbed a belt, and I slapped it right up here and, just as I looked up, I saw little black mice turds comin' toward me, and I said, 'Bombs! Hey! Get the hell out of here! Bombs. They're going to go over! Fuck over!' And Blam! I outrun those bombs and jumped in that stairwell. I threw my hands over my head, solid concrete all around me. I had to run from the gun to the hangar and jump through that door. And I didn't even hit the deck before I heard three big rolling horrendous explosions. It seemed to me just like a wave, you know how you shake a big carpet, exactly like that, three big ominous horrendous rumbles—rumble, rumble rumble, boom! The hangar was a-shaking, glass was falling down, a ton of glass fell on me. I got that cut on my head. I know my scalp was cut, and that was where the most blood come out of me, because these shrapnel wounds, they were just kind of a dull puncture, and evidently closed up right away.

"Whammo! I whirled right around and started to run right out and back to my gun and, hold it, you fool! Possibly, delayed-action fuse. I knew about these things, and I hunkered down there, finally said, 'The hell with the God damn fuse.' I run out there, and one of those bombs had made almost a direct hit on that God damn gun. The crater was nearly twelve feet in diameter. The center of the crater might have been six or eight feet from the first tripod of that gun. It did not knock the gun over, but it almost completely covered that big pile of ammunition. There was a whole bunch of belts of ammo under the gun, and they were all practically covered with sand and little fine broken bubbles of cement.

"Earlier, just as those bombs were about to hit, I saw two sailors running close to this hangar, Bucky Walters and Christian Guiness. Bucky was badly injured. The bomb just picked him up and slammed him full force right into the side of that hangar. He was a big heavy kid, a strong bastard. Christian Guiness was more my size, small and wiry. He got right to the middle of the hangar, and there was a door there. He grabbed the handle, but the door wouldn't open more than a few inches. He took his two hands and tried to jerk it open. It was tied shut with that great big five-six-teenths wire they use to bind up bundles of reinforcement steel. Somebody had wired the damn door shut from inside, and he got his hands in there just as the bombs hit. The concussion blew that God damn door shut, and it just smashed every damn bone in his hands. He got over it, though. He went around for a long time with little splints on his fingers, putting tension on each finger to keep it straight. He went around squeezing tennis balls, and they put him to making macramé. That's a funny thing: He made a beautiful red, white, and blue belt for Alice, with a square knot, and nice mother-of-pearl. Alice wore it quite a while. She had a real slim little waist."

As the attack wound down, Finn waited around a while longer.

"I thought there might be somebody coming and, sure enough, I looked way up, five or six miles, and saw a little black speck, a seagull. But I said, 'You couldn't see a seagull up there.' I saw it was moving, and here this guy come, in nothing flat. I watched just long enough. You could see it passing trees, going by, and I started to shoot at it. Then I said, 'You God damn fool, it's four or five miles away. Save your ammunition!' I swung around with him, and all of a sudden he disappeared behind this smoke. Our planes were burning out there in the bay, that's how low he was. I could see he was coming like hell. I followed him. The minute he come out, I swung my gun to him. I said, 'I don't give a shit if he's ten miles away, I'm gonna get on him, give him some elevation and lead and try to squirt out everything in this gun.' I didn't know how much ammo I had left. I was just shootin' whatever was in there. All right . . . I waited, pulled the gun down, held it right there, waited. Hey, at the speed he was goin', he should have been out of there, he ain't coming out of there. And I swung my gun like this. I didn't have to move that God damn gun, I just swung it back, just straight and he flew right out of that fuckin' smoke.

"He came out I'm thinking maybe a few hundred yards away. As soon as I could, I pulled the trigger. I started firing at him. His propeller had picked up a wreath of black smoke that was trailing in a big disk with his propeller, and he came boilin' right down that God damn gun barrel. There was no way in the world that I could have missed him. I figured I got possibly eight and definitely three or four rounds by the time he passed over my head. When I whirled around to try to see where he went, he had disappeared behind the buildings. There was no way I could have seen him after he cleared the other side of the hangar."

Was this the plane that crash-landed that afternoon, piloted by Fusata Iida?

"There was no way in the world I could know if I got him or not. If I didn't hit him, it was just a God damn miracle, because I was a good shot with a machine gun. It was just a fraction of a minute, seconds, that he was in that sight and over my head. The air pressure of that plane, from flying so close to the ground, pushed me down to my knees. I come right up, and I thought that I would swing the gun around no matter where he was, but I couldn't even see him. He must have made a veer to the right. He went up there and crashed in a wide-open field. He was killed, and I saw his body. The thing of it is, I don't know if this Fusata Iida crashed at the first of the battle and was already down, or during the middle of the battle.

"If it was him, he must have gone past me and swerved to the right and made the landing in a quite wide swale, they call it, up by the officers' quarters. Right there's a marker that says this is the impact site of Lieutenant Iida. He did not hit there. He hit the ground way back here; they know that when he hit the ground his engine tore loose from the plane and rolled on up the hill like a ball.

"I was at the sick bay when they brought his body from the crash site which was, oh, maybe one hundred and fifty or two hundred yards from sick bay. Someone said, 'Hey, we got a dead Jap out here.' I found out where they had him, on the door from an old house. He was layin' on that door out on the lawn full length. His face was upturned and I would swear he had on a light green summer flying suit, and he was missing one foot. Some guy had cut it off at his ankle. Suppose his foot was caught in that plane, he could have been thrown out of the plane, I don't know. Okay, he had one foot. I went over and looked right down in his face, and I felt sorry. I said, 'You poor son of a bitch, you got killed.' A few minutes before he was trying to kill everybody on the base. His face hadn't had time to swell or turn blue; it looked to me like it was a little misshapen.

"I later on heard this Marine Corps officer telling how he was scattered all over. They took a body bag and picked up part of him here and part of him there and part of him over here. That God damn pilot, I saw him, and all he had was one foot missing. He certainly had his arms and his legs and his head. I don't think they even had the term *body bag* at the first of the war. Of course, they could have had an old sack. Another guy said he saw that plane come in from over the piling and it was on fire, and it hit and burned. Well, God damn it, that plane was not burned."

Finally, the battle was over. The Japanese had launched 330 planes from six aircraft carriers two hundred miles away. Thirty-two planes did not make it back to their ships. Nineteen Americans were killed at Kaneohe, two thousand at Pearl Harbor.

"That last plane left me madder than hell. See, I was still mad that we didn't have gun mounts. Little pieces of shrapnel had cut a hole in my shirt and stuck in my chest bone. I thought when I pulled the shirt off, it would pull the shrapnel out, but it was stuck in me. I jerked it out and threw it on the ground." Finn went to sick bay for first aid and then went back out, cleaning up and preparing for a possible second attack. He was held in the hospital for treatment from 1 P.M. on Monday, December 8, until December 24. "I was on crutches for quite a while."

Finn was decorated several months later. "I got the Medal at one P.M. on September fifteenth, nineteen forty-two, on board the USS *Enterprise* in Pearl Harbor. It was awarded by Fleet Admiral Chester W. Nimitz. He made a good speech. I still remember his words. He said, 'Do not think for an instant that we have the enemy on the run. He is a tough, sagacious, brave, determined enemy.' Then he said, 'But we are making progress,' so that made me happy. Then he come up, praised me, said laudatory remarks about my 'magnificent courage,' one thing and another. I've got a copy of that. But I wasn't being courageous. All I was doing, I was pissed off and mad, and I was doing exactly what I thought I would do if there ever come a war. But I never dreamed that I might fight in a war. You didn't think of that. But anyway, he came up to me, and he had kind of a little bit of an old farmer way of talking—you know, he was born and raised in Texas—and he said, 'Finn, it gives me great pleasure to pin, or, ah, hang, this medal on your neck. Pin, or, ah, hang this medal around your neck.' I was standing there, of course, I was naturally at attention, here was my admiral. The ship was under repair and there was more racket around there with air hoses and crap all over the deck and banging and hammering everywhere. But during that ceremony, they stopped all the noise. Nimitz gave out twenty-five awards. I was number one in line. I think there were two Navy Crosses, and other awards."

More than fifteen Medals of Honor were awarded for action on December 7, nearly all of them for rescue. Finn's was the only Medal of Honor presented to an individual who actually fired back at the enemy that day. On October 6, two weeks after he was decorated, Finn was commissioned an ensign. The following May 1, 1943, he became a lieutenant (jg). He was promoted one last time, in July of 1944, to lieutenant (sg).

Once out of the hospital, Finn started a gunnery school on the base. In addition to his ordnance duties, he was made the Norden bomb site mechanic. "Oh, Christ, that was something I did my damndest to get out of. You cannot be a bomb site mechanic and run an ordnance gang." Several months later he was transferred to the Naval Air Technical Command in Norman, Oklahoma, then went to aviation aerial free gunnery instructors' school in Pensacola, Florida, and from there to stops in Detroit and Chicago and back down to Jacksonville.

John and Alice adopted a baby boy in 1944. Finn retired from active duty in 1947, nearly twenty-one years after his mother had signed so he could join the Navy. He spent some time in the junk business, then in 1958 he and Alice moved onto ninety-three acres out in the country. "I wanted a place to ride my motorcycles, shoot my guns on my own property and collect my junk. I never dreamed though that I'd end up with a hundred fifty head of cattle. At one time we had twenty horses." The cattle went, eventually, and Finn was down to one horse.

John and Alice were together sixty-six years. Alice died December 17, 1998. "Alice was healthy as a pig, but she was just torn up by arthritis. The last two years, the poor thing, she couldn't do anything. She was eighty-eight when she died. She was ready to go. She lived a good long life."

The one thing Medal of Honor recipients share, Finn said, is that they have "whatever it takes to go out and do what they did to get the Medal of Honor, whatever it is—the guts, the courage, or whatever. They had the guts, and stupidity too. I didn't have enough sense to come in out of the rain. But I was mad a lot of the time, pissed off. I can truthfully say I don't remember being scared to death. But I was God damn mad. Anger, hunger, and sex; those are the greatest instincts that we've got. Those are things we are born with. What else is there?"

FIVE

Vernon Baker

Buffalo Soldier
92d Infantry Division
Castle Aghinolfi, Viareggio, Italy
April 5, 1945

*"I heard that black units took up and ran, but I had no actual knowledge
of that happening. I know for myself and for my platoon, and especially for
those nineteen men, when we got in that firefight on that hill on the fifth of
April that, if I'd had a little higher rank and if I'd had a company like
that, the war wouldn't have lasted long. They were that good."*

Vernon Baker at eighty-three in
December 2002 with his ever
reliable M-1 Garand, kept
"always loaded" in the bedroom
of his home in the hills outside
St. Maries, Idaho.

Photo by Tom Davenport

After Vernon Baker's wartime lieutenancy in the 92d Infantry Division expired, he joined the
82d Airborne, became a sergeant, then joined the 11th Airborne and volunteered to fight in
Korea. Instead, he wound up in Alaska, then back in the States. Here, at Fort Campbell, Kentucky, in 1951, he wears the parachute insignia along with his first lieutenant's bars. Under the
U.S. on his left collar is the Combat Infantryman's Badge, and just below that is the ribbon
that signifies the Distinguished Service Cross. On his left pocket flap is the insignia for a Presidential Unit Citation awarded to the 11th Airborne for distinction in World War II.

VERNON BAKER lives way out in the Idaho sticks, about two hours from Spokane, Washington, and south of Coeur d'Alene. We spent about two hours talking in the parlor one summer morning. I didn't get to see the hide of the cougar he shot when he was seventy-five because someone was still in the bedroom, where it lay stretched on the floor, but we had a good visit. He keeps a loaded World War II–era M-1 rifle in his bedroom. I wouldn't fool with him.

"My grandmother, Dora Baker, had the worst disposition of anybody I have ever seen in my life. She was the meanest woman I had ever run across, spiteful—it seemed like she hated everybody. She would scream and yell and shout, and it surprised me that Grampa was so calm and cool with her. I never heard him raise his voice to her at all. After I grew up, I realized she suffered from rheumatoid arthritis and couldn't walk. She was confined to a wheelchair for twenty-two years. When I was a kid I hated her. I didn't realize she was in pain twenty-four hours a day and that really affected her."

Vernon Baker was born in Cheyenne, Wyoming, in 1920, to Manuel Caldera and Beulah Baker, who were killed in a car accident when he was four years old. Vernon and his two sisters were reared by their grandmother, Dora, and their grandfather, Joseph Samuel Baker. The two ran a boardinghouse. Mr. Baker was chief air inspector with the Union Pacific Railroad. He had his own office. He had come to Cheyenne from Buxton, Iowa.

Vernon idolized him. "I tried to follow in his footsteps. We were sitting out on the deck talking one day, and I said, 'Grampa, when I grow up, I want to be just like you.' And he said, 'No.' He said, 'No, boy, you don't grow up to be anybody else. You want to be yourself.'

"One of my favorite traits when I was small was eavesdropping because I wanted to find out what was going on. Al Palmer was Grandfather's best friend, and when they would get together, I would sneak in the room and hide behind his chair and listen to their conversation. This particular time there was a railroad strike, and Mr. Palmer asked him, 'What are you going to do, Joe?' Joe said, 'I'm going to work. I don't have any reason to strike. I don't belong to any unions or anything, and I'm going to work.' And Al said, 'Well you know them guys out there are picketing the shops, so how are you going to go to work?' And Grampa said, 'Well, I'll tell you what happened yesterday. I went to work and I had my .45 in my overalls. A few men stopped me and I pulled my .45 out and put it in my hand, and I walked on through, and I went to work.'

"That's the kind of man my grandfather was. He took no shit from nobody."

He also taught Vernon how to shoot. Grandpa Baker had a sense of humor but he didn't show it "unless something was real funny." The shooting incident took place during a hunt for sage hens. "Mr. Palmer was out with us and Grampa said, 'Boy, I'm gonna show you how to shoot this shotgun now.' He said, 'When we walk through here and one of them sage hens gets up, I want you to knock it down.' I was twelve years old and, oh, boy, he's going to let me shoot his shotgun. It was a double-barreled 12 gauge with two hammers. He showed me how to break it open, put the shells in, close it, and pull the hammers back. I remember pulling both hammers back, and when I got them back, he said, 'Now, put it up on your shoulder and fire. Get that forward trigger.' Well, I had my fingers on both triggers. And he said, 'You ready?' I said, 'Yessir!'

"He said, 'All right, fire!' And I pulled both triggers. It knocked me right on my ass. And that was the first time I ever saw Grampa guffaw. He just stood up there and looked at me. Well, Mr. Palmer was a little more serious than Grampa at that time, so he picked me up and said, 'Now, you see what happens when you don't listen?' I said, 'Yessir!'

His grandfather eventually bought him a .22 rifle and told him every time he fired a shell, he had to bring home meat, prairie dog or jackrabbit, so Vernon became a very good shot. At the rifle range in basic training, he qualified as an expert marksman. This was to prove even more significant when he went into combat in Italy.

Baker learned to read early, but got in and out of trouble. He spent several months at Father Flanagan's Boys Home in Omaha, Nebraska, and then was called home after his grandmother died. He worked shining shoes, making $25 and $30 a week during the Depression, and then as a redcap, or porter, on the Union Pacific. He hated both jobs, which entailed taking too much "guff from assholes." He and a companion, James Horn, still boys, had a thrilling run of several days with two adult women, a pair of carnival dancers called Red Top and Geneva. He eventually finished high school and worked summers on the railroad. In 1940 his grandfather died of prostate cancer.

When Vernon developed a yen for a "hot number" named Leola, his sister Cass suggested he consider the Army and the Quartermaster Corps instead. Vernon also thought that if he had a regular income, Leola might agree to marry him. But his visit to the recruiting office in April of 1941 ended unpleasantly. "The first time I went in, this big old fat guy looked up at me and said, 'What do you want?' I told him I wanted to enlist. He said to me, 'We ain't got no quotas for you people.' "

Vernon went home in despair, but a month later, at Cass's urging, he tried again. This time he encountered a different recruiting officer who, to Vernon's surprise, began asking him questions and writing things down. He said, 'What branch would you like?' I said, 'Quartermaster,' and then watched upside down as he wrote Infantry. But I didn't argue with him because I was in. I was sent to Camp Wolters, Texas, where racism hit me square in the face."

First, though, he tied the knot with Leola on June 25, the day before he left for the Army. When he reached Camp Wolters he found out, in a letter from Cass, that Leola had moved in with an old boyfriend the day Vernon left town. He never saw her again.

Baker had gone to Fort Leavenworth, Kansas, then took a train to Mineral Wells, Texas, where he caught a bus to Camp Wolters. As he got on, he put his duffel down and went to take a seat up front. But then the bus driver spoke. "He said, 'Get out of that seat, nigger, and get back in the back where you belong!' " Back home in Wyoming, Vernon had been condescended to and ordered around, but no one had ever spoken to him like that. "That was a wakeup," he recalled, and a narrow escape as well. "Yeah, because at that time I would have gone on to fisticuffs. I probably would have got killed. They probably would have hanged me. Texas was bad then. This old guy came up and took me in the back and sat me down and educated me there on that bus ride to Camp Wolters. I was mad, and I half listened, but the guy got through to me, so I realized, 'Oh, okay, keep your temper in check, watch what you're doing.' I wasn't thinking about Grampa then, but after I got away, I began to think, you know, 'Grampa's right.' He told me explicitly, 'Don't hate. Because if you hate, hate will destroy you.' "

After basic training, Baker was sent to Fort Huachuca, Arizona, where, because he could read, write, spell, and operate a typewriter, he became a company clerk. In 1942, a white officer told him to sign up for Officer Candidates School and he did so, receiving his commission as a second lieutenant on January 11, 1943. "They were organizing an all-black division, the 92d, in three regiments, in three different places. It was the Buffalo Division, and we were Buffalo Soldiers, a name given to black units during the Indian wars because our black skin and nappy hair made them think we were like buffaloes. I couldn't understand why they organized us in three different places. Of course we were segregated, and that may have had something to do with it."

This was June or July of '43, and the division had come together at Fort Huachuca. "All the officers on this particular day were called up to headquarters. And they wouldn't let us all inside the division headquarters. At that time when you went to headquarters and you were black, even if you were an officer, you went in the back door. You didn't walk in the front door at division headquarters. We were sitting under a tree at the back, and the chief of staff, I can't remember his name, I don't want to remember his name, came out, gathered us all together under a big tree and said, 'Well, you know why we're all here. We're gettin' organized. And all the white boys have been going overseas, and now it's time for you black boys to go get killed.' He said 'black boys.'

"That was it. And a lot of the officers had a chance to ask for a transfer out of the division. A lot of 'em did. They turned around and said, 'Shit, I ain't going.' "

Black newspapers and organizations such as the National Association for the Advancement of Colored People had repeatedly petitioned the government, and President Roosevelt in particular, to grant blacks a significant role in wartime industry and all branches of the military. Resistance was intense, and bigotry ran bone deep.

Indeed, racism was institutionalized in the United States Army. For example, a study, produced by field-grade students at the Army War College in 1937, four years before the war, concluded, "As an individual, the Negro is docile, tractable, lighthearted, carefree and good-natured. If unjustly treated, he is likely to become surly and stubborn, though this is usually a temporary phase. He is careless, shiftless, irresponsible, and secretive. He resents censure and is best handled with praise and by ridicule. He is unmoral, untruthful, and his sense of right doing is relatively inferior. Crimes and convictions involving moral turpitude are nearly five to one as compared to convictions of whites on similar charges.

"On the other hand the Negro is cheerful, loyal, and usually uncomplaining if reasonably well fed. He has a musical nature and a marked sense of rhythm. His art is primitive. He is religious. With proper direction in mass, Negroes are industrious. They are emotional and can be stirred to a high state of enthusiasm. Their emotions are unstable and their reactions uncertain. Bad leadership in particular is easily communicated to them."

This attitude did not give black units much chance for success; it was compounded by the Army's thinking that white southerners were the best suited to command black units because they "understood" the Negro. All company commanders and senior officers in the 92d Division were white. Lieutenants and noncommissioned officers were black.

Baker encountered prejudice in his own platoon. "They were all from the South, and they were all illiterate. They were big. I was five feet five and weighed one hundred and thirty-nine pounds, twenty-two years old. They were seven to nine years older than I, and they thought I was the 'white man's nigger,' a 'smart nigger.' We had a hard time until we got on the ship and began talking to one another.

Then I became their mother, their father, their sister, their brother. I wrote all their letters for them, read all the letters to them, and in the process we got together. We went as a combat team. We reverted from the 25th Infantry Regiment to the 370th, altogether a little more than five thousand men. But we were still part of the 92d. We were the first unit to go over. We got to Newport News, Virginia, and we saw one great big ship sitting there, the *Mariposa*, an ocean liner that had been converted to a troopship, and they put the whole combat team on that one ship."

The division crossed the Atlantic without an escort, landing at Naples, and then encamped in an old volcanic crater for a few days. Once resupplied, the units moved out, to Civitavecchia and from there up the west coast of Italy, toward Pisa, Lucca, and the front lines. It was July of 1944.

"Right after we got over there, we went on a night patrol. They said blacks couldn't fight at night, and that's all we did. Our first three or four months of combat was nothing but night patrols. Reconnaissance." Baker saw several of his own men killed as he learned how to function in combat. Early on, he lost three men on patrol. Their deaths haunted him, he said, "because I sent them there. I placed them in that position. I said, 'You go right here, and you wait there.' When the Germans hit us we were just getting organized to move out, and I had told those three men to go cover us. They got it, just like that. They were exposed. It was stupidity on my part, I realized. I still feel it. It was a dumb thing to send those men up there.

"Combat is a learning thing. If you give an order, and people get killed or hurt, it's a learning experience, and you keep that in the back of your mind: Watch out for this kind of situation. You keep that in your mind and don't repeat it. That was my philosophy. I tried not to repeat things. I kept pulling things back out that I had experienced before. I tried to keep everything in my mind as what should we do in this situation, what should we do in that. Or if a new situation comes up, either do this or that, because if you don't, somebody's gonna get killed, and it may be you."

Baker made it from July to October without injury. "We crossed a canal near Seravezza to capture a farmhouse, and Lieutenant Frazier became the first officer in our company to get killed. He and three or four of his men got killed in this very same area doing the same thing they told me to take my platoon up there and do. We went across this canal where the bridge was blown, and the road continued on up by this house we were supposed to take. I led the platoon with my platoon sergeant. There was a stone wall, and I told the rest of the platoon, 'You stay here.' I took the platoon sergeant and two more men and we went up off the road and around the house. It was very dark. We went almost all the way around the house, and I looked up and saw this silhouette of a German soldier standing on the skyline, and he must have seen or felt our movement because it was black dark. He shouted something in German, and I fired at him. He dropped and fired back.

"When I dropped I fired also, and as I was doing this, I felt something hit me, right here in the wrist. Well it didn't hurt. It was something like a sting. And I kept firing and he stopped, so I told the platoon sergeant, 'Let's go up and see.' The German was only five or ten feet from the corner of the house we were supposed to take. He was lying there dead. I kept feeling a little tingling in my arm but never paid any attention to it. We broke into the house and cleaned it out. There were five more German soldiers in there, asleep. We caught them asleep, and we did them in. This was about two o'clock in the morning. They didn't hear my exchange with the sentry because the walls on that house were about four feet thick.

"I left two men in the house and went back outside. There was a warehouse on the other side of the road and down the hill and we went there. Lieutenant Montjoy, my company commander, and I walked in. As my eyes became accustomed to the gloom, I saw big naval shells about waist high, standing, aligned all the way around the damn warehouse, with wires going from one to the other. I turned around, and I said to Montjoy, 'We better get the hell out of here.' And he looked. He was a light guy, and he got pale. He said, 'Oh shit, let's get out of here.' "

When they returned to the command post, Baker got into a mild altercation with Montjoy and the platoon sergeant, who kept telling him he had been hit. He kept denying it, right up until the moment he passed out. "When I woke up, I looked into the brown eyes of a pretty Italian woman, who was asking if I wanted a cigarette. Oh, that was a good day. I was sent to the 64th General Hospital right outside of Pisa. I was there from the middle of October to December twenty-sixth. The bullet broke a couple bones in my wrist. I've still got a piece of metal in there holding the bone together."

When he came out of the hospital, Baker finally settled on a weapon of choice. He chose the M-1 Garand, the rifle carried by most GIs. "We went over to Italy with 1902 Springfield bolt-action rifles. I was no stranger to guns, and I had a feeling for weapons. When I went over as an officer they gave us those .30 caliber carbines, and I thought it was a pretty spiffy little weapon until I saw a German take about six rounds from one and keep on coming. And I said, 'Uh uh,' and I traded it to a tanker in the First Armored Division for a .45 caliber Thompson submachine gun. I remember we were in a firefight one day, and I threw up that Thompson and it chattered, and I could see each of the bullets going out of the barrel, and I said, 'Uh uh.' It was effective only at very short range. So when I came out of the hospital on the twenty-sixth of December, I went and got an M-1. It was a .30-.06, with an eight-shot clip that ejected automatically when it was empty. I loved it. It is a beautiful rifle, it really is. I got one settin' in there, in my bedroom.

"On the fifth of April, 1945, the whole Buffalo Division—twelve thousand to fifteen thousand men—was spread out at Querceta. The whole front moved. The objective was to end the war. This was the last big offensive in that part of Italy. Our objective was the Castle Aghinolfi. On our right were the Japanese-Americans, the 442d. My outfit, the 370th, was going up toward the castle. We were all on foot. There were no tanks because of the terrain. Our objectives were Hills X, Y, and Z, and then the castle, which sat right up on a knob overlooking the Ligurian Sea, part of the Mediterranean.

"Captain John F. Runyon came to the unit about a week before the push. He brought with him a Lieutenant Botwinik. I can't remember the name of the other lieutenant. I was the only officer in the company until Captain Runyon and the other two came. White officers were always coming through to get their tickets punched, get 'combat experience,' and move on. At that time I never thought too much about it because I figured, 'Well, they're white. They don't want to be with us anyway, and the hell with 'em.' But that was one of the things that rankled most of the black people who saw or figured out what was going on. I never paid much attention to it because I had a job to do and I had men I had to teach, and I wanted to do my job and the hell with anybody else.

"I was still a second lieutenant. I stayed a second lieutenant from January first, nineteen forty-three, until May of nineteen forty-five, when the war was over. I was the executive officer, but Runyon made me the weapons platoon leader, which I didn't want—mortars and heavy machine guns. I was a rifleman. I had six grenades to start that morning, two bandoliers of M-1 clips with forty-eight shells each and one clip in the rifle, and a .45 on my hip. Runyon led us and he went rock to rock. I was right on his tail, and I passed the word back. Stay on the rocks. I never thought about mines, but there were mines all over that place. As we got up on the crest and started east, I heard explosions behind us. We got separated from the mortar squad, and I don't know to this day what happened to them. They most likely got caught in the minefield. When I heard the explosions, I thought it was our artillery barrage. Artillery was supposed to precede us, but it didn't.

"The hills, X, Y, and Z, were interlocking and there was high ground, very high, up on the right. This is where the Japanese were, the 442d, and up on Hill X, there were these wires running down all over the place. They were coated in yellow plastic—the first time I had ever seen any plastic wire. I carried a pair of wire cutters with me for barbed wire during patrols. I kept them right next to my .45 on the side. I took those wire cutters out, and I cut that wire. Every time we come across it, I cut it. As we were going up, I'd see some men and they would pick the wire up and glance over at me, and I'd cut that sumbitch. It felt real good. I don't know, but I'm thinking that was what got us up to the castle, because we cut all their communication lines. Because they were strung all the way across, crisscrossed, like a spiderweb almost, there were so many wires. I guess if we hadn't cut those wires, they would have known where we were step-by-step.

"I had twenty-six guys. I had lost the mortar platoon, but some others guys came along. I don't know what happened to Runyon. He faded away, and then when we got up to where we could see the castle, all of sudden he was there. I can't say he hid. I don't know where he came from. The first German machine-gun nest was just going up the tip of X, the first hill. I was coming from the flank. I had no idea there were any machine-gun nests or anything. All I wanted to do was get my men up there near that castle in one piece. I happened to look over, and I saw movement, I saw two helmets. Now, all the time the artillery was boom boom boom and boom boom boom, all across the whole front. There was so damn much noise you couldn't even hear yourself think.

"I saw these two helmets and fired at them from about thirty yards. I fired, and I walked over and looked, and there they were. My men kept coming. I don't know why, but I was ahead of every-body. When they came up, I left a couple of my machine-gun guys there and we went on.

After a while, off to the side, I saw some things peeking out of the ground. It was between six A.M. and seven A.M. that April, just beginning to get light. You could make things out. I saw holes, a lit-tle mound, with some holes with these two cylindrical objects pok-ing out, and I said, 'Oh, damn, it's an observation post.' I crawled up there and threw a grenade in the slit, and boom! I came back around the other way, because I saw dust blow there, and I found the entrance and peeked in. There was two guys in there, gone. I think they were dead.

"I went on up the next hill, and then I saw two more heads bob-bing around, and I shot. I shot at the object. I shot at what I saw, what I saw moving. I know I'm a good shot, but there was luck to that, too. I just shot. And there they were, two more guys lying up there. It was another machine-gun nest. I left two more machine-gun guys there with the water-cooled .30 caliber, the good one. I left them there and came on back, and we got all the way up. And right out there at the edge I met Captain Runyon. We were standing there looking at the Castle Aghinolfi. But there was a deep-assed draw, I'd say a young canyon, maybe a couple hundred feet deep, between us and the castle.

"We were standing there trying to figure out how to get across, because halfway up on the other side of the draw everything was exposed. If we went to our left, we could go down. We could see all the way to Highway One along the coast. We were sitting there trying to figure out whether we should go left or right, when this guy came out on the path down below. It was brush covered, and you couldn't see unless you were almost on it. This German came out, and I saw his helmet come up, and he stopped and looked up us and threw this damn grenade.

"And Runyon yelped. He threw his hands up as I was veering across him to shoot the guy, and he almost knocked the rifle out of my hands. I got hold of the rifle and the guy almost got out of sight around the corner of the path before I shot. I hit him twice. Well, Runyon disappeared. The grenade had landed right at our feet and nothing happened. But it never registered on me. I said, 'I'm okay, I'm fine,' so I went on down the path. The rest of the guys are still coming. 'I'm all by myself. There's nobody there but me.' "

Why did he go down the path? "Jesus Christ, I don't know. After I shot the guy, I think I was a little curious to see what he looked like. I went down the path and turned him over. He was a young kid—eighteen, twenty years old. So then I went on, and all this other shit happened. The kid's dugout was empty, but I went on down until I came to another dugout that was sealed shut with a Volkswagen car door over the entrance. I used a grenade to blow the door open. Then this guy peeped out, and I blowed his head off, and threw another grenade in. I checked inside, and there were three more dead Germans. They had been having breakfast.

"The path went all the way down, but I said, 'Bullshit, I ain't going down there.' We were three miles behind the German lines, and it was between eight and nine o'clock. I went back up and found Sergeant Dickens, asked him, 'Where's Runyon?' He didn't even know who Runyon was. I said, 'The company commander.' 'Oh, he went back up to this little stone house.' I think it was a stable of some kind. So I walked up there—and Runyon was sitting there on the floor, and he had his hands around his knees, and he was white as a sheet, no color at all. He hadn't been in combat. And then he said, 'Baker, can't you get these men together out there?'

"And I didn't lose it. I said, 'I'm doing the God damn best I can, Captain.' And he said, 'Well that's all right. I just wanted to know.' Then I looked out the door and there was a stone wall going up the hill, and Lieutenant Botwinik was up here. He had four men with him, just sitting down behind the wall. Then, all of a sudden, here come the mortars. As I looked out the door, I saw a mortar round coming down, three feet long, big son of a bitch. I can still see that damn round coming down and hitting that wall. I thought Botwinik was dead because it landed right on top of him on the wall, and he disappeared in all the dust and dirt, and I said, 'Oh shit, he's gone.' And I looked out, and here he come staggering down the wall. He was about half blind. He got in, and Runyon hadn't moved. He was just sitting there, rocking back and forth. Then Runyon kind of moved and got to him and took him over and brushed dust and stuff off his face, and then he turned to me and said, 'Baker, I'm going back for reinforcements.'

"I looked at him, and I'm not going to tell what I thought." Pressed to continue, Baker said, "I started to shoot him. I did. I started to kill him. But then, I said, 'No, uh uh, whoo.' It was bullshit, but I didn't say it to his face. I just looked at him and said, 'All right, Captain. We'll be here when you get back.' Runyon took Botwinik and the radioman, so we didn't have any communication, and he went back and told Colonel Murphy, our battalion commander, that we were all gone.

"Earlier, Walker, our artillery spotter, had tried to get artillery support against the mortars, and nobody would believe we were there until Walker yelled and screamed and cursed so on the radio, and then all of a sudden we could hear our antiaircraft—boom boom boom and then chirrup chirrup chirrup. They came right over the crest of that hill and down at the castle. There were no planes for them to shoot at, so they used those 90 mm antiaircraft guns as supporting artillery. After that, one of the mortars got Walker's radioman and the radio, and then Runyon took the other one. I never realized until after the war that he had taken the radio. I didn't have any communication at all. I didn't think about it because when he left, the mortars started coming in again.

"We set up a perimeter in a little depression almost at the edge of the draw. You could look down and peek over and spot them. Well, the Germans knew we were there, and they kept mortaring and they kept mortaring and they kept mortaring, and every time I'd look up, a mortar round would fall and one of the men would fall, and I said, 'Shit.' Every time a man died, I went and took the dog tags off him, lifted them up over his head. I had a pocketful when we got back. After a while, the Germans came out and attacked along the wall. I told the men, 'Lay still and shoot at movement.' And that's what we did.

"The enemy sent guys out with stretchers and blankets and stuff. They knew where we were, but the mortars weren't taking too much effect on us because we were in that little depression. So here they come with those stretchers, between eighteen and twenty men with four stretchers. They had a flag with a red cross on it. My men wanted to shoot, but I told them, 'No, just hang steady, no, no.' Because if they were medics, you don't want anybody shooting your medic. And when the Germans dropped those stretchers and took the blankets off, they had machine guns. It was incomprehensible to me that somebody would use a symbol of mercy to commit a crime. I saw where there were some dirty things done, but that was the dirtiest thing I ever saw. I told my men, 'Hit the bastards!' All we had was our rifles, but that M-1 was something else. If you had fifteen or sixteen men, and each one of 'em's got an M-1, you had pretty good firepower. We blasted them out before they could set up."

Why did Baker and his men stay after Runyon left? "Dumb. That's the only way I can figure out. Dumb. But we were fightin' a war. And we had something to prove, and we did that. Of course nineteen men died up there. I've thought about that a lot. We were out there all day. When we headed back, there were seven of us left and myself. We lost two on the way back, so when I got back down we were six.

"I heard that black units took up and ran, but I had no actual knowledge of that happening. I know for myself and my platoon, and especially for those nineteen men, when we got in that firefight on that hill on the fifth of April that, if I'd had a little higher rank and if I'd had a company like that, the war wouldn't have lasted long. They were that good.

"We saw two more machine-gun nests on the way down, and Johnson, my drunkard who kept getting himself in trouble and getting busted, appeared from somewhere with a BAR, Browning Automatic Rifle. There were two machine-gun nests we had bypassed going up. They were firing back down the hill. They were busy. I looked over at Johnson, and he was using his BAR to fire at those machine guns. So I waved him over and he came standing up, and I was afraid for him, and I kept yelling at him, I said, 'God damn it, Johnson, get down!' And he said, 'God damn it, Lieutenant, I'm gonna be here when you're gone! I'm all right. Go!' And he kept those machine guns suppressed while I belly-whopped to them. I had three grenades left, and I used two, one on each outpost.

"I had sent my men ahead of me, and they found a tank and took it out by dropping grenades inside. When I saw the turret there and smoke coming out, I just kept going, we all kept going, straight down back to Highway One. Back on the road, I sent the men to report in to the CP.

"And then I went and vomited my guts out. That was a horrendous day, I'll tell you. I'd never seen so much blood shed in all my life. I didn't count the number I'd killed. I was just working on adrenaline and reflexes, trying to stay alive. That's all. Didn't eat all day. I had a canteen of water on me. That's all."

By his account, Baker had single-handedly killed seventeen of the enemy, taken out four machine-gun nests, an observation post, two bunkers, and perhaps critically disrupted enemy communications by cutting all those yellow wires. The Germans pulled out that night.

"There was a call from Colonel Murphy when I got back to the CP. He was a lieutenant colonel, our battalion commander, and he was the only officer who said thank you. First thing I walked in the door, he said, 'Runyon was here.' And I knew, he didn't have to tell me, I knew Runyon had told him we were all dead."

Vernon Baker was awarded the Distinguished Service Cross for his efforts that day. Remarkably, Captain Runyon received a Silver Star. How this came to be, Baker said, "I don't know. He had some buddies up in Division because that's where he was when he came to us. He disappeared after April fifth. I never saw him again until the Fourth, when I got the Distinguished Service Cross and he was standing to my left." More than fifty-five years later, Baker received a message from a Runyon via the Internet. "I think it was a woman's name. She wanted me to get in touch with her, but I'm not going to because I don't have anything to say to them."

After reporting to Colonel Murphy, Baker asked the Jeep driver to take him to Regimental Headquarters, a three-story villa with an underground tunnel, so he could drop off the dog tags of his slain men. There had been a lot of artillery all day, and everybody inside the place was wearing a steel helmet. "Colonel Raymond Sherman, the regimental commander, never asked about the dog tags. The only thing he asked when I walked in, was, 'Are you just out of the field?' I said, 'Yes, sir.' He said, 'Where's your helmet, Lieutenant?' I said, 'Back in my quarters, sir.' And then he started. He didn't have a word of thanks or ask what did you do or what happened up there or nothing. He just started chewing my ass because I didn't have a helmet on. He was just stupid. He said he wanted me to lead a patrol back up there next morning. I could have shot him.

"Next morning I went to the 473d. The company was an all-white unit that had been put together from various service units. They had no combat experience at all, but they were lucky, because the Germans had moved out. When I took them back up on that hill, there was not a sound, not a sign. The only people up on that hill were my dead men. The Germans had taken their weapons and their shoes and socks. Boots and socks. They were all barefooted. You can see what condition the German Army was in when they had to take boots and socks off dead men." The Germans were gone from the castle, too. So the division had accomplished its objective, and Vernon's platoon had played a significant part, especially in cutting the wires. "I guess so," he said. "But we didn't get any thanks for it."

The European war ended not long after, on May 15. That same month Vernon finally made it to first lieutenant. Colonel Murphy brought him his bars and pinned them on. In mid-June Vernon got a message to report to Major General Edward M. Almond, the commanding general of the division. "And I was wondering, 'Oh shit, what have I done now?' What did I do, or what did I get caught doing? I'm young, the war was over and I had cut some didoes [shenanigans]. I got a Jeep and a driver. Headquarters was just outside of Genoa in a big castle. I was ushered in, and you know when you're going to meet the CG, the big shot, you have to sit around and wait. Finally I was told, 'Okay, Lieutenant, go in there and report to General Almond.' So I went in, and he was standing by a big window looking out over Genoa. The door closed behind me, and I stood there and waited for him to turn around. Finally he did, and I saluted and said, 'Second Lieutenant Baker reporting, sir.' He didn't even return my salute. He just walked over and looked at me and poked me in the chest and said, 'I want you to write me a report of what went on on that hill April fifth.' And I said, 'Yes,' and I didn't even get the 'sir' out of my mouth and he said, 'Dismissed!' The bastard. So I went back and wrote my report.

"Later on, we were in Viareggio, and I got a message to be there for the Fourth of July medal ceremony. And, you know, protocol has it that the highest award goes to the person who stands on the extreme right in a medal ceremony. Guess who stood on the extreme right—General Almond. He got the oak-leaf cluster to the

Silver Star. And Runyon was down on my left, getting his Silver Star. I can't think of the name of the general who handed out the decorations. I got a photograph of the ceremony, but I don't know where it is. It all just pissed me off, so I hid it someplace."

Back in April, Vernon's division had followed the German retreat from Italy. In Milan, on the trek north, Vernon saw and photographed the corpses of Mussolini and his mistress, Claretta Petacci, and watched their bodies hoisted feetfirst as they were hung by partisans from the concrete beam of a bombed-out building.

In September of '45, in Genoa, Vernon hooked up with a fiery young Italian woman named Giovanna Sanna. Wildly in love, he stayed in Italy as long as he could, returning to the States in February 1947. The ship from Italy stopped in Southampton, England. "We pulled in there because of the storms on the Atlantic. They told us we could go into town but don't stay too long, four or five hours. So I walked through the streets, and the weather was terrible. I found myself a little cafe and went in and sat down and had a cup of tea and a scone or whatever it was. This young lady, I think she was a prostitute, she came and sat down and said, 'Hi, guy.' I asked if I could get her something and she said, 'No, I just have a question to ask you.' I said, 'Okay.' And she's leaning over toward me and she said, 'Would it be all right if I see your tail?'

"I said, 'Ain't this a bitch? Where you get this that I've got a tail?' She said, 'Well, your buddies tell me that you black guys have tails.' I said, 'Well, wherever you got the information, I don't have a tail, and I'm not going to bare my ass to let you look at me.' She said, 'Wait, don't be offended. I just wanted to see.' Vernon laughed at the memory, and asked, 'What you gonna do?'

"My commission expired in June of forty-seven. My Aunt Cord talked me into reenlisting. To stay in, I had to go down to master sergeant." He joined an all-black unit in the 82d Airborne, eventually went to photo school, served in Korea after the war there, and then for an extended period at Fort Ord, California, and did his last tour in Germany, where he retired in August 1968.

"I have no complaints at all. I saw a lot of prejudice fall by the wayside. This was the only country I had, and I knew things would get better. I just felt it in my heart. I came to the realization that America, the United States, was growing up. Look at Colin Powell."

Responding to the 1937 summary about blacks from the Army War College, Baker said, "Reading this, I could begin to hate again, but now, I feel it's just from somebody who doesn't know and has his own idea about people that are of a different color or a different ethnic group, or a different religion. I think it's something that came from way back in prehistoric days, and it's been carried on up to now. I had problems with some of the white fellas after the Army was integrated in forty-eight, and I told many of 'em, I said, 'You look at me, and look at my color on the outside, but I'll tell you one damn thing: We get out there and something happens, your blood is just as red as mine, and my blood is just as red as yours. We all bleed the same color.' "

After getting out of a second marriage he'd made during the war, Baker met and married Fern V. Brown, a divorcée with two daughters. They married in June of 1953 and had another daughter together. During a yearlong tour of Korea, the Bakers adopted a fourth child, a nine-year-old girl, half black, half Korean. After retiring from the Army, Baker went to work for the Red Cross for twenty years. He spent 1969 in Vietnam as a Red Cross counselor. His marriage to Fern lasted thirty-eight years, until she died of a heart attack in January 1986.

Seven years earlier, Baker, who was a member of the National Rifle Association, read in its magazine, *American Hunter*, a piece about elk hunting in the Red Ives Peak country in northern Idaho. In 1979 he went up there with a friend and shot an elk. In 1987, with his wife gone, and yearning for more solitary surroundings, he bought a twenty-five-acre property way out in the country, near St. Maries, Idaho, gave the kids the California house, and moved up there for keeps. It suited him. He was sixty-seven years old.

A year later, sitting at a restaurant table in Spokane Airport, he flirted with an attractive blonde, Heidy Pawlik, who was sitting nearby. It turned out she had been born in Germany and lived in Pennsylvania. They kept in touch, until Baker finally invited her for a visit to Idaho. Subsequently, she came to stay, and they married four years after that.

In March of 1996, Baker was sitting at the dining-room table when the phone rang. "Heidy usually answers the phone. But I picked it up and said, 'Good morning.' The voice on the other end said, 'Mr. Baker, Vernon Baker?' I said, 'Yeah.' He said, 'What do you know about the Medal of Honor?' And I thought, 'Who in the hell is this nut?' and I started to hang up the phone. He said, 'Don't hang up! I'm Professor Gibran and I'm a professor at the Shaw University in North Carolina, and the Army has given us a $350,000 grant to investigate why no black Americans received the Medal of Honor during World War II.' And I said, 'Um, yeah, this is another one of those committees they dream up to investigate, and then all of a sudden they're gone.'

"Well, he said he'd like to come and talk to me, him and a Colonel Cash. He's deceased now. So I said, 'Okay.' We met them over at a hotel in Spokane for a couple of days, spent the time talking. Then, all of sudden, reporters started calling, and then people started showing up at the door, wanting interviews." A Spokane newspaper reporter, Ken Olsen, did a series on Baker for the *Spokesman-Review*, and they collaborated on his autobiography, *Lasting Valor*, published by Genesis Press in 1997 and then in paperback by Bantam in February of 1999.

"I received the Medal the thirteenth of January, nineteen ninety-seven, from President Clinton," Vernon said. "Seven were awarded, but I was the only one still walking around."

What finally, after all those years, was going through his mind as the President of the United States put the blue ribbon of the Medal of Honor around his neck? "I was thinking about nineteen men left on a hillside." Reliving this moment, five years after receiving the Medal from the President, Vernon Baker wept.

SIX

Desmond Doss

Conscientious Objector
Okinawa, May 5, 1945

*"That skinny pharmacist's mate from Georgia who's getting
the Medal of Honor is the only CO I consider to be on the level."*
— *Harry Truman*

by Robert M. Bush, CMOHS photographer

Desmond, photographed during a
luncheon at the annual convention
of the Congressional Medal of
Honor Society, held in Shreveport-
Bossier, Louisiana, at Barksdale Air
Force Base on September 11, 2002.

Desmond Doss in Okinawa atop the Maeda
Escarpment, over which he lowered the bodies
of between fifty and one hundred injured GIs.
The rope he used hangs down from the cliff.

90

OUTSIDE THE HOME of Desmond and Frances Doss atop Lookout Mountain in Rising Fawn, Georgia, just over the border from Chattanooga, stands a ten-foot replica of the Statue of Liberty, the emblem of Doss's 77th Infantry Division. He discovered it some years previously in an antique shop in Chattanooga. It was expensive and he didn't want to buy it. But his first wife, Dorothy, pointed out all the money he had saved over the years by not smoking and suggested he take that money now, and buy the statue. Doss did.

Desmond Doss was Sergeant York without the rifle.

"Why be a noncombatant? In my case, it's what I wanted because of this picture here of the Ten Commandments and the Lord's Prayer." Desmond Doss, who was born February 7, 1919, gestured at a poster encased in plastic and framed in wood, hanging on the wall behind his living room sofa. A little scene accompanied each of the Commandments, which encircled the Prayer, spelled out elaborately in eleven different kinds of type. The panel for the Sixth Commandment showed Cain holding a club, with the slain Abel at his feet. A beam of light flashes down while Cain holds his left hand to his brow.

"My dad bought it at an auction for seventy-five cents when they first started housekeeping, and so the picture's over a hundred years old. And when I looked at that picture, I came to the Sixth Commandment, Thou Shalt Not Kill. I wondered, how in the world could a brother do such a thing? It put a horror in my heart of just killin', and as a result I took it personally: 'Desmond, if you love Me, you won't kill.' And He says that every man is your brother.

"And when I was eighteen, in nineteen thirty-seven, I registered, like anyone else, with my draft board in Lynchburg, Virginia. I believed in serving God and country. I took medical training, and I did what I could in preparation for getting into the Medical Corps where I could serve God and country without going against the dictates of my conscience. My pastor, R. F. Woods, went with me. We were Seventh-Day Adventists. I wanted to be known as a noncombatant, but the Army had no such classification. I had to accept

Conscientious Objector status or face a court-martial. It meant you were going in with religious scruples. Now, I did not want to be known as a CO because they were refusing to salute the flag or serve the country in any way, shape, or form, and they were having demonstrations.

"Congress signed into law that COs could not be forced to bear arms. President Franklin D. Roosevelt and George E. Marshall, chief of staff, signed it, showing their approval. Adventists would not volunteer but would wait to be drafted. That's why I didn't go in until April first, nineteen forty-two. In addition to the Sixth Commandment, there was also the Fourth, to remember the Sabbath and keep it holy. Now, Saturday is the Sabbath to Adventists and they worship on that day and don't work. But, you know, Christ healed on the Sabbath. It's a type of work I could do seven days a week. That's why I wanted to get into the Medical Corps.

"I was working as a carpenter in defense work in a shipyard in Newport News, Virginia, and my boss offered me a deferment. But I did not feel it was essential work, so I refused, because I was in good health and I did not want to be known as a 4-F or draft dodger, and I felt it was an honor to serve God and country. I didn't feel like I was any better than anyone else. I could serve my country for twenty-one dollars a month. That's what we got when we went in. We had a joke in the Army: 'You know how much I get? No. Twenty-one dollars a day! What? Yep, once a month.' "

The first thing the Army did wrong was to assign Doss to a rifle company in the 77th Infantry Division at Fort Jackson, South Carolina. Desmond went to the chaplain and got himself transferred to the medical department, as a bona fide objector. This was only the beginning of Desmond vs. the U.S. Army. On his first night in the service, as he knelt at his bunk to pray, the other recruits hooted and threw boots at him. Desmond confronted one ordeal after another as he faced down a succession of officers at bases in Louisiana, Arizona, Pennsylvania, and Virginia who sought to compel him to hold a rifle or a hand grenade or a knife, tried to make him work on his Sabbath, refused to grant him passes so he could go off base to attend services, and in general sought to make his life miserable. He was transferred back to the infantry, threatened with court-martial, and one officer even tried to get him out of the Army on a Section Eight, as a mental case. None of them succeeded. Desmond never hesitated to go over his officers' heads. On one occasion, his father appealed on his behalf all the way to Washington. This got him reinstated with the medical department. He carried around a note from General of the Army George C. Marshall saying he was entitled to practice his religion.

Doss had a knack for knots, partly as a result of learning all about them as a Junior Missionary Volunteer in his church, and during training in West Virginia an officer engaged him to help the men with knot tying, which was useful in scaling or descending steep slopes, crossing rivers, and in other areas. On one occasion, two men were using each end of a long rope, so Desmond took the middle part, doubled it, and began to practice with it. He threw a bowline, a strong knot that can be untied fairly easily, and found he had two loops that would not slip. He was to remember this long afterward in a deadly place on Okinawa.

On August 17, 1942, not long after finishing basic training, Desmond married his first wife, Dorothy Schutte, of Richmond, Virginia, also a devout Adventist. Their marriage was to endure eight months short of fifty years. That November she gave him a Bible, which he carried throughout extended combat in Guam, Leyte, and Okinawa.

She inscribed these words:

Dearest Desmond,

As you read and study the precious promises found in the word of God contained in this little Bible, may you be strengthened in whatever trials may come to you. May your faith in God bring comfort and peace of heart to you, that you may never be sad or lonely no matter how dark the way seems. If we do not meet another time on this earth, we have the assurance of a happy meeting place in heaven. May God in His mercy grant us both a place there.

Your loving wife, Dorothy.

"When we went overseas," Doss said, "I was assigned to the 2d Platoon, Company B, 1st Battalion, 307th Infantry. I had three months' training to be a medic at Fort Jackson, South Carolina." After more than two years of training, the 77th, the Statue of Liberty Division, shipped out for Hawaii and then, in July of 1944, landed at Agat Bay on the island of Guam. "Brother! Talk about rain! It was coming down like out of a bucket, and the tide was in, and we had to get out about a half mile from shore. The fellows coming in held their rifles over their heads. The vehicles were waterproofed to run underwater, and I saw Jeeps with fellows standing on the seats steering the things to shore while stuff floated away. On shore there were dead Japanese everywhere.

"Once we got there we had these tanks and these two-and-a-half-ton trucks and bulldozers pushing through the ruts, mud, soupy mud—knee deep. The fellows in the platoon were cussing up a streak because they were so mad. I found out that didn't do no good, and through my mind, I was humming to myself "Onward, Christian Soldiers." Now, I had a number of experiences on Guam. The brass said, 'Don't touch anything, marking pens or anything,' because the Japanese booby-trapped things. I was going along this trail when—Boom—there came this big noise, and I heard three men screaming, calling for a medic. I got to these three men, and they were still sizzling from being hit by a white phosphorous grenade. Phosphorous sticks to the skin as it burns. They were the first ones I treated in combat. Even the trails, those that weren't guarded, were booby-trapped. So we had to head across the brush. You could hardly crawl under it with a pack.

"Now the Army has ways of getting jobs done. We were given a three-day issue of K rations. You could eat it all at once, or you could make it last, they said, because there would be no more until we got the roads open so the trucks could get through. I myself was living off coconuts and dog biscuits, we called them, a kind of hardtack that came in K and C rations we were sure were left over from World War I. The rations were mostly pork or bacon and cheese, and Adventists don't eat pork, so I had to get by on the dog biscuits and, I tell you, those things are strong. The other folks couldn't eat them. I've even seen a dog turn his nose up at those things.

"Anyway, we were at a standstill, and I saw some coconut trees, and I went out to get myself some coconut and I no more than got to the trees, and brother, I began to get sprayed with machine-gun fire, and I knew I was a dead duck. It was the first time I was out in the open being sprayed with a machine gun. Well, luckily, those Japanese had had a lot of sake, whiskey, and man, they were so drunk they couldn't hit a boxcar. I didn't drink coffee or tea, let alone whiskey, but this was one time I was sure glad they were drunk. Otherwise I would have been shot to pieces. I ran and jumped into a ditch near the road. We found empty bottles all around their position later.

"The Japanese were out to get the medics. To them, the most hated men in our army were the medics and the BAR men, the Browning Automatic Riflemen. They would let anybody get by just to pick us off. They were taught to kill the medics for the reason it broke down the morale of the men, because if the medic was gone they had no one to take care of them. All the medics were armed, except me. There was no evidence but your aid kit to show that you were a medic. Even though I was unarmed, the men wanted to get close to me. I had to shoo them away. They said they felt safer with me.

"I made it a practice to go out on patrol with the men. The non-com [a noncommissioned officer, such as a sergeant] warned me not to, but I told him, it may not be my duty but it was what I believed in. I knew these men; they were my buddies, some had wives and children. If they were hurt, I wanted to be there to take care of them. And when someone got hit, the others would close in around me while I treated him, then we'd all go out together."

Captain Leo Tann, the medical officer at the battalion aid station, also warned Doss against going out on patrol. Toward the end of the campaign on Guam, he made Desmond a litter bearer, probably to keep him from going out with the men.

For most of November 1944, the 77th was aboard ship, steaming toward New Caledonia for rest and relaxation, but then the transport changed course for Leyte in the Philippines. The American advance had slowed, and the Japanese command had declared it would make the Leyte campaign decisive. Desmond's division landed first on a secure beachhead on the east coast, at a place called Dulag, but two weeks later it was pulled out and transported by ship around the island, south and up the west side, to invade just below Ormoc on December 8. The Japanese, expecting reinforcements, thought it was their own forces landing, instead of the Americans, and did not contest the beaches.

"We saw plenty of combat in Leyte. In fact, that's where I lost two of my closest buddies, Clarence Glenn and Herb Schecter, a Jew." They had been together from the beginning. Back in the States, Glenn and another medic named James Dorris had attended to Desmond's duties while he was off on Saturdays, and he filled in for them Sundays so they could attend Mass. All three were married, and off duty they socialized.

"I tell you it was all in the goodness of the Lord I'm alive because I went at risk of my life to save them. Somebody said, 'Doss, do you know Glenn's been hit?' I said, 'No, why didn't they tell me?' He had gone against orders to take care of someone up on this plateau, and he got shot. I went to try to take care of him, but there was no way I could go into this open field—it was just sagebrush—and take care of two men by myself. And then I met another medic, Herb Schecter, a Jewish fella, and he volunteered to go with me. Schecter went to see Glenn, and I got to this other fella first. Blood was running down his face and eyes, and he was groaning and calling for a medic. I took water from my canteen and washed the blood out of this man's eyes. Man, when his eyes came open, his face just lit up. If I had not received any more than that smile, I'd have been well repaid. He thought he was blind.

"I called over to Schecter and asked, 'How's Glenn?' 'Bad, come over.' That's where I made a bad mistake because, man, the Japanese started firing for all they were worth. I hollered to Schecter, 'Hit the ground! Play dead!' I told the wounded soldier to work his way out and down the slope, and I crawled over to help with Glenn. He had received several slugs in his body. I don't know if he recognized me or not. We rolled him onto his poncho and laid him flat to the ground to keep from being hit, and we dragged him down and away, over a couple of dead Japanese, on the lowest terrain we could find.

"When we got to where it was safer, I took a machete and chopped down a couple of bamboo poles to make a litter. Captain Vernon, the commander of B Company, offered me some men for a rear guard and to help with the litter. It was hot, and Glenn was heavy, and the snipers were shooting at us all the way back. Man, I was getting weak as a kitten. I could hardly keep walking, and I didn't have a dry thing on my body. As we were coming into the bivouac area, I checked on Glenn, and he had passed away.

"The shock was more than I could handle. I lost all my will to live. When the doctor saw me, he just gave me a handful of pills that knocked my lights out. I didn't know nothing until the next day. I made up my mind then I didn't even want to look in the face of my men anymore. My goal was to take care of them as quick as possible and get them to the hospital because minutes could be the difference between life and death.

"One day some time afterward, Schecter and I and some other litter bearers were evacuating wounded across the Ormoc River. It was hip deep and a hundred yards wide, but no cover. We got across and, going up the bank, Schecter, who was up on the right corner, got shot in the back by a sniper. The bullet went between me and one of the men carrying the back of the litter, and hit Schecter. He dropped the litter and the wounded man fell off. The other two and I got the wounded man to the litter Jeep. Then we went back and got Schecter. We carried him to the Jeep and just as we were putting his litter on the back, the Japanese began to spray us with machine-gun fire. Everybody forgot about everything but Number One. The driver took off like a bat! I shoved Schecter's litter up as far as I could and was just barely able to hold on to the back end of that Jeep with the ends of my fingers. I tell you the GI was driving that Jeep for all it would do, and I was doing more sailing than running, but I knew, if I didn't hold on, that was going to be the end of me.

"After he got out of range of that machine-gun fire, he slowed down. But Schecter never regained consciousness, and he died. Now I had lost my two very closest friends, one a Catholic and the other a Jew. One thing I liked about Schecter was that he was religious, and you'd be surprised how much our beliefs are alike in the Bible. We became close friends despite our differences."

The captain in command of B Company, Frank L. Vernon, liked to disparage Doss and other medics as pill rollers and "chancre mechanics" because he thought they were too quick to send a man with jungle rot or a fever back to the aid station or the hospital for treatment. The medics despised him, Desmond said. But there came a day when Vernon's feet were so bad he had to have help from a medic and Doss took care of him, administering ointment and bandages. "I told him to stay off his feet and keep them dry, knowing he wouldn't do either one. He tried to say something in the way of an apology but couldn't get the words out.

"About that time, the B Company aid man died of pneumonia, and I asked Captain Tann to take me off litter duty and put me back with the company as an aid man. He wanted to know if I was crazy; I said, No, I wanted to be with my old buddies. He let me go. When I got there, Vernon didn't exactly welcome me, but he did say if something wasn't right in the company, I was to tell him, and he'd make it right.

"The Ormoc campaign ended with a victory, and the 77th was sent to a rest area. I stayed in a pup tent with Dorris, and slept and slept, for about two weeks." Doss was recommended for a Bronze Star. He had been promoted to Private First Class by now, and his pay was up to $54 a month. His outfit was put on a troopship called the USS *Mauntrail*, which, late in March 1945, debarked them on the southwest side of Okinawa, which was to be the scene of some of the bloodiest, nastiest fighting in the entire Pacific Theater.

American forces had cut the island in two, and the 77th was working its way southward toward a big grouping of limestone hills heavily occupied, and fortified, by the enemy. A big brown rocky ridge called the Maeda Escarpment stretched across the island west to east. Covered with heavy boulders, the escarpment sloped up sharply, culminating in a rock cliff ranging from thirty to fifty feet high. From it, the Japanese could see American forces at sea on both sides of the island. The battalion was to capture the escarpment.

"We moved up there, to the base of the cliff, in the dark. There were big rocks and lots of crevices, good cover for us. Lieutenant Gornto and Sergeant Potts climbed the cliff in the afternoon and found emplacements and concrete and steel pillboxes up and farther back. When they came down, they sent back to battalion headquarters for rope, demolition materials, and flamethrowers. The following morning, I went up the cliff with two squads, and we tied a rope up there. Although the squads were supposed to attack, we were driven off by mortars."

Back at the base of the cliff, Captain Vernon reported to the battalion, which ordered B Company to attack again next day. The battalion also sent three large cargo nets, the type that was thrown over the sides of the ships for debarkation. Because Desmond had shown himself adept with knots, Lieutenant Gornto, the platoon commander, asked him to help secure the nets to the top of the cliff. Desmond and a few others went up with ropes, pulled nets up, linked them together with two-by-fours, and fixed them in place so that the entire platoon could scale the cliff at the same time, instead of one by one. The first objective was a large pillbox only yards from the edge of the cliff.

"Before we went up the face of the escarpment, I told Lieutenant Gornto that prayer was the greatest lifesaver there was, and I didn't think any of us should go up this cargo net we had put up the day before until we prayed. So the lieutenant called the platoon together. He said, 'Doss wants to pray for us.' I took off my helmet and some of the others did too, and I prayed to the Lord to give the lieutenant wisdom in how to give his orders because our lives were in his charge. I prayed also that He give us wisdom in taking all the safety precautions we could. May we all come back alive.

"I knew that was a mighty big request, and I didn't know how it could be done, but I believed God was to save our lives in some way—because the men seemed to have so much confidence in me. They faithfully believed in the prayer, that God was going to do something—and He did. We went up first against this Japanese position, got pinned down and thought we could not move. While we were there a message came from battalion wanting to know what my losses were, and I didn't have any. Then we heard that A Company had been shot up so badly it couldn't move, and we had to take that whole thing by ourselves. Well, our bazooka man fired a few times until we could see an aperture in the side of the dome of this pillbox. Then our automatic riflemen laid down fire from the flanks, while somebody else ran up and threw a satchel charge into that aperture. Then we had the flamethrower. The man with the flamethrower ran up and threw a burst of fire down on this position. If you've ever been behind one of those things, they are hot. I've been behind it, and it was almost hot enough to scorch my eyebrows. I actually saw the Japanese run in flames, and it was almost like wax. They didn't have a shred on. They were just cooked.

"Doing things like this, we were able to knock out seven or eight of those Japanese positions before we again contacted A Company, which had five men killed in the first charge. They had failed to reach their objective, and we had captured a large area at the top of the escarpment. After we contacted them, they wanted to know how many of our men had been killed. And as far as I knew, when the day was over, I didn't have a single man killed. I understand only one fellow, I think a sergeant, was hurt by a falling rock. The captain wanted to know how in the world it was done. Know what the answer was? They all said it was due to Doss' prayer. And that report went all the way back to division, all the way back to the States."

The area, on top of the escarpment and below, was honeycombed with tunnels and caves, some as much as three stories deep, interconnected by ladders, and the Japanese moved about at night—slitting throats, throwing hand grenades, and terrifying the

American soldiers. Desmond's company was in action for nearly a month. His citation recounts several instances of his dashing out into the face of open fire to treat and carry off wounded men. For Desmond Doss, it was a way of life.

One day after they had been in combat for some time, "Captain Vernon came to me and asked if I would mind going up to be with the men because, he said, 'You know, Doss, you're the last medic we have.' I told him I would but first I would like to finish my private devotions. The subject was 'Following Christ.' He started to say something, but then he kept quiet and waited, and I found out later I was holding up the whole battalion."

On May 5, 1945, a Saturday and Desmond's Sabbath, Company B was ordered into another assault, which it thought was going to be fairly routine but instead turned out to be part of the biggest battle for the escarpment to date. "I thought the main job was done, but it wasn't. And this time practically everything we tried went wrong. We were trying to blow up this cave, and the Japanese managed to pull the fuses out, so it was decided that there was only one thing to do, and we got some tin from someplace and tried to funnel gasoline down on the position. That didn't work. So in the end, men threw five-gallon army water cans filled with high-octane gasoline down there, and then some phosphorous grenades. It must have been an ammo dump, because the whole mountain just seemed to quiver when it went up. You wouldn't think anything could survive it.

"Everything that had looked so peaceful the day before happened to be camouflaged trenches. They threw all the concealment off and out they came from both sides. It was like hitting a hornet's nest with a stick. There seemed to be more of them than there were of us. We had orders to withdraw and then it turned into a panic, and our men just fled back down the escarpment.

"We had a lot of wounded lying around, and I had my buddies there, and I couldn't give up. I had a Japanese aid kit, two American aid kits, and my pockets were stuffed with bandages. I couldn't just abandon my men. They knew if there was any way possible I could take care of them, I would. So I dragged the soldier nearest to the edge over to a litter and a supply rope and rolled him on and tied him down, and then started to lower him. He almost fell off before it got down, and it took too long. Then I remembered that bowline knot I had practiced with when all the rope was in use back in West Virginia. I felt like the Lord brought it to my mind. So I shouted down for them to keep the litter and just free the rope. I pulled it back up, doubled it and tied my bowline, and now I ended up with two loops instead of one.

"I got another wounded man, put one of his legs through each loop, doubled and tied it around his chest underneath both arms and still had enough to wrap around the stump of this tree, and all I had to do to lower him was just slack off on the rope. And then they untied the rope under the arms, slipped it off the legs, and I pulled it back up and used the same loops for the legs over and over. You can see how much quicker and safer it was."

For five hours, most of the time by himself, his fatigues caked with blood, Desmond Doss lowered wounded men down the thirty-five-foot cliff one by one until he had removed them all. To this day, he cannot explain why the Japanese did not come and finish him off. He wasn't even wounded. His citation states that he lowered seventy-five men, and that number is a compromise between Desmond and the military. "There were one hundred and fifty-five went up and fifty-five got themselves down, so they wanted to say I lowered one hundred, but I refused. They wanted to know how many I took care of. I said, 'I don't know.' I don't see how it could possibly be more than fifty. So they're the ones who changed it from one hundred. I wanted fifty, and they made it seventy-five. I don't want ever to say I took care of seventy-five. All I want to say is I was just thankful the Lord was able to use me, and forget the number. It's not the number: It's doing the best you can.

"And this is another place where we sort of disagree. To sum up my award now, you say I saved a life because I lowered a man down a cliff? That's like you say the operation was a success but the patient died before we could get him sewed up. That's not saving.

Of the men I took care of, a number of them didn't survive. Did you save any, Doss? You didn't save his life; you did the best you could. And that is the reason I don't like it said I saved so many lives, because it couldn't be. I just did the best I could."

When Doss came down the escarpment after letting the men down, his uniform was stiff and filthy with dried blood. He was sent to B Company headquarters, where they gave him clean fatigues. Then he went off by himself to read his Bible and thank the Lord that He could use him. While he was gone, the commanding officer of the division, Major General A. D. Bruce, came all the way up to the aid station to congratulate him for his action. They missed each other. Much later, Bruce was to give Doss some of his own battle stars and to inscribe a photo with these words: "To Desmond T. Doss, Medal of Honor, an outstanding godly hero of the 77th Division."

Company B was given two weeks of rest and then ordered to make a night attack at a place called Chocolate Drop, a mile or two past the escarpment. The men moved in a column of threes, and it was so dark Doss put little patches of white adhesive tape on the back of each man so they could see to follow each other. "We were ordered to hit the ground, facedown, no looking around when a flare went up. We went with fixed bayonets, no ammunition, radios off. If there was anything you couldn't take care of with a bayonet, you were out of luck, because under no condition were we to give our position away. We had to take this mountain at dawn by surprise. But what happened was, all the artillery didn't land where it was supposed to, and different platoons started shooting, and the Japanese started throwing grenades at us.

"I was in a shell hole with two other men when a grenade came right in at us. The other two managed to get out, but I was on the upper side, and I knew I had no way of getting out without being blown up. So I just threw my left foot back to where I thought it was, and I no more than did that and it felt like I went sailing through the air. I threw my foot back to find out how far it was, but it was also the only way I could save my life. The grenade went through my double-soled combat boot and fractured a toe and the fragments went up my legs and buttocks. It almost knocked me out, and I realized I was losing a lot of blood. I treated myself several times for shock, elevating my legs, when I realized I was about to pass out. Orders came to withdraw, and after I crawled away I found this other fellow who was shot through the shoulder. I used his shovel to clean out a shell hole for protection for us. Next morning, when it got daylight, I could see just inches from my helmet an artillery shell that didn't go off. If I had hit that shell with my shovel during the night, there wouldn't have been a spot left of either one of us."

The company commander, Vernon, had been hit in the face with a grenade fragment and Doss treated him. "I told him he needed to go back to the aid station, but he said he couldn't. He was acting battalion commander, in charge of all the troops trying to take that mountain by surprise. I found out later he was killed next morning when a mortar hit his command post. I will say this about him: He was a real soldier. He didn't like me because I spoiled his men, taking care of feet that were nothing but a mass of raw meat. He had no good name for any of us, not even doctors. All we were was just a bunch of chancre mechanics. We did become friends, though, after I treated him that time."

Finally four men and a litter came for Doss, who had seventeen separate shrapnel wounds in his feet, legs, and buttocks. They came under fire from artillery and tanks as they worked their way back toward the aid station. The litter bearers hit the dirt, dropping Doss who came sharply into consciousness from the pain. Lying nearby was another soldier, unconscious and bleeding with a severe head wound. Doss rolled off the litter and, despite the bearers' protest, persuaded them to take the other man, who appeared to be more badly injured.

After a time another soldier, walking wounded, came along and offered to help Doss make his way. As they hobbled along, Doss's left arm around the soldier's neck, a sniper bullet passed through the arm, breaking the bones above and below the elbow. They took cover, crawling into a shell hole. Doss had the soldier, Lewis Brooks of Richmond, Virginia, break down his rifle, discard the barrel, and use the wooden stock to make a splint for his broken arm. As they continued onward, still working toward the aid station, Desmond Doss finally passed out.

It was the end of his war but nowhere near the end of his troubles.

"The bullet was still in my arm when I was in the hospital in Hawaii. They couldn't take it out because all three bones in my left arm were shattered. They had put a plaster cast on the entire upper part of my body, from my waist to my neck. It held my arm out parallel with the ground but bent at the elbow. In the ambulance on the way to a hospital ship in Okinawa, I realized I had lost the Bible Dorothy had given me. I had read in it almost every day from the time I left her, all the way through Guam, Leyte, and Okinawa. I pleaded with the driver to ask my buddies at the aid station to look for it.

"The ship took me to Guam, and they flew me to Hawaii, still in that smelly cast. I finally got it off and in two months I was back in the States in Fort Lewis, Washington. From there they sent me to Swannanoa, North Carolina, where I saw my parents and, finally, Dorothy. I heard from the medical battalion; they sent an article about me in the division newspaper, and there was talk of a medal. It also reported that Vernon was dead. The big news was, they found my Bible. The whole company had gone looking for it. It came back waterlogged with the cover falling off. Dorothy had it rebound."

By now he had made corporal. After the bones in his arm had healed sufficiently, the bullet was finally taken out at an army hospital in Staunton, Virginia, in October 1945. A colonel came to tell him he was to receive the Medal of Honor.

On the day Desmond Doss went to meet Harry Truman, he wore a corporal's stripes on each arm, the Statue of Liberty patch of the 77th Division on his left arm, two small gold horizontal stripes representing two six-month periods overseas, a hash mark for three years in service and, over his left breast, ribbons signifying the Bronze Star for valor, with cluster, the Purple Heart with two oak leaves, the Good Conduct Medal, the American Defense Campaign, the Asiatic Pacific Campaign, Guam, Leyte with a beach-

head landing arrowhead, Okinawa, and other decorations. He also
wore the combat medic badge and, over his right shirt pocket, a
small blue ribbon representing a presidential unit citation given the
1st Battalion, 307th Infantry, "for assaulting, capturing, and securing the escarpment."

Fifteen men received the Medal of Honor from Truman on the
White House lawn on Friday, October 12. General of the Army
George C. Marshall, whose personal order had shielded Doss as a
Conscientious Objector, was there, as were Doss' parents and, of
course, Dorothy. Truman took his hand and held it throughout the
reading of his citation.

Doss was to spend the next five and a half years of his life in hospitals. Just before he was about to separate from the Army, he had
an X ray for what appeared to be pleurisy and was found instead to
be tuberculosis. He and Dorothy had a son, Tommy, born September 15, 1946, while Doss went in and out of hospitals. Before it was
over, he had a lung and five ribs removed. In October 1951, he was
released from the hospital in North Carolina. In the following year
he began making speeches in front of Adventist groups, often
demonstrating how he had made his knots back on the escarpment.

After years of strain, Dorothy had a nervous breakdown, and
Doss got her into an Adventist sanitarium in Wildwood, Georgia,
near Lookout Mountain. He was doing maintenance for a children's institution up there when he acquired some property, four
acres for $50 an acre, with a trailer to live in. Buying bargain mate-
rials as they became available, Desmond managed to cobble
together a three-room structure for himself, Dorothy, and Tommy.

He wasn't doing very well financially. Then, in 1959, he was persuaded to go to California, supposedly to discuss a Hollywood
movie. Instead he found himself on the Ralph Edwards TV program, *This Is Your Life*. Officers and men of B Company were there
to tell how Doss had saved their lives. He came away from that with
a power saw, a station wagon, a tractor, and enough money to
increase his Lookout Mountain property to thirteen acres.

In 1967, a book about Desmond titled *The Unlikeliest Hero:The*

Story of Desmond T. Doss, the Soldier Who Wouldn't Touch a Gun,
by Booton Herndon, was published.

Desmond's hearing had diminished gradually over several years
until in 1976 he became totally deaf. He attributed this to the
experimental antibiotics he had received for tuberculosis, killing
the nerves in his ears. But in 1998 he underwent surgery for a
cochlear implant, connecting the nerves in his ears to a magnet
implanted in his skull. He had to learn to hear again and to lip-read.
While it wasn't the best, it was a wonderful improvement over total
silence.

In November 1991, Dorothy Doss, who was fatally ill with cancer, was killed in an accident on the way to the hospital. On May
14, 1993, Desmond drove up to the Chattanooga National Cemetery near a tree dedicated to Medal of Honor recipients with
Frances Duman of Wildwood and proposed to her, not far from
Dorothy's grave. They were married on July 1 of that year in Wildwood. Three hundred people showed up for the wedding. Members of a trio, Dona, Anita, and Roby Ann, sang a Warren Wilson
song, "Jesus, You and I."

Part Two
THE KOREAN CONFLICT

THE FORGOTTEN WAR
The Korean Conflict
June 1950–July 1953

The Korean War began on June 25, 1950—roughly five years after the end of World War II—when ninety thousand North Korean soldiers crossed the 38th Parallel into South Korea, took by surprise and overran four Republic of Korea divisions, and seized the South Korean capital of Seoul in three days.

Korea was divided at the 38th Parallel into separate occupational zones by the Soviet Union and the United States when World War II ended. Rival governments were created in 1948. In the south, the United Nations took over Korea as a mandate and established the Republic of Korea on August 15, 1948, with Syngman Rhee as president.

The Soviet Union then established the Korean Democratic People's Republic in the north, with Kim Il Sung as premier. His announced goal was to reunify Korea. Hence the invasion two years later. The United Nations Security Council then passed a resolution calling for cessation of hostilities, withdrawal of North Korean forces north of the 38th Parallel, and for all members of the UN to help execute the resolution. So the Korean "war," never actually declared by the United States, was a United Nations "police action."

The truce would not be signed until July 1953, three years and a month after the North Koreans invaded. About 33,600 Americans were killed in the fighting.

Following the capture of Seoul, the North Koreans drove southward toward Pusan at the bottom of the country but then General Douglas MacArthur, in a brilliant maneuver, landed a force at Inchon just west of Seoul, on September 15, and came in behind the North Korean Army, recapturing Seoul twelve days later.

United Nations forces then took the initiative, advancing into North Korea in the late fall, spreading across the peninsula as they moved toward the Yalu River, where North Korea bordered Red China. There was talk among the Americans of being home for Christmas. Instead, the Chinese Communist Forces, called CCF, counterattacked in bitterly cold weather on November 24, taking UN and Republic of Korea forces by surprise, overrunning and driving them southward. To the east, around the Chosin Reservoir, the 1st Marine Division fought ferociously to stave off annihilation. It was in this area that Bill Barber and Hector Cafferata, from November 28 to December 2, stood firm as their company survived against extraordinary odds.

It was also in this area at this time, December 4, that Thomas Hudner crash-landed his Corsair in an attempt to save a fellow pilot, Jesse Leroy Brown.

Marine and Army units withdrew, fighting as they went, all the way to Hungnam on the Sea of Japan, where 105,000 American and South Korean troops were ferried back south to Pusan by dozens of ships. There were more than 7,500 American casualties, with 1,500 dead or missing. The war was six months old, and the North Koreans were back in control.

Matthew Ridgway took command just after Christmas of 1950, overseeing a force of 365,000 men, consisting of ROK forces, seven U.S. divisions, and units from eleven UN members. The Chinese and North Korean forces arrayed against them totaled 486,000, with a million more Chinese waiting near the Yalu River.

American forces withdrew fifty miles south of the 38th Parallel, relinquishing Seoul, while Ridgway regrouped and then started the

Eighth Army northward in Operation Thunderbolt. It was as part of this offensive, near Osan, south of Seoul, that Lewis Millett led on February 5, 1951, what has been called the last bayonet charge by a full company in military history.

Pushing north, American forces retook Seoul on March 14 and continued northward. The Chinese, in the largest single battle of the Korean war, launched their spring offensive with 250,000 men. Five U.S. Army divisions, the 2d, 3d, 7th, 24th, and 25th, met them in central Korea around the 38th Parallel. To the west, three Chinese divisions crossed the Imjin River. It was just south of here that Hiroshi Miyamura and his machine-gun squad set up on April 24 and 25, near a place called Taejon-ni. He left there a prisoner of the Chinese.

By the end of May, American forces had established the No Name Line, extending from Inchon eastward, north of Seoul and northeast across the 38th Parallel—all the way to the east side of the country. On May 15, thirty enemy divisions struck the UN lines, and the paratroopers of the 187th Airborne Regiment were sent eastward from Seoul to strengthen the lines. It was here, on May 31, near a place called Wontong-ni, that Corporal Rodolpho Hernandez stopped an enemy attack and very nearly died.

Truce talks began July 10, 1951, at Keasong, and military action slowed down. The following May, with negotiations stalled, General Mark Clark took command of the forces in Korea and stepped up military pressure in an effort to break the stalemate. The war dragged on through the summer, fall, and winter and into the new year.

In February 1953, Marine Lieutenant Raymond G. Murphy took part in a companywide attack on Ungok, which he described as part of a series of actions designed to show the North Koreans they could not win a miltary victory, and thereby help induce them to reach a settlement. Although the raid on Ungok was disastrous, the United

States, North Korea, and China signed on July 27 the armistice that ended the war.

And, as Ray Murphy pointed out, Hiroshi Miyamura went home.

One hundred and thirty-one men received Medals of Honor for action in Korea. Only thirty-seven survived combat.

SEVEN

Thomas Hudner Jr.

Navy Pilot
Korea, December 4, 1950

"But Jesse was alive, and it looked as if he needed nothing except a good tug to get him out of the airplane. I wouldn't even have considered it if I didn't know the helicopter was coming. Because I don't think anybody could have survived that night. It was fifteen degrees above zero. My thought was, if I go in I might save his life. I just didn't think very much about hurting myself. I just felt that, for what it was, it was worth taking a chance."

Photo by Kristian Koslowski

Tom Hudner, at seventy-eight, in September 2002, stands in front of the North Bridge in Concord, Massachusetts, where an exchange of musket fire between American militiamen and British Redcoats across the Concord River on April 19, 1775, marked the beginning of the American Revolution.

Here is how Tom Hudner described the circumstances of this photograph: "It's a couple days after President Truman has fired General MacArthur and the President has received a lot of criticism. And so we're on the Rose Garden steps and Daisy Brown, the widow of Jesse Leroy Brown, the fellow I tried to pull out of this airplane, was there; she was escorted by a black Navy lieutenant. So after he put the Medal around my neck, the President started to leave and, as he turned around on these Rose Garden steps, he stumbled and the black lieutenant caught him. He wouldn't have fallen on his face but still this guy said, 'Well, Mr. President, I hope you know somebody here is still supporting you.'" It was Friday the thirteenth, April 1951.

THOMAS HUDNER lives in Concord, Massachusetts, where an exchange of gunfire in April 1775 between British Redcoats and American militia marked the beginning of the American Revolution. He and I spoke in his home on December 5, 2001. "In the last two weeks," he said that day, "several things related to December fourth kept coming up and I kept thinking there's something about December fourth, I'm sure, but I don't have it on my calendar. Then I suddenly realized it was the fifty-first anniversary of my crash." As we drove off after the interview to get something to eat, Hudner said abruptly, "I wish I was young again. Why? Because there's so many things I can't do anymore. When we were younger, we did them all and took them for granted."

Tom Hudner went to the Phillips Andover Academy, then graduated from the Naval Academy in Annapolis after three years, in 1946, with James B. Stockdale, Jimmy Carter, and Stansfield Turner. Stockdale was to receive the Medal in 1976, following almost eight years of resistance as a prisoner during the Vietnam War. Hudner, a 145-pound running back, played junior varsity football with Stockdale at the same time Glenn Davis and Doc Blanchard were national figures, starring on the Army football team at West Point. In scrimmages, Hudner was given a bralike overgarment with the name of Glenn Davis stenciled across the front, and then ordered to carry the ball against the first-string Navy defense. "The junior varsity was cannon fodder for the varsity," he recalled.

Receiving his wings in 1949, Hudner was trained to fly a single-engine attack plane called the Corsair on and off the carrier ship *Leyte*, based in Quonset Point, Narragansett Bay, Rhode Island.

"It was a good airplane," he remembers today. "Everybody liked the Corsair. It was very distinctive because of its dropped wing. It came into the fleet the last year of World War II. Initially it had some undesirable characteristics that made it dangerous to men aboard ship, but the company finally ironed those out so we considered it a comfortable and safe airplane. The nose was so long that when you came up behind the carrier, if you were too long in the groove, you couldn't see the stern or the landing signal officer. So the conventional approach was the racetrack pattern in which you'd try to be turning all the time you were approaching the ship so you'd have good visibility except when you straightened out. Your hope was that when you straightened out you were headed right at the mid flight deck, hoping you were close enough so you wouldn't lose sight of the signal officer.

"The Corsair weighed twelve thousand or fourteen thousand pounds, and our approach speed was about eighty-five knots. Nowadays aircraft weigh easily fifty thousand pounds and their approach speed is easily one hundred and thirty-five knots but with the angled deck and the optical landing system they have now, with the emphasis on aviation safety, the landing accident rate today is only ten percent of what it was those days. The flight deck was nine hundred feet long then, whereas now they're almost eleven hundred feet long. It never occurred to me until a while ago that the flight deck on that carrier was long enough so you would have to be Tiger Woods hitting his driver three hundred yards to span the length of it."

In May 1950, Hudner's carrier, *Leyte*, of the Essex class, was sent to the Mediterranean. They called the carriers in the Mediterranean the "Dancing Fleet," because so much socializing went on in port. With the Cold War already well under way, there was a great deal of concern about the Soviets, and the American military was considered a strong presence crucial in that part of the world.

Tensions erupted into war on June 25, 1950, when the North Korean People's Army crossed the 38th Parallel and attacked South Korea. "Korea took almost no part at all in World War II. We hardly knew where it was. The Japanese had possession, and after World War II the Soviets and Americans divided it."

Hudner's group got word of the invasion the following day, June 26. "We thought we would not be involved because we were so far away, but on August eighth we awoke to the sound of the helicopters and were told another carrier had just arrived in the Mediterranean to relieve us so we could go to Korea. We were sent there because we had been operating a couple months so we were better trained than any other carrier available at the time." The United States had about twelve carriers, including several smaller ones, Hudner recalled. The *Leyte* was too big to go through the Suez Canal, so it was back, past Gibraltar, across the Atlantic to Norfolk for ten days, on up to the home port of Quonset Point on Narragansett Bay, Rhode Island, then down through Panama, up to San Diego, out to Hawaii for a day, to Japan for a day, then to the operating area off the east coast of Korea. "So our first day of operations was about the eighth of October, almost two months and roughly twenty thousand miles from the Mediterranean."

There were eighty-five planes on the ship and about 115 pilots, including Jesse Leroy Brown, the Navy's first black aviator. Tom Hudner was his wingman. The Corsair was designed as a fighter "but we used it mostly as a fighter-bomber throughout the rest of the Korean War." It had six wing-mounted .50 caliber machine guns, three on each wing, and it could carry two five hundred-pound bombs or eight two hundred and fifty-pounders. It also could carry eight rockets and napalm.

The beginning of these operations on October 8 occurred three weeks after the landing at Inchon, which had turned the war around. At the time, United Nations forces were moving quite rapidly up north. "We were there to support our troops. There was talk then about how far we'd go and the Yalu River, the border, was being talked about all over the world [as to whether the UN forces would cross it]. General MacArthur was anxious to go as far north as he could. Truman and the Brits especially were very concerned about Chinese warnings not to get too close to the Yalu, but MacArthur was so successful at Inchon that he rolled all over the North Koreans in his determination to go north. Truman met him on Wake Island and gave him the Distinguished Service Cross. When you have four stars you don't just give the guy a Good Conduct medal." (MacArthur had previously received the Medal of Honor for his defense of the Philippines.)

Hudner was not greatly apprehensive about his first foray into combat. "I remember seeing the first tracers from the antiaircraft guns coming my way but the North Koreans didn't have much at that time, and almost all they had was supplied by the Soviets. There was enough so we had to be careful. Our planes would come back with small-caliber holes in the underside, the fuselage, and wings. The Chinese would lie on the ground as we flew over and they'd fire at us. We used to fly in groups of four and most of the time we flew fairly close together, as a single unit."

"We wanted to hit troop concentrations more than anything else. Railroad trains were a favorite target. When they heard planes, they'd try to get into the closest tunnel and hole up there. We also would be preassigned to bomb industrial sites—power and manufacturing plants." A bombing run on a plane would start about ten thousand feet but in close air support "we were probably flying about a thousand feet, cruising about one hundred and fifty or one hundred and eighty knots." There were jets at the time, Hudner recalls, but their fuel supply limited them to ninety-minute flights, whereas the Corsairs could stay up for three hours.

"Our first flight, as I mentioned, was on the eighth of October, and our last was the twentieth of January, nineteen fifty-one. We were desperately needed back in the Mediterranean, and the Navy was getting carriers into commission as quickly as they could. We belonged to the Atlantic Fleet and we were on loan, much to the discomfort of the Mediterranean Fleet Commander."

In fact, Hudner flew about twenty missions. "After I crash-landed, I couldn't fly for about a month. I hurt my back. It was December fourth, nineteen fifty."

As dramatic as Hudner's story is, that of Jesse Leroy Brown, whom Hudner tried to save, is a story in itself, and indeed, a book has been written about him. Called *The Flight of Jesse Leroy Brown*, it relates his dreams, struggles, and achievements before he met his death on the cold ground of North Korea that December day. The two men were one year apart in age, Hudner the younger at twenty-six, but their backgrounds were remarkably different. Given the segregation policies in the military through World War II, there were very few black officers in the Navy at the time of the Korean conflict. Brown started out as a naval air cadet and won his wings as a midshipman. In that program, Hudner said, he would have had to serve twenty-four months as an ensign before being commissioned a lieutenant junior grade. "So Jesse went through the program a year before me as a midshipman and, when I reported into the squadron in early November of 1949, Jesse had been there almost a year. He was married—he got married in flight training, which was illegal, but he'd been hassled so because he was black. There was real bigotry at that time. He married his girlfriend to protect himself. He needed support. But I never heard of anybody in the squadron who didn't like him. Some were devoted to him; other people just liked him.

"I knew nothing about him until I got my assignment in November nineteen forty-nine. Our squad was a pretty small group of about fifteen pilots and three or four officers with a support group. We got to know each other pretty well. We didn't socialize a lot. Because he was married, he'd go home all the time. There was not a startling difference between the ranks even though he was still only an ensign, and as JGs the others of us clung together. I had a friend from the Naval Academy aboard ship. Nobody cared about color, no way. He was just another one of the guys. He was given credit for the good things he did, and got his butt kicked just as hard as anybody else when he didn't get his job done. However, there were aviators in the fleet that were just so antiblack they would speak about it. I never heard anything dire happen to him or criticism of him by anybody except for these people who didn't know who Jesse was; they criticized him just because he was black. At that time almost all the stewards in the wardroom were black. They just idolized him and deservedly so. And they made sure he never had to ask for anything—he was a real gentleman."

Once in Korea, they would make combat flights two days out of three. And the three-hour flights, Hudner remembers, were very tiring. "I remember how exhausted I used to be just being in that airplane for three hours, the tension, not so much afraid of being shot at—we were being shot at—but it was just wearing."

On December 4 Hudner and Brown flew off the *Leyte* in a group of six. "We four were together and the other two were about a mile away. You fly a loose formation because most of your attention is on the ground looking for targets, and you're spread out pretty much so you're not going to run into each other. We did have visual contact, and you had to have pretty good weather almost all the time. We were flying in mountainous country, and you had to be very careful.

"We were about forty-five minutes into an armed reconnaissance mission, looking for targets of opportunity, when Jesse was hit. At that time the Marines and the Army were in a desperate withdrawal from the Chosin Reservoir. The Chinese attacked just a week after Thanksgiving, and this was less than a week into this whole withdrawal thing and every aircraft available to the Air Force and Navy was out providing support for the troops. Except on this day we were flying armed reconnaissance.

"We assume Jesse was hit by some ground fire. The first we knew was he called out and said, 'I think I've been hit, I'm losing power, and I'm going to have to land.' We were up in the mountains at that time and almost the whole area was covered by scrub pine, and yet one of the other pilots saw a clear area and directed him toward that. He barely made it because he was almost on top of the mountains.

"There was not enough room to bail out, and if you did you'd get killed down in those trees. It was better to ride the plane down. We were circling as he went down. I was calling to him on the radio with a checkout list: Make sure your shoulder harness is locked, lock your canopy open, be careful of your airspeed so you don't stall. But he hit the ground with such force that when he came to a stop his aircraft was actually bent at the cockpit twenty or thirty degrees and his canopy had slammed shut because the lock didn't withstand the force of the crash."

Because of the condition of the aircraft, Hudner said, "we were convinced he had perished in the crash. We were flying overhead talking among ourselves, saying, 'Jesus, Jesse's dead,' and our flight leader left us to climb to a high altitude so he could get better radio reception to ask for a helicopter, and while he was up there, we saw that Jesse had opened his canopy and was waving to let us know he was alive. . . . but he didn't get out of the cockpit. Some smoke was coming out from the end of the cowling, not great volumes of it but some, indicating a fire of some sort from the nose of his airplane. And then the flight leader called back to say they had acknowledged his call and that a helicopter would come along as soon as they could get it up there.

"I was getting quite concerned about that smoke and felt that in the time it took for the helicopter to get up there, the smoke could develop into flame.

"So I took a lot of things into consideration and made the decision to land as close to him as I could and pull him out of his cockpit and wait till the helicopter could come."

Asked why he thought he could land without injury and still be of some use, Hudner acknowledged, "They don't have that in the handbook. We used to talk, barely a year after I got my wings, that if you ever have to make a forced landing, do it with your wheels up. I just felt the worst thing that could happen was I could hit a rock which was covered by the snow. On the upslope I had to fly down a little bit low and fly up to cushion the landing on the snow." But he miscalculated the rate at which the plane was dropping "so, when I hit the ground, God, it was hard. I thought, God, what the hell am I doing here? But Jesse was alive and it looked as if he needed nothing except a good tug to get him out of the airplane. I wouldn't even have considered it if I didn't know the helicopter was coming. Because I don't think anybody could have survived that night. It was fifteen degrees above zero. My thought was, if I go in I might save his life. I just didn't think very much about hurting myself. I just felt that, for what it was, it was worth taking a chance."

Hudner had an extremely difficult time simply climbing up onto the slanting, slippery wing and was forced to hold on to the edge of the plane merely to look down at Brown. "When I got to him he was conscious. He saw me coming up to his airplane, and his first remark was something to the effect, 'Tom, we got to figure a way to get out of here.' Those were not his exact words, but he was very calm. I couldn't believe he was so calm. There was about a foot and a half snow on the ground, and it was fifteen degrees. He had pulled his helmet off so he was bareheaded and he had dropped his gloves and his fingers were literally frozen solid in that short a time. The reason he had taken gloves off was he tried to unbuckle the chute and had dropped his gloves beyond his reach. He was sitting there doing almost nothing. As the aircraft bent at the cockpit, it pinned his leg in so his knee was caught between the edge of the cockpit and the hydraulic control panel. I used to carry one of these Navy wool watch caps, and I went and got that and pulled it down over his head, and I had a white silk scarf I wrapped around his hands so he could get some sort of warmth. The snow had the soles of my boots packed like ice and I couldn't get footing. I was able to pull myself up to look into the cockpit but I had to hold on with one hand all the time. Even with the one hand it was difficult to reach in. I had no leverage, no hold, no way to provide him any help at all. I didn't call for an axe until I'd gotten up to look into the cockpit. I was thinking I could pull him out, but I couldn't. So I ran back to the airplane and turned on my radio and asked for a fire extinguisher and an axe and then I went back to the airplane.

"Pretty soon I scooped up some snow and threw it into the cowling, but it didn't do any good at all. Jesse talked without any strain, but then he would stop talking. It wasn't really a situation where you could carry on a good conversation, so it was difficult for me to know whether he was semiconscious or too tired to talk or just cold. He didn't mention anything about being cold.

"It was forty minutes before the copter came. This was probably about three P.M., and the copter pilot and I didn't work very long after that." The fire extinguisher lasted about three squirts and the axe bounced harmlessly off the metal of the fuselage. The helicopter pilot, Lieutenant Charles Ward, climbed up on the fuselage to get a look at the pilot so he could pretty well see what the situation was. "Then he told me away from earshot of Jesse, he said, 'I don't know about you, but I have got to get out of here because it's getting to be dusk and this helicopter doesn't have any ability to fly in these mountains after dark. It's your choice if you want to stay, okay, but I've got to go.' Of course, that would have been suicide for me to stay, so I went back to Jesse and told him we were hoping to get some more equipment and we just couldn't move him without it. And sometime during this time he said if anything happened to him to tell his wife, Daisy, how much he loved her. He really, he really did love her. I just have no idea what was going through his mind.

"All I can say is he was unbelievably calm. He gave me support instead of panicking. Had the situation been reversed, I'd have been saying, 'Get me out of here!' He was, just matter-of-fact, saying, 'We got to figure out some way to get out of here.' And he wasn't begging or anything. There was nothing like, 'God, don't leave me.' He was a very religious person. So I said, hang on, we'll be back in a little bit, we'll get some tools to get you out. I don't know if he heard me. It was a miracle that he had survived, that he had lasted as long as he did. There was a period when he said nothing at all and I didn't know if he was unconscious or just tired, or had nothing to say. And in my mind I have to think he was unconscious if not already dead by then. I have to think he had expired by then."

Although there were enemy in the area, Hudner saw none. "It could have been all those airplanes. There were at least fifteen airplanes flying the site. They probably didn't dare show themselves."

Hudner was taken to a place called Hagaru-ri and then to Koto-ri. The weather was so bad no one could come for him from the ship until December 7.

Back aboard, Hudner was called up to see the captain on the bridge. "He said, 'What I'm planning to do is send a helicopter to the crash site with a flight surgeon to get Jesse's body out of the airplane and bring him back to the ship.' But I told him in those conditions and the distance over hostile territory and the fact that the helicopter would be overloaded with three people would be very very dangerous, as nice a gesture as it was.

"So the backup plan was to send a flight of Corsairs and some Skyraiders to the crash site and drop napalm on it. So they did. And so it was a Valkyrean funeral for Jesse. The pilots who dropped the napalm said his body had been stripped of all its clothing. I think, if they could have, they would have pulled his body out without the distraction of having somebody constantly shooting at them. So our two airplanes and Jesse's remains are still up there someplace."

Over the years Hudner received conflicting reports about whether the wreckage of the planes remained. "The fuselage was metal. The wing and part of the tail surfaces were cloth. I don't know if they still exist or not."

Hudner met Brown's widow, Daisy, for the first time on Friday the 13th of April, 1951, when he went to receive the Medal of Honor from President Truman. "They invited her to attend that. I remember she was really quite a lady. She was so gracious at a time of great celebration for my family and me, and it was only four months after her husband was killed. I've seen her several times, as recently as a couple of weeks ago down in Mississippi. Both of them grew up in Hattiesburg, and she has never left there."

The friendship between Hudner and Brown's widow has endured over time. On Veterans' Day, November 11, 2001, Hudner went to Mississippi State University to present Daisy Brown, a retired schoolteacher, with one of the medals given as a gesture of appreciation by South Korea to Americans who had served during the conflict. "After the presentation they put her on the spot, and she spoke two minutes. She was very articulate in expressing her appreciation to the people who had recognized her for what Jesse had done."

Mrs. Brown remained a widow for ten years after Jesse's death, then married a retired master sergeant, who died about 1990.

"I'm a terrible correspondent, and she is too," said Hudner. "We don't even exchange Christmas cards. A lot of times we hear about each other from other people."

How many people told Hudner he was crazy for trying to crash-land a Corsair under those circumstances? "About ninety. I have to admit I was very lucky. I did hurt my back enough so I couldn't fly for about a month, but there was no permanent damage. I had back pains for six or eight years, and since then my back hasn't bothered me at all.

"I know a lot of people were pissed off about it because they said, 'You know, it was bad enough to have to go pick one person up but now you put yourself in a position where the rescue pilot is that much more exposed.' Well, a lot of things they call foolish until they're successful; then it's called daring.

"I never lost any sleep over it, although there were some things I didn't consider at the time: The helicopter was a questionable performer at that altitude. I didn't think of that. Somebody later on pointed out to us that at seven thousand feet it didn't have the lifting power to take off. All this is under normal circumstances. If you weren't rushed by the tactical situation, a report of enemy troops in the area, the coming of darkness, all this stuff. If you had a discussion leader who said, okay, now, guys, give me the pros and cons of this—it didn't happen. I was so damn lucky it turned out okay."

Hudner said that, despite his nomination for the Medal, he didn't think the captain was very happy about it himself. "He had the same reason others did, that I endangered the helicopter pilot, put a lot of other people at risk in other planes. Somebody told me this captain, my captain, had put out the word that if anything happened to any of our people he didn't want anyone to ruin an airplane by helping somebody else out. This was before Jesse went down. If I had heard that, I still might have helped him because here was involved the life of a guy we all knew and he was a hell of a lot more important than an old broken-down World War II airplane, even though they were desperate for aircraft."

Hudner eventually got into jets and made captain in 1965, three years before he married Georgea Smith, who had three children. Her husband, also a Navy flier, had been killed in a car accident in Jacksonville, Florida, in 1963. "I met Tom in nineteen sixty-five at a party after moving to San Diego," she recalled. "He was forty-three, a bachelor, and I had three children. We dated for three years, very casually, until one day my daughter Shannon, who'd been born in sixty-one, said to him, 'Why don't you marry my mommy?' That may have given him the idea. Remember, he was a bachelor for a long time. But the idea of taking on three kids—I guess that must not have scared him. But these were good kids; he was very fortunate. But I would never have done that, married a man with three kids. Another time we were in this stupid little kitchen I had and he just picked Shannon up, because she was there probably, and she looked up at him and said, 'Do you know you have hair in your nose?' That's the way to date." This apparently did not dissuade Hudner, for he and Georgea married in August of 1968. "Our son, Thomas Jerome Hudner the third, was born three years after we got married, in nineteen seventy-one."

Hudner retired at the end of March 1973, worked as a consultant for a time, got involved with the USO, and eventually became commissioner of Veterans' Services for the Commonwealth of Massachusetts, a position he held for ten years, before yielding it to another recipient of the Medal, Thomas Kelley of South Boston, in April 1999.

Asked about the impact of the Medal on his life, Hudner said it had given him the opportunity to go places and meet people that he would never have had as a simple Navy captain. "The Navy did not make a lot of to-do over it, whereas in the Marine Corps it means an awful lot," he said. In civilian life, it made no difference except "I was always at the head of the table. I always appreciated getting a good seat. But, you know, most people don't even know what the Medal of Honor is."

Even so, he said, the Medal did not shape his life, even though it was a big part of it. He said some recipients lived only for the annual convention and other Medal-related events. "That's not me," he said. "I feel sorry for them."

He said he had two commitments as far as the Medal was concerned. One was to veterans, many of whom are awed in the presence of a Medal recipient. He went out of his way to see them and do what he could for them. And the other was to young people, to help guide, teach, and inspire them as citizens and patriots. He lamented the failure of American education to adequately present the history of the nation, especially its founding and other instructive eras, to young people who, he said, seemed to have no clue as to where we come from, or how we got here.

"I wrecked an airplane and I didn't even get the guy out of the wreckage. I happened to be an aviator but an infantryman can dig deep enough or fast enough to get away from the gunfire, but he'll jump up and pull a buddy to safety. It's an attitude that is latent for the most part in normal life but comes out when you are suddenly confronted with life or death in a situation like that. And I don't think a lot of kids recognize the love one person can have for another that sometimes comes out only in time of war.

"That's why veterans always want to get together for silly, stupid reunions. It's memories of times when these people would do anything for one another, groveling around, or being shot at four thousand feet, trying to get something accomplished for absolutely nothing at all but the satisfaction that they maintained what freedom they could for the country—because freedom for the U.S. means freedom for the whole world. If we weren't out there, the world would be absolute chaos."

EIGHT

William E. Barber
Hector Cafferata

The Captain and the Private
Fox Hill/Toktong Pass, Korea
November 28–December 2, 1950

*"Pass was not a very good descriptive of the area. We had a very
unimproved road going to Yudam-ni in the north, and we had to hold on. . . .
I had two hundred and forty guys, positioned in an oval shape alongside the
road, facing a Chinese regiment, a thousand or twelve hundred of the enemy.
The first night the Chinese came in, mainly from the northwest,
I had no help except my own people."* —William Barber

*"To tell you the truth, I did it. I know I did it.
Other people know I did it. But I'll be God damned if I know
how I did it. Put it that way."* —Hector Cafferata

Colonel William Barber at the 1999 Medal
of Honor Society convention in Riverside,
California. Barber died on April 19, 2002,
at the age of eighty-two, not long after he
granted the following interview.

by Robert M. Bush, CMOHS photographer

This formal portrait of Marine Captain William
Barber was taken in 1952 following the battle of
Toktong Pass near the Chosin Reservoir, Korea,
November 28–December 2, 1950, for which he
was awarded the Medal of Honor.

Hector Cafferata, at the Patriots Award dinner during the 1999 Medal of Honor Society convention in Riverside, California.

by Robert M. Bush, CMOHS photographer

Marine Private Hector Cafferata, shortly after receiving the Medal of Honor in November 1952 from President Harry Truman, who had to tread on Hector's toes in order to secure the ribbon around his neck, leading Cafferata to remark years afterward, "The little bastard ruined my shoes."

IN LATE JANUARY 2002, I spoke with William Barber in his home in Irvine, California. "I'd been in good health all my life, better than good," he said, "and then I had a heart bypass in June two thousand, and I had pneumonia and several other things go wrong. I was in a hospital bed a long time, and now I get kidney dialysis three times a week." In addition, he had just learned that he had a cancer in the spine. "They say it's treatable. That's all I know." Three months later, on April 19, Bill Barber died. He was patient during the conversation, and candid with a stranger.

William Barber was a twenty-five-year-old Marine Corps lieu-tenant in his first war. Korea was still to come. "We landed on Iwo Jima the nineteenth of February, nineteen forty-five. I commanded a Marine Corps rifle platoon. I ended up the company commander in the last two weeks because everybody else was dead. It was tough combat, but we were tough."

On February 23, the fourth day of the invasion of Iwo Jima, he witnessed the flag-raising on Mount Suribachi that was captured by Joe Rosenthal in the most famous military photograph ever taken. The image became an icon not only for the Marine Corps but for America itself. "Somebody said, 'There's the flag.' Somehow we saw it when we looked back. Iwo was only eight square miles. We could see it, and we knew there was a tough fight going on for Suribachi. It's very real—the thoughts, the thrill, the added deter-mination that it brought to the company. It meant we were now in control of the place. But your thoughts at that time are not organ-ized. They flow through the mind, get interrupted and then some-thing else comes along. I am always reluctant to try to find words, so I simply say: 'It meant a lot to all of us.' "

In thirty-seven weeks of combat on Iwo Jima, 60,000 Americans killed 22,000 enemy soldiers, while 6,800 Americans were slain. Barber, shot in the finger and bleeding from a concussion, was taken off the island for treatment, but he made his way back and went on to receive the Silver Star.

When World War II ended, Barber served with the Occupation forces in Japan. "I was surprised the Japanese were so compliant. They were very bold soldiers. On Iwo and elsewhere in the Pacific, they were very determined to kill one of us for every one of them, and we had to dig them out with grenades and flamethrowers." Barber came home in the beginning of 1946, and was sent on recruiting duty, eventually landing at Camp Lejeune as company commander. He and his wife, Ione, had married in 1942. They had two daughters and a son.

"I was a company commander from 1947, then assigned to Altoona, Pennsylvania. By then I was a captain. I was an instructor with a group of reserve companies. I had to recruit reservists. I was there until 1949, and then in 1950 I got hurry-up orders to Korea.

"I was in Korea just thirty-nine days, serving with Fox Company in the Seventh Marine Division. The company had gone in on the Inchon landing, then went around and up the east coast to Wonsan. This company was not very good, not very well trained. They were almost all reservists. I was getting them trained when this group of Chinese came in, a Chinese regiment, a thousand or twelve hundred enemy."

In fact, 120,000 Chinese communist soldiers had crossed the Yalu River about forty miles north of Hagaru-ri with the intention of annihilating Republic of Korea and American Army and Marine Corps forces that were working their way north around both sides of the Chosin Reservoir. Somehow the enemy went unnoticed. The Main Supply Route, or the MSR, as it was called, forked at Hagaru-ri, at the south end of the reservoir. Eight miles out of town, up the left fork, was a place called Toktong Pass. This was where Barber and his 240-man company were directed to dig in and keep the road from being cut in two by the Chinese, who wanted to isolate and wipe out a Marine unit up the road at Yudam-ni. After the action there, the pass became known as Fox Hill.

"Pass was not a very good descriptive of the area. We had a very unimproved road going to Yudam-ni in the north, and we had to hold on. The first night the Chinese came in, mainly from the northwest, I had no help except my own people. I had artillery from Hagaru the second day, and I had air power. The Chinese would come at night because they didn't want to face the planes during the day.

"I had two hundred and forty guys, positioned in an oval shape alongside the road, facing a Chinese regiment, a thousand or twelve hundred of the enemy. The first night the Chinese came in, mainly from the northwest, I had no help except my own people. We were surrounded and outnumbered. The Chinese were courageous, tough, and tenacious, but they weren't very well organized or very well skilled.

"The battle began the night of November twenty-seventh–

twenty-eighth. I was shot on the morning of the twenty-ninth. I took a large number of casualties the first day—probably twenty-two killed—and I had a number of wounded. Then, in all, I probably lost twenty-six or twenty-seven killed out of two hundred and forty. I'm not in favor of talking about this because, well, they learned so fast, these young Marine reservists. The first night was when we lost so many before they became convinced they had to do certain things. From then on, they all got better. If I compare it with Iwo, and I can't, the Marines I had on Iwo were so well trained, so skilled and competent. But in any event, on balance, we put on a good five days there at Toktong Pass.

"On the morning of the twenty-eighth, I had orders to go back to Hagaru, about eight miles. But I had dead and wounded and by that time I didn't have any radio communications. I had a radio but nobody I could contact with it. I wrote a note and sent it to the regimental commander. I said, 'We're surrounded and receiving heavy casualties, request resupply of ammunition.' I didn't know when I sent my message that we were facing as many enemy as we were.

"Then the colonel sent me a message saying I could move out and link up with another company. But I knew how important this piece of real estate was, so I sent back a message saying I could hold on if I could be resupplied by air and get air power. I was shot in the hip at three in the morning. Oh, I could walk, I could hobble around." Barber's Medal of Honor citation says Barber often moved "up and down the lines in a stretcher to direct the defense" and encourage and inspire his men. But, he said, "somebody added that for drama. I might have been on the stretcher some, but I had Marines there to hold me up and help me out. They rigged a sort of crutch or cane for me, and that's how I got around."

"The bulk of the Chinese force would leave each day, and then they would come back again at night. But they had snipers who would shoot at you as you walked around during the day. We were very busy in the daytime. We had certain things for the Marines to do and get everything squared away—I'd have them take care of their weapons, get some chow, change their socks, get ready for night, and sleep. There was no hot chow. It was all C rations. We had little tins of canned heat, and you could take C-ration coffee and melt snow, heat water, and drink that. Some would build little fires during the daytime when you didn't have to worry about being observed. The cold was exaggerated in most reports afterward. It was cold. It would get down to twenty-five below zero at night. You see reports where it was a lot colder than that. We had pretty good gear, Korean boots, parkas. The wounded got frostbite. I never got frostbite. If my Marines did what I did, they wouldn't have frostbite. But some got it. I wanted them in the fighting holes taking care of themselves, and getting their weapons in shape for the night.

"Hector Cafferata was in my company. He was a real stalwart. He prevented the real overrunning of our lines that first night. He was in a fighting hole with one of the reservists who'd been with him in high school in New Jersey, and his holemate had his glasses blown off, lost them in a grenade concussion, and he was scrabbling around for them. He said, 'I can't see.' Cafferata said, 'You don't have to see to hold these clips.' So he loaded the clips for Cafferata, and Cafferata held them off with his M-1. He was an amazing man."

Hector Cafferata barely made it to Korea in the first place because, as a member of the Marine reserves in Boonton, New Jersey, he had grown somewhat lax about attending meetings and ended up being placed on inactive status. "I didn't have time to fool around and go into these meetings where you didn't do nothing but sit around and bullshit. I always wanted to be a Marine but World War II was over, and I didn't think there'd ever be another one. You know. You were a kid in World War II. I was a Marine-happy kid and I was always gonna be a Marine. But then the war ended. I'll never forget how sad I felt when the war ended. I mean, my dad was over there and here I'm sad because the war ended—only because I was going to be a Marine. But I couldn't see being a peacetime Marine. . . . I was gonna go off to war, you know? Jesus Christ, what a dope. I don't know. I guess it was an adventure. So I missed the big one, but God damn it, after my little training episode in Korea, I'm glad I did. I'd probably have got myself killed. Anyway, I'm glad to know the Skipper liked me."*

Here is how Hector remembers that first night in combat:

"They called it Fox Hill, after Fox Company. I guess the proper name was Toktong Pass. It was almost dark when we got there that afternoon. We got up onto the hill and, Christ, nobody knew what the hell was going on. A couple guys got nervous that night and started shooting at shadows and we threw up some flares. Later on, I don't know what time it was, but I heard gunfire, and Benson [Cafferata's foxhole mate, Kenneth Benson of Newton, New Jersey] and I jumped out of our bags, and the Chinese were about thirty feet from my hole. I just started shooting. We were out front, like an outpost. I don't know what the hell we were doing out there. The other two guys, who were supposed to be awake, I don't know where the hell they ended up. They either got killed or pulled back. They never woke us up. They probably didn't have time to wake us. I know one guy was captured that night in a sleeping bag.

"I got wounded around eight o'clock the first morning. They hit us about one in the morning, and it was about seven hours later that I got shot. Anyway, we jumped out of our bags and started shooting. We had M-1s. There was no way we could hold there, so we stayed just long enough to figure out where the MLR [Main Line of Resistance] was, and then we fought off the first charge and then fell back to the line. When we got there, down in this little wash, there was a bunch of wounded and dead laying around, so I said, 'Shit. We gotta stay here.' And when Benson and I fell back, we happened to hit a hole that was shot up between the Third and Second Platoons. So we were filling the hole, plugging the gap.

"Then I had the shit scared out of me. A Chinaman come up on my right side about thirty yards away and threw a satchel charge in the God damn wash, and shit went flying all over the place. The explosion really scared the crap out of me, but I calmed down after that. You know you're scared, but fear comes in waves. It seems to come and then you conquer it, and then something else gets you up, and you're scared shitless again. You conquer that, and you know you can't let it get you. I seemed to have a debate going on between my feet and my brain. My feet were telling me, 'Let's get the hell out of here.' My brain was telling me what the hell we were gonna do. That was the kind of thing that was going on with me.

"All I had on was a pair of socks. I fought all night in socks and no parka. I didn't have time to get dressed. There was about six inches of snow, and it was about thirty degrees below zero. My feet felt like two blocks of ice. I was a pretty big guy and the bags we had were mummy bags, and you can't get in a mummy bag with a pair of boots on, and you can't get in there with your parka on, so you had to take them off."

It was a moonlit night and flares were going off, and visibility was not a problem, Cafferata said. "Some of them I shot I could see their faces real clear. There were times I thought, 'Oh, shit, look at this, the poor son of a bitch.' I had to shoot them, you know? But I could see them plain as day. Right in the face. It's one thing when they're out farther and they're just arms and legs, but when you can look 'em right in the puss, and then you shoot the poor bastard, you know, I felt bad shooting them. But it was life or death; that's the name of the game. But I think about it now and I think, What a waste.

"I didn't have to do much aiming. I had a rifle ever since I was twelve years old and had been a hunter ever since. All I had to do was put the gun up to my shoulder and just shoot. There were times I wished I had a pump shotgun. That would have been better. You shot them dead center in the chest. The M-1 was a good stopper. They dropped when they were hit.

"And all night long there was grenades coming and I had an entrenching tool [a small shovel with a two-foot handle, used for digging foxholes], and I would take the entrenching tool and whack the grenades. The Chinese were coming and chucking grenades, and I was about the worst baseball player you ever saw, but for some reason or other—maybe because I was scared shit-less—I didn't miss them.

"I had my entrenching shovel in my left hand, the rifle in my right and there were times when the grenades would come three or four at a time, and I'd pop 'em back out or they'd go over me. All I wanted the grenade to do was not land in the ditch with me. So all I'd do was whack it away. I might not whack it too far but those grenades they had weren't that powerful, and I'd knock it away just far enough and duck down so it couldn't do damage.

"To tell you the truth, I did it. I know I did it. Other people know I did it. But I'll be God damned if I know how I did it. Put it that way.

"If I had to shoot at someone who was coming at me, I'd just lay the rifle right by my left thumb over the shovel handle and shoot. You didn't even have to hold with the forearm. I fired so much that the top cover of the barrel turned to charcoal, and it was catching on fire. I had to put it out with snow. That's how much I shot it that night. I fired hundreds of rounds. I probably had maybe two hundred and fifty rounds on me that I fired. Did I take a man down with every shot? Well, I sure as hell should have. There were some that were out there a-ways, but if I seen 'em I shot at 'em, and I didn't worry about how far they were. I shot a lot of the poor bastards. As a matter of fact, along toward morning, I was doing a little crawling around looking for ammo."

The Chinese had all kinds of weapons. "They had a burp gun with a drum magazine on it. They had carbines, they had M-1s, they had Enfields, they had Springfields, they had Nambus, they had a collection. I don't know how the hell they kept ammo for them. They had Thompson submachine guns up the kazoo. They probably took 'em from Chiang Kai-shek.

"When that grenade went off," Cafferata said, "Benson got flash-blinded. It knocked his glasses off and cut him a little bit in the face. He couldn't see. He was bleeding. But I didn't have no time to see how bad he was hurt. So then he was loading the rifles. I'd empty my rifle and hand it to him and grab another one. If I could load, I'd put a clip in quick enough, then I didn't need his rifle. But if I didn't, I had another one loaded and ready."

In January 2002, more than fifty years after the battle, because of a mix-up in paperwork, Kenneth Benson was awarded the Silver Star for his action that night. "We hated each other," Cafferata said jokingly. "He went to another school in Jersey, and then we both started playing semipro football. We used to beat the shit out of each other. And then we end up in the same foxhole together. He's a great kid. I mean, he didn't panic. He stayed right with me. You know, one dopey reporter, and you can quote me, she said to me not long ago, 'Well, what about Benson?' I said, 'Benson was a cool guy, he helped me, he didn't panic.' So she says, 'What would you have done if he'd have panicked?' I said, 'I'd a probably panicked right along with him.' What a dumb question.

"I was belting back hand grenades all night, and I threw back a bunch too." At one point a grenade landed near some of the wounded, and Cafferata ran over and grabbed it. "When it went off," he said, "it didn't go off in my hand. It went off as I threw it, but my hands were kinda frozen, and it just kinda blew the meat off some of the fingers. Don't make it worse than it is. It didn't blow no fingers off like you see written in some articles. I didn't have time for it to hurt. It happened in the middle of the action, way after the guy threw the satchel charge.

"Just before dawn I took these three prisoners. I don't know where the hell they come from, but they were unarmed. They just surrendered to me. So I laid them down one on top of the other after I searched them, and it wasn't long after that dawn broke and the Chinese seemed to pull back. Then three of our guys come down, and I handed the prisoners over to them, and then I went looking for my boots. That's when I got hit again.

"I went out by myself and then I got shot in the muscle of my right arm, and that screwed up my arm pretty good. I was laying on the ground and the son of a bitch kept shooting at me. I guess somebody poured lead down his direction and he quit. Then I got up and ran back, still in my socks. I never did get my boots. At some point I got hit in the chest, and I had blood all over me. God damned if I know how I got it. It wasn't a bullet, but there was a little hole in my chest. It bled like hell, and my lungs filled up with blood.

"I come back when the firing stopped, and we staggered down to the aid tent and got checked in by the corpsman, Red somebody. Later on in the afternoon, Benson's sight got better, and he went back out and fought with the outfit, and he helped me down the mountain when we got rescued five days later and fought our way down to Hagaru. Then later he was fighting his way out, heading down to Koto-ri when he got hit in the shoulder and ended up in the hospital with me.

"We got to the medical tent probably about ten o'clock in the middle of that first morning. I had bad feet, the meat off some of my fingers, a bullet hole through my arm. As a matter of fact I found the hole in my chest because I was wondering how come I'm so God damn sick. Then I started peeling through two shirts I had on, and my long johns, and when I got there, boy, there was blood all over. I had the corpsman put a bandage on it. Wasn't long after that Benson and a sergeant come in to see how I was, and I said, 'Guess what, I'm shot in the chest.' They both looked at me like I just died. They couldn't do nothing for me in the tent. Couldn't do nothing when we got down to Hagaru either. It was like I had double pneumonia. When I finally got to an Army hospital, they worked on me there, kept doing chest taps, sucking that fluid out of my lungs.

"At one point the skipper, Captain Barber, comes in the tent and he says, 'Men, if we get hit hard tonight, we might not be able to hold, so if that's the case, we're going to take the tent off you.' Which meant we'd get overrun and probably wouldn't make it out of there. He said they were going to take the tent off the wounded, which I was one of. Then he left the tent and, you know what I thought right after? Boy, is my mother gonna be pissed off I got myself killed.

"I couldn't have crawled five yards. I was really sick, and I was so disgusted with myself. I'd always been tough, and here I find myself weak as a kitten, can't do anything. I had a Thompson submachine gun and a machine pistol in my sleeping bag in the tent, and the funny thing about that was, I was so God damn weak, if I'd have went to pick it up I'd probably shot my feet off."

When told what Barber had said about him—that he kept the lines from being overrun—Cafferata said, "I'm glad to hear that. He was one tough guy. He was a quiet guy, and he did a lot of thinking. But when he took over the company, whoo, I don't know, he wasn't too happy with what he saw. He was respected by the people in Fox Company. We respected all our officers. We had good officers. We had seven officers in the company, and six of them were wounded on the hill and the seventh got killed taking the rest of the company down the road from Hagaru. One killed, and all the rest wounded. So they weren't sitting back in some CP [command post] with the boys. You know that's important.

"And Barber was holding everything together. Because, Jesus Christ, they told him to leave and the only way he could leave was to gather his troops that weren't wounded and get on the road and try to fight his way south, which probably would have got the remainder of the company killed or wounded. He would have had to leave us at the mercy of the Chinese, and they didn't have too much mercy. We'd have all been killed anyway. I don't think I could have survived as a prisoner. I'd sure as shit do something and get myself killed. That was a real mess. We were awful lucky we got out of that."

The First Battalion, 7th Marines, led by Lieutenant Colonel Raymond G. Davis, broke through to Fox Company the morning of December 2, 1950. The Marine garrison at Yudam-ni, up the road, had fought its way back toward Fox but was still hemmed in by enemy. Davis helped them break through and then led the entire force back down to Hagaru-ri and safety. Two years later, Davis would receive a Medal of Honor along with Hector Cafferata.

How was it possible that the American command could be talking of getting the boys home for Christmas and not be aware of tens of thousands of enemy soldiers closing in? "That's the question that has always pissed me off," Cafferata said, "because we had Thanksgiving dinner down at Hagaru, the twenty-fourth or the twenty-fifth, and we got hit the night of the twenty-seventh. And you know, the God damn American Army was off to our flank, thirty miles away, getting the shit kicked out of them by the Chinese. Now why in the hell didn't they let us know that the Chinese were there in force like that? We could have pulled our boys back from up there on the Yalu, we could have gone all the way back, got together at Hagaru, and we could have really put up a battle, you know what I mean? We wouldn't have took the casualties we took.

"The Army didn't tell us. The Army ran it. We were just part of it. And if it wasn't for a Marine Corps general, O. P. Smith, we'd have been in dire straits. He's the guy who wouldn't let them spread us out as much as they wanted to. He went cautious, built up supplies, made an airfield. He did things that MacArthur and that jerkoff friend of his, Major General Edward Almond (see chapter 5), didn't want us to do. That's what saved our butt."

Cafferata spent the next eighteen months in hospitals in Korea, Japan, Hawaii, California, Texas, and Long Island. "The bullet that hit me in the arm cut the nerves, and that's why I have a wrist problem. They kept trying to get my arm put back together, but they couldn't do it. They tried like hell, but they couldn't get the two ends of the nerve to stretch so they could suture them. I had a lot of operations on the arm.

"I got out of the hospital in June or July of fifty-two and went back home to the job I had before I went in the Marines. Later I ran a sporting goods store in Caldwell, New Jersey, ran one up in Dover, sold guns and ammo wholesale, bought a bar, and eventually got a job with the Division of Fish and Game in New Jersey. I retired in nineteen ninety-four. All I do now is hunt and fish, and think about it. My hand is fine, but because of the wound I can't pick it up. In other words, my wrist drops. When I have a gun in my hand and my hand around the pistol grip, I can move my trigger finger. I can button my shirt, but I can't eat with my right hand. I gotta write left-handed." Cafferata and his wife, Doris, raised four children. They retired to Venice, Florida, from Alpha, New Jersey, in 1998.

He was nominated for the Medal by Lieutenant Robert McCarthy of Asheville, North Carolina, who commanded the Third Platoon. "Hector was at the end of my platoon, joining the Second Platoon to me," McCarthy said. "He was able to fire down this draw and he was flat killing Chinamen, I'll tell you that. I figured he killed close to a hundred of the enemy but we only wrote

it up for thirty-six because we didn't think they would believe it."
McCarthy said he and Barber were both wounded by the same bullet, when they stood up to ascertain whether a group of men some distance away were Marines or enemy. "They fired one bullet that hit me in the upper thigh," McCarthy said, "and it hit the small of my stock and knocked me on my butt. Barber was bent over. The same bullet hit him in the crotch and cracked his pelvis bone. I had a through-and-through bullet wound, but he had a more painful situation. He was fortunate that he was able to walk, with some help. I was very annoyed by the obituary release in the *New York Times* that said Fox Company was a scruffy bunch until Barber took over. That's a damn lie." McCarthy said half the company consisted of regulars and half of it was reserves, and that it was squared away before Barber showed up. McCarthy said it was he who had nominated Barber for the award, as well as Cafferata.

Cafferata said, "Would you believe I never knew I'd been put up for the Medal of Honor? Then I got a telegram. It said, 'You have been awarded the Medal of Honor. Come to Washington and get it.' I called them up and told them I'm not coming. Mail it to me. They said, 'No, get your ass down here.' So I went." Lieutenant Colonel Ray Davis, who retired a general, and Staff Sergeant Robert Kennemore, who fought the same action north of Yudam-ni, received the Medal on the same day with Cafferata, November 27, 1952, from President Truman at the White House.

"Yeah," said Cafferata, who was six feet two and weighed 220 pounds, "and the little bastard ruined my shoes. Because you know he was a kind of a little short guy and I'm standing at rigid attention, as high up as I could get, as straight as I could get. And he steps up, and he's trying to get his arms around me to snap the ribbon behind my neck and I'm just too tall. So now I have to kinda slink down. So I'm slinking down while he's standing on my spit-shined shoes. So anyway, he ruined my shoes, and I kept them, with all the smear marks, for about twenty years. Then I threw them away."

NINE

Lewis L. Millett

The Last Bayonet Charge
A Hilltop in Korea
February 7, 1951

*"I believe in freedom, deeply believe it. I believed that,
as a free man, it was my duty—and I'm not Jewish—but I
thought it was my duty to help the Jews be freed of a son of a bitch like Hitler.
That's why I deserted and went to Canada: to fight against Hitler.
I've fought in three wars, and volunteered for all of them, because I
believed as a free man it was my duty to help others under
the attack of tyranny. Just as simple as that."*

Lew Millet, eighty-one, at his home in Idyllwild, California, in the fall of 2002. He retired as a full colonel.

Photo by Eddie Adams

Lew Millett as a rough, tough, grenade-toting, bayonet-brandishing mustachioed Army captain who feared no man.

143

IT WAS COLD and frosty the January morning I drove up a steep drive-way and parked beside Lew Millett's chalet-style home in Idyllwild, California. His son met and led me to a basement entrance, explaining that he and his father had been sitting down there watching a movie called Anzio, *with Robert Mitchum, on the VCR. I remembered the picture and, as I entered a room crammed with memorabilia and clay sculptures, I said, "How's the movie, Mr. Millett?" And he replied, "Pretty good. I was there, you know."*

If America has a warrior class—and it does—Colonel Lewis H. Millett, U.S. Army Retired, belongs at the head of the line. As his son Lewis Jr. remarked, summarizing his father's exploits over three wars in North Africa, Italy, Korea, Vietnam, Laos, and Cambodia, "He makes Rambo look like Captain Kangaroo."

"My family settled in Gloucester, Massachusetts, in sixteen thirty-five," Lew Millett was saying. "I'm not an American. I'm a Yankee. My ancestor, Thomas Millett, was killed in an Indian attack on the Brookfield Massachusetts Bay Colony in sixteen seventy-five. And later on Milletts fought in the Revolution and got a land grant, in Maine. I went back to look at it. They got the side of a hill, rocks. I'm a descendant of soldiers, mainly militia." Millett joined the Massachusetts National Guard in nineteen thirty-eight when he was an adolescent.

"I graduated from Dartmouth High School in New Bedford, off Cape Cod, in nineteen forty. I joined the peacetime Army in nineteen forty—the Army Air Corps, before there was an Air Force." He was sent to Lowry Field, near Denver, to learn about machine guns. Later, in Louisiana, his unit and others trained with toy rifles because there were not enough real ones to go around. "We had broomstick machine guns. They cut a hole in a two-by-four, stuck this broomstick in, and put it on a pedestal to act like a machine gun."

In October of 1941, two months before the Japanese bombed Pearl Harbor, President Roosevelt made a speech saying that no Americans would be fighting on foreign soil. Young Lew Millett promptly deserted the Army. "The war was going on in Europe. I deserted the Army, hitchhiked to Canada in uniform. I started out with another guy. He turned back at the Canadian line, lost his nerve. I always wondered what happened to him. We tried to go in uniform, and they wouldn't let us in. I went home to get some civilian clothes, and went back over near Fort Kent, Maine, to Edmonton, New Brunswick, where I enlisted." Basic training included instruction in hand-to-hand fighting with the bayonet, which, ten years later, was to prove useful.

"There was another American, who had worked to get a bad-conduct discharge out of the Marine Corps because he wanted to go to Canada, too, and rather than desert he got a bad-conduct discharge. We had to take tests and all that, and we passed with very high marks. They sent both of us to Ottawa, to the National Research Council. It was radar school, classified and very secret. And here I'm a deserter and he's a bad-conduct discharge, and they sent us because we had high IQs."

Millet was sent to England to be a radar specialist, but by then the United States had entered the war. "I go to the embassy in London and ask how I can get back to the American Army because we're fighting now. They said, 'Just wait for the announcement and you'll be transferred.' The American Army didn't know anything about me because I came from the Canadian Army. I had to give them my serial number when I enlisted and all that."

In August of 1942, Millett was sent to Ireland, assigned to the 27th Armored Field Artillery, 1st Armored Division, and on November 8 he landed in Oran, North Africa, at a place called St. Leu. His first contact with the Germans came at Medjez-el-Bab in Tunisia. "They took one-third of our combat team because they didn't have enough gas and oil to send the whole division across. They sent one combat team across North Africa to try to take Tunis. Of course, the old adage is 'If you're going to walk piecemeal, you get defeated piecemeal.' That's just what happened. We hit Rommel's people, and they creamed our ass.

"During combat, a half-track [vehicle with wheels and tracks, like a tank] was parked next to a pile of wheat or grain as big as a

garage, and the shelling caught the grain on fire. So I ran back to
get the vehicle and drive it out. Unbeknownst to me, they put a
camouflage net over the top when they parked it and put straw on
top of the camouflage net. I ran the artillery fire to get in, and I had
a hard time starting it because I didn't know there was a push button. By the time I got it started the fire from the haystack had got
to the camouflage net and the hay on top of there, and I'm driving
across country on fire. And I get out there and realize it's on fire
because smoke started coming in. And it was full of ammo. I drove
it away from our troops. The bags for the 105 [105 mm howitzer]
caught fire and made a flash. I rolled out of the vehicle, and it blew
up. And that's what they gave me the Silver Star for."

The following February, as part of a counterattack at Kasserine
Pass, Millett shot down a Messerschmitt with a pair of .50 caliber
machine guns his outfit had jury-rigged on the back of a half-track
because there was so little in the way of antiaircraft armament. He
made corporal after that. Eventually he was to receive the European
African Campaign ribbon, with seven campaigns and three amphibious assault landings—in North Africa, at Salerno, and Anzio, Italy.

"All this time I'd been getting partial pay because they didn't
have my records. I'd already fought six months in Africa and six
months in Italy. I had the Silver Star. I was a buck sergeant. Now
my records come in. I get about two thousand dollars in back pay.
And they court-martial me.

"It was all done in Washington, D.C. They said, 'You'll court-
martial him, and you'll do this, that and the other' . . . but I never
appeared before a court-martial. We were in Naples. The lieutenant, George Crick, said to me, 'You were court-martialed yesterday, found guilty of desertion, fined fifty-two dollars.' Then, a
week later, they made me a second lieutenant. Mark Clark pinned
the bars on me."

During the campaign up through Italy, his artillery outfit was
taken out of the First Armored Division and attached to the all-
black 92d, where it was to provide direct support for the front lines
near the Cinquale Canal north of Pisa high up on the west coast of

Italy. Millett was a forward observer, which meant that his job was to go forward, locate targets, then call back and order artillery fire. The Battle of the Cinquale Canal was to be Millett's last major action in Italy. He was too busy to be scared or worried, he said.

"The battle was brilliantly planned. They found out that most of the canal could support tanks. There was hard rock under the sand in the Ligurian Sea. So we went up the beach and then went inland behind the German lines. I was on the extreme left flank as a forward observer for one of the rifle companies from the 92d. And the Germans make contact, and I'm firing, and Coleman, my radio operator, is pulling on my leg. What's the matter? We're by ourselves. The company had taken off.

"So I go back to cross the canal, and a captain tells me to go in, find a major in there, find out where he wants me to go. So I went to the infantry major, a black major, and he sent me inland, along the canal. There was a big farmhouse the Germans had reinforced with pine logs. We were very well protected in there. I called artillery down on our position.

"Most of the infantry took off, but the tankers who'd lost their tanks, who'd been knocked out, were fighting as infantry. There were three different FO [forward observer] groups there. We were surrounded for three days. There were fifteen or twenty of us, including a few blacks. One night the Germans had us surrounded, and they were throwing grenades into the house. One landed on the chest of Coleman. It blew him up. We went out one night, the third night. And I remember we were walking along the canal and crossed where there'd been a bridge. And there was a German, evidently wounded, lying there saying, '*Trinkwasser. Trinkwasser* [A drink of water].' I can still remember that very vividly. We didn't stop." For his part in this action, calling in artillery on their position in the farmhouse, Lieutenant Millett received a Bronze Star.

The war in Italy ended April 29, 1945, and Millett was home by June 1. After being discharged from the Army, he joined the Maine National Guard, and subsequently began attending Bates College in Lewiston. The Army had called for volunteers to return to active duty, and Millett had volunteered for June of 1949, following his graduation, but he got called up in January, which kept him from obtaining his degree. [After the Korean War, he received a degree in political science from Park College in Missouri.]

He was sent to Japan, where he wound up as an education adviser on MacArthur's staff for six months, and went from there to the Eighth Field Artillery. The Korean conflict, as it was called, began June 25, 1950, when the North Koreans crossed the 38th Parallel, midpoint in the country, and drove south. Again, Millett was a forward observer. Stationed far south in the Pusan Perimeter, he called down an artillery barrage on his position, halting a North Korean tank attack. For this he received an oak-leaf cluster. A few months later, this time well up north of Seoul with the 25th Division, again acting as a forward observer, he was wounded in the leg by shell bursts the same night Capt. Reginald B. Desiderio, commander of Company E, 2d Battalion, 27th Infantry, was killed.

"When the Chinese first attacked Task Force Dolvin, we were in support. Easy Company of the 27th held a hill just north and was protecting the task force. I was with the force as a liaison officer, and I remember Desiderio coming by and taking his troops up the hill. I told him, 'When you get up there, give me a call. I'll fire from here.' He got seriously wounded reinforcing, died up there. He had mortars and got shot too. In fact, I got wounded there, right after I talked to him. Shrapnel knocked me down. I couldn't understand why I went down. I didn't feel it.

"So we're going down the road in an ambulance convoy and hit this ambush. Well, I was in the last vehicle, and I'd refused to give up my rifle, my M-1. I said, 'I'll give it up when I get to the hospital.' I rolled out of the ambush. Two guys followed me, and I crawled toward the enemy position. And they're firing. So I fight my way out of it and then go back to the front. They had set up the ambush so that anybody going to the rear would be running into machine guns. Because they think you're gonna run away, you do just the opposite, and you can get out alive. I met back up with the unit and stayed with them until the next day. I rode a tank out.

"I'm evacuated to the hospital. You go to the MASH hospital and there's litters all over the place. And you're not gonna get immediate service unless you're bleeding to death. I look around and see this. The wound had stopped bleeding. I was lucky. It just missed the artery. Later on, they operated and took the shrapnel out."

Recovering from his leg injury, Millett became an aerial observer in a two-seater Stinson, seeking out enemy positions and calling in artillery. On patrol, he spotted a fighter pilot, John Davis of Pretoria, South Africa, who had been shot down behind enemy lines. He directed his pilot, Captain James Lawrence of Pittsburgh, to set the plane down on a road and put the South African in the Stinson. He stayed to fight off an enemy patrol until his plane came back for him. The South Africans presented Millett with a bottle of scotch for saving Davis.

Millett's next move was to volunteer for transfer to the 27th and command of Desiderio's Easy Company. This was not an enviable post because Desiderio, who was to receive the Medal of Honor posthumously, had been enormously popular with his men. Although he was an artillery man, Millett also had served with rifle companies in World War II. In the latter part of December 1950, he took over the company.

"And in that period of time, the Chinese said the Americans were afraid of the bayonet. And I said, 'I'm gonna teach those damn Chinamen something,' because both my great-grandfathers fought in the Civil War, and you know damn well they used the bayonet all the time. So I said, 'We'll teach those bastards.' And I had to scrounge bayonets because a lot of people had thrown them away. We had to sharpen them, so we got the Korean women to do it.

"The funny part is, I didn't know American bayonet drill. I knew Canadian, so I had to teach them the Canadian drill. So I taught them and said, 'The next attack we make, it's bayonets.' We made three attacks. The first one was probably against an outpost, a platoon or small company, and they ran. Before we even got in the holes with them, they ran, which allowed us to shoot them in the back.

"And then the next day, they fought until we got real close to them, and then they ran. That was a company. Then I missed a day because we were off on a flag-protection mission. And then the fourth day, February seventh, they were commanded by a major, and they fought us.

"There was a line, and supposedly we were not attacking to take ground. The enemy had gone as far as they could go and had, what would you call it, fingers, out? And we were waiting for reinforcements, to reorganize and all that. And [General Matthew B.] Ridgway wanted us to knock off these people, not to take territory, but to kill as many of them as possible.

"I think most of them were Chinese because they had the quilted uniform and all. They were dug in on a line, a linear defense, alongside a road. We were going along the road. I had the left side; the right side was Fox Company. The enemy had set up their defensive line on this ridgeline that crossed the road. There was a hill line parallel to the road—Hill 180 it was called—and I had a platoon up there to protect my flank. We were just making an approach. One of the guys in the platoon spotted some movement on this ridgeline and alerted me."

Millett had two tanks with his company. The Chinese opened fire as he deployed his two platoons. Millett jumped on a tank and began returning fire with a .50 caliber machine gun. Directing the gunner to take over and provide covering fire, he jumped down and ran to his men. "They were in the low ground and I just alerted them, 'Fix bayonets and follow me!' "

He then led a charge across a hundred yards of icy rice paddy to the base of the hill. "I started out yelling and screaming. I taught the people. We had a pamphlet, Chinese words, *she lie sani* or something like that. Means 'I'm gonna kill you with a bayonet.' I don't know how true that is."

Asked about the wisdom of a charge across one hundred yards of open ground, he replied, "I'm an arrogant son of a bitch. I don't believe anybody is gonna kill me. Every time I got hit, I couldn't believe it. You feel invulnerable, you know? During the charge I got a grenade fragment in my left leg. We're running straight at them. The smartest thing is to run as fast as you can to the bottom of the hill because if you get to the base, and if they don't have anybody there, they can't see you. We had to reorganize, wait for the others to catch up, stuff like that."

In his two platoons, he had roughly sixty men, stretched out in a line about two hundred feet long. "We all start charging up the hill, and they're shooting down and throwing grenades. They went to grenades more than anything else, which was kind of stupid because they're heaving them and ducking back into their holes. And the grenades are coming through the air, and you're going right or left, trying to get by so they won't hit you. The only thing about it was, some of them would be strewn along on the ground. That's where I got hit in the shins. The grenade they had was a potato masher. I think they took tin cans and filled them with powder and put them on a potato handle. And when they blew, very few people got hurt bad, unless you came underneath it or something like that. Later on they got better grenades.

"At the crest of the hill, they were in an inverted V—I don't know why—three people in it, and they had an antitank rifle, shooting at the troops. I came in on their right. And the first guy, the gunner, didn't even know I was coming. He turned just as I hit him in the throat with the bayonet. The other two . . . all the noise and grenades going off, all the noise of battle, people don't hear, especially if you're coming in at an angle. He was at the point, and the other two were at each end of the V. The next man reached for a pistol, and I got him in the throat. About that time the third man turned, and I lunged forward and the bayonet went into his forehead, like going into a watermelon."

Millett said he had two Browning Automatic Rifles per squad for extra-heavy firepower, all facing about one hundred and fifty enemy on the hilltop, most in individual foxholes. Later on, the Army historian S. L. A. Marshall would write that forty-seven of the estimated two hundred enemy on the hill were killed, eighteen by bayonet. Other reports said sixty enemy received treatment for wounds later. But Millett thought they killed them all. Four Americans in the assault were killed by sniper fire.

"They didn't count these people until two days later and someone came up and said fifty-seven, but we killed them all. What we did was, we'd throw them down the hole and cover them up with dirt and use the hole for ourselves. Then the Turks came up and relieved us, and they did the same thing."

S. L. A. Marshall also described the assault as "the most complete bayonet charge by American troops since Cold Harbor," scene of a spectacularly unsuccessful assault in Hanover County, Virginia, by Northern troops in June 1864 in America's Civil War.

Decades later, the Class of 2001 at the War College gave the artist Don Stivers $20,000 to make a painting of Millett leading his men up the hill. "I went back there when they were making the presentation," he said. "Shinseki, the chief of staff of the Army, was there. The class had the painting. Three things are wrong in it. One bayonet is too long; the guy that's right behind me should be black—Green, the only black in the unit; and there were only two tanks, not four. Otherwise, it's not a bad picture." The description of the painting says the men left a bayonet stuck in a crack in a rock holding a sign that read, "Compliments of Easy Company." That was half true as well, Millett said. The bayonet, he said, was "right up the ass of the Chinese commander," adding, "He was supposed to have been a major. We left it stuck in his ass with a sign saying, 'Compliments of Easy Company.'

"It is war, you know, and these were . . . gung-ho guys. We actually danced on that hilltop, waving our rifles and saying, 'We're good! We're good! We're good!' I wouldn't be alive today if they weren't. You don't go charging up a hill with just a bayonet against armed enemy all by your lonesome."

So Millett led three charges with the bayonet. For the second action, he received a Distinguished Service Cross. For the third, he was awarded the Medal of Honor.

After the third attack, "Gordon Mercer, my battalion commander, ordered me not to lead any more bayonet charges. I was pulled off the line in June, once the recommendation for the Medal of Honor had gone back to the States. They send you back because most people, in all the wars, they get recommended for the Medal of Honor, and then they get killed. So once the citation gets to a certain level, they start pulling out the guy recommended for the decoration. They flew me home, on a commercial flight." President Truman put the ribbon holding the Medal around Millett's neck on July 5, 1951. Millett recalled Truman saying, as he did almost every time he presented it, that he would rather have the Medal of Honor than be President.

By June of 1952, Millett was on reserve duty in Maine. "I was stationed at Indiantown Gap, and I went to New York for a shindig with all the big shots. They asked General John R. Hodge to have a picture with me, because I was a most highly decorated person and he was a four-star general. Well, he was five feet two, I was six feet tall, and they wanted him to put his arm around me. I said, 'Just a minute, General, come with me.' And I went over to a stairs, had him stand on a higher step, and he thought I was a pretty shrewd son of a bitch. So he asked for me as a junior aide. I knew nothing about the Army then. All I did was fight wars. I never had any training until I was a major, and they sent me to school. I never went through any training in the American Army until then, except as a machine gunner in the Army Air Corps back in the States, when I first enlisted.

"I started out as a captain, worked for Hodge a year until he retired. After reserve duty in Massachusetts, I went to Greece, as a captain and a major. I was an adviser to the Greek airborne, and I wasn't airborne qualified. So they sent me to jump school in Germany, and then I went back to advise the Greeks, for almost two years. I came back to the States, went to school at Fort Benning. By this time they figured I should have some training, so I took an advance course for company-grade officers, then I went to the 101st Airborne for almost two years.

"I started Recondo for the 101st. We were on maneuvers, and I took a unit, infiltrated through the lines, and captured the 82d

Division headquarters. I got a call to report to General West-moreland. I said, 'Oh shit, I really screwed things up.' He called me in, said, 'That was a beautiful job you did; you got another one. You're gonna get every soldier in the division who's a specialist and train them to be field soldiers.' So that's where Recondo came from: It stood for reconnaissance/doughboy. Westmoreland dreamed that up.

"It was two weeks' training and it was so tough almost everybody had to go through twice. Most of them couldn't read maps in the first place, and most of the brigade commanders hated my guts because I was flunking all these guys. Later on I went up to the 82d Airborne and started a raider school there, too. Same thing.

"After I retired I went to a VFW [Veterans of Foreign Wars] convention in Tennessee, and there's one small group there of a chapter, all black, and I'm walking across the hall, and one of these blacks is in front of me, and he's got a jacket on with a great big arrowhead, which is Recondo. And I said, 'One of those damn Recondos!' And he turned around, he was gonna hit me, and he says, 'Major Millett!' And he grabbed my arm and took me over to introduce me to all his friends and he said, 'When I was going through this man's training in the 101st, if I ever met him in the streets of Nashville, I was gonna kill him.' He says, 'And I go to Vietnam. And this man saved my life, I don't know how many times.' " Millett teared up as he finished the story. "It was worth it, you know," he said.

"I went over to Vietnam in 1960 and started the rangers for the South Vietnamese in Na Trang. They didn't have much fighting then. I was the first man to rappel from a helicopter in Vietnam. We only had one chopper, and it belonged to the president, Diem. I had to borrow it to demonstrate what you could do with a chopper, dropping troops into action. I came back to the States.

"Then in 1968, I went to Deputy Chief Thailand, that was the name of the unit I was in. It was a cover for Laos, because we weren't supposed to be there. We lived in Thailand, worked in Laos. We had to go in civilian clothes, no IDs, fly Air America. I had an Air America contract for ten million dollars a year. I was taking soldiers out of Laos, training them in Thailand, taking them back."

His last combat assignment was as an adviser to the Phoenix Intelligence Program. "They called us murderers. What we did was set up ambushes on the outskirts of villages so that when underground agents would go out to make contacts, we'd either kill or capture them. We wanted to gain intelligence to find out who these people were. Most of them would not be captured, and they'd fight and of course get killed. And the media called us murderers. Of course we didn't get good publicity out of Vietnam anyway."

Lew Millett retired in 1973 as a full colonel. He had battlefield promotions to corporal, sergeant, then a battlefield commission to second and first lieutenant. In Korea, he was promoted to captain after three months in combat. In addition to the Medal of Honor, he was awarded the Distinguished Service Cross, the Silver Star, three Bronze Stars, three Purple Hearts, two Legions of Merit, the Air Medal, the French Croix de Guerre with palm, the Vietnamese Cross of Gallantry, and various other awards and citations. He refused all U.S. decorations for his actions in Vietnam, declaring that he was not there for recognition but to provide freedom for people under attack by the forces of tyranny.

He had served in combat as an antiaircraft machine gunner, a tank commander, a forward observer, an artillery gunner, a reconnaissance sergeant, an infantryman, a paratrooper with eleven jumps in Vietnam and five jumps in Laos, and an intelligence officer. He was first man to rappel from a helicopter in Vietnam and the last man to lead a full company in a bayonet charge.

Hence, as a retiree in Abilene, Texas, he was understandably annoyed when President Gerald R. Ford granted amnesty to those who had evaded the draft. Millett's son, Lewis Jr., recalled what happened: "Dad said there're still POWs held in Vietnam, and he himself never got amnesty for going to Canada to enlist in their military and fight the Germans. He was on national television for two days, with a picket sign, all dressed up in dress greens with his medals and everything. He was picketing in front of City Hall, in Abilene, and then he went to the post office and picketed there. And Ford pardoned him."

Millett laughed to hear the story. "I'd forgotten all about it. But I was the only Army colonel ever convicted of desertion and subsequently pardoned by a President—thirty years later. And got away with it. It was like when they court-martialed me. They did it just to clear the record. I was only making a statement against draft dodgers. It's illegal, you know. An officer can't just go and do things like that, in a uniform."

Millett married an Abilene woman, Winona Williams, in 1951. She was part Cherokee. They had four children, Lewis Jr., Timothy, Elizabeth, and John. Staff Sergeant John Millett, their youngest, died with 248 members of the 101st Airborne, part of the multinational peacekeeping force, when a DC-8 they were on crashed in Gander, Newfoundland, while returning from an assignment in the Sinai December 12, 1985.

Millett was elected justice of the peace in Abilene and served for a year. Then he got sick, thought he had cancer, went to Tennessee for treatment, and ended up a deputy sheriff of Gibson County. Later on, Lew and his wife, Mona, moved to Idyllwild. She died in 1993. They had been married over forty years.

"I've never worked at a job to make money," he said. "Always some service, justice of the peace or chamber of commerce, something like that. I'm sergeant of arms in the Medal of Honor Society. I think it's a great honor. I was elected ten years ago, for life."

Of his fellow recipients, Millett commented, "I think most of them try to live up to the Medal and protect and not disgrace it. I have not met any that I would say did not deserve it. And they're a hell of a gang of people. You got every conceivable race, religion. What they have in common is courage, or the absence of fear in a critical situation. It's having courage when it counts.

"I believe in freedom, deeply believe it. I believed as a free man it was my duty—and I'm not Jewish—but I think it was my duty to help the Jews be freed of a son of a bitch like Hitler. That's why I deserted and went to Canada: to fight against Hitler. I've fought in three wars, and volunteered for all of them because I believed as a free man it was my duty to help others under the attack of tyranny. Just as simple as that. Now, I'm so damn old I can't do it. But that's my belief; if free men don't help others to retain or regain our freedom, then we'll lose in the final analysis."

TEN

Rodolfo Hernandez

Son of Migrant Workers
187th Airborne, Korea
May 31, 1951

"I said to the gun, 'Speak to them, Baby Doll.'
And she spoke."

Rudy Hernandez at seventy-one,
in his home in Fayetteville,
North Carolina.

Rudy Hernandez as a young soldier, newly decorated, after fearful combat in Korea. The scar from
an enemy bayonet is visible under his lower lip.

158

*CORPORAL RODOLFO HERNANDEZ was so badly torn up and had
bled so heavily following his bayonet charge into a crowd of enemy
on Hill 420 near Wontong-ni, Korea, on May 31, 1951, that the soldiers who found him early that morning thought he was dead. He had
been shot, blown up, and stabbed. A large part of his skull and part
of his brain were gone. He had been bayoneted in the back and
through his lower lip. He was placed in a body bag and carted off the
hill. Then someone noticed a bit of movement from inside the bag.
He finally came to a month later in a hospital in South Korea. He was
paralyzed on his right side and could not move. He could not talk. He
could not swallow. After being stabilized, he was moved to a hospital in Japan and from there to Letterman Hospital in San Francisco.
He was twenty years old.*

*Words come slowly today. He speaks haltingly, slurring a bit, and
grows annoyed when he can't find the word he is searching for. He
lives in Fayetteville, North Carolina, near the military home of his
old outfit. His wife, Denzil, helps him through the rough spots.*

"I was born April fourteenth, nineteen thirty-one, in Colton,
California. My folks followed the crops. They were migrant workers. They picked cotton, oranges, grapes, string beans, strawber-
ries, boysenberries. My mother, Guadalupe Perez, was born in
Mexico City; my father was born in Texas. They married young. My
mother was about sixteen. They had eight children, five boys and
three girls. My father's name was David.

"At the end of nineteen thirty-eight we went down to Bakers-
field. My brothers and my sisters were in school, not me. You might
say I was playing hooky. I got through elementary school, eighth
grade. Nobody could handle me, but I didn't get in trouble with
the law. I was too young to get any jobs. I went in the service in
1949, in Fresno. I was seventeen, I got my mother to sign for me.

"When I finished basic training in Ford Ord, California, they
marched us down to where they assigned each man to a division.
Before this started, the sergeant asked, 'Does anyone care to go to
the Airborne?' And I said, 'Yeah, yeah, I do!' And that was that. I

got a seven-day leave and spent it with my mother. After that they took us by train down to New Orleans, and it stopped and they told me to get off, go somewhere and stretch my legs. I went into a restaurant for colored folks, and they wouldn't serve me. I said, 'Why? Why? Why?' They said, 'Because you are white folks.'

"The train took us to Fort Benning, Georgia, and I had five or six weeks of parachute training. I made my five jumps, and they assigned me to the 511th Regiment, 11th Airborne Division, in Fort Campbell, Kentucky. Only then it was called Camp Campbell. When the Korean War broke out in June of nineteen fifty, I was assigned to the 187th Regimental Combat Team. I became a BAR man, Browning Automatic Rifle. It was heavy, but you could walk and fire it at the same time. I called it Baby Doll.

"We went by train to Camp Stoneman near San Francisco. Then the whole regiment took a boat to Japan, in August nineteen fifty. After a few days in Japan, they flew us down to Korea, near Seoul. The first time we went into actual combat, I felt like Superman. I had my BAR, I had my ammo clips. And all it took was for one artillery round to go over my head and make me a small thing, like an ant crawling. I knew I was in for a real interesting time.

"We made our first combat jump behind enemy lines north of Pyongyang on October twentieth. The whole regiment was involved. The First Battalion dropped at Sukchon and my battalion, the Second, landed near Sunchon, about twelve hundred men. We were trying to save our buddies who were taken prisoner, but we were too late. They were killed two hours before we jumped. We jumped from real low, about eight hundred feet. My parachute opened, and then I was hitting the ground. I had my BAR. We started moving toward our objective. There was an enemy soldier that encountered me, and I shot at him. He must have ducked, but he was ready to surrender. So I gave him to one of my backup guys. We took the town and set up roadblocks. A few days later we moved down to Pyongyang.

"In February, Valentine's Day, we were involved in an operation that I knew we were not going to come out of alive. My BAR wouldn't fire, and the priest was right there talking to each man who passed by. I'll never forget that. I took my BAR apart—there was something wrong with it—and I put it back together, and I started walking, and I said to the gun, 'Speak to them, Baby Doll.' And she spoke. I was relieved."

Hernandez saw a good deal of combat that month. In one incident, he said, "nearly everybody who was up on the mountain got hit, and we were pinned down. And I got this urge that was my 'inner man' coming out, so I got up and came out, run run run and shooting shooting shooting. Bullets were flying all around everywhere, and I got to the first hole and I shot them, and I went after another foxhole and they were firing and firing, but they didn't hit me, so I fired back and killed them. My buddies were right behind me. We killed fifty guys and took out three foxholes."

Hernandez said he was not scared when the bullets were flying because his "inner man" took over in those situations and he followed the impulses dictated by that presence.

Shortly afterward his feet became frostbitten so badly he was unable to walk, and he ended up being sent to Japan for treatment. "I was at the aid station with some guys who had visible injuries. With me there was no visible hurt, but they patched them up and sent them back to the front lines and sent me down to Japan. That was something I couldn't understand.

"I was in Japan about two weeks, and a guy in my company who had been injured in a practice jump said we were going to make another combat jump. So I don't know what happened to me; it must have been that 'inner man' again, but I went to my doctor and told him I wanted to go back to Korea. No sooner had I told him that than I was a regular Army man again. It was my 'inner man' running wild, wanting to get back into action. The doctor said, 'I'm not going to keep this guy in solitude.' I was like Rambo. I joined my company and was issued a rifle and within a month I was made squad leader. My battalion commander called me a cook's helper. I don't know where he got that from.

"When that action occurred on the thirty-first of May it was my 'inner man' taking over again. It was raining, and we got pushed off Hill 420, and then we pushed them off, counterattacked and took it back. They must have been a special regiment because they all looked like they were six feet tall. I was struck all over my body by grenade fragments, and artillery shrapnel caused my skull injury at the same time. I was firing, and then my weapon jammed, and this shell fragment went through my helmet. Our leader ordered us to withdraw, but I was bleeding badly, so I took my rifle and fixed the bayonet and I had six grenades in my foxhole and I threw them at the enemy and then I yelled, 'Here I come!' " Hernandez paused, then laughed. "It must have been my 'inner man' telling me to attack. I don't know what the other Medal of Honor recipients say, but with me it was that 'inner man.'

"I charged the foxholes with a bayonet on an empty rifle and killed six guys. They bayoneted me here in the back and in the lip. They were coming at me. I got them with the bayonet wherever I could. I even kicked them." Hernandez fell unconscious to the ground. His foxhole mate said afterward that Hernandez had stopped the enemy charge. Later, his unit retook the hill and found his "body" twenty-five yards out in front of his foxhole next to the corpse of an enemy soldier.

Rudy's wife, Denzil, listening to his account of the battle, described what then happened. "He was put in a body bag. They said he was dead, but somebody happened to see a slight movement of his hands. When we went to the dedication of the Korean War memorial in Washington, D.C., in nineteen ninety-five, the medic, I believe, that picked him up was jumping over chairs to get to him and when he did he said, 'Rudy, you was dead!'

"Rudy told me," Denzil continued, "that when he was injured he couldn't even swallow, and he almost starved to death for water, because he couldn't tell them what he wanted.

"He had to learn to speak all over again, like a child. He would say the ABCs and nursery rhymes. He had to learn how to walk again, and how to write with his left hand. When they put him in the hospital, he couldn't swallow. He said a real pretty nurse came in, and she kept trying to get him to open his mouth and finally he said, 'Ahh.' His mouth came open and she dropped a little bit of ice cream into it."

It was in Japan, Hernandez continued, when "I started getting my memory back. When they sewed my lip back together, they gave me a smile no one could erase because of the way they stitched it. They put a sort of a smiling face on me. Somebody wrote an article about it called, 'A Touch of Smile.' I'm like Raggedy Andy."

A more recent skull surgery left him bald, and he grew a beard to cover the scar under his lip. Today, Hernandez's right arm tends to rise at the elbow and the fingers on that hand are bent and twisted. "That was from the skull injury," Denzil explained. "When you get hit there, that controls movement, and that's why he was paralyzed down his right side. He has a plate in his skull."

He received the Medal of Honor from President Truman in the Rose Garden on April 12, 1952. By that time, he was able to say a few words. He was told he could bring one guest. His brother Thomas accompanied him from Fresno.

With no more than an eighth-grade education, Hernandez attended Fresno City College for three years, studying business administration. About ten years after Korea, he went to work as a counselor for the Veterans Administration in Los Angeles. He married a California woman, Bertha, and they had three children. "I retired from the Civil Service in December 1979 after seventeen and a half years because I couldn't handle the telephone."

He got divorced and moved to Fayetteville, to be near the home of his airborne unit. A second relationship failed, and then he found Denzil through the Christian Dating Service at the Fayetteville Community Church.

"You see," said Denzil, who was born in 1935, "I had never married. I kept my grandmother, my father's mother, thirty-some years, and I was a bookkeeper for an office in Whiteville that does millwork all over North Carolina, South Carolina, Florida, anyplace. One of my friends, she said, I have something for you. I want you to fill it out and send it in. You know, you fill it out just exactly like you are, what you like, what you do and everything. It was about a month before I even mailed it out. So later on, I got a telephone call. It was Rudy, and he told me all about himself, but he did not tell me he was a Medal of Honor recipient. He doesn't like for people to know he's one.

"So he came to see me, and it was on a Saturday and I was in the house doing my chores. The doorbell rang, and he was standing there smiling, and he took me out to dinner, and then he asked me if he could come back. So he came back, and he kept coming." They were married in the First Baptist Church in Clarkton on March 4, 1995.

When they first married, she said, "I had a hard time understanding him. He could not speak as well as he does now. He has improved greatly."

Hernandez drives, and functions reasonably well, but still his life can be an ordeal as a result of his war wounds. Despite the permanent disability and years of struggle, he said he did not resent his condition. "I feel lucky to be alive. I shouldn't be here. I should be dead."

ELEVEN

Hiroshi Miyamura

Corporal, Third Infantry Division
A Hilltop in North Korea
April 1951

*"When I started thinking about my life from the time I
went into the service, and how I came through, I said, 'There has
to be someone watching over me.' And that's when I said,
'Hell, I must have a guardian angel.'"*

Old soldiers (left to right) Hiroshi
Miyamura, Ray Murphy, George H.
O'Brien Jr., of Midland, Texas, and
Robert Simanek, of Farmington
Hills, Michigan, stand in front of a
statue of Murphy in Pueblo,
Colorado, his hometown, during its
unveiling on September 21, 2000.
All four received the Medal on the
same day, October 27, 1953, from
President Dwight D. Eisenhower.
They get together at least once a year.

Corporal Hiroshi Miyamura, who weighed
ninety-eight pounds when he came home
from Korea, had regained some weight by
the time this picture was taken.

HIROSHI MIYAMURA and his wife, Terry, were extremely hospitable to my wife and me at their home in Gallup, New Mexico. A fellow Medal recipient, Raymond G. Murphy, and his wife, Mary Ann, drove over from Albuquerque to spare us the need to make that trip. We all had dinner one night, lunch the next day, and the Miyamuras and the Murphys insisted on being hosts. We visited the Navaho war memorial to Vietnam veterans at Window Rock in Arizona. In Gallup, we drove past Miyamura Boulevard and Miyamura Park.

"You know what I really think? I had a guardian angel. When I look back at what I went through, being drafted, why I didn't go overseas when I was supposed to, the hernia, a lot of guys I trained with getting killed, guys I was supposed to have been with. And then that night, even before that. I could hear the bullets cracking by my ears, why I didn't get hit then. Other actions, shells dropping all around you. It's just that you gotta, the way I feel, you don't think about it. You just think about what you're supposed to do, and your training will come into play. You start doing things automatically. It's not that I was trying to become a hero. I was trying to do what I was supposed to be doing, and what I was trained to do."

About one hundred and twenty thousand Japanese-Americans were hauled off to internment camps three months after the attack on Pearl Harbor. But the City Council of Gallup, New Mexico, distinguished itself in remarkable fashion when it voted against the internment of its approximately thirty Japanese-American families even though federal authorities had seized their cameras, radios, and firearms. One of these citizens was Yaichi Miyamura, who ran the OK Cafe. He was Issei, a first-generation Japanese-American, distinguished from the second generation known as Nisei. Yaichi had come over from Kyushu in 1906 and had been left to raise seven children ranging in age from four to seventeen after his wife died in 1936. One of his children, who was eleven years old when his mother died, was named Hiroshi. A grade-school teacher found that difficult to pronounce, so she called the boy Hershey. The name stuck, and today, Hershey is often referred to as Gallup's favorite son.

"I didn't really know what was happening in the first part of the war," Hiroshi Miyamura said. "I felt like a lot of them who volunteered out of those camps to fight for this country. I considered it an obligation. I considered myself an American, because that was what my dad said I was. I never resented anything. I was in no position to say if they were wrong or right. I really didn't know many Nisei growing up. We all felt we were Americans, and that was the way we were brought up, and that was the only way I thought. This is the only country I know. My father's restaurant served only American food."

Even though Miyamura knew virtually no other Japanese-Americans, he was placed, when drafted, in such a group. "The 100th Infantry Battalion, consisting for the most part of members of the Japanese-American National Guard in Hawaii, was the first all Japanese-American combat unit. Hawaii was not a state then, just a territory, and they wanted to show our government that they were good, loyal citizens, and that was one way they could show their loyalty—by going to war. A lot of them were in ROTC. Did you know the 100th Battalion had the highest IQ of any battalion in the U.S. Army? Because most of 'em were college educated, or in college. A very intelligent group of guys. They trained in Wisconsin, then were sent to North Africa. And they did so well there that one general said he wanted more of these soldiers, and that's when they decided to start drafting. Up until that time, the Nisei were not allowed to be drafted or even join the Army. So they asked for volunteers. A lot of guys volunteered from out of the internment camps."

As noted in chapter 3, the 100th Infantry Battalion was fighting in Italy when the 442d Regimental Combat Team was formed in 1943. The 100th was then folded into the new outfit as the first of three battalions. The 442d won seven Presidential Unit Citations, and its members earned more than 18,000 individual decorations, including one wartime Medal of Honor, 53 Distinguished Service Crosses, and 9,486 Purple Hearts. The 100th and 442d fought in eight major campaigns in Italy, France, and Germany, including Anzio, Monte Cassino, and Biffontaine in France. In May of 2000, forty-five years after the war ended, nineteen Distinguished Service Crosses that had been awarded to veterans of the 100th and the 442d were upgraded to Medals of Honor following a review of service records of Asian-Pacific Americans.

"I was assigned to the 100th, Company D, a heavy-weapons company—that's when I got into the machine guns. We had finished basic training in Camp Blanding, Florida, when they sent us to Camp Shelby, Mississippi. That's when I lost contact with all the guys I trained with, because I was one of the few that was sent to the 100th. They had just finished basic training for this replacement group, we got our equipment, boarded the train the first part of April in forty-four, and then, before the train pulled out of the station, they called several of us off. We were given the reason that we were not yet nineteen. They had a law that you could not be sent overseas if you were less than nineteen. Yet there were some guys still aboard the train that were eighteen. Anyway they took off, and I was reassigned to Dog Company, and I had to undergo heavy-weapons basic training with the machine gun."

After thirteen weeks, Miyamura was given a furlough and went home to Gallup, where he met a pretty young woman named Teruko. Her family had just relocated to Gallup following release from an internment camp in Poston, Arizona. They had spent three years in the camp, and she had graduated from high school there.

Miyamura returned to Camp Shelby, Mississippi. "Within a matter of a week or so we were told to get ready, we were shipping out." His nineteenth birthday, October 6, had come and gone. "So we boarded a train to Fort Meade, Maryland. We were there for two or three weeks of training. Before we went to the ship, we were given a full field inspection and a physical. They wanted to make sure we had all our gear. And during the physical a lieutenant colonel examining me said, 'Do you know you have a hernia?' I said, 'No.' I didn't even know what a hernia was. He said, 'Don't it bother you?' I said, 'No.' He said, 'We're gonna send you back to Camp Shelby Hospital and have you fixed up.' So then I got separated from my group of machine gunners I trained with.

"Anyway, I reported to Camp Shelby, and they operated and made me stay in bed for seventeen days. After convalescence, I was in the next group that was ready to go. They had just finished basic training. We were not called replacements for the 442d. We were called the 171st Separate Battalion, all Nisei. We boarded the *Patrick Henry* in Norfolk, Virginia. Five days out of Naples, Italy, we heard over the ship's loudspeaker that the war in Europe had ended."

Did he feel cheated to miss out on the action? "I don't really know what I felt. I got written up in *Stars and Stripes* that I had missed going overseas twice before and the third time the war ended."

Miyamura went home in June 1946 and was discharged at Fort Meade. At first he thought he'd reenlist for a three-year hitch, but he never did anything about it. He decided to go to the Milwaukee School of Engineering on the GI Bill, intending to study air-conditioning. But when he came home for the holidays a cousin who was a car mechanic suggested he come work for him. "So instead of going back to school, I said, 'Okay, I'll stay and help.' In the meantime I get married to Terry, June twentieth, nineteen forty-eight, and I didn't even think of going back to school, because I was busier than hell at my cousin's shop. He had a government contract. But the following year, forty-nine, things started slowing down and we were in a kind of a depression. And when this officer came by, in June, to ask if I wanted to reenlist for another three years, I was ready. I was getting bored, and everything else. I didn't tell Terry I'd reenlisted for another three years.

"Well, you know, the next year, June of fifty, the Korean War started, so I got my notice to report in August. They sent me to Fort Hood, Texas, for nine weeks. They called it a refresher course. All we did was march with full field pack every day. It was really hot. After nine weeks, we boarded a train, and the train came right through Gallup, and it stopped. I asked the commander if I could run home. I said, 'It's only about three or four blocks.' There were two other Gallup fellows with me. He said, 'Okay, you can run

home, but when you hear that whistle, you'd better be back here.'
So we did.

"Terry happened to be home by herself that day. She was staying
with my father. There were no kids yet. I went back and boarded
the train, and we went to Camp Stoneman, California. I was flown
to Japan on a commercial airliner and finally ended up on the
southern island of Japan, Kyushu. I was told to join Company H of
the 7th Regiment of the Third Division. I had no idea who they
were. I came to find out later the Third Division made a name for
themselves in the European Theater during World Wars I and II.
Their history goes back a long way, very distinguished. I was
assigned to a machine-gun platoon. I had made corporal shortly
after I joined the unit, and was put in charge of a machine-gun
squad, twelve or fourteen guys. They kept shifting them around.
We had a water-cooled machine gun and an air-cooled, both .30 caliber. You got a first and second gunner on each gun because you
have to have one guy feeding the belt in order to keep the gun from
getting jammed. Most of the other guys were ammo bearers.

"Within a month we boarded ship and went to Korea, landed in
Wonsan, North Korea, in November of nineteen fifty. We ran into
small-arms fire right away, nothing big. From there we made our
way up to the Yalu River. It was just cold, you were cold and miserable. For boots, we had these snow packs, they called them, and
you were supposed to change the felt. They gave us felt liners to put
in there, but our lacing was always frozen and you couldn't even
undo it, so how could we change? But we were told we gotta
change: During our way up there we had so many cases of frostbite
that the commanding general said the next case of frostbite he's
gonna court-martial somebody. We ran into weather that was thirty
and forty below zero. The guns? Oh, yeah, We learned that if you
had any oil at all on them, it would freeze whether the breech was
open or closed. So you didn't oil them. We had to keep a vehicle
running all night long, so you could pull the others to get them
going in the morning. We had Jeeps, mainly. We had machine guns
mounted on them.

"This was more toward the eastern side of North Korea. You heard of the Chosin Reservoir? Those guys were to the left of us. Part of our unit was left to defend as the troops started by, on the retreat. It was the Tenth Army. We were spread out too damn thin. MacArthur didn't think the Chinese would cross the Yalu.

"I was told to dig in and sit there and watch them. We were always on top of a mountain. Through binoculars we could see the Chinese mass on the north side of the river. It was frozen. That's how they got across so quick. But, my God, once they started, it was like ants coming down a hill. Jesus. But you know, from a distance, it looked like every one of them had a weapon. But actually one in nine had a weapon. The others had wooden rifles. With binoculars I could make out they weren't real guns. Because we were so far north, our own Navy Corsairs were strafing my position, and I got orders to get off that mountain, to make my way down to the main road that was the only road that led from North Korea down to the south along the eastern side. It was really a mess. It was snowing, colder 'n hell, and I remember catching a ride on a tank.

"Once we made our way down to a certain point, we were told we were going to defend a perimeter while all the troops were evacuated. There were ships waiting in the harbor. This was in Hungnam. All the time we were up north we never got enough food, and when we reached this area we saw what looked like miles of rations stacked high. So they said, 'Go in, help yourself, take whatever you want.' I'll never forget that day. You'd open up a can, eat a little, throw the rest away, and look for something else. These were ten-in-one rations, they call 'em; gallon cans.

"Next we boarded ship and we heard a big explosion. They told us they were destroying all the ammo and the supplies left over from the retreat. We made our way to Pusan, a large port down in South Korea. We got off the ship, went to a staging area, got new equipment or whatever we needed, clothing, got on trucks; and headed up north again. We made our way up past Seoul, fighting all along the way, nothing real big.

"As machine gunners we were always assigned to different companies, rifle companies mainly, to give them more firepower. And we were always getting put up on the tops of mountains. In April of fifty-one there was a lull in the fighting. That's when the enemy were regrouping, and we were waiting to see what was happening. We were also being supplied with ammo.

"Finally, our group was situated just south of where the Hantan comes into the Imjin River, near Taejon-ni. It wasn't too far from there that I was given the area perimeter to cover, up on top of a mountain again. The rest of the company was down near the CP, the command post, I was told later. I didn't have any communication. During most of my encounters, I was never given or issued a radio or radioman. Just this one time, a runner from the company came up during the day—and that was the last time I saw them. He wanted to know if I had everything I needed. That's when he told me they were going to assign these four riflemen to my squad. We were already dug in, had a trench dug, the gun had a covering, two guys around each gun. Most of the guys in between had M-1s. I always had a .45. I got hold of a carbine, and an M-1.

"There was another machine-gun squad, a section two, just to the right of me, in a lower area, so we were covering the low and the high ground.

"I also had two cases of grenades, about a dozen in each case, just loose in there. You know how, in the movies, they just pull 'em out and fling 'em? Well, you don't just pull 'em out. There's a cotter pin that holds the lever, and it's spread out. I had to squeeze them in together so I could pull the pins out easier and faster. So I did that to all of them so I could heave it fast at night when I had to grab one.

"The runner who came up said the company knew the enemy were going to come. I didn't think they were gonna get across that river that quick because we had to use pontoons to get across. I often wondered how the hell did they get that many men across that quick. I heard different stories about how many they were. It seemed to me like a helluva a lot of 'em, that's all I could think. Several hundred, at least. The snow was gone, but the nights were very cold, but that particular night I don't remember being cold. I don't know where I put my duffel bag with all my belongings. All I remember is I didn't even have a fatigue jacket on, just my regular khakis.

"As it got dark, I was wondering where they were going to come from. We were camouflaged pretty good, so it's possible they couldn't see my position. We were spread out pretty thin, too. The other squad was to the right, the company was down more to my left rear, way down. This is a mountain, not a little hill. There were other battalions and companies to my left, but I never saw them. The 7th Regiment was down to my right. They called it the Kansas Line, I believe. I've often wondered where I was because I was one of the guys who never paid any attention to where I was at. I never thought of the town; I could have cared less. I rarely saw civilians.

"They hit us on the twenty-fourth of April, at night. The Chinese had all the firepower they needed then. You could hear them. Sound travels a lot more than you would think because everything is so quiet. They were rattling, it seemed like tin cans, blowing bugles, whistles and just making all kinds of racket. That kind of gets you on edge.

"Anyway, they were making all kinds of racket, just a lot of vocal sounds, nothing we could understand. I told the machine gunner on my right to start firing if he saw anybody. I was constantly looking. We didn't have the luxury of night binoculars. I saw a flare go off but didn't see movement, but I knew they were on the move. And that's when he opened up. I started firing in that same direction.

"Pretty soon, the guy comes up to me, the gunner. I never liked to tell this story because I don't want them to get the wrong impression that I was doing any more than what I was supposed to do. He came up to me, he says, 'It's gettin' too hot, I want to get out of here.' So I got madder 'n hell, and I almost, I had my pistol, I was ready to shoot him. I told him, 'Get back!' He said, 'It's hotter 'n hell, I gotta go!' So I told him, 'Get the H out of here!' I don't even know where the second gunner was. I never did see him.

"So I don't know to this day whether he told the rest of the guys at the other gun that I told 'em to get out." But didn't he send some men out himself? "Well, not until later, after I had fired most of my M-1 and carbine ammunition. Then I started throwing grenades. I could see them behind me, the enemy, they were on the skyline. They had made their way around our position."

Because the gunners had left?

"Well, that I don't know. That's where I might get court-martialed. I didn't know what the other guys were doing. It was just as if I were fighting my own war. Not exactly alone. There was still half my squad there, but I didn't know what they were doing. Anyway, at one point, I was firing like hell at these guys in the back, and I didn't know how many more were gonna come up, so I went to the second gun. That's when I discovered they were gone. I said, 'My God, what happened to those guys?'

"So I showed the rest of the squad how to get out where that second gun emplacement was, crawl out the opening, make your way back, and go down the hill. I knew we were surrounded, and I did not want all of us to get captured. So I told 'em, 'Leave.' Six, maybe seven, guys left. One of the fellows who had stayed with me, his name was Martin, he told me later when he came to Gallup to look me up, he said a couple of riflemen that were there in the trench were so scared they wouldn't move. He had to get them going. But anyway he did, and they all made it back safely.

"The original group, the gunner and all, one of 'em got shot, and a couple of other guys got wounded, not seriously. They all made it back all right."

Why did Miyamura stay?

"Like I say, I was fightin' my own war. Why, I don't know. I just got so mad, I guess. I can't explain it. I find out later, I'm that way. Once I get mad, I don't know what I'm doing. Really. You hear of guys losin' it? That's why I don't want to get mad. But what woke me up, here comes bombs, white phosphorous bombs, landing right around my position. I said, 'Geez, our troops must figure there's no one else up here now.' That's when I decided I'll make my way down the hill. I fired the machine gun, the first one when the first gunner left, but I couldn't do the belt, too. It fired just so much, then it jammed. I put a grenade in the breech, and it went off and blew it up. The other gun was gone. They took it with them.

"The boxes of grenades were all gone, the carbine ammo, the ammo for the .45, all gone. So I started making my way down one of these trenches with the M-1 after the bombs fell. In North Korea there were trenches all over these mountains because we went up and down them. I was making my way down this trench, and here comes this Chinese soldier and we meet face-to-face. I recognized his head cover; it wasn't a helmet, it was like a cap. I stuck him with the bayonet and, and as I was pulling out, I shot him at the same time. I didn't see him with the grenade in his hand. He apparently had the pin pulled because when I pulled back, I fell and was on my back, and I felt something hit my leg, and I just kicked back at it, and it went off. A fragment of shrapnel got buried in the soft part of the leg next to my shin, but I didn't know I was hurt.

"I got up out of that trench; I started crawling and halfway running down this mountain, toward the company where I told the guys to go. When I got down to the road, I didn't know the Chinese had strung a barbed wire. I didn't even know there was a road. Somewhere along the way I lost the M-1. I still had my .45 though. It was rugged terrain.

"I got down to the road. I saw one of our tanks. That's why I didn't see the barbed wire. I heard the tank's engine revving up. I waved to him, and that's when I ran into the wire. It was still dark, but I could just see the silhouette. He apparently didn't see me because he turned around and took off. I dropped down to get underneath the barbed wire. I went another fifty feet or something, and I passed out. I don't know exactly how long I lay there. But I do remember it was just starting to get daybreak. I could hear troops going by me, a lot of troops, but no one stopped to shake me or poke me or anything. I don't know whose troops they were. I was down. None of 'em stopped to see if I was alive. Finally, after all the noise died down, this guy calls out in English, 'Get up!

You're my prisoner. Don't worry. We have a lenient policy. We won't harm you.'

"I realized I was wounded when I tried to get up. I figured I'd better follow him, see what's going to happen. He leads me across to their troops and they were massed, Jesus. They tried to poke me, but they knew they couldn't do anything because they wanted prisoners. We had so many of theirs, ten to one or more, and they were looking to exchange down the line, so they wanted American prisoners. Anyway, he leads me to an area where there are other members of my company—none of my squad but some guys from the second squad; they were all hurt. This kid tells me afterward, the reason why he became a POW also, he had a bad hand and I said, 'How'd you get wounded?' He said when they started overrunning his position, he had a grenade in his hand, and they told him to drop it. I said, 'You did what?' And he said, 'Yeah, well, I more or less threw it at 'em, but it killed four or five of them,' and it also hurt him in the hand and hit a couple of other guys, tore a big hole in one of our guys. So I helped bandage them up. We all had a package of sulfa powder and stuff. We were told to wait.

"None of us who were wounded got any treatment from the Chinese. Then I ran into the other squad leader, Joe Annello. He was shot in the butt, so here we go hobbling down the road. I was helping him the best I could. He could hardly walk. I tried to help him, but after a while I couldn't do it anymore. I told him, 'Joe, I gotta set you down here.' So I put him under a tree, and I thought, 'Geez, that's going to be the end of him.' Because I figured they'd just shoot him.

"Then, when I got home and got discharged and was working for a store, he comes walking through the door. By God, that was the biggest surprise. He told me the Chinese got him and nine other guys, who were wounded, and could not walk altogether, and just left them there, figuring they were going to die of starvation. One of the ten guys was able to make his way back to our lines and let 'em know that nine guys were still up there. Meanwhile, they had to eat whatever they could find to survive. Well, eventually our troops did go up there, find 'em, and bring them back—after twenty days, he said. He stayed in the service and eventually became command sergeant major of the division.

"It took us over thirty days of walking from April to the end of May to finally reach our camp. The food they gave us they claimed was the emergency rations their own troops ate. It was a fine powder, ground up, of millet, barley, and rice. You know what talcum powder is like? It was just about that fine. They gave each one of us a sack, about so long, and two or three inches in diameter and said, 'This sack has got to last you a week.' And what you have to do is take a glob of it, put it in your mouth and drink some water. When it goes down in your stomach, it'll swell and make you feel full. The big problem was, they didn't give us water. We had to find it wherever we could, so most of us would get dysentery.

"A lot of the fellows claimed they could not eat that stuff, they would not eat it, and so we lost a lot of 'em along the way. I tried to get the younger guys to eat. Because I had dysentery, it'd go right through me, but I kept eating it. When they realized how thin they were getting, and weaker, they tried to eat it but it was too late. Their stomach juices wouldn't digest any of it. We lost a lot of 'em along the way.

"We had to make so many kilometers a day. The first week or so we were being strafed by our own planes, napalm. It killed a couple of our guys. When we rested for the night, we were in the clothes we had and, the farther north we went, the colder it got and we couldn't even sleep. I kept cleaning the wound in my leg and bandaging it and watching it, and by God, by the time I got to the camp it was almost healed. The shrapnel was still in there, but it did work its way out eventually.

"What kept me going was seeing these young kids—I was one of the older guys, I was twenty-four, and these guys were seventeen, eighteen years old. You'd see wounds that were a hell of a lot worse off than yours, and you'd see them keep going. I said, God damn, if they can go, I can keep going. Eventually maggots would form in those wounds and, not knowing, we thought that was it, they had it. But then we found out the maggots would eat all the poison and drop off and pretty soon they're healed. A lot of them healed along the way, without any medical attention and very little food. So that tells you how much punishment a human body can take. But there again, it depends on your willpower, and your body makeup.

"When we got to the camp, oh gee, I thought, we got it made. We thought we were going to get better treatment and medical attention, better food—but it wasn't any better. They put nine of us in a room that was nine by nine. The only heat was a flue that ran under the floor. A Korean farmhouse is a mud hut with maybe two or three rooms in a row, with the kitchen on one end. The flue runs underneath the dirt floor. During the winter months, that's what keeps the house warm. But during the summer, it gets hotter than hell. You can't even sleep on the floor. Only when the peace talks started a year later did they allow us to build bunks to get off the floor."

For the first year of his captivity, Miyamura's wife, Terry, had no idea if he was alive or dead. All she had been told was that he was missing in action. "When I first got the telegram," she said, "I thought he was coming home, but it was an MIA telegram. They didn't know. I don't think any wife ever thinks, especially if it's MIA . . . You never give up hope. You just know he's coming back."

Miyamura said the peace talks started a little over a year after he had been in the camp. "We lost a lot during that time, just about a man a day. We started out with two companies of maybe two hundred a company. I don't know many of us made it. They had a detail that would take them out and bury them. I went into one area, a makeshift hospital with guys just lying there with beriberi. The only shot we ever received was for cholera, and I believe it was a square needle. Each one of us carried that scar all the time we were in there.

"We did get a package of their tobacco. I had two other guys give me their rations because they didn't smoke, but the big problem was paper. The Korean huts had paper on the walls, with glue backing. I should have quit then. But, hell, no, I started rolling them with that kind of paper.

"There was no toilet paper. You had to do with what you could find. The Koreans themselves used corncobs and I said, 'Jesus, I could never use one of them.' We ended up using our old clothing, something like that.

"My dysentery wasn't near as bad as it was in the beginning. When the talks started, our treatment improved. I guess getting off that diet of that powdery stuff helped, and boiling the water helped. But I'll tell you there's nothing like having dysentery in the winter, because our latrines were outside, and they were nothing but slit trenches. To squat there in the freezing night . . . Most of us had night blindness. We made jokes when the first guys had it. They said, 'Oh, I can't see.' All you could see was a dot. Eventually eight of us came down with it. Malnutrition causes it.

"I was flat on my back most of the time I was in the camp. To get out of the work detail, I volunteered when the company commander asked if there was anyone who knew how to cut hair. I had very little experience, but I figured, hell, I could do it. And you know I never used a straight razor in my life. But someone in the camp knew how, and showed me how to keep the thing sharp with a strap, how to strop the razor, and they gave me a pair of scissors, taught me how to keep them sharp. These guys were all from the, I don't say hills, but the country. American ingenuity, I mean, there was always a kid who'd come up with something, like mixing that powder with water to make little patties and toast them on hot rocks, making them much easier to swallow.

"You find out you have to work together. You can't do it yourself. Each guy would contribute something, and that's how you eventually make it. But you had to have something to keep you going. If you didn't, you just didn't make it. You also had to have the willpower, you had to want to do it, because if you gave up, you had no hope."

Was that what kept him alive?

"You know what I really think? I had a guardian angel. When I look back at what I went through, being drafted, why I didn't go overseas when I was supposed to, the hernia, a lot of guys I trained with got killed, guys I was supposed to have been with. And then that night, I could hear the bullets cracking by my ears, why I didn't get hit then. Other actions, shells dropping all around you. The way I feel, you don't think about it. You just think about what you're supposed to do, and your training will come into play. You start doing things automatically. It's not that I was trying to become a hero. I was trying to do what I was supposed to be doing, and what I was trained to do.

"When I started thinking about my life from the time I went into the service, and how I came through, I said, 'There has to be someone watching over me.' And that's when I said, 'Hell, I must have a guardian angel.' And even to this day, the things that happen, it seems like there's someone watching."

Miyamura's prison camp was closer to Seoul than the Yalu, near the 38th Parallel. "It was over three or four months before we were released. They assembled us in an area, and they'd call out the names of the guys who were going to be released that coming week. You really didn't know when your name was going to be called. We were the last group in our area. Finally, they put fifteen or twenty of us on a cattle car and then on a truck and took us up to Freedom Village. There was a bridge. When we crossed over, there wasn't a sound made because we were still in a state of shock. Disbelief, because we heard it so long, and then wondered if we were ever going to be released.

"They stopped on one side. We walked across to our side, which was nothing but a compound made of tents. There was a pole with an American flag flying. The first person you saw was a guy that would delouse you before you went into the compound. Spraying and delousing us. The medical officer would give us a quick lookover, and we were told to go and take a shower, the first in two and a half years. Then they gave us a pair of pajamas and a robe and told us to go lie down on a cot.

"I was resting, and some sergeant comes up to me and says, 'There's a guy from your home state wants to talk with you.' I said, 'Who?' He said, 'I don't know. Just follow me.' So I follow him into another room, nothing but lights in that room. A desk and a commanding general standing at the foot of it, a brigadier general of the Third Division. His name was Osborne. I was told to go up and see him. I'm wondering, 'What the hell am I going to see him for?'

"And he tells me, he says, 'Do you know you received the Congressional Medal of Honor?'

"All I could say is, 'What?' I'll never forget that. 'What for?'

"Then he asked me to relate my story. Why? I figured. Hell, I said, 'Geez.' I figured I might get court-martialed. And I told him I just felt I was doing my job, doing what I was trained to do. I didn't think I was a hero deserving of the Medal. That's when he told me the reason they didn't let my family know was they were afraid of reprisal from the enemy. Even though they finally released names and all, they still didn't let my wife know I'd received the Medal. They just told her I was alive.

"Then we were sent to a port of debarkation, and I was given a choice of flying home or going home by troopship with the rest of the fellas. I figured, geez, that's a good time to recuperate, get built up a little. I think I weighed ninety-eight pounds. That ship took nineteen days to reach San Francisco. I was seasick I think eleven days on that boat. I went to Italy and back on a ship, never got sick. I went over the Japan Sea, one of the roughest, never got sick. And here was the smoothest ride back home, and I got sick. Anyway, we docked in San Francisco and I was the first one to debark. They gave me that honor."

Miyamura's young wife, Terry, and his father, Yaichi, and other family members were waiting at the bottom of the gangplank. "He was in uniform," Terry remembered, "real thin, but he still looked handsome. I guess they had cut his hair. I don't know how long I hugged him, but I guess it must have been a little too long. But you know, for me and him, it seemed like just a short time we were hugging. It was a long time that he was gone. I heard he was missing, but I just never gave up. You don't."

Hiroshi Miyamura and six others, including four Marines, received the Medal of Honor from President Eisenhower on October 27, 1953. Four of them—Miyamura, Ray Murphy, Robert E. Simanek, and

George H. O'Brien—still get together along with their wives once a year. Murphy lives a couple of hours away, in Albuquerque.

After receiving the Medal, Miyamura went on a tour of various cities for eight months, speaking on behalf of a Japanese-American group, meeting with city officials, and trying to promote better understanding between the Anglos and the Japanese-Americans. Returning to Gallup, he helped run an auto-parts store for several years and then took a plunge, opening his own Humble Oil gas station three miles out of Gallup on Route 66. It was against the advice of all his friends. Even Terry was opposed, but the business flourished. "The opening day was one of the biggest gas days I ever had, and it was a storm, all day. The company guys couldn't believe it. I felt I was an honest person, and it got around. And whatever I said to the customer, whatever the car needed, they said go ahead, and they never doubted whatever I told 'em." The citizens of Gallup, including the Navajos, still stood up for a native son.

Miyamura retired in April 1984. "I almost went back to school, but I couldn't concentrate. I found it harder to get along with people. And physically and mentally both, I didn't think I could do it. I was starting to have a lot of problems with my stomach. I wasn't able to sleep good at night. You know, after all the pressure and stress is gone, then you start thinking about things that happened before, especially during the years in service.

"I didn't have nightmares, but I would wake up in the night and not be able to go back to sleep. Then I was having a lot of physical problems, vomiting, stuff like that. They never could tell me exactly the cause. See, eventually, they discovered this poststress syndrome where you've got things that show up much later in your life, and that's exactly what was happening to me. Things I never felt before, thirty years later. That business had kept me so busy I didn't have time to think of anything else. Plus raising three children." They were Mike Yaichi, born in 1954; Pat Hiroshi, in 1955; and Kelly Hisae, in 1958. "All my kids are doing well, and they're in good health. So that's why I say, you gotta have someone watching over you."

Receiving the Medal, Miyamura said, affected him in a lot of ways. "I was the type of person, and I still am, who always wanted to be in the background. I'm a good listener. I'd rather be a listener than the one up there doing the talking. All through my school years, I could never get up in front of a class, and talk, read even. But wearing the Medal requires us to be in the public's eye, especially for the youngsters, the schoolkids. We get asked to talk to them whenever we attend the Medal of Honor conventions. That has changed my life.

"And I feel I have an obligation to my own race, to help better them because of what they have gone through. I'm more representative of them. I feel that's an obligation, to make fellow Americans know that we participated in the war. I was relieved when these twenty-one medals [to Asian-Americans in May of 2000] were upgraded. That's going to relieve me a lot of making appearances, stuff like that.

"I've been to so many places, met so many people. Whenever we have these conventions, you always meet the elite of the city and the state. And then the privilege of going to Washington, sitting with the Joint Chiefs of Staff during inaugurations. All the military organizations have banquets for us, and they foot a lot of the bills. So we meet so many people that you would never meet in your lifetime. Foreign dignitaries, go to embassies, stuff like that.

"I've always believed that we had to prove ourselves. And, you know, the men from the 442d helped me realize that. I just took it all for granted. I grew up in Gallup with all the different minority groups, never thinking that I was anything special, or different. We all felt that way. But I knew eventually, especially when our ancestors started this war against our country here, that things were going to be different, and the guys in the 442d helped me to see that clearly, and understand what we had to do."

TWELVE

Raymond G. Murphy

Captain, U.S. Marines
The Battle for Ungok, Korea
January 31, 1953

"What is it... Something in the water out there in Pueblo?
All you guys turn out to be heroes."
—President Dwight D. Eisenhower asked that question when
he awarded the Medal to Captain Raymond G. Murphy, a native
of Pueblo, Colorado, at the White House on October 8, 1953.

Murphy stands beside his statue in
Pueblo, Colorado, shortly after it was
unveiled during the Congressional
Medal of Honor Society convention
held there in September 2000.

A second lieutenant during the
battle of Ungok, Murphy left
the Marines as a captain.

WHEN MURPHY received his Medal in 1953, there were two other recipients, William Crawford and Carl Sitter, who also hailed from Pueblo. A fourth man from the town, Drew Dix, was to receive the Medal for action in Vietnam, inspiring Pueblo to designate itself the Home of Heroes, establish a memorial, and commission statues of the four men. "They held the Medal of Honor convention in my hometown in two thousand," Murphy recalled, "because there were four of us still living. The sculptor worked on those statues for a couple of years and even brought us in a couple of times for consultation. I'll be darned if two of us, Bill Crawford and Carl Sitter, didn't die before they had a chance to see their statues."

A high-school athlete in three sports, Murphy went to junior college for two years and then attended Alamosa State Teachers College. "I was in my senior year in nineteen fifty when the Korean War broke out. The Marine Corps started a crash program for officers because this country used to have—I don't think we do anymore—a tendency to demobilize after a war. They didn't like wars. And they got caught. As some people would say, they got their tit caught in a wringer. So they come with the biggest officer candidate school crash program in the history of the Marine Corps. Because General Douglas MacArthur was screaming he wanted a brigade for amphibious purposes. So they came up with this. They went across the country offering it at colleges and universities. To get in, you had to have a degree and you had to finish regular boot camp at Parris Island.

"This recruiter out of Pueblo signed up four of us, but only two of us went. This was in the fall of fifty-one. I had graduated in May from Alamosa. I had gotten a teacher's certificate. I'd studied physical education. After we graduated, the Marines swore in, out of boot camp, eight hundred fifty of us from around the country. You had to go through regular basic officer training at Quantico, but you got the second lieutenant bars when you came out of boot camp, which was unusual. Basic officer training was five months but ours went through in two and a half. Talk about ninety-day wonders; we were shorter than a ninety-day wonder.

"We were called Special Basic Class. We have reunions now. The bulk of that class went to Camp Pendleton, California, to end up in Korea. Pendleton is basic infantry. We were training in a battalion, but all of a sudden the Marine Corps got in trouble. They were losing second lieutenants. That's where you have the fastest casualty rate among officers, second lieutenants who are up front, leading the men into battle. So they jerked out about fifty of us and put us on planes and flew across the Pacific. The rest came over by boat. The troop transports were these old prop planes, and it took a while to get across in those things in those days. They had side canvas seats and there were stretchers up top that you could sleep on, if you could get up there fast enough.

"We went from El Toro to San Francisco to a small island called . . . I got CRS, you know what that is [Can't Remember Shit]—a small refueling island and went on from there to Okinawa, then to an air base in Japan. Overnight in Tokyo, then we took off in the morning and landed at Seoul. We spent one night, and the next morning they trucked us to the front lines. This was May or June of fifty-two. I was put in with Baker Company, Fifth Marine Regiment, but only for a little over a month. After a certain amount of time at the front, companies would be rotated back, put in what were called blocking positions. And when they did that, they said to me, 'Well, you've only been here a month, so you can't be rotated.' So they moved me across the Imjin River and put me in Able Company. I spent the rest of my time there in Able Company.

"The guy I was replacing was due for rotation. After one night there, they had a big attack on. I didn't participate. I just sat there in the bunker watching him do it, until the next day came, and he said, 'Murphy, it's all yours.'

"Was I scared? Oh, I guess I'd say I was scared shitless. But you didn't have much time to stop and meditate on it. There were nights during this period of stagnation in the Korea conflict in fifty-two and fifty-three where you didn't get much sleeping. You were one of three things each night: You were either on patrol, or on outpost in front of the line, or in the trench line. You didn't get to go to sleep until daylight. Everything took place at night. The patrols were for reconnaissance plus trying to grab communist prisoners, any live body. The patrol usually was a reinforced squad, which is three fire teams of four each. A lot of times we were reinforced with a four-man machine-gun unit.

"You wore the cold-weather combat boots if you had them. When I first got there they were having trouble because they found out after the Chosin Reservoir that they didn't have the necessary cold-weather gear. Some of our people still had the old canvas gaiter-type of boot from World War II.

"On November fourth, nineteen fifty-two, I led a patrol in an action I thought I was going to be court-martialed for. It was a night deal, and I was out with this heavy squad, to get captives. It was close to Panmunjom, where the talks were going on. There was a no-fire zone and we weren't allowed to go there, at all. We were skirting around the zone, and I had my squad spread out a little. We knew there was an outpost—four or five people—because we could hear them talking. They were probably as nervous as we were. I was trying to move my men. I'm going to get a captive, anybody.

"I had a brand-new corpsman. I was not too sharp about this, in that he had just come to the front, and I didn't interview him. That was something an officer should never fail to do. And I didn't do it. He was beside me going up toward this outpost. And as we were creeping and crawling up to get to these guys—you could hear them, you knew they were there—something happened to this corpsman. He got shook, and he threw a grenade.

"But it wasn't a regular grenade. It was a phosphorous grenade that corpsmen carry for when you want to call in a helicopter to pick up somebody. And he threw this. And, shit, that thing just lit us up—all off a sudden it's like Times Square—and that was the death of the operation. We began taking fire, men were getting hit, and I had to get them out of there. That part of Korea was very similar to New Mexico. It had big arroyos, gullies, and I got the men down there and found out how many were hurt. I had three bad ones, stretcher cases, and I told my squad leader, I said, 'We're going to go down through the corridor, the no-fire zone.' That was the road the talkers went on each day, to talk, you know, trying to stop the God damn thing.

"And my corporal says, 'Mr. Murphy, that's the no-fire zone. You can't go down there.'

"I said, 'We're goin' down the road.' The men were shook. But I wanted to get these wounded guys back. So we got down there on the road, and we're walking. It's a really dark night, and Headquarters is trying to call us on the radio. They want to know where we are, what we're doing. They've got a pretty good idea what we're up to. And I told my radio man, 'Shut it down. Act like it's not working.' And you know, soon we hear trucks, engines running, and they're sending them out with no lights on, about six Army trucks to get us the hell out of there. Which they do, and we get back, and I'm thinking, 'Shit, I'm in big trouble. Boy, I'm going to get court-martialed for going in the no-fire zone.'

"And instead of a court-martial they gave me the Silver Star. But that came after I was wounded and I was being treated in a Navy MASH [Mobile Army Surgical Hospital] unit.

"We saw a lot of combat. The way this goes is the United Nations got tired of trying to negotiate with the communists. So at the end of fifty-two, beginning of fifty-three, they had a campaign on to do something real big, to make five big assaults against the communists, trying to shake 'em up and get them to start talking seriously. And my company drew the short straw. We got the first assault.

"My company commander was a guy named Blanchard. He was called Doc. At that time anybody that had the name Blanchard was called Doc because of the football star by that name who was playing for Army. Anyway, our Blanchard was a mustang, meaning he had come up through the ranks of enlisted men. He was a nice guy, but he was eager. The way my company was selected to make this attack, I believe, was that Blanchard had gone back to Division and volunteered for it. He was eager. And so what happens? Why, we start practicing for the attack and before we get done, Division tells him he can't go. And he asks why? Because, they say, you're too old. He was over forty. So he had to stay back on the line, and our executive officer, Lieutenant Dave Fauser, took command of the company.

"I was supposed to leave on the thirty-first of January. Our contracts were up, but I stayed. I had been with these guys too long. It would have been walking out on them. A sergeant said to me, 'How come you're not rotating?' I said, 'I have a couple of days, I'll go through this one.' He said, 'Mr. Murphy, you're going to stick us [up in the front] in the attack.' I said, 'No, I don't think so.'

"Our purpose was to capture this stronghold called Ungok. The communists had been there for some time. It was well mined, and they were well dug in. Ungok was a long ridge, all torn up and blasted from artillery and mortars and planes for a couple of years. You had to go from the MLR, the Main Line of Resistance, which was the front, down through various arroyos, and then up. We were three platoons lying in arroyos on the second of February waiting for morning." Two platoons were to make the assault. Murphy's was to stay in reserve and handle evacuation.

"There were forty-eight in a platoon, but they were reinforced with machine guns, mortars, and BARs, Browning Automatic Rifles. Just before daylight of the third, they made the assault. We waited down below. Then, sometime during the morning, I said, 'Something isn't right up there.' The attack was under way, but nobody was coming down—no prisoners, no sign of anybody. I said, 'We're going to go up.' So I went with some of my men, and it was a mess up there. All the sergeants were gone, killed or wounded, all the officers. There were three officers, one for each platoon. Fauser, who had been put in charge after Blanchard was told he was too old, led the first platoon. He had part of a hand shot up. Then each platoon had a staff or a tech sergeant. Some had corporals.

"The mess was in the trenches. I first encountered a big trench, and there was a bunch of Marines just standing around up top, and I said, 'Get down, God damn it! You're standing up there in silhouette.' And then this other group was trying to get a guy out of the trench on a stretcher and they were really screwing it up. The stretcher had got stuck on the edge of the trench. So I went down there, and I lay on this wounded man and told him, 'Put your arms around my neck.' Then I told these guys to pull me up, grab my arms and help me up. I couldn't lift him without help. So they pulled me up with him on me. Some of the trench had filled in with dirt where it had been hit with mortars and artillery and I could walk out with him. Then I told some people to take him to the rear.

"I was leading both platoons, I was the company commander now, and I spent all day going up and down the hill trying to get the wounded out. I don't know how many times I went up and down that hill. I had to lead some assaults to get to some of our wounded and the KIAs [killed in action]." Seventeen marines died and about seventy-five were wounded in the attack that day.

"I don't know how many I saved. It's hard for me to be strong on details of what happened that day. I don't recall shooting two guys with a pistol, like the citation says. People ask me, but it was a confusing time. It really was. To get the Medal you have to have three nominees, witnesses. If they said that's what I did, I'm not one to argue with them. I've only known one recipient in our [Medal of Honor] Society who told me many years ago he wasn't scared and he knew what he was doing in his combat action. Well, most of the people around me at that time and after say that's a bunch of bullshit. You don't get in the infantry and not be scared.

"I just don't remember. I'll tell you one thing I remember: When it got close to the end of the day, I told somebody in my company we were going back up one more time, and I found a whole four-man machine-gun crew, all of them dead. So we started lifting them up, dragging them, trying to get them off as fast as we could. Marines don't leave their dead. That was our way. We had to get them out. I don't know what the hell they were killed by. I didn't have a chance to follow up.

"Anyway, I was pulling a guy by his shoulders, over rocks and through brushes and stuff, and all of a sudden I look down at what

I'm pulling, and he's naked. His pants were ripped from shell fire and then got torn off as I dragged him. And I thought, 'Shit, even in dying up here you can't have any privacy.' There was no dignity in death. You could see the enemy. They were going around, dodging behind bushes and stuff, hiding. I lost every weapon I had. I lost my .45. I lost my carbine. I had at least one M-1 that I lost. I would pick these guns up and use them on the way up and then, when you're busy getting a stretcher or moving wounded, you shitcan your weapon. I would pick up whatever was handy on the way back up. I ended up the whole day not only hauling stretchers, but with a BAR, a Browning Automatic Rifle. I don't know how that happened.

"They sent Charlie Company up the various arroyos to help with stretchers. They didn't send anybody up into the hills, maybe because it got so screwed up. I didn't have my radio very much after it became apparent we had to get a lot of wounded out. There was very little fighting by my platoon because of the wounded. This went on all day, from 6 A.M. to dark.

"I had wounds up and down my back and on my hip and my leg. All the damage was on my left side, from shrapnel, artillery or mortar, except I'd had a bullet through my fingers. I didn't notice the blood during the action. It's hard to concentrate on a wound unless it's something real serious, you know, like an arm taken off. I was too busy trying to move around and get to people.

"Did I consider the attack ill-advised? I can't really say that. I was not on that level to decide whether it was ill-advised or not. They went on, and they had the full five assaults they planned, and then the cease-fire was signed later that year and Hershey [Hiroshi Miyamura] got out of the prison camp, so maybe they accomplished what they set out to do.

"All I know is once you're through something like that, you want to go home. I was taken to a Navy MASH unit about midnight. I partly remember the MASH because they were working on me, and this one doctor says, 'It's a good thing you got a big butt. You might have been hurt seriously otherwise.' And I said, 'You're a smartass, aren't you?' Because I wasn't a very humorous person. Then later I was put on a train and taken to the coast and put on a hospital ship, the *Jutlandia*. It was Denmark's only contribution to the United Nations effort. I heard 'em say they wanted to leave the wounds open. I guess that was part of the cleaning process. I know the first night on the *Jutlandia*, I'd had some medication that put me in a kind of coma, and I woke up and there on my chest is a medal, a Purple Heart. I said, 'What the hell's going on?' Some of the guys who were lying next to me said my captain, Blanchard, and my colonel, Lew Walt, had come in and handed them out."

Lew Walt was a highly decorated veteran of World War II who was famous in the Marine Corps, became a major general by the time of the Vietnam War, and retired as assistant commandant of the Corps. "Back when I was about to go out on that night patrol to try to get some prisoners, I was down in the CP with Blanchard, and he said they wanted me to take some reporter from the *Boston Globe* out with me. And I said, 'Oh, shit, I already got too many people to watch over.' And Blanchard says, 'I don't think you got a choice in this, Murphy.' I said, 'Can I ask somebody else?' He says, 'You can go as high as you want.'

"So, you know where I went? I went to the colonel, Lew Walt. He had gone to the Colorado Aggies when I was in high school. My brother played freshman football there, and when Walt was a senior he was the number-two punter in the United States. Well, I went to Walt, by radio, before my patrol. He had the Fifth Regiment. I told him what I wanted, and you know what he did? He said, 'Murphy's the boss out there. The reporter doesn't go.' Now you know he was God to me."

Following treatment in Japan, Murphy continued convalescence at Mare Island Naval Hospital in San Francisco. "I was there about two months, and all of a sudden the admiral who's head of the naval hospital comes to the ward one day and said they were going to have a parade and give out some medals. I think he said, 'We're going to do six or eight, and yours is the highest.' And I said, 'What do you mean?' And he said, 'You're getting the Silver Star.' This was for that night patrol.

"I got out of the Marines in April nineteen fifty-three and went to graduate school that fall at Springfield College in Massachusetts. I got a master's in Recreational Youth Leadership. Meanwhile, that October eighth, fifty-three, I received the Medal of Honor from President Eisenhower outdoors at the White House. There were seven of us, four Marine and three Army. These were the first medals he gave out as President. I was so shook up I couldn't remember what he said. He made that remark about what is it with these people from Pueblo, something in the water? I didn't remember. The press picked it up."

Murphy married in 1958, and he and his wife divorced after eleven years. They had a daughter, born in 1958, and a son, born in 1960. In 1969, Murphy remarried and he and wife, Mary Ann, had a son, born in '69.

"After graduate school, I became director of recreation in Natick, Massachusetts, then went to Santa Fe, where my brother was the mayor, to help him run a bowling alley for fifteen years. Then I went to do counseling work for the Veterans Administration in the regional office in Albuquerque. I retired from that in ninety-seven. I now volunteer at the VA in Albuquerque. Mondays I work escort, taking people in wheelchairs and stretchers from clinic to clinic. Tuesdays I work the information desk.

"I recently found out—my son came across this book in the library—that one of my favorite baseball players was flying support for us that day, and he got hit by small-arms fire and crash-landed on his way back to the base. His name was Ted Williams.

"Back when I was in officer school at Quantico, Virginia, a friend from Pueblo and I went and saw his team, the Red Sox, play the Senators [now the Minnesota Twins] in Washington, and he didn't hit a ball out of the infield, and I remember thinking, 'Shit, I'll never see that man again.' Well then, when I got to Natick, Williams— maybe the greatest hitter who ever lived—had come back. He got out of the military, rejoined the Red Sox, and I got an opportunity to see him play about six more times. I even saw his final game, when he left after hitting that last home run. He was the only Major

Leaguer I know of that got called back for Korea. I heard after Ungok we lost a tank commander and we lost another officer who was flying close air support. I didn't know that was Ted Williams. He had to crash-land going back to base because the controls of his Corsair had been shot up.

"He was a big hero of mine."

Part Three

THE VIETNAM WAR

THE WAR NOT EVERYBODY WANTED
Vietnam

A major buildup of American advisers and support personnel in Vietnam began in February of 1962, when John F. Kennedy was President. By the end of 1963 there were thirteen thousand military personnel in the country. United States involvement was seen as necessary to help deter the spread of communism, which was the government of North Vietnam under Ho Chi Minh. South Vietnam was likened to a domino which, if captured, would lead to a succession of countries in the region falling, like dominoes, to communism.

Authorization for American involvement came in August of 1964 when the U.S. Congress passed the Tonkin Gulf Resolution, based on reports of an alleged attack on an American destroyer in the Tonkin Gulf by North Vietnamese patrol boats. The attack, as James Stockdale reports in chapter 22, never took place.

The war was to continue for almost ten years, until January 27, 1973, when the United States, the South Vietnamese, the Vietcong, and the North Vietnamese signed a peace pact in Paris.

By March 29, American forces were withdrawn as the last 590 American prisoners of war, including Jim Stockdale, were released by the North Vietnamese. A second accord, strengthening the cease-fire, was signed June 13. The North Vietnamese then proceeded to overrun the country, seizing Saigon, which had been the capital of South Vietnam, at the end of April 1975.

An unusual aspect of the Vietnam War was an intense adverse political reaction in the United States. All America's wars have had resisters and protesters—but not to the degree provoked by our country's involvement in Vietnam. It cost lives, resources, and even the presidency of Lyndon Baines Johnson.

At the height of U.S. involvement, there were more than 500,000 American troops in Vietnam. The number of Americans killed in action totaled 46,163. Medals of Honor were awarded to 238 combat participants. One hundred and fifty were awarded posthumously.

Most of the eleven recipients who tell their stories here served in various parts of Vietnam in 1968 and '69, when the fighting was at its height.

THIRTEEN

Paul Bucha

West Pointer
Vietnam
March 16, 1968

*"My first sergeant, Harjo, is back at base camp, and I call him
and say, 'Top, we got trouble. The resupply missed us. He says, 'I'm coming.'
On this next helicopter, I see this nut standing on the skids as the chopper
descends. He's standing on the skids, kicking out the boxes [of ammo].
And then, then he jumps down beside me and he says:
'I missed the last Alamo!'"*

Photo by Eddie Adams

Paul Bucha, who donated his Medal
of Honor to the United States Military
Academy at West Point, is pictured
here at the age of fifty-nine.

An exhausted and emotional U.S.
Army Captain Paul Bucha wipes
tears from his eyes as he works the
radio. Bucha and two men from his
company were photographed
here at first light on March 19, 1968,
at the battle site near Phuoc Vinh following three days of ferocious fighting. They did not expect to survive.

Photo by Earl Van Alstine

PAUL BUCHA met with me in the den of his home in Ridgefield, Connecticut, for a couple of hours on a snowy January morning. He took a lot of phone calls. At fifty-eight, he had a number of business enterprises going. He was very proud of his son and three daughters from his first marriage, and very happy in his second, to Cynthia Bell of Cornwall, New York. He was patient, candid, and extremely thoughtful.

To fashion an effective fighting unit, Captain Paul Bucha, one of two *living* graduates of the United States Military Academy at West Point to hold the Medal of Honor, did everything from getting into a fight with an enlisted man to biting the head off a chicken.

An All-American swimmer, he attended the academy from 1961 to 1964. On May 12, 1962, he was one of two cadet athletes who, because of a big water polo meet, were excused from the mess hall the day General Douglas MacArthur was to make his "Duty, Honor, Country" speech, quite possibly the greatest speech by a military man in the nation's history. Bucha recalled, "A classmate named Grant Fredericks and I thought we were the cat's meow. We said, 'Aren't we hot shit!' And after the match we went and sat on the steps of the mess hall and thought the guys would say, 'You sons of guns. How did you get out of it?' Then they opened the door, and you couldn't hear a sound. We wondered what happened. No one said anything to us."

Because he finished in the top 5 percent of his class, Bucha qualified for a two-year stint at Stanford, where he earned an M.B.A. Then, in 1967, he went to Fort Campbell, Kentucky, as an airborne ranger captain. Two brigades of the 101st Airborne Division were preparing to ship out to Vietnam. Bucha's colonel directed him in August of 1967 to form what was to become Delta Company, 3d Battalion, 187th Infantry. At the outset, Bucha was the only man in the company. "We were the fourth rifle company and the last battalion of the last brigade, which meant I was last."

Bucha had to scrounge up an outfit that came to be known as

"clerks and jerks," including clerks, cooks, mechanics, artillery-men, and a bunch of bad guys he transferred from the stockade. "My first sergeant, Austin Harjo, a Creek Indian from Muskogee, Oklahoma, had been in the 187th in Korea, and he'd been to Viet-nam with the first brigade. He was a great guy. He taught me an enormous number of things. And he would look at one of these guys and tell him, 'You say, "Sir" to him,' and the guy'd say, 'If I don't, are you sending me to the stockade so I don't have to go with some guy from Stanford University to Vietnam?' And Harjo said, 'No.' Then, bam! He hit him. But that was the way it was. And then I had a group of guys who were speechwriters. They were all assigned to me as combat infantrymen. What's your background? Oh, I have a master's degree in English from Brandeis.

"So I had a bunch of bad guys and a few smart guys. When you think about it, a pretty good mix. Of my first twelve or thirteen guys, nine had failed advanced infantry training."

Like a Dirty Dozen?

"More than that. The Dirty 164. And they're sending guys from everywhere, anybody they could find."

Bucha immediately sought to instill discipline by making his company run longer, harder, faster, than any of the others as soon as he got them. "I had to be sure I could run farther and faster than any one of them. I had the airborne and ranger patches, so that made me different. I could not afford to fail. But when I finally got the whole company, and we'd go for a brigade run, we were the last company, out of sixteen. I told them, 'That's okay. We're gonna pass everyone.' Delta Company, coming by! And we'd pass them and do circles, like the movie *Stripes* a little bit. But very disciplined.

"Officers would say to me, 'Where you going?' And I'd say, 'Sir, we're going to the field.' And we'd run, and be gone. It got to the point where our guys were cocky. Our saying was All the Way, Sir! and I told them, 'Officers hate saluting large groups. So put your damn hat on, a little bit of a rakish angle, and when you see an officer a hundred yards away, you yell that at the top of your lungs and hold that salute:

"All the way, sir!"' And finally the officers would turn their backs when they'd see the Rakkasans of Delta Company coming.

"I had this man, Sergeant Griffin. I had seven or eight black guys from Chicago. Most of the unit was black and Latino, but these guys, they were tough nuts. All you'd want in war. And Griffin looked like he should have been a starting halfback in the NFL. He emerged as the leader of this group. Originally, they were all spread out in different squads, but I said, 'What the hell, I'll put them all in one squad.' I called him in and said, 'Griffin, I'm gonna make you a squad leader, and here's your squad.' 'Oh, my God, no, I don't want to be a sergeant. Oh no! Not with these guys!' I said, 'Well, they're your guys.' So I stapled on E-5 stripes, made him a squad leader. But it was informal.

"The rank is in the top five of enlisted men, which meant normally you'd go to the Top Five enlisted men's club. I made Griffin the squad leader. So we're out in the field, we come in on a Saturday, and I get a call at two in the morning: 'Your men have been in a fight.' So, like, what else is new? I go down there, and there's Griffin up against the wall with his guys. And the MPs are there, and the MPs' jackets are ripped and filthy. I said, 'Griffin, what happened?' He said, 'Sir, I threw a right, man, I nailed . . .' 'No, no, no, what happened?' He said, 'Well, I went in the club with my squad, and they told me I'm not allowed in there. But you told me I'm a sergeant, aren't I, sir?' I said, 'Yes, you are.' He said, 'Well, if I'm a sergeant, I'm an E-5. Aren't I allowed in the Top Five Club?' I said, 'Yes, you are.' He said, 'Well, a first sergeant told me I wasn't and everybody else said I wasn't because I'm not a real sergeant. So what am I? Am I a phony-ass sergeant or a real sergeant?' I said, 'You're a real sergeant.'

"So I said to the MPs, 'Look, this is my problem, not yours.' They said, 'Like hell it's not ours.' I said, 'Wait, I'll take it from here. I'll punish them suitably.' I got them back in the barracks, and we had a one-hour discussion. I said, 'Okay, let me explain what the problem was. It's not your fault; it's mine.' " Bucha saw to it that Griffin was made a "real sergeant."

"One of the first weeks we had the company the colonel said to me, 'You're junior, so you have to teach survival training.' That's like, cooking in the field, killing game, eating raw stuff. Now the key to that is always getting their attention. And West Point had taught me that. Back at the Point, the survival training was taught by this recondo, Sergeant Hunt or Jones, from Fort Campbell. And he'd stand there, and the way he got our attention, he'd reach into a bag and then pull out a live snake, and bite its head off. Live. Sometimes the snake would bite him back. He'd spit it out, and it'd be biting his tongue. As the senior cadet, I would go there every two days to watch this class, knowing full well he was gonna ask me to do it. And I'd gotten my brain set. I'd have done it. Again, what could happen to me? I'd have bitten the head off the snake and chewed it. I was ready for this. Whatever he did, I was willing to do. But he never called. He never asked me to.

"So I'm sitting there at Fort Campbell thinking, 'How do I get these guys' attention?' It's during this whole time when D Company, my company, is trying to look for its identity. So I said to a ranger-qualified NCO of mine, 'Dicky, quick, get me a bunch of chickens. Get me a thousand chickens or five hundred chickens, something like that.' So he did. These crates of chickens arrive, and they are the ugliest, skinniest-looking chickens. I don't even know where they came from."

Bucha recalled with a smile that he was in the field, a junior guy teaching survival training because no one else wanted to, and he was standing in front of five hundred airborne troopers who thought that they were tough. They were sitting on the ground, and no one was paying attention.

"And I'm supposed to teach. So I said, 'Today, we're gonna cook chickens.' And no one is listening. I said, 'You're gonna have to learn to take a fowl, kill it, and cook it.' Still no one's listening. So I said, 'The first thing you have to do is kill a chicken. How do you kill a chicken?' A guy says, 'Cut its head off.' I said, 'Dicky, give me a chicken.' I went whack with my bayonet, and I said, 'That's right.' I cut about four chickens' heads off and threw them in the audience. Now people are looking.

"I said, 'How does an airborne trooper kill a chicken?' And remember, we're all airborne, but Dicky and I are the only two airborne rangers. Now, I say, 'A *grunt* just kills it with his knife, but what's an *airborne trooper* do? He wrings the head off the chicken with his bare hands.' I said, 'Dicky, give me some chickens.' Whack! And I'd snap these chickens' heads. And I'm starting to get people listening. Then I said, 'How does an airborne *ranger* kill a chicken?' Big chubby kid in the front says, 'He bites the head off!' I said, 'You're right!' Come up here, soldier. 'No, sir!' And then the place was quiet. I said, 'Dicky, give me some chickens.' And I bite the head off one. Give me another one! That was good—and the feathers!'

"And I'm throwing these chickens into the crowd. By then, you could have heard a pin drop. I said, 'Okay.' I'd done like five of them, so I look at Dicky, and he says, 'Ten hut!' And boy, everybody all jumped up. And we had a good survival class. They took their chickens, killed them, cut 'em open, cleaned 'em, cooked 'em in cans and ate 'em.

"I get back to officers' call on Tuesday and walk in. Colonel Larry Mowry, who's dead now—he's my mentor in the company— he says, 'What the hell did you do?' I said, 'What are you talking about, sir?' He said, 'Did you bite the heads off chickens?' I said, 'It was an attention-getting step.' He said, 'I didn't ask you why. I just want to know, Did you do it?' 'Yes, sir.' He said, 'You're nuts.' 'Thanks a lot. It worked, sir.' 'Don't do that anymore. It doesn't set a good example.'

"I mean, it was that kind of thing with my men. And we got to Vietnam in November nineteen sixty-seven, some 120 days after I started putting the company together, and we were sitting there at Camp Alpha, and I went to my bunk and there was this big, big enlisted guy sitting there, obviously stewed or stoned. I said, 'Soldier, please get out of my bunk.' He said, 'F you.' I said, 'Please, get out of my bunk. The company's forming up. I have to get out there.' He said, 'I'm not getting out of anybody's bunk.' I said, 'Come on, get up, soldier.' He said, 'What are you gonna do, make me?' I said, 'Well, if I have to, I guess I will.' And he stood up. All of a sudden, we fell down outside the tent, and my company was formed up, and there was this big guy I was on top of, and we were hitting each other, and my company was formed up. They were at attention. And I was rolling around with this guy. Finally, I got up, and he got up and I said, 'You'd better get out of here.' And he said, 'Yes, sir,' and he left. About twenty minutes later I was in front of the company, and Major Homer Holland from West Point came and got me. It had been reported that I had a fight with this enlisted man.

"And my guys are all proud of this. If you want to say who pulled the short straw, it would be my guys. They got me, this guy who went to Stanford Business School, teaching surfing and scuba and stuff. And then, too, they said I got the short straw. I got all these rough-necks. But if you're going to war, that's the kind of crowd to go with."

They flew from Fort Campbell to Saigon and then to Phuoc Vinh. "We took trucks, and we were scared. I mean, we were scared to death. Everybody was scared. Always scared.

"No one wanted us in base camp because we would cause trouble. We get to Phuoc Vinh, and the first thing we do is build this Tori gate that is the symbol of the *Rakkasan*. Everybody said, 'What are you guys, nuts?' I said, 'The hell with it. Rakkasans, baby. That's us.' And not to be outdone on the good side of things, we said, 'We're gonna build a chapel for the chaplain.' So my men went and borrowed a Marine Corps mess tent. How they did, I don't know, but it arrived by helicopter. We put the mess tent up, probably one hundred by thirty, and that became the church. My guys did the sandbags, did it all. They didn't bitch about anything.

"We were out on patrols all the time. Never did they leave us in. And they had this thing called the Dong Nai Bridge, the First Infantry had said was the hottest spot, and they were always in combat down there. So they assigned my company. We built our bunkers and went on our patrols, and we didn't have a round fired, which led me to believe this was just people shooting, making up that they were in combat there. You see something, you shoot at it. Our guys wouldn't do that. So pretty soon, we get logs, and we build this floating dock. We put up a sign called THE BEACH, and we would swim in the river, and we'd eat and go on patrols. We were in heaven. We were supposed to be in this worst place in the world, but it was like R and R for us."

Over a four-month period Bucha's unit encountered considerable combat, without taking any casualties. "It was great, but it wasn't good. We created a mystique. We'd go out on ambushes at night. We were always on rocket patrol. Wherever we'd go, people would be getting shot up. We'd go there, and we wouldn't get shot up. It has to do with luck. And it has to do with the guys. We did stupid things in the minds of others, but we were really, I think, very good. I liked to move at night."

Bucha recalled some examples of operations he passed on that he considered foolish and dangerous. "So we just kept moving at night. The brigade commander would give me our mission, and we'd go do it. What we were doing was somewhat unconventional. I mean, we're in a rocket belt. We're the only unit running north of Bien Hoa, trying to catch the guys shooting the rockets into Bien Hoa. I had three tanks, five scout Jeeps. Our idea was, we probably won't catch 'em, but if we keep moving, then they can't stay in a place. So we will disrupt their ability to fire. That's got to be a mission accomplished. And they would say, 'Well done. Now you're gonna go here.' And then someone else would come in, do it their way, and either it worked or it didn't work. We did it our way. We didn't shoot any rounds. We never got anybody hurt.

"If you shoot into a village, someone shoots back at you. If you don't shoot at the village, they might not shoot back at you. Our men had a very strict fire discipline. It was rules of war, and our guys followed them. Let me give you an example. One time, I put Sergeant Estada, the former pistol team captain, a brilliant sergeant, out on ambush and said, 'Here's the signal: Two radio clicks means they're coming; one radio click says I don't see anybody.' All of a sudden . . . two clicks. I'm waiting, and I should really hear this fire go off because it's about a mile away. And nothing. Then I hear one click. Two hours later, he gives me a three. It means he's abandoning the ambush site. He comes back in, and I said, 'What the hell happened?' He said there were a couple of guys with guns, and women carrying supplies. 'I didn't feel right.' Well, he might have fired on that group, and some of them would have gotten killed. What would you report? Two men killed, and five women and four children? And he chose not to do that. He had discipline. This wasn't the target, in his opinion."

On March 16, 1968, following the Tet Offensive, Bucha's company was put out as the point unit. He had a reconnaissance platoon with him as well.

"We were in contact with the enemy for about three days. They were withdrawing. We were pushing and pushing them. We were hitting their rear guard. We were beyond artillery range. I had resupplied everybody, and then command said, 'You can go into a night defensive perimeter.' I said, 'No, we're gonna keep moving.' And hell, it was dusk, and we moved into the jungle, and the lead unit says, 'I see some people carrying water. Request permission to fire, recon by fire,' which was a method of saving people's lives. A lot of people say no, we've got to sneak up on them. But I figured we just resupplied here, had six helicopters come in, we're not kidding anybody. So I said, 'Go ahead and recon by fire.' It's a way of triggering an ambush before you're in the middle of the killing zone. And they did that, and nothing happened. And we went another hundred yards, and nothing. Then all of a sudden the whole mountain just . . . boom!"

Progressing through thickly foliaged, hilly terrain, the Americans had come upon a reinforced battalion base camp of the Vietcong's Don Nai Regiment. In a short time, thirty of Bucha's men had been wounded and two were killed. His citation describes the site as a bunker, but Bucha recalls it as fire coming from the Y of a tree about eight feet up. Whatever it was, Bucha crawled forward to within twenty feet and stopped the enemy fire with grenades.

"I said, 'Okay, let's get everybody out of here.' This was bad news because everybody was being fired at from everywhere. I said, 'Holy shit, this is a big unit. Withdraw back to a perimeter.' Because

it was night now, and we didn't know who we were up against. And
we had no artillery. And we went to a small clearing. Then they said.
'Second Platoon is cut off. They've been ambushed, the guys taking the wounded back have been ambushed.' There was this Lieutenant Jeff Wishik, and his RTO, Calvin Heath, was with him. And
I said, 'How far are you?' They said, 'We're about fifty yards outside your perimeter.' And there were only eighty-nine of us total by
now. I got on with these guys who were calling me. They said they
were all over the place, everywhere. I said to Calvin, the radio telephone operator, 'You got to trust me on this one. Turn the radio off
and tell everybody to feign death. Just pretend you're dead. Play
dead. Don't talk, breathe, do anything.'

"I couldn't think of anything else to do. I heard the radio go off,
and that was it. I knew generally where they were." There were
about ten out there with Wishik, all of them surrounded. Bucha's
perimeter was about half the size of a basketball court, just large
enough to bring in a helicopter. He had about eighty men. "Hell,
half the group was wounded in some way. Nicks, scratches, cuts.
And I was thinking, 'What the hell do you do now? We're too tiny.
We're obviously a small force. We're all down.'

"At the very beginning, I wasn't *concerned* about getting killed.
I *knew* I was *gonna* get killed. I figured they'd just come running
over us any minute now. It's just one of those things that happens.
You say, 'Shit, this was a mistake.' And my thought was, 'What a
terrible place to die. I don't even know where I am. I know where
I am on a map, but there's no name. Where was your son killed?
He was killed in Saigon, Rangoon, the Bridge at the River Kwai,
the Argonne . . . Coordinates 6565444 . . . What a shitty thing!'
That's what I was thinking. And then this young radio telephone
operator comes in and he says, 'Oh, sir, we're kicking the shit out
of them, aren't we, sir?'

"My other guy was real experienced. Dave Dillard is on both my
radios transmitting what's going on. He's telling the colonels and
everybody everything we're doing. And now it's pitch-black, and I
say, 'I got an idea.' They obviously don't know much about us, or

they'd have come in here. If I have everybody firing, it's pretty easy to see we're a pretty small group. So I'm gonna be the only one firing, and you know it's not one guy. But you don't know how many others there are. And at the same time, we don't have mine fields, so we're gonna create our own mine fields by throwing grenades at random intervals at different points, all around the perimeter, as far as you can. And that will expand our perimeter. So if I said to you, 'One o'clock, two grenades.' One goes ten feet, the other goes thirteen. If you're the guy trying to infiltrate and you can hear 'em, you say, 'Ooh, I don't want to go there.' All of a sudden, boom boom. I say, 'Two o'clock, four o'clock, six o'clock, three o'clock, three grenades each.' And you do that all night long, that's kind of creating your own mine field."

Meanwhile Pfc. Calvin W. Heath of Norwich, Connecticut, Lieutenant Jeffrey Wishik of Montgomery, Alabama, and three others lay among the enemy, playing dead. Bucha had helicopters high above; colonels, generals, and the helicopters flying lower were taking intense ground fire. "This made me think, 'Holy shit, that's a big unit that's shooting at the helicopters.' So right away I came to my conclusion that this is not the best position in the world, but it seems we've established a status quo. Stay where you are, keep this thing going; and I had the guys throwing the hand grenades put claymores out also. Everybody moved out twelve feet, stopped, twelve more feet, stopped. Put out your claymore, come back." The claymore is set off by hand, and it has a back blast that is quite severe, which is why you have to get it out at least twenty-four feet from your perimeter. "I said, 'Plant that out. If we're ever overrun, at least we've got our ass covered.'

"And as with the grenades, I said we could use an M-79 to do the same thing." Bucha then called in his sergeants and outlined his idea: Since the M-79 could function as a grenade launcher, firing a large round that explodes into shrapnel, he called in all that ammunition, and directed that the grenades be distributed evenly among everyone. He told the sergeants to tell everyone to stay down, that he and the sergeants were going to be the only ones moving, so if the VC were looking, they should see only one guy. He also told the sergeants to tell the men, 'If you hear a sound, throw a grenade.'

"So we're firing away, every ten seconds, in different directions. So all around is boom! boom! Plus we've got fifteen helicopters flying, and they're strafing." He had alerted them not to fire in the tree clump fifty yards south, where Calvin and the others were playing possum.

One helicopter pilot came in to take out some wounded, cutting his way in through the canopy with his chopper blades. "And off jumps the padre. He says, 'I think you need some last rites.' I said, 'Oh shit, this is the last thing I need.' Then the brigade commander comes in second, he kicks his crew out, and he's taking fire going out. So they're all above watching what's going on; they can see what's going on. I can't see squat. This is all at night. They drop off these beanbags, little bags with a light on top to mark our perimeter. And then comes Puff, C-130, says, 'Hi, I'm Puff the Magic Dragon, and they're blasting all around us.'

"And we're running out of hand grenades. We need a lot of hand grenades. We're into this like three hours and it's getting pretty intense. They bring in a helicopter with ammunition and they get so much ground fire, they miss us and they drop it off where the enemy is. I said, 'Oh shit.'

"My first sergeant, Harjo, is back at base camp, and I call him and say, 'Top, we got trouble. The resupply missed us.' He says, 'I'm coming.' On this next helicopter, I see this nut standing on the skids as the chopper descends. He's standing on the skids, kicking out the boxes [of ammo].

"And then, then he jumps down beside me and he says, '*I missed the last Alamo!*'

"And he goes around issuing hand grenades. And he's giving them out and comes back, and he's giving me an update because all my lieutenants are shot, my platoon sergeants are wounded, so he is now the new man. He says, 'Okay, we've got this well in hand.' Meanwhile, we're bringing in the dustoffs, medevacs. I would stand up with the lights, and they would bring it in, and people said,

'Don't stand up.' I said, 'I've been standing up all night.' I mean, if they wanted to shoot me, they'd have done that a long time ago. And things seemed to be coming along."

Nothing could be done for the guys playing dead. Bucha declined an offer for a reinforcement company, saying it would be too dangerous. "They'll be ambushed as well. We'll be all right. We seem to have this one under control. Lo and behold, we get through the night. As soon as I saw the daylight, I said, 'Thank God. Let's get some patrols out. Let's go find our guys.' "

Bucha's company suffered 11 dead, 35 wounded. His citation says 156 enemy lay dead around them.

"Pretty soon we hear this voice: 'Hey! We're over here!' It was Calvin, the radio telephone operator. To get to us, Calvin had to kill a guy with a bayonet. And Calvin got a Silver Star for this—thirty years later.

"I'll digress: Calvin lives over in Norwich, Connecticut. He's a Nipmuck Indian. He got dusted off that morning, and was gone. I didn't hear from him for years. Then one day he called me and said, 'Sir, I need some help.' 'What for?' 'Psychological benefits.' I said, 'That's okay. Your VA will cover it.' He said, 'I don't have any VA benefits.' I said, 'Calvin, you got wounded in combat. You got a Silver Star, what do you mean, you don't have VA benefits?'

"He said, 'I never got any Silver Star. I got a dishonorable discharge.'

"Now, what happened was, all his wounds were in the back because the claymore hit him in the back. And he had stayed that night, covering Jeff Wishik, his lieutenant, who was wounded badly, too, and they had both killed NVAs with their knives. Blood all over 'em. And the NVAs had sat on Calvin and Jeff Wishik and eaten breakfast. They were still alive. So anyway, all his wounds are in his back because of the ambush, and his father and everybody was convinced he was a coward, shot running away. And he never got any medals because the damned general didn't have time to go give him the medals. And his company commander who was at Fort Carson said, 'You're a phony. You don't need . . . get him out of the hospital.' The doctor said, 'He needs help.' 'No, he doesn't need help.' Because there was no documentation for his story. So he finally said, 'Hell with it,' and went AWOL.

"Now, he was not a college graduate or anything. Young kid. They finally catch him, send him back to Fort Harrison. If he signs these documents, they'll let him go, which gives up all his VA benefits, everything. I resubmitted his story, with documentation, and we got him his Silver Star.

"So we were having this ceremony at this monument in Norwich two years ago, and this congressman was reading the citation, and I interrupted. I said, 'Just a second. I'm gonna tell you what this young man did, and I don't need to read it.' But I had trouble . . . You know, his tribe's there, and I said, 'I just want you to know, he's getting a warrior's medal. That's the Silver Star. That's the medal given for people who fight. That's a special medal. I don't have it.' And his tribe was just like . . . And his congressman was standing there. And Calvin said, 'Excuse me, sir.' He takes the medal off.

"I thought, 'Oh God, he's gonna throw it, or do something.' Then he walked around behind the monument there, and he came up to me and said, 'Sir, will you put this on?'

"He said, 'I don't need it from a congressman.' And my daughter Becky was there. And she was crying. They gave Calvin his back benefits. They gave him a check for twenty-five grand. He sent his sister and her husband on a trip. He calls me once every two months or so. We're working to get his discharge reclassified as honorable. And he said, 'Boy, I'm a hero in the town.' I said, 'Calvin, remember those who treated you like a hero before you got that little piece of metal. All the rest are phonies.' He said, 'I know that, sir.'

"I put sixty-six guys in for medals at our base camp at Phuoc Vinh. The general came and pinned on like thirty of them. And then he didn't put the paperwork in, so a couple of them got Silver Stars, but there's no record of it."

Bucha thinks there should have been a Presidential Unit Citation. His men put him in for the Medal of Honor, which he received from Richard Nixon at the White House in May 1970.

"I thought long and hard about turning it down. But a sergeant who was interacting with me about the trip to the White House said in very blunt terms, 'Who do you think you are?' He said, 'It's not yours to turn down.' I said, 'I don't see it the same way.' He said, 'Well, what don't you see?' I said, 'I don't see crawling through a hail of fire in a bunker [in the citation]. He said, 'Where does it say crawled?' So I said, 'I didn't think it was any big deal. And the wound was painful, but I didn't notice it until the next morning.' He said, 'Did you stand up with lights?' I said, 'Of course, but I didn't think it was risky.' He said, 'Well, that's your problem.'

"So then we tried to use it as a platform to convince others to stop calling Medal of Honor men heroes, get rid of the word *winner*. Talk about recipients. . . . Then, as president of the society in ninety-five, I tried to present it as a vehicle. . . . We've received these medals on behalf of others. The important thing is to recognize that we are not special, and we are not different. We just were in a strange confluence of events, time and circumstance, where that which each of us has within us emerged, both in those who wear the Medal and those who do not. So the important thing is to encourage respect for the potential that exists in people. Just as my men, who were written off by everybody, proved to be these fantastic, wonderful, legendary guys."

Back in the United States, Bucha wound up at West Point from 1969 to 1972, teaching history, economics, and national security. He wrote a course in accounting while there.

Bucha became a Young Turk. He had long hair and never wore any ribbons. The only insignia on his uniform blouse were the CIB, the Combat Infantryman's Badge, and his jump wings. He agitated for a kind of change at the academy that he later came to regret. "We were full of ourselves, young officers. We had come back. We had all been well educated at the finest schools. We had guys who were Ph.D.'s from Harvard and Stanford. We knew better. My military career was mismanaged by me from the day I graduated, but I knew better. And we were critical of West Point being a trade school. And thought it should be a university. In hindsight, that was a mistake because I think West Point is an institution unique in its commodity, called leadership.

"It's not an academic institution. If you want to become academically polished and well read, go somewhere else. But we criticized it in our conceit—unfounded conceit, youthful arrogance, if you will. And West Point responded, and now it's trying to be an academic institution. And it's not. I think the cadets come to West Point to learn about a way of life. A life of being a leader based on the premise of honor. You can go serve your country anywhere. You don't need West Point just to serve the country. The academy must do something that enables service to country to be better performed here than anyplace else. West Point is leadership.

"I'm lucky, and I have to say, bringing it full circle, a lot of what I can do today, what I have the ability to do, comes from the way I was taught at West Point. So I'm beholden to them, to the institution."

Bucha left the service in 1972, and went to work for H. Ross Perot, who ran for President in 1972, with another Medal recipient, James Stockdale, as a running mate. Bucha worked for Perot on Wall Street and then started his international operation. He represented Perot in Iran and moved from there to Paris. In 1979, he resigned to form and run his own company, an international marketing and consulting business. This focused on trade with firms interested in selling United States products and services abroad. In 1984, he switched to real estate, went back to consulting, and in 1997 took over a company called Delta Defense, which makes environmentally friendly nontoxic, frangible ammunition. "It'll kill you," he said, "but you won't die of lead poisoning." He also was affiliated with a steel company and a tin-plate producer.

In November of 1997 Paul Bucha presented his Medal of Honor to the United States Military Academy at West Point. The superintendent of the academy, Lieutenant General Dan Christman, said Bucha donated his medal "to inspire generations to follow and symbolically give back to this institution what it gave to us."

On that day Bucha told his audience, "Leaders should be competent, professional, and have the absolute intestinal fortitude to use the last ounce in you to minimize the risk to the men and women in your command. I want this to be a reminder to each and every one of us, and every one of the men and women that you command, that we have the potential to do something extraordinary under certain circumstances. This is where this medal belongs, because this is where young men and women are learning to lead troops."

FOURTEEN

Alfred V. Rascon

Medic
173d Airborne Brigade, Vietnam
March 16, 1966

*"I somehow ended up being selected to become a medic.
Everybody thought that was cool, but I wanted to be in the infantry.
Little did I realize that was cannon fodder."*

Rascon and his wife, Carol, at the
annual convention of the Congressional Medal of Honor Society in Boston, October 2000.

by Robert M. Bush, CMOHS photographer

Photo by Tim Page

Al Rascon, badly shot up, is helped toward a
dustoff helicopter by two GIs in South Vietnam on
March 16, 1966. He became an American citizen
the following year.

I MET AL RASCON early one evening at his spacious, well-appointed home at the edge of a cul-de-sac in Laurel, Maryland. It was Christmastime. His wife, Carol, was there, as were their two children, Amanda, fourteen, and Alan, ten. A fire was blazing, the Christmas tree was brightly decorated, and the Rascons were gracious and accommodating. Except for a painting on the wall, there was no sign of any military connection. Rascon and I faced each other across a table at the edge of the kitchen while Carol and the children sat behind us near the fireplace in the den. After a couple of hours they went off to bed; Rascon and I spoke for almost four hours.

He was born Alfredo, in Chihuahua, Mexico, on September 10, 1945, and brought into the United States as an infant, most likely illegally, by his parents, Andrea and Alfredo. "They came like a lot of Hispanics, looking for a better life. My dad was the youngest in his family. They had a fairly large ranch in Chihuahua, but he decided to come to the States in the forties and that was how we ended up in California. You get incongruent stories as to what really happened. I remember very distinctly being in L.A.—but I also remember going back to Mexico in 1951—and coming back legally and getting a green card.

"They were poor individuals, both of them. In Oxnard, a military embarkation port north of Malibu, my dad worked wherever he could find jobs, mostly as a laborer, working in the fields, picking lemons. I remember being very young going out and picking lemons with him. It was very traumatic for a young kid, probably under ten, getting up at four A.M. to pick lemons. It wasn't exactly my cup of tea."

When they first moved to Oxnard, Rascon says, "I remember for a very long time we had the largest door in the whole entire neighborhood. My door opened from top to bottom and vice versa, and not from side to side or left to right, and I didn't know it was because we lived in a garage." They stayed there for a couple of months, moving a few more times, before settling in La Colonia, the Hispanic section. Military personnel going to and coming back from Korea would give the little Mexican boy leggings or patches. He especially admired the paratroopers with the airborne insignia on their garrison caps, and even made himself a parachute. He read comic books about tough Army guys like Sgt. Rock and played in the back of a secondhand store that sold Army/Navy stuff. Sometimes his mother found him asleep back there amid the helmets and boots and leather jackets from World War II.

"We never knew how damn poor we were until years later. We were just a raggedy-ass bunch of kids who'd go out and have BB-gun fights, lemon fights, or go down to the railroad and check out the hoboes. I had my little toy soldiers. I was happy."

His playmates called him "Güero, the white guy—I didn't look Hispanic." A long time afterward, maybe fifty years later, Rascon was asked to speak at a Veterans' Day service in Oxnard. "There were pretty close to thirty guys there with families, grandchildren—they all came to see me. They were white and black and Hispanic, and they were so proud of me, the fact that I had moved out of what we were.

"The irony of the whole thing was that it didn't impact on me until later that I was literally a guy born in Mexico—until when I was in high school—and then that was an embarrassment for me. Everybody was born in L.A. or born in Oxnard or born in Anaheim. I was born in Mexico, and I tried to treat it very secretly. It was not shame; I guess it was more ignorance. Hey, it's not your fault where you were born; it's not your fault how you're brought up, either. Now I don't have any problem with it.

"High school was good because I merged with everybody, and most of my friends were the Anglo-Saxons, the white kids, and they never looked at me like anything other than who I was. The most sobering thing was as a junior or senior being invited to dances at friends' houses and being ashamed to tell them where I lived. They knew I lived in La Colonia, but they never knew where. They would come back and drop me off at a residence I would find, probably the best house there."

Some white guy gave Rascon an old tennis racket, and he learned to play, lettering all four years on the varsity. "I could play basketball really well, and baseball. The only problem was my stature. I'm not quite five feet seven. I could never quite compete with the other guys because they were taller. I played varsity football, but I was maybe one hundred and ten pounds wet so I was basically cannon fodder. I sat on the bench most of the time, but I didn't give up.

"The sad thing was your future was picked out at the school not by what you did but by your nationality. A lot of us in La Colonia were not allowed to take college-prep courses. They wanted you to take shop or some other 'ash and trash.' Instead of taking English one, you had to take English seven. I got straight A's in English and math and everything I was doing, but you could never quite get into the biology class or the chemistry class because they were never prepared [they couldn't deal with it] for that."

College appealed to Al, but he didn't know it was possible to go without having any money, so he persuaded his parents to sign so he could join the Army in August of 1963. "It was kind of neat because it was like *Pee-wee's Big Adventure*. There was no height or weight limit. I wanted to be a paratrooper, a ranger, join Special Forces, be a jungle-warfare expert, and I wanted to be in the infantry.

"What I didn't realize was that, once you finished basic, they could make you whatever they wanted you to be, whether it was a cook, mechanic, or candlestick maker. Your destiny was in their hands. I somehow ended up being selected to become a medic. Everybody thought that was cool, but I wanted to be in the infantry. Little did I realize that was cannon fodder."

He was given fourteen weeks of medical training at Fort Sam Houston in Texas, where he found out you had to be over twenty-one to join Special Forces, you had to be a senior noncommissioned Army officer to go to ranger school or to get jungle-warfare training. "It's the Army at its finest, but I didn't care. I was so awed by everything in my environment changing so traumatically that I didn't have time to dwell on that, other than the fact that I was going to jump school at the Fort Benning School for Boys." After

four weeks and five jumps, Rascon was assigned to the medical battalion of the 101st Airborne, then abruptly reassigned to the 173d
Airborne Brigade (Separate) and sent to Okinawa.

So in about four months Peewee from La Colonia had his first
train ride, in a sleeper to Texas, jumped out of airplanes in Georgia, flew to Oakland, and rode a troopship to Japan. This was January 1964. It was only the beginning.

After a year and four months, on May 5, 1965, his unit was
deployed to the fourth landing in Vietnam. "We were the first Army
unit to go. It was a good thing we were an airborne brigade separate because we had the M-16s when nobody else had them, and
we had rucksacks. We'd been experimenting with the M-16s and
rucksacks, jumping with them."

He ended up with the Reconnaissance Platoon of the 173d, from
May 1965 until March 1966, "when I got nailed."

"We were going out in the field all the time. What people don't
understand is that Vietnam was a situation where sometimes you
walked out in the woods for days and didn't see anything, and other
times you landed and immediately you were involved in a firefight.
We had plenty of operations, a couple of dozen maybe, lasting fifteen seconds, sometimes twenty minutes or less. Probably the most
pivotal ones were in September, October, November, and March.

"The first time I was wounded was on September twentieth,
nineteen sixty-five. I was hit in the forearm. I was crossing a rice
paddy when the guy in front of me by the name of Boots gets hit.
Boots was a Texan, and he's hit in the fleshy part of the calf, I see a
piece of tube steak flying out of him, and I was hit probably one
tenth of second thereafter. Both of us were caught in the rice paddy
we were crossing. Maybe a portion of the recon platoon had already
cleared the rice paddy. Behind us and to the right there was a
machine gun set up, and I guess the guy was asleep and he woke up
and saw us crossing and he opened up on us. We had two snipers
shooting at us at the same time and we lay in the rice paddy five or
ten minutes until the firefight terminated. We never did catch the
people who shot at us, but I think we ended up killing the sniper.

They claimed that I was one of the guys that took the sniper out. We were medics at that time, but we carried M-16s. So the first thing you are is a soldier, an infantryman, and then you go into the medic mode. This is a new Army.

"Anyway Boots is lying there yelling every profanity in the world and I'm saying, 'Boots, Boots!' He's on the other side of the dike, probably not more than two feet away, but for me it's a lifetime. Don't forget you've got the old heart failure there [abject fear], and you don't know what's going on, and I'm trying to find out how bad he's wounded and I finally figure out that he's yelling every profanity not because he's got an open wound and he's lying in the rice paddy but because the leeches have gotten to him. The slimy little animals have bit into him, and he's yelling more about that than he is about being hit.

"I can hear our platoon sergeant, Jacob R. Cook, on the embankment. He's already cleared it, and I can hear him yelling every profanity and apparently what's happened with him is his M-16 was jamming. Initially when we were in Vietnam circa 1965 in June and July, the M-16s would jam. They ended up putting a ramming rod in the side to eject a round. But at the time, when an M-16 got jammed you had to come back and field-strip it. Later Cook told me he had got a Buck knife from his wife the day before and he was able to use that to eject the cartridge."

A medevac helicopter came for Boots, but Rascon's wound was slight so he stayed with the platoon. Their attackers had left. "Everybody went into the wood line where the guy had shot at us with the machine gun, and we hadn't gone five minutes and I remember picking myself up off the ground with a ringing noise in my ear. Then immediately somebody said, 'Doc, get up,' and I went up to the front and I remember seeing two guys up at the point. An individual by the name of Sergeant Larry Pierce, an E-5, had seen a land mine made by the Chicoms. It was lying off the trail and it had wires on it. He saw that and he saw it was going to come back and impede on all of us, so he threw himself on it.

"So here I am with two people up front and one had his leg

mauled, gone, and one had his arm dangling, and they're both trying to tell me, 'Don't worry about me, Doc. I'll cover you.' And I
never thought about this insanity until years later, asking myself
how in the heck were these guys going to cover me? One could
barely see, and one of them is missing an arm. They were telling me
go look for Sergeant Pierce. I turned around, and small trees and
small branches were gone, they were cut down to maybe a foot off
the ground from the explosion by the land mine. I finally found
Pierce about twenty feet from where the explosion had gone off.
This guy is bleeding to death on me, and he's got more holes in him
than Carter has liver pills, and I remember trying to stick an IV in
his leg someplace, and we're trying to take care of other guys and
they're telling me, 'Don't worry about the other guys. You take care
of Pierce.'

"But what ends up happening is that a month later Larry Pierce
was to be the first noncommissioned Army officer in Vietnam to get
the Medal of Honor.

"Of course he didn't make it. The battalion chaplain by the name
of Major Frank Vavrin guided us to a helicopter, and we finally got
Pierce and other people on it. What I didn't realize was I had him
barely alive. I don't know how many IVs I stuck into him, but what
happened later on we found out a piece of the shrapnel was embedded in his heart. So it didn't matter what I was gonna do. He ended
up dying in flight before he got to the hospital.

"And later on Sergeant Cook told us that Vavrin, the chaplain,
said to him, 'Do you think God would get mad at me if I carried an
M-16?' But that's how intense things were the rest of the day. He
ended up taking the M-16 of one of the guys who was injured.

"A couple of weeks later we were in another firefight and we
ended up leaving the area, and this is how insane it was sometimes—the firefight was going on up front but it was not impacting
on us, so we were eating our lunch. Then I went up and there was
a bunch of guys injured and I remember crawling up to a guy lying
there and he was going blue on me and I couldn't find an exit or
entry hole in him but I knew the guy was dying on me and I had no

idea why, and I started giving him mouth-to-mouth resuscitation, and the guy barfed in my face. Then I felt something in his belt buckle; there was a hole, and I finally reached down his spine and I felt a small protrusion. What happened the guy had got hit dead in the belt buckle, dead center in the belly button, and the bullet had apparently jammed inside around the backbone. I could just feel the back of it. I had no idea who the guy was. I just remember he died there.

"But you get on with your life, okay? My experiences had already led me to getting my hands on somebody's innards and . . . you name it. Blood has a very distinct smell; it has a coppery, earthy smell to it. I remember that very clearly, and I remember getting my hands in blood and they would get sticky and you would have it on your uniform. These were things you never thought of but now you'd go, oh my god, these are not sanitary conditions, but when the thing hits the fan it's going to be like that no matter what.

"And even then there were always comical incidents when these things were going on. I remember this big black burly guy, and he was lying there and I was trying to haul him to a safe area and Frank Vavrin had a 35 mm camera in a case around his neck and we were trying to haul this guy off, but he was too big for me and Frank came over to help and finally the guy who I thought was injured so very badly just got up and walked away. What happened was he got mad at us, not because of me, but because Frank kept on dragging him and every time he would drag, the camera would swing back and it kept hitting the guy in the head. So, as bad as he was, he finally got up, and I guess he took care of himself. . . . But Frank was always there for us. He was the battalion chaplain, but somehow every time the thing would hit the fan he ended up with us."

Rascon's recon platoon was a composite of three other platoons, like a mini-company, consisting of at least fifty men. "But there was just one medic, and that was me. They didn't want anybody else. Once I took off on leave, and they were mad because I was going away for a while. At first I stayed with the medical platoon, but the recon guys went back and told them they wanted me to be housed

with them. So I became the first medic to live with the recon platoon. Most medics would get assigned to other companies out of
the medical platoon. But we had a mutual respect. I would take care
of them, and they would take care of me."

Medics carried two types of bags: The smaller one, called an M3
wasn't sufficient for combat. The larger bag, the M5, which looked
like a large attaché case about six inches thick, was too heavy for
Rascon. "That was overkill, okay? So me being a streetwise kid, I
realized I couldn't carry my food, three hundred rounds of ammunition and my hand grenades, my water, my M-16 and do everything I was supposed to do because I was so small. I used to carry
a serum albumin, a half pint of blood expander, like plasma, and it
came in a little canister with an IV, a rubber tube with a .12 gauge
needle, a horse needle. But the problem with these little canisters,
they end up being heavy and I had bandages and other things to
carry, so I went to Sergeant Cook and said, "Can I have some of the
guys carry their own medical stuff?" And I ended up strapping
their canisters on the backs of their rucksacks with green Army
tape, so when they got hurt, I'd just rip it right off and start giving
it to them. And I ended up teaching the enlisted men and some of
the NCOs how to do that, so they ended up being mini-medics.
That facilitated a lot of needs right there because in combat you
never knew whether one person was going to get hurt or six, and I
couldn't do all things to all people. Probably the most important
thing at that time is you're a nineteen-year-old kid and you've got
to learn there are people who are gonna die and other people that
can be saved, and that was the reality. Nobody talked about that
when you were going through medical training.

"When we went out on our first patrols we carried our food in
tins, and they were heavy. So then I realized I didn't have to carry
a lot of food because the other guys would carry everything in the
world with them and sooner or later they would come down the
path and dump some of their load and I would just pick up their
cans and eat what they had, cocoa or canned bread or peaches or
something. So, you know, you learn by experience."

Rascon also saw that the North Vietnamese carried hammocks, and with his sergeant's approval, he bought nylon and parachute line and had hammocks "small enough to fit in your pocket" made so the men didn't have to tote blankets. The hammocks also doubled as stretchers for the wounded.

"On November fifth we wound up in another operation, Hill 65, which ended up being a day in which the First 503d was surrounded by a North Vietnamese regiment as they came into a small valley, and within a couple of hours there were a lot of Americans killed or wounded. A short round from a mortar coming off a helicopter hit our battalion command post and the North Vietnamese, charging with bugles, swept us twice. They came at us head-on and went through us twice, hand-to-hand combat, that's how close it was. The recon platoon was a kilometer and a half away, and we were hearing this hellacious firefight going on. Later on we found out maybe twenty-five Americans were killed, and fifty or a hundred wounded, which was peanuts because they ended up counting bodies, and they had over five hundred North Vietnamese dead all around them, so we kicked the holy hell out of them. And this was not the day when they would come back and make up things. For this battle, the First 503d was to be given the Presidential Unit Citation. And one individual, a Spec-5 or an E-4 named Lawrence Joel, he ended up being the first medic to get the Medal of Honor in Vietnam. He was hit and kept himself alive by giving himself quarter-grain syrettes of morphine so he could keep on taking care of people. So here I am with two guys all of sudden I know personally and well from the First 503d, one on September twentieth, Larry Pierce, and Joel on November seventh, who get the Medal of Honor."

On March 15, Rascon's platoon and other units were finding plenty of signs of the enemy—substantial caches of ammunition, weaponry, and rice, including some MAT-49s, French paratrooper mini-submachine guns evidently captured after the surrender of Dien Bien Phu. Around six next morning, the 2d 503d, a sister battalion, was on the verge of action. "We're at Point A, they're at Point

B, already in the Landing Zone, like the center of a small soccer field. And they were going to send probing patrols. Unbeknownst to them, they were surrounded by a reinforced North Vietnamese regiment and a supply helicopter was bringing them these containers of hot food and eggs, when a North Vietnamese who was chained to a tree shot down the helicopter, and that was the start of the firefight for that day. Had the guy waited like ten more minutes the 2d 503d would have been all over hell's half acre, remember? But instead everybody hunkered down where they were.

"So all hell was hitting the 2d 503d, and then in an hour or two it got worse, and they decided to commit two of our companies to help. The recon platoon was told to take the point, and they were moving us at a good pace. I remember seeing trees all soot from napalm, which ends up like a charcoal jell, and in my own Tiny Tim mind I said, 'God, I'm getting dirty.' We were probably a good three hundred meters from the 2d 503d and we were seeing bodies—two, three, four, five—all over the place we were headed into. They were dead North Vietnamese. And all of a sudden the patrol stopped and Ray Compton, the sergeant who had the point squad, came back and told Cook they have North Vietnamese up front setting up an L-shaped ambush, and he was not sure if they were there to take us out or they were waiting for probing patrols from the 2d 503d.

"In seconds the decision was made to take them on, and I think they saw us but we ended up firing the first shot. The M-79 grenadier told me he was told to go up front, and he said he had hardly fired when they opened up on us and that was it.

"I could hear us firing, I could hear M-16s, I could hear hand grenades going off, I could hear heavy machine guns going off, hear the AK47s, and you could hear the North Vietnamese talking and you could hear us yelling and there was organized chaos. I'm talking about branches falling, small trees falling from the intensity of the firefight and you don't dig in, you just go take 'em on, and whoever's got the biggest toys is going to win.

"Put yourself in a one-lane bowling alley and the North Vietnamese are down where the pins are and the lane is the trail. We were never on the trail; I guess they thought we were going to walk on it, but we were off it. And I don't know why or to this day how one of our M-60 machine gunners ended up being on the trail. I don't know how he got there, but that ended up being Thompson, a strapping young man over six feet, black, a gracious guy, everybody liked him. He ended up lying on the trail and facing the enemy and he was being shot at.

"I remember trying to get up to the front and Cook telling me, 'Doc, don't go up there; you're going to die. Wait for somebody to come back and provide some cover fire.' But I took off anyway. I remember lying off the trail to Thompson's front and to the right, and I tried getting up there, and I could hear my guys and see them providing cover fire and a couple of guys tried to get to him but they couldn't do anything. Every time you stood up you were getting shot at or you were getting hit. I think I tried it two or three times, and I could hear somebody yelling, you know, 'Cover Doc! Cover Doc!' And I got onto the trail, and I remember lying behind and between his legs and he's being hit—what I remember is every time he got hit, I knew it because he was shaking. I could feel it but I couldn't see it. It couldn't have been that hard to realize the guy was being hit gravely but I didn't realize that, I wasn't thinking that logically, I'm thinking this guy's down, I got to help him. I couldn't grab his head and I couldn't see how bad he was hit, so I turned around to cover him and see how I could take care of him, and that's when I was shot.

"It hit me in the hip, went up my spine and came out my collar bone. I don't remember that, though. I just remember it was like somebody slapping me. I was still trying to see what was wrong with him, and I dragged him off the trail, I just remember rolling him off or something, and I think then I realized the guy wasn't about to make it and I just left him there. People were still yelling and people were still firing at each other and Gibson—the other M-60 machine gunner—kept on yelling for ammo, so I crawled up to him and I did not necessarily think about the fact that he was out of ammo as the fact that I thought he had been shot. I was right. He had been shot in the leg, and I didn't know where. I kept trying to give him some aid, and he kept telling me to get the hell off him and leave him alone and a few other profane words. His concern was not for himself, but he was trying to provide cover fire for everybody. And I kept on telling him I think something is hurt and let me take care of it. He kept on telling me, 'Doc, get the hell away from me.' I ended up in his pant leg, I don't remember if I put a compress on it or I just ripped his pant leg off, and he kept yelling he was running out of ammo.

"And I remembered Thompson had two bandoliers, and I made it back to him and took off the bandoliers and gave them to Gibson and he put his M-60 back in action. Don't forget all this was going really quick, and I didn't know what was going on, but there were hand grenades going off all over the place. One went off very close and nothing happened and another went off at a distance, and I remember my head going around in circles. I was hit by shrapnel, hit in the face and in the chin and the cheeks and the back of my head and I think a few places in my body. I thought somebody had ripped my head off. I remember my face was inflamed and I couldn't speak or do anything. I started to hyperventilate. I lay there almost in tears. I thought I had lost my face. You bleed a lot from your face, and blood was just gushing out. Then I thought that was going to be the end of it, I wasn't going to play anymore, and you know my vanity, I kept thinking why me, in the face? Finally I just calmed myself down and got on with my life. More hand grenades were going off." Nearby a grenade landed in front of Jerry Lewis, whose best friend, Neal Haffey, was watching. He told Rascon later, "I saw the hand grenade lying in front of Lewis, Lewis looked at it, Lewis looked at me. Lewis was my best friend. We had plans."

The grenade killed Lewis, Rascon recalls. "Haffey decided enough was enough; he was going to try to get out of that area. A little movement was enough for somebody to see him, and I saw somebody on the treeline pop him with an AK47, probably no farther then ten feet away, shot him in the back or in the hip, and all he was trying to do was get to his buddy Lewis. At that time they were throwing hand grenades at him, and I made my way to him; it could have been ten yards or ten feet, everything was going in slow motion. I mean everything stops, and everything is exaggerated. Very clearly you could smell the cordite, you could smell the weapons. I remember making it to Haffey, and I threw myself on him and—remember I said I didn't want to get dirty? —well, Haffey was lying next to an area they had napalmed, and it was full of soot and I threw myself on him, and that was when the hand grenades went off and I got nailed. And he was okay, but the first thing came out of his mouth was we were all gonna die, and I told him we were okay. He was worried about Lewis, and I told him I would go back and check on Lewis.

"Then I was to find out years later, last year, I was lying. Neal Haffey said, 'Doc, you covered me, you saved my life.' And I said, 'I didn't save your life. I was just trying to do what you would have done for me.' And he said, 'You lied to me.' and I said, 'Why did I lie to you?' And he said, 'Well, you grabbed me and you were telling me to shut up, everything was going to be all right, and you were going to take care of me and Lewis, but you were bleeding. You couldn't even talk, your mouth was ripped open from top to bottom, you were all full of blood. You were lying to me.' "

Rascon then went to check on Lewis. "I don't know how I never got shot that time. When I got there he was plenty dead. I didn't even know who was back there. I found out later it was Lewis because he had red hair. He was a carrottop. That was it, there was nothing I could do, but I never got touched. I don't even know how I got back there, don't know what the time frame was, whether it was a couple of seconds or a minute or what. Only thing I remember to this day is I looked to my right and saw three stripes. It was a sergeant. I had no idea it was Sergeant Compton, our point squad leader. You could hear Sergeant Cook and Sergeant Cunha yelling, 'Let's go!' And 'Let's flank 'em!' and I guess the rest of the company was trying to get to us, but it was every man for himself up at the point. Compton was already wounded when I saw him. I saw hand grenades get thrown at him, and I was close enough that I made my way to him—I don't think he knew what was going on—I know I knocked him down and covered him and when the hand grenades went off, I got hit again. Gibson thought it was rather comical, he said he saw me and Compton flying in the air. He said my rucksack and helmet flew off. I don't remember that. I hated helmets anyway. I tell everybody the firefight lasted ten minutes, but it couldn't have. It probably lasted a good twenty."

Rascon remembers he tried to take care of Compton. Then "I don't know whether I went back to take care of somebody else or went looking but then everything just went quiet. You could hear the bush, you hear the company coming up on the flanks. What happened apparently was Cook and Cunha managed to flank the bad guys and chase them out of the area.

"There were fifteen guys in the point squad involved in the action, four up front. We had two dead, Thompson and Lewis, and eight wounded."

Rascon was walked and carried to a helicopter that had been transporting chaplains. "Apparently, just to give me some cover, you know, just in case, one of them gave me last rites, because I was pretty well banged up. I'm bleeding from the head and my mouth is ripped open." He was flown first to a battalion aid station, "where they try to stabilize you, give you emergency first aid and get you back aboard for the next trip."

"They get me there and my concern is with my face. It was my only concern. I only care about my face. And everybody else was concerned about my back. This guy starts going into my back and I'm going, 'Hey! I got other things to do. Don't be sticking your hand back there.' They were trying to figure out where the round was. They didn't realize it came out over here (touches back of neck). They put me in another helicopter, a regular supply helicopter, and I was medevacked to the 93d field hospital at Bien Hoa, and I remember the guy was mad because I kept bleeding on his helicopter. I remember him mouthing off. The irony of this whole thing was when I was medevacked to Japan, I saw the guy there. He ended up being shot two weeks later. He got his karma. You know, what goes around, comes around.

"So we landed at Bien Hoa and the nurses and corpsmen came running up, and the first thing—I didn't realize—they did was go after you with scissors and strip your clothes off, see where you're wounded. I didn't realize I still had my M-16, between my legs, and I was really worried about the fact that I was going to lose my M-16, and I'm also concerned about the fact that these people are going to see my private parts. What happens is I'm vain. But the nurse very subtly and quietly says, 'Son, I think you've got other things to worry about.' So they took off my clothing and stripped my boots off and I'm laying there under a sheet and somebody told me they were going to give me my M-16 back later."

He was placed in a triage area, somewhere near the middle, which reassured him because it indicated he was not in imminent danger of expiring. "Next morning I woke up and I was in bed with clean sheets and IVs in me. They still had not taken care of my mouth or my face, and I'm still mad about that. I still have a chunk in there they never took out. I have a six-inch scar in the back of my head."

He had three operations on his back. How is it today?

"It's bad. It's really bad." He adds, "I live with it."

The recon platoon had scarcely returned from patrol when somebody borrowed a Jeep. "They came to see me at the hospital, and I was kidnapped. They told me they'd got permission to take me back to the battalion. They would feed me and get another medic from the medical platoon to come and take care of my dressing and the drains in my back. That lasted for all of four days because I started going into a fever and finally Cook got enough smarts to realize I was really in bad shape. So they managed to con some guy over at the brigade, and they took me over there like they had just found me or something. . . . and the next day I was medevacked to Japan. That's how bad it was. I was sent to Johnson Army Field Hospital in Japan, an orthopedic hospital, and I ended up spending two months." He got in trouble with the nurses for popping wheelies in the hall in his wheelchair.

Rascon never knew that he was recommended for the Medal of Honor. Late in May 1966 he was sent to the States to be discharged. The following February he received a yearbook and a Silver Star. "I thought that was kind of neat, but then I read the citation and realized it told maybe ten percent of what happened that day, so I just got on with my life."

In 1993, twenty-five years later, his wife, Carol, persuaded him to sign up for a reunion of the 173d in Washington, D.C. It was the first he had attended. "Sergeant Compton came up to me and said, 'How does it feel to be a Medal of Honor recipient?' And, I said, 'How do I know? I'm not one.'

"Eventually they found out the nomination or the packet somehow got lost and never went up the chain of command. Frank Vavrin, the chaplain, was really the guy that instigated all the follow-up."

As the effort to obtain the Medal for Rascon was going forward, Rascon recalls, somebody asked Sergeant Cook or one of the others involved, "Why would anybody want to change history?" And the answer came: "Nobody wanted to change history. They just wanted to correct it."

Suspended from a blue ribbon, the Medal of Honor was placed around the neck of five-foot seven-inch Alfred V. Rascon from Oxnard, California, at the White House in February of 2000 by President William Jefferson Clinton. In his talk, Clinton noted that in 1951 when Al was seven, he had made his own parachute. "I jumped off the roof of my house and I didn't break anything other than my wrist, even though I fell on my head. And the president said that's when I made my first parachute jump, and I had a couple of malfunctions, but that did not deter me from becoming a paratrooper after all."

After leaving the Army, Rascon went to college in Santa Barbara, working full-time simultaneously, and graduated with a degree in business. In 1969 he went back into the Army to attend Officer Candidates School. Commissioned on February 20, 1970, he did a second tour in Vietnam as an adviser, then from 1976 to 1984 he served as an Army liaison officer for the National Guard in Panama.

In 1985, the same year he and Carol were wed, he joined the Drug Enforcement Administration, and two years later he went to the drug financial terrorist branch at Interpol, working all these years for the Department of Justice. He became inspector general of the Selective Service, retiring in January 2001. That spring he was appointed director of the Selective Service. Despite Al's injuries, the Rascons and their children dwell comfortably today in Laurel, commuting distance from Washington, D.C., where they work—a lifetime away from a little garage in Oxnard, California, where the door opened upward.

FIFTEEN

Jack H. Jacobs

82d Airborne
Adviser to South Vietnamese
March 9, 1968

"If you have to defend liberty, you got to defend liberty.
It's as simple as that. But I found the actual combat a horrible, horrible thing,
to be acutely avoided. Whatever you can do, it's best to avoid it. . . .
I was scared all the time I was in Vietnam.
I didn't enjoy it for a second."

Jack Jacobs at fifty-eight
in December 2002.

Photo by Eddie Adams

Jack Jacobs made captain in the 82d Airborne in
June 1968, following his last combat in March of
that year. He received the Medal of Honor in
September 1969. This was the official photo
taken shortly afterward.

"I HAVE NO time now," Jack Jacobs was telling me. "I'm retired and you know the more retired you get, the busier you get. I'm involved in a wide variety of things. I own a construction company that does building in Connecticut, principally, an investment company that buys properties, and a construction company that builds them out. I'm a partner in a property company in London, where I own quite a bit of property. I'm involved in a company that produces security systems and a network messaging company. I'm involved in a billion different things. I spend a lot of time on MSNBC as a commentator. It started out as military stuff but since I have a banking background as well—when I came out of the Army I went into the investment banking business—I tell them what to think about Enron and so on." He has to get his diary out to report what else he's up to. "I can't say no. If I find something I'm interested in, I'll go ahead and do it. . . . Am I compulsive? I don't know. It must be compulsive. I'm sure it's compulsive. I'm supposed to be retired."

Jack Jacobs is the only living person of the Jewish faith to hold the Medal of Honor, but he is by no means the first. Since the medal was created, thirty-one members of his faith have received it. When he says "we," however, he refers to other members of the Medal of Honor Society. "We're a dwindling asset," he says. "When one of us is gone, he's gone forever. I mean, this stuff is important. And you can't get them back."

He describes himself as "one of those guys who was born old." His family moved from Brooklyn, New York, when he was eleven or twelve to Woodbridge, New Jersey, not far from where he lives now, in Millington. In high school, he was small, and not at all athletic. "I'm not trying to be pejorative about myself, but I was a combination goofball and intellectual." He wrote for the literary magazine and the student newspaper and was manager of the track team. Later on, after military service, he became a runner and participated in three marathons, the last around 1990.

After high school, Jacobs went to Rutgers University, where he majored in political science and joined the ROTC (Reserve Officers

Training Corps), partly because it paid $27 a month. "That wasn't the only reason. It interested me. I thought about a career in the service. I really wanted to be a lawyer, but I had no money to be a lawyer. I was eighteen when I got married and I had a baby daughter, and I was going to school full-time and working full-time and then when I graduated I couldn't go to law school but I did have a reserve commission in the Army so I asked to go to the Army right away." He had to request a waiver to get a commission because you had to be five feet six and Jacobs, at five feet four, "was nowhere near" that height. He weighed 120 pounds. "They gave me a commission which committed me to three years, and I expected to serve three years and get out and go to law school. I blinked and the next thing I knew I had been in the Army for almost twenty-one years. It's a bit like Yogi Berra once said: 'When you get to that fork in the road, take it.' I kept taking these forks in the road."

He was sworn in as a second lieutenant with orders to go to the 82d Airborne. "I had asked for airborne because as a new lieutenant I made two hundred bucks a month and if you were a paratrooper you made an extra hundred." He got through jump school and became a platoon leader in the Second Battalion, 505th, spent a few months at Fort Bragg, North Carolina, and was ordered to Vietnam as an adviser in March 1967.

"I argued strenuously that I didn't want to go as an adviser. I wanted to go with my unit because the Third Brigade of the 82d, which we were part of, was shortly to get orders to go to Vietnam. But they said, 'No.' I said, 'Why not?' They said because you've got to go as an adviser because you've got a college degree, that's why.'" The thinking at the time, Jacobs said, was that officers who had college degrees might be more adaptable than those who did not, would do better in language school, fit in better with the South Vietnamese, and so on.

Was the fighting ability of units a concern? "The South Vietnamese were never highly thought of but one thing in retrospect that is of interest to me is the perception now that a lot of soldiers are only as good or as bad as their leadership, and they were taught a lot of bad lessons. For example, go out, contact the enemy, drop a lot of bombs on them, and then go in there. But that doesn't work in that environment. What you're supposed to do tactically is use all your indirect fire, bring it all to bear and move while all this fire is going in there. But we didn't do that. We tried to bomb the shit out of them, and then move in."

Did Jacobs worry? Did he ever think about getting killed some-time in the future while getting paid twenty-seven bucks a month back in ROTC?

"Absolutely not. It never crossed my mind. Young people don't have enough peripheral vision, they can't see very far into the future. Toward the end of my college career, the war was starting to heat up and a lot of people were against it already, but I figured they probably didn't know what they were talking about. There were no big protests at Rutgers, but the tenor of the intellectual discourse was decidedly against American participation in the war. Later on, I had a fairly grown-up view of what war was really like and that the chances of getting your head blown off as an adviser were just as good as anywhere else: It's all a matter of luck, most times, anyway, all things being equal. So it's irrelevant whether you're standing in a bar that gets mortared or lying in the middle of a rice paddy get-ting shot at.

"I remember George Aiken, this senator from Vermont, got up in the Senate—and this was long before we made that huge commit-ment of forces in Vietnam, still relatively early in the conflict—and Aiken was a Republican who was pretty much to the right, he said, 'I've got a great idea: Why don't we just say we won, and go home?'

"And of course, ten years later, that's exactly what we did. Fifty-eight thousand lives later. And now we know from the tapes that came out from Johnson, he said, 'This sucks. This is a big mistake. I'm going to live to regret this. I know we're doing the wrong thing, but what can you do?' He was very badly advised. He had rotten advice from his civilian assistants, and even worse advice from the military. [Secretary of Defense Robert] McNamara was probably the wrong guy in that job, and [General William] Westmoreland was a complete numbskull. I mean, he's a great guy and I'm sure he's a patriot, and one should never confuse respect for people's motives with respect for their intellectual acuity, and he had lots of the former and none of the latter, none whatsoever. He was absolutely the wrong guy for the job.

"And it may very well be that you couldn't have picked the right guy for that job. There may not have been a right guy for that job." For example, what was Jacobs thinking at the time? He was an intellectual. "I considered myself patriotic, very much so. I thought all those who were somewhat to the left of center were lazy and self-serving; I thought they were probably lazy bastards who were trying to stay in school as long as they possibly could. Like most people, I thought I had a lock on the truth, I thought they were being naive. In retrospect, I believe by accident, they turned out to be strategically correct. There were lots of people who were strategically correct, like George Aiken, not by accident, and a lot of people who were strategically wrong, not by accident, like Westmoreland, and McNamara and McGeorge Bundy [national security adviser to Presidents Kennedy and Johnson] and [Bill] Moyers [special assistant to LBJ, speechwriter, and later White House chief of staff] and that whole mob, they were all wrong on purpose. Not that they didn't know better, some of them did know better, but they were just wrong, on purpose, following a political expedient. There was an old saw in the press at the time that went, 'They told me that if I voted for Barry Goldwater [versus Lyndon Johnson in 1964], we'd be involved in a decade-long war in Vietnam, and I voted for Goldwater, and we were.' "

On the verge of entering the war in Vietnam, he was not worried that he'd be hit himself. "You don't think you're going to get shot. And, as a matter of fact, even when you get shot, you think it's a big mistake. Your first reaction—it's a bit like getting cancer or something, there's all this denial, you say, well, this is not really happening. This actually is not supposed to happen to me. It's supposed to happen to that guy over there. Then, of course, you realize that it is happening to you and it isn't a movie and you're not watching somebody else. If you had a high degree of confidence you were going to get killed, nobody would ever go to defend this country. I think one of the things that motivates you to do so is not only your inherent patriotism and your desire to do the right thing, but also at least the hope that it ain't going to happen to you. Otherwise, you just wouldn't do it. Only a maniac would do it, and most people aren't maniacs. So I think you start with a high degree of confidence that it's not going to happen to you. There was another old saw back then that said: 'If you go in the Army, you're either going to go to Vietnam or not; if you're not going to get sent to Vietnam, you don't have to worry; if you go to Vietnam, you're either going to get wounded, or not; if you're not going to get wounded, there's nothing to worry about; if you are wounded, you're either going to die, or you're not going to die. Well, if you are not going to die, you have nothing to worry about; and if you are going to die, you can't worry . . . so don't worry.'

"I mean there's this fatalistic view, but I think you structure the future in your mind in a fashion that makes it easy for you to do what you have to do. Because if you couldn't do that, you wouldn't do it. In retrospect, I knew we're seventy-five percent water, it's just a bag of water, and if you get a hole punched in, it's going to leak, and then you're going to be a deflated balloon.

"Now, I had that all figured out: I really believed that was too simplistic a view. I don't think young people think they're invincible at all. I certainly didn't. I knew I was totally and completely vincible. But my view was the law of averages was such—and this was all wrong, clearly—was such that bad things were not going to happen to me: They were going to happen to somebody else. Based on skewed thinking, I manipulated my view of the law of averages in a way that would satisfy my own view of what my future ought to be. I don't think people go in there and say, 'People are going to shoot me and I'm not gonna fall down.' No no. I think that's too simplistic. I think young people think it's going to happen to that other guy. I'm not going to be that guy who gets killed. Now, I know that the more time you spend in combat, the more certain it is that you are going to get killed. Oh absolutely, if you continue. The chances of rolling heads one hundred times in a row are very close to nothing."

Jacobs received advisory and language training at Bragg, then was sent to Fort Bliss in Texas for still more language study. "Eight weeks, mornings and afternoons, so I had a lot of Vietnamese language training. Don't ask me why they picked Guy A or Guy B. Knowing bureaucracies as I do, the choice was completely irrelevant. They had to have a certain number of guys do it, so they said, 'You guys go.' Vietnamese is a very easy language to speak, but it is much more difficult to listen to, to understand and read—it's like Chinese and Thai, it's all tonal. Each word has a half dozen different meanings depending on the tone you put on it. So if your accent's crappy you can't make yourself understood. But if you know what you want to say, chances are whoever you're talking to will be able to pick it up in context, but if you're listening to somebody, and you have only a rudimentary knowledge of the language, you're not going to pick it up."

After Bliss, Jacobs was given a month's leave to spend with his wife and—two children by now—a daughter and a son. He arrived, at twenty-two, in Vietnam the first week of September 1967. "Vietnam was one of the few places that turned out to be exactly as I expected—the sight, the sound, the smell. We broke through scattered clouds and there was green Vietnam and we landed and they kept the airplane running, refueled it hot, and guys were getting on to fly back, yelling, 'You'll be sorree!' and all these guys nineteen years old, they looked like they were one hundred and nineteen, and all us young guys getting off the plane. It was exactly as I expected it to be."

The new advisers were bused to downtown Saigon, to a place called the Kelper compound, a group of buildings cordoned off by barbed wire and a guard shack. "They had a snackbar. I remember the "Ode to Billy Joe" played over and over and over, and now anytime I hear that all I can think about is Kelper compound. They gave me a tiny room I shared with four other lieutenants that was right over the exhaust of the diesel generator that provided electricity for the place."

After a few days Jacobs' name came up on a bulletin board saying he was going to some popular force battalion, but then those orders were canceled. He was being sent to a different unit, "and the reason was a bunch of advisers had been killed in the unit I was going to." His orders directed him to the 2d Battalion, 16th Infantry, Ninth Vietnamese Infantry Division, situated in Sadec in the Vietnam Delta. The first stop was Cantho, where the plane damaged a nose wheel on landing, so he scrounged a ride to Sadec with a couple of helicopter jockeys who stopped by. From division headquarters "they ultimately sent me down where my battalion was located out in some province, the last province on the right-hand side of the Mekong River before you get into Cambodia. That's where I started out, and that's where I finished up."

A captain and two noncommissioned officers were there when he arrived. The captain and one of the sergeants rotated out not long afterward. "Now I was the ranking officer, with no combat experience." Luckily, he still had with him Staff Sergeant Romero Garcia Ramirez from Raymondville, Texas, and the two of them were to be wounded together some months later. "The South Vietnamese were glad to have us around because we could provide them with air strikes and we could get them stuff. Occasionally, infrequently, they would accept our advice. The more they would accept it, the better off they were tactically, but they were averse to accepting advice.

"One thing I have told a lot of people is that we probably don't understand [anything] about any of the places we have to operate in. There was a saying, something of a gag, we would say to the Vietnamese, 'Well, you're a lifer in Vietnam.' But that was precisely the point: When we went to Vietnam, we brought America with us. Not in my units because I was an adviser, but the American units by and large brought the country with them—they had showers, movies, candy bars, chewing gum. And not only that, if you survived you were only there twelve months and you went back home. But a Vietnamese soldier was there until he died. If he'd get wounded, they'd take him and patch him up and send him back. He didn't have any Chicago to go home to. Your average working-class Vietnamese guy was going to a unit and would get wounded until he was killed. You have a different view of life and a different view of the world when you are in that kind of environment than you do when you say, 'We're going to Afghanistan, we're going to blow up all these bad guys and when we get sick of it we're going to go home.'

"In addition to that, most of the Vietnamese units, certainly the ones I was with, had all their families with them. So you're in a compound with three hundred soldiers and you're also in a compound with three hundred soldiers' mothers-in-law, and their kids and their wives and so on. You have a different view of life when your family is at risk. I think under those circumstances they're going to say, 'I'm going to listen to this guy? This adviser? This guy's going home. What the hell is he? He may know a lot but what does he care? He's here for practice.' We didn't understand that then, and I think we still don't understand it. I think the very few who understand are the guys who spent some time with Vietnamese. Special Forces guys understood, advisers who spent a lot of time there, they understood.

"Because that never got communicated, there was this cultural gap, to use the cliché. Sure the Vietnamese were reluctant, they didn't want to fight. They were true believers, but they were reluctant participants. The kids were all conscripts, and they were going to get their brains blown out. They weren't interested in fighting. And this is to say nothing of all the strategic errors we had made when Ho Chi Minh asked for help. I mean we advised them during World War II and they asked us to help them throw the French out and, because we were afraid of pissing off de Gaulle—who, by the way needed a great deal of pissing off, if you want my opinion—we decided we weren't going to do anything about it. We would have solved a lot of problems if we'd just told de Gaulle to get the hell out, if we'd helped Ho Chi Minh and got rid of those guys and been done with it.

"But we couldn't distinguish between Ho being a Nationalist on the one hand and his being a communist on the other, any more than today we can distinguish between Osama bin Laden's being a Muslim on the one hand, which by the way is completely trivial, and a revolutionary on the other, which is really what he is. Ho Chi Minh really was a Nationalist, a revolutionary. So they say Osama bin Laden is a fascist."

Jacobs saw his first combat about three weeks after arriving in Vietnam when the Vietcong attacked a prison in a nearby town in the middle of the night. "We drove them off, killed some bad guys, lost some guys. It was the middle of the night, the same atmosphere as you saw in that nighttime combat scene in the movie *Platoon*, shooting tracers, can't see anything, don't know where the bad guys are, don't know where you are, total confusion. It was just like that. Ramirez was there, and we were looking out for each other. The whole thing lasted a couple of hours and in the dawn we saw the carnage and went back to our compound, about a mile away. They didn't get the people out of jail. Along the river there were guys lying in wait for us on the bank, and we lost a couple of guys when they started shooting at us.

"It was very scary, and I remained scared the entire time I was in Vietnam. I believe anybody who says he wasn't scared in combat is lying, or has got amnesia. I was always scared. I think it's good to be scared. It's a sign of intelligence. Anybody who's not scared is deranged."

Jacobs said he got along very well with the battalion commander, Colonel Hong. "He spoke reasonably good English, better than my Vietnamese, and I spoke pretty good Vietnamese. We got along, but he was frustrating because he didn't always take my advice. As a matter of fact, he almost never took my advice. He wasn't that old himself, less than forty, and he took pains to explain stuff to me. When I first showed up he made sure I was part of the briefings. They liked Ray, too. He was a swell guy, even-tempered, very steady, they liked to see that. They didn't like to see maniacs and people running around with their hair on fire, because they're taking the long

view—they're going to be in Vietnam forever. So if somebody comes
in with his hair on fire, they're going to shut him out completely."

Eventually an infantry major by the name of Nolan and a staff
sergeant from Maui joined Jacobs and Ramirez as advisers. "That
was the complement of the advisers when the action happened in
March some months later. But this was toward the end of sixty-
seven when the Vietcong and the North Vietnamese Army farther
north were gearing up for this big offensive, Tet, that was going to
take place in a couple of months. Of course we didn't know that.
There were a lot more enemy around, and we had a lot of combat
the end of sixty-seven and the first month and half of sixty-eight.
We saw a lot of action for four months. We took a lot of casualties
and the bad guys did, too. It was movement to contact mostly, large-
scale movement, sometimes by helicopter, sometimes on foot,
sometimes by boat. We were right near the Mekong River and the
Vietnamese had these old LSTs, and we'd go downriver to a nearby
province and make an assault.

"As time went on, Colonel Hong would ask me more and more
about strategy. When the major came, he'd ask us both what we
thought and we'd have conversations about what we should do, that
sort of thing. I think it was real unusual for the Vietnamese to take
any kind of advice. Hong was an adequate commander. You have to
remember a lot of these guys who rotated through there didn't have
years and years of experience either. The guy he replaced had been
killed. He was subsequently wounded one day and replaced by his
executive officer, who was not competent, who was in command of
the battalion the day I got wounded, March ninth [1968]. So some
of these guys were extremely good; the large majority of them were
okay. Competence is like deciding whether someone's attractive or
not. It's really a subjective evaluation. It was the company commanders who really had to be competent. You'd get into a firefight,
maneuver your platoons around, get stuff accomplished. They were
more important than the battalion commander."

On March 9, the battalion got on some boats, landed, and made
an assault in the direction of a checkpoint where they expected to

find the enemy. "We ran into a very large force, Vietcong, guys who were good at what they did, two hundred to three hundred guys. They sprang an ambush on us, and we had a lot of guys killed and wounded right away. There was a huge firefight that went on for some time." Jacobs and Sergeant Ramirez were with the lead company, in the thick of the fighting, in an exposed position, while Major Nolan and the sergeant from Maui were with the battalion commander in the next treeline to the rear.

"We were calling in air strikes on the radio, talking to an American forward air controller who was piloting a fixed-wing single-engine Piper Cub overhead. We'd talk to him and he talked to the F-4s or F-100s, whichever happened to be delivering the ordnance.

"The VC were established in a fortified position consisting of logs and dirt bunkers. With so many people wounded right away, the first thing I did was not call in air strikes; the first thing I did was try to help the wounded. Ramirez was wounded, I was wounded." In fact, Jacobs was hit in the head by shrapnel from an 82 mm mortar round, "the same round that hurt Ramirez, killed the S3 [the operations officer], killed the radio operator, killed two other guys, and wounded a bunch of other people." Jacobs had just taken his helmet off to scratch his head when the round landed. "A piece is in my nose, I still pick pieces out of my face, bits of steel, one over the right eyebrow. The main piece followed the contour of my skull and went out. I was very lucky. My face was pretty well busted; there was a lot of blood.

"I remember Ramirez, who had three sucking chest wounds, picks up the radio and calls. Our call sign was Snow Flanks Three Two—call signs were all organized to be difficult for Asians to pronounce. One time we were Bourbon Bucket. But this time we were Snow Flanks, and I was Three Two Alpha and Ramirez was Three Two Charlie. Ramirez picks up the handset that's attached to the radio that's attached to the dead radio operator, and he says, 'This is Three Two Charlie. Three Two Alpha [Jacobs] is hit real bad, an' I don' think he's gonna make it.' " Jacobs goes on, "Ramirez staggers, you know, he's got three sucking chest wounds, he's really sick. So I pick up the radio and I say, 'This is Three Two Alpha. Three Two Charlie is hit real bad, and I don't think he's gonna make it.' And the guy on the other end of the radio—I can't remember who it was—he said, 'Hey! This is no comedy routine. You guys get to work!'

"It seemed funny even then, I gotta be honest with you. I patched up Ramirez real quick and got him back to a small treeline. I think before that time the S3 who was wounded had been blown into a small canal, so I went and got him." Jacobs gave instructions for the headquarters company commanding officer "to deploy his people forward to engage the enemy because we sort of had a flanking position on them, if he would get some of his guys to roll 'em up. Anyway, he just sat there, so I took some of the guys, said come with me—guy with a machine gun, a couple of riflemen, and we went forward and killed a lot of the bad guys, collected up some wounded guys and brought them back. We did this a few times. I put a bandage on what I thought was a big wound. I was bleeding a lot, and it doesn't take very long when you lose a lot of blood to become really ineffective. You get tired, you start to feel sick. Your pulse goes up, blood pressure goes down, temperature rises and you just get flat physically ill. And when you start to feel really sick then you realize you probably are not going to make it.

"I wasn't hit again during the action. I was very lucky not to get hit again. My carbine was useless. I remember in the second contact I had a pistol and tried to shoot it at a guy who was standing about five feet away, and I missed him completely. I'm a terrible pistol shot. Thankfully the guy next to me had an M-60 machine gun on a sling, and he killed the guy. Otherwise I would have been dead, because I unloaded my whole pistol at him and missed. I could have thrown the pistol at him and done more damage. So I wasn't carrying the pistol anymore, I wasn't carrying the carbine, but I had an M-16. I liked the M-16. My recollection is hazy at best, but I ran out of ammo, and picked up an M-60 machine gun because the machine gunner I had brought forward, he was killed too, and I used his machine gun.

"That gun weighs twenty-three pounds without ammo, so it's best to be shot from the ground, but you can carry it if you're strong enough. If it's got a sling that runs over the top, you can sling it over your shoulder like Rambo did, you know? But twenty-three pounds is very heavy—it's twenty percent of my weight. I was carrying it for a while, but I ran out of ammo. It just had a short belt on it. And when that ran out, I used an AK47 for a while because the bad guys had AK47s. There were lots of them lying around. There was no paucity of weapons lying about. There was no problem getting weapons. Bodies were all over the place. Bad guys were wandering around, grabbing weapons from our guys and shooting the wounded.

"But it didn't look like *Ben Hur* or anything like that. I mean, it wasn't masses and masses of people. They were like isolated pockets where stuff was going on and you'd encounter it quite by accident. You'd be going forward, and there'd be a couple of bad guys in a foxhole that they'd dug and you'd be on the side of them, and you ventilated them, you know? You shot them before they even saw you.

"I was extremely low to the ground, as low as I could possibly get, and I would try to go forward to my left to get around to their flank and to the bank. There was some foliage and cover there and so, while it wasn't easy, it was not impossible to get some concealment. There was also a canal bank, so I could scoot along that. But God forbid they should ever get to the back of me by the canal bank. I would have been done for, really."

Sometimes people were with Jacobs during the action, but much of the time he was by himself. Why did he keep doing all this, when he was so badly injured?

"Well, you do what you have to do. There's an anecdote about an old great Hebrew scholar, I think it was Hillel. Some rich guy who's very wealthy, from some small town, goes to the rabbi to consult him. He says, 'Listen, I paid for everything in this very poor town, and now they come to me and say they need more money, and, you know, what am I gonna do? What am I supposed to do?'

And Hillel answered his question with another question. He said, 'If not you, who?' And to the extent I thought about anything during the action that's what I thought about. I mean, if I was not going to do it, who was? I mean, I'm not a particularly brave guy, but who's going to do it? So, you know, you do what you have to do . . . in the end.

"I was trying to get guys who were already wounded back to areas where they could be taken care of. To the extent that I encountered any bad guys, I'd get rid of them, but I wasn't going to be some one-man assault wave, or anything like that. I was just trying to get these wounded guys out of the area. That's all I was thinking about. It wasn't like I weighed the alternate missions and made some rational choice. I just decided it was the easiest thing to do. Initially some of the others helped, but I was so far forward I was the only guy there. I have to tell you, it wasn't necessarily like I said, 'Oh well, I'm going to do this myself.' That's the way it turned out to be geographically and tactically. You know, you always press your luck a little bit, everybody does, so I wound up finding myself a little bit farther forward than I probably should have been. And that's when I encountered some of the VC who were shooting our guys and taking off their weapons. And I encountered some who were shooting at the ranger battalion across the rice paddy.

"It happens, stuff like that happens, and you do what you have to do and you don't think about it. People who do these sorts of things are not tactical geniuses. You follow your heart, you follow your training, and you do what you can do, and often guys don't make it. And there are lots of guys who did similar things and never got cited. There's lot of actions that have taken place where guys have done extraordinary things, where ordinary people have done extraordinary things that never got to the level of being published.

"That's the way combat is. That's ordinary people doing extraordinary things. There are lots of instances in which people have done really quite extraordinary things, and I don't know if they got anything or not." Was Ramirez decorated? "I don't know. He helped get the wounded. I would hope he got something."

Meanwhile Ramirez's lungs were collapsing and he was bleeding heavily into them, with blood streaming from his mouth and nose, but he made it in the end. "I helped him partway. He's a *big* guy. Some of the Vietnamese I carried, some of them I dragged, but at the end of the day what really saved us was that Major Nolan called in a helicopter." Nolan and the sergeant had been in thick of the action as well, Jacobs recalls. By the time he found them, "I was very ill. Of course they were horrified to look at me because I was a mess. They told me to lie down so they could get the doctor. We had a Vietnamese medical doctor to see to me, and he started fooling around, and I think they gave me an IV, then they said, 'Okay, get up,' because we were going to go where the landing zone was for the helicopter . . . and I couldn't get up. I flat couldn't get up [Jacobs laughs]. I was conscious, but I just couldn't get up.

"As I recall we were picked up by Navy gunships, old B Model Hueys from a landing ship located in the Mekong River someplace. I vaguely recall one of them getting shot down, and then Nolan called a helicopter to a different position and it didn't get shot down but it took a lot of fire, and he threw me and Ramirez and a couple of the worst wounded guys into the helicopter, and we took off. Nolan did it. He got us out. They took us to an aid station of U.S. Ninth Medical Battalion." In fact, it was Major Nolan who recommended Jack Jacobs for the Medal of Honor.

A year and a half later, in September 1969, Jacobs, with his wife present, received his citation, along with three other Army guys, Pat Brady, Jim Spraybury, and Bob Patterson.

Jacobs was laid up for a couple of months, sent back to the States, and reassigned to Fort Benning, where he took command of an OCS company. He had been a captain since June of 1968, following his last combat that March. After some months at Benning, he found that some West Pointers in the area were being asked by the Army if they'd like to go to grad school and, typically, Jacobs wanted to know, Could he go too? Get yourself accepted, he was told, so he got himself into Rutgers and over the next two years earned a master's in international relations and two minors,

in comparative politics and constitutional law. He even managed
to get a teaching assistantship, which paid $8,000 a year, doubling
his Army pay.

In all his years in the military, Jacobs said, he never encountered
discrimination because of his faith. "Never," he said. "Not a whim-
per. I'm serious. Never to my face, not at all. Of course it's very difficult to be discriminatory when you got to say yes, sir, no, sir all the
time. I mean I was an airborne officer. But I never did, I'm happy
to say."

By and by, he was asked to go teach at the Military Academy at
West Point, even though he was not a graduate. "But they said they
don't want you until nineteen seventy-three, and it's now seventy-
two." I said, "So what have you got in mind?" They said, "We'll
send you to Korea." I said, "I don't want to go to Korea; Korea's
too cold." They said, "Well, the only other short tour we have is
Vietnam, and we can't send you to Vietnam because you're a Medal
of Honor recipient, and you can't go to Vietnam again. We don't
like you to go to Vietnam again. We'd prefer it if you didn't do it."
Yes, no, yes, no, they finally said, "Okay, you can go but you've got
to go work in the headquarters there." So I said, "Okay. When I got
there, I went to Camp Alpha or whatever the heck it was, I called
the airborne advisory team and an NCO named Sergeant Rick
Biondo happened to answer, and I said, 'Let me talk to the senior
adviser.' Not here. 'Deputy?' Not here. 'Administrative officer?'
Not here. I said, 'Where is everybody?'

" 'Well, they're all up at Quang Tri, trying to take the province
back because the bad guys are attacking the 72d. What can I do for
you, sir?' I said, 'Well, this is Captain Jacobs and I want to get in
the airborne advisory team.' He says, 'I know a guy over in the
orders section.' He came by in a couple of hours with orders,
picked me up and got me my uniform squared away, and we flew
up to Phu Bai, an airport south of where the airborne division was
located. We got picked up by helicopter, flew into Fire Base Sally,
which was the headquarters of the airborne division and the advisory team. They gave me a bunch of ammo, I got onto another hel-

icopter, and we flew into the First Airborne Battalion. This all happened relatively quickly. As we were going in, the helicopter got shot down and landed on a bunch of guys who were already wounded.

"And I said to myself, 'What have I gotten myself into?' I must have a bad case of amnesia. I was in exactly the same position that I had been in five years before." Jacobs laughs low. "You forget, you know. You ask a woman who has just given birth, 'What do you think of that?' 'Oh,' she'll say, 'it's a piece of cake. Let's do it again.'" He laughs again.

"It was a completely different war now because the enemy had tanks, artillery. This is now the Fourth of July, nineteen seventy-two, when I went over for the second time. I came home the second week in January seventy-three, six months later. I was in combat the whole time."

Jacobs viewed combat as "absolutely deplorable," adding, "It's a hideous thing and should be avoided at all costs. But that didn't stop me from engaging in it, and I would do it again if I had to. If I'm not going to do it, who's going to do it? Of course," he said with a laugh, "I'm almost sixty years old and it's too late for me. But if you have to defend liberty, you got to defend liberty. It's as simple as that. But I found the actual combat a horrible, horrible thing, to be acutely avoided. Whatever you can do, it's best to avoid it. I was scared all the time I was in Vietnam. I didn't enjoy it for a second.

"But I was a professional soldier, and you do forget what it's like. Memory makes you forget all about stuff. The job was to fight and to teach people to fight, and so that's what I did. I'm an extremist. So if I do something, I usually do it all. I don't do half of it and then stop. That's the kind of person I am. When I became a civilian, I jumped into it. I became an investment banker, became a managing director of Banker's Trust, I mean I don't do things half-assed, pardon my French."

Did he ever question his own acumen? "I still wonder about it, in retrospect, all the time. I'm not a very bright person, in the end."

He made it home and went on to teach for more than three years at West Point. "So I'd been through all three ways you commission people: I went through ROTC, I commanded an OCS company, and I taught at West Point. We had a great department, I mean really classy people, excluding me, of course." He taught international relations and comparative political systems, mainly to first-classmen (seniors).

He and his wife divorced after twelve years of marriage. Jacobs was single for a few years before remarrying. He and his second wife, Sue, have been together twenty-three years. They have a son, Zach, eighteen. Heather, from his first marriage, is thirty-seven, and her brother David is thirty-four.

As for the impact of the Medal on his life, Jacobs says, "It has made me more aware of a number of things. First of all, how important each person's contribution is to society and his fellow man. It's something you know about, but you don't think about it. I mean, I certainly didn't think about it until after this action, and now it's something I think about all the time. Also, there is the perception that I am representative of other people. I'm also representative of an ideal, and it's very important that I continue to be true to that ideal. I have to assume everybody is looking at me, even though they're not. I have to be true to myself and true to what I think are ideal principles."

What does he consider ideal principles?

"I wouldn't be able to enumerate them. It's sort of like the guy said, Justice Potter Stewart, when presented with the opportunity to rule on whether something was obscene or not, he said, I don't have to tell you what it is; I'll know it when I see it. And I think it's a lot like that in combat. If you were to ask somebody before he went in, 'Are you going to be able to acquit yourself honorably?' he'll say, 'Yes'—without knowing what that circumstance will be."

SIXTEEN

Nicky Daniel Bacon

Staff Sergeant, U.S. Army
Tam Ky, Vietnam
August 26, 1968

*"I got my boot heel shot off, I got holes in my canteens, I got my rifle grip
shot up, I got shrapnel holes in my camouflage covers, and bullets in
my pot. A bullet creased the edge of it, tore the lining off.
All that stuff, and I suffered a major explosion that everybody seen,
blowed me in. Actually it probably saved my life. They was tearing
me up with machine-gun fire, and I just got blowed into a hole.
They thought I was dead. They just stopped firing at me."*

Nicky Bacon, president of the Congressional Medal of Honor Society from 2002 through 2004, with General H. Norman Schwarzkopf, U.S. Army Retired, at the Patriots Award dinner at the annual meeting of the society, held in Shreveport, Louisiana, September 2002. Schwarzkopf received the award, given annually by the society.

by Robert M. Bush, CMOHS photographer

A mustachioed First Sergeant Bacon,
pictured just before his retirement in 1984.

IT WAS the first morning session of the annual meeting of the Congressional Medal of Honor Society in September 2002 and its president, Nicky Bacon, was eager to call the meeting to order because the secretary for Veterans Affairs, Anthony J. Principi, was expected shortly, and he was on a tight schedule. But there was no flag to pledge allegiance to. The meeting could not start without the pledge. So Bacon looked around the big hall at Harrah's Hotel Casino in Shreveport, Louisiana, then called four women in blouses variously designed with the American flag to come forward. He stood them in front of the podium, joined the audience in reciting the pledge, and the meeting went forward.

Nick Bacon was born November 25, 1945, into a farm family in Caraway, Arkansas. "When I was six, we lost the farm. Cotton prices fell, the whole nine yards. It happened all over Arkansas, Oklahoma, lots of places. It was kind of like the old stories back in the 1930s, *The Grapes of Wrath*, so we moved to Arizona. I remember when we first got there it was very difficult, and it wasn't long after that my dad got very sick with polio. I remember working a lot, and I remember my mother working hard all the time. I had five sisters and two brothers, and my mother took care of all those kids, did the washing and ironing and would work in the fields or do anything else to help support and maintain us kids. My dad was in the hospital eighteen months. I don't know how they paid for it. There was no help with money, no help with rent or anything. As kids we learned to live like that. We lived in a little town real close to Phoenix, called Peoria. Arizona at that time was farmland. You could get in the air and fly over the valley and as far as the eye could see it was just farms. Now you see houses instead, and golf courses.

"I dropped out of high school after ninth grade and went to work—for seventy-five cents an hour. I worked on a farm for a couple of years, bucking bales, driving Farmall tractors, irrigating—everything you have to do on a farm in Arizona, which doesn't have rain. We irrigated everything and raised produce, lettuce, onions, cotton. It's not hard on your back if you keep your tractor job. You want to keep your tractor job. I hated picking cotton and that other stuff. I've done my share of it. And I'll guarantee you one thing: I've never, ever went back to it once I was old enough to hold a man's job. I'll Sheetrock, I'll do concrete work, I'll do a lot of heavy things. But I'm not picking no damn cotton.

"I went in the Army when I was seventeen, just to get the hell out of Dodge. My mother's brother was wounded in Europe in World War II. He was always a hero to me, always red, white, and blue. His name was Herschel Meadows but we called him Uncle Peewee. He was tiny but he was a man. He was a mean little sumbitch, tougher'n nails. He wouldn't tell you a whole lot about what he did. He would tell you what other people did. We'd go, 'How'd you get shot, Uncle Peewee?' And he'd say, 'Well, I was in the wrong place at the wrong time.'

"He encouraged me a great deal. He was able to use his GI Bill to go to school. He went to Los Angeles and was making good money, so he was the example to live by: Go in the military, serve your country. You're supposed to do that. It was only right anyway. You don't have a good job right now, so you need to go in the military and get your education. My mother had to sign, but I lied. I signed the papers for her. I took them home, didn't tell her until after I turned them back in. I just told her I was going to enlist. She asked me, 'How can you do that? You're not old enough.' And I said, 'Well, I just did.' And that was that.

"I joined the Army September tenth, nineteen sixty-three, went to eight weeks of basic at Ford Ord, California, then eight weeks of training for a heavy-weapons infantry platoon. I did have a choice. I went into heavy weapons because I figured with them you wouldn't have to walk very much, wouldn't have to carry stuff. I went to Fort Polk, Louisiana, for BUT, Basic Unit Training. We did a lot better, longer training in those days than they do today. We learned how to function as a unit. After that I went to the Eighth Infantry Division in Wurms, Germany, early summer of 1964. The whole time we were out constantly on freezing-cold exercises in the mountains, Graffenwehr and Baumholder, all those places that a soldier hates with a passion. Germany in the wrong places is a very very cold country. The wind blows, the snow falls, it's cold. We slept in the same kind of foxholes in the same snow the GIs slept in during World War II. Only difference was we were walking in their footsteps in the freezing weather without the real live ammunition coming back at us. I hate cold weather. I made about eighty-three dollars a month, sent half of it home. I was there a year and a half, came home Christmas of nineteen sixty-five because we received orders for Vietnam.

"Then early January nineteen sixty-six, my friend Ronnie Baker and I were in-country, Vietnam. He came from my hometown, went with me to basic, heavy-weapons training, Germany, Vietnam, and we were assigned to the same outfit for one year. We both survived, came back, then he went back with another unit and I went back with Americal Division. This guy got wounded seven times on different occasions with the Fifth Mac. He's got just loads of Purple Hearts.

"People get killed. That's how come they sent replacements over there. First tour we were replacements. They sent us to Long Binh, O Camp Alpha I think they called it. We were supposed to be assigned to the First Cav Division and instead they tore up our orders. We were screaming that we're heavy-weapons infantry, and they made us overnight into infantry. We were assigned to the old Second 16th Ranger Recon Platoon, so we never got to use our great talents and skills in heavy weapons. We became grunts overnight.

"The Second 16th was nothing but a light infantry unit. They were still called rangers. Our base camp was at the edge of Binh Hoa, big enough for only one company at a time. From there we went all over, to the south, all over the Central Highlands, the old plantations. We even went over into Cambodia when we weren't supposed to be there. When you came back they would take the map away from you and you would get dots on your map showing where you'd "really" been.

"We went down to the Mekong Delta a couple of times. I couldn't stand it down there. From our base we went down through a dry area, then did a sweep across this muddy swampy area. We hadn't had any resistance. We figured there was nothing there. We were just on a sweep. We were waiting for the boats from the Mobile River- ine Force to extract us, but before the boats got there I guess the Vietcong thought we were pushing them to the river. They defended themselves with hand grenades so we ended up in this big fight with grenades, and that was the biggest mess I ever got into in the Delta.

"We were crawling in the mud, rolling in the mud while we waited for the boats to get us out of there. We killed a lot of them [Vietcong], but you'd get so muddy. They would just wobble up in that mud and grass and you couldn't find them. If you didn't hit them with a rifle round, you couldn't kill them. Sometimes they'd find a rock and throw it, see if you moved. And if you moved, the next throw would be a real hand grenade and pretty soon you'd be doing the same tricks as them. You'd be throwing handfuls of mud to see if you could get anybody to move. We were finding each other by noise. You couldn't show yourself. They'd put one right on you. Water don't bother grenades. That was the craziest mess. I've been in lots of firefights, I've been in lots of ambushes, I've watched lots of people get blowed up on booby traps, but I have never been in anything that I hated worse, or felt so helpless, as I did in that mud. You can't do a damn thing in the mud.

"To give you an idea of the Delta, helicopters couldn't land for your wounded. You had to low-crawl with them, and pull them up and the helicopter door gunners would reach down, and you had to feed the bodies up because you couldn't stand up. You'd sink. There were no dikes. We were right next to the river, and it was just that flat, messy piece of shit.

"My first tour we saw a lot of combat. The first time I got shot at was a real weird scenario because I was pulling point. I had never seen any combat, and I walked out into this very small clearing, sur- rounded by jungle and everything, and I see two dinks eating. One's got a weapon against a tree and one's sling-arms, with his weapon slung on his back. Well, I've got a machete in my right hand and I've got my weapon slung behind me, too. I don't remember much about it. All I know is, I dropped the machete and I swung the gun around, I suppose, I don't really remember. All I remember is, I was out of ammunition. I had gone through a twenty-round clip just as fast as I could. The adrenaline was stomping, and I'm just shooting the M-16.

"It was a piece-of-shit weapon back then too. It jammed a lot and the bolt was no good. But thank God that time it didn't jam. A lot of times in combat that original bolt would jam and you had to get a ramming rod and drive the bolt back down with a bullet that was stuck in the barrel. The rejection mechanism on the bolt would just miss it. This is good for the record because we went from a great weapon, the M-14, to the Mattel Shooting Toy; that's what we called it.

"They worked out all the problems and it's obviously a good weapon now, but I remember being in a firefight, getting the shit kicked out of us, and people hollering, 'Throw me a cleaning rod! Throw me a cleaning rod!' With the friggin' weapons jamming all the time, we had more cleaning rods than we did rifles. I had a lot of personal hangups with the M-16 at first but, after they worked it out and I got used to it, I wouldn't carry anything else because, hell, you'd carry three hundred rounds of that little 5.56 shell. The M-14 was a 7.62, a big old long heavy round. We carried the same ammo pouches for both but you could get way more ammunition in them with the M-16. So you never ran out. You could always have two magazines taped together in your weapon back to back, then you had five in each ammo pouch, carrying two ammo pouches. You had twelve magazines.

"When we had the old weapons back in World War II, a lot of times people would get out there and get in a firefight and run out of ammunition. I never ran out of ammunition. I have fought all night. You would blow through your first, blow the shit out of your basic load, trying to kill everybody, but when you're reloading, then you're thinking, I better start conserving.

"So I saw the two VC, the next thing I knew my clip was empty and these two guys were dusted. That was my indoctrination to killing the enemy. I didn't feel anything about it. Still don't. Really, I've never, ever thought anything about killing enemy. I've always looked at 'em as, they were the enemy. I had compassion for the people, the women and children. I liked the Vietnamese people. I've been over there since. I don't have any hatred. The war was never personal with me. It absolutely was a game of survival. To me, it was always a game of survival, and I've never given it any thought other than that.

"I thought about getting killed myself, at first, but a person gets calloused to that. You know, after a while you're calloused and you kind of accept the fact that there's a pretty good chance you ain't gonna make it out of here: You're an infantryman. But you also got a good chance of leaving wounded. We called that Early Out.

"You're kind of worried the first two months, and the last two months. In between, you didn't really give a shit. And I wasn't married. I pitied those who were because they had a lot more to worry about, kids and a wife. And I always figured, Hell, who's going to miss me for very long? You know your family loves you but, truly, you just don't have a whole lot to worry about.

"I read something one time that says something like, 'War is a young man's game.' As you get older, you would like to think of yourself as tough and that you could still strap it all on and head for the boonies, but you can't do that. Wars are fought by young men. Strong, brave young men. I can look at people, my friends, like Robert Howard [Medal recipient], and I know what a man he was. Hell, I was in great shape. I was a great jungle warrior. Mike Thornton [another recipient]. Mike's still a rough, tough old fart, but I tell you, he couldn't hump the boonies very long today. None of us can. It's a young man's game, and I look at them and sometimes I envy them because I was never prouder, I was never in better shape, I was never more sure that I stood for something in my life than I was when I wore the uniform. When I retired, I couldn't replace that, and I had a very rough time adjusting.

"After my first tour I went to Hawaii and trained troops with the 11th Light Infantry Brigade for combat in Vietnam. I was a buck sergeant, and I helped train the troops there, and I rotated back to Vietnam with them. I didn't have to. I didn't have to go, but I went back with them because the company commander was a great man. He's still alive today, Captain Bill Treadwell. We called him Big T. He wanted me to go back with him. He was 'prior,' he was a veteran. The battalion commander was a veteran, there was a couple more veterans there, and that was it, for the whole battalion. The rest, all those kids, were newbies, shake and bakes. They kind of made you feel guilty. You know, you do all that training and then let them go die, because they don't have proper leadership. So I volunteered to go back with them. January of nineteen sixty-seven I went back. This was the 11th Light Infantry Brigade. I was a squad leader. The 196th was already over there and the 198th went over before we did. We went over and then they activated the colors for the American. We became the American Division.

"Big T and I had a special bond, and I was only a buck sergeant. He was a great infantry officer: He was tough, he was demanding, but he never asked the troops to do anything he wouldn't do. He would put as much weight on his back as anybody did, and he was a big man. Everybody'd get down to one hundred and forty, one hundred and forty-five pounds in the jungle. Real big people would get to one hundred and fifty, one hundred and fifty-five. Big T held a lot of weight. I don't mean fat. He had big bones and, sweat—I've seen him soaking wet every day. Never stop, never look back, never say nothing discouraging. Never cuss command, never did any of that stuff. Just humped, and took care of his men. He'd pick up a rucksack and say, 'Come on, son.' The guy was phenomenal in the jungle. I figured, well, if he's that good here in Hawaii, and if I'm going to have to go back to Vietnam anyway, six months or a year from now, I'd just as soon go with Big T. If I'd waited, I wouldn't have had a choice. There's a lot of units you want to go with, and a lot you don't. So I said, Okay, I'll go.

"I guess I went back over August or September of nineteen sixty-seven. By the time of the Tam Ky action, on August twenty-sixth, nineteen sixty-eight, for which I received the Medal, I'd had so many battles under me and firefights, I had everything there is to have. I have been in the Highlands, I have been to the DMZ, I have been a sniper on a quick kill team.

"Did I enjoy combat? Yeah. I enjoyed the game. It's not something you would just dream up to do every day. Honestly, I was good at it. It's the simple things that make you good. It's not that you can shoot better than anybody, or run faster than anybody. Your senses are very very sharp. You learn to cook and eat what's out there. You learn where to find water. It is the skills and senses that you develop in combat that make the difference. For example, you know where not to walk, simple as that. If it's too easy, don't do it. There's going to be something you're going to step on, and somebody's going to get blown to hell. If it looks too easy, it is.

"Don't let nobody smoke around you anywhere when you're in a dense area. If you want to smoke out in a rice paddy and it's the middle of the day, hell, they can see you anyway. But if you're in the jungle, and you're trying to be quiet, don't ever light a cigarette. The smell is just as important as the visual. Don't leave anything behind that they can use; use everything you can that they leave behind. You just develop skills and senses. It is a lot of common sense, but it's common sense that's based on learning.

"You teach the simple things. You teach the radio operator: One, don't let that antenna stick up above you. Tie that son of a bitch down to the radio. Put your poncho over the top of it, so it doesn't look like a radio. Don't ever come running to me with a handset in your hand. You get down somewhere and you pass the word that I got a call on the radio. Don't run behind my ass. Don't ever holler Medic and call him out into the open, or I'll shoot you myself.

"There's one hundred thousand ways to make booby traps and killing devices. You better learn to recognize them because, if you don't, you're going to die. Bouncing Bettys, you know, they'll take you off at the waist. You're gonna be a double amputee.

"Never put a new man on the point. You see that on television a lot. But point men are very skilled. If you had a good point man, he liked it. He didn't want somebody else getting him killed. Because, normally, if you're on point, you don't die. It's the third or fourth man that gets nailed. Even with a booby trap. You hit a booby trap and you've now made three or four steps forward and, even with a grenade you've got four seconds, and if you're moving, you go Oops, and keep walking. You got four seconds, and the grenade takes out the third or fourth man.

"And you don't want a dumb ass on your best weapon, like the M-60 machine gun. You want somebody that's strong enough to handle the gun, somebody that's good enough and brave enough to stay with the gun, because it will draw fire. And you want to have two good ammo carriers with him. Because, with a machine gun, its rapid rate of fire can be a lifesaver. It's big enough to do some damage. Another thing you want is a blooper gunner, an M-79 grenade launcher, who can hit things without sights and going through all that phony shit. A good gunner doesn't have to run the sights out. You got to know who your skilled people are, and how to use them. And you know how to protect them. You teach the simple things.

"You develop skills to stay alive, and you keep your people alive with those same skills. They got all these modern devices now, direction finders and all, but in the jungle in those days you had to be very very good with a compass and a map. Every tree looks the same, especially under a triple canopy. You better know how to shoot the compass from one tree to another, you better know how to crawl around it and start at the same spot and not lose a degree here and a degree there because, at the end of the day, you lost a lot of degrees. And as soon as you come out of that shit, you hope you know where you're at, because you're gonna call in artillery and you're gonna need to know.

"And all the time you're counting paces, so you know how far you've come. I'm gonna have two counters going. Even if you're crawling, you're counting paces. And if you're smart you'll carry a little rope, or string, and tie knots in it. Every time you go one hundred meters, you tie a knot. That's how you do it when you can't see nothing.

"I've got one Purple Heart, and I guess I could have had three

or four. It's my fault but the infantry didn't give out Purple Hearts
for little bitty stuff, and you wouldn't take it anyway. I suffered a
concussion in the battle of Tam Ky. I was bleeding from the ears
and nose, had shellshock. I didn't take anything for that.

"General Westmoreland was at the White House for my Medal
ceremony, and he came in before the President. My family was
there, and he came over and introduced himself and then came
back to me and said, 'Why didn't you get a Purple Heart for that
action?' He had talked to my battalion commander, the company
commander, the troop commander. He had eyes that could stare
through you and he just kept looking at me and he says, 'I can't
believe this shit. I can't believe you went through all that without
getting hit.' I said, 'Sir, as far as I know, with the exception of this
concussion, I did not get hit with a bullet.'

"I got my boot heel shot off, I got holes in my canteens, I got my
rifle grip shot up, I got shrapnel holes in my camouflage covers, and
bullets in my pot. A bullet creased the edge of it, tore the lining off.
All that stuff, and I suffered a major explosion that everybody seen,
blowed me in. Actually, it probably saved my life. They was tearing
me up with machine-gun fire, and I just got blowed into a hole.
They thought I was dead. They just stopped firing at me. They
shifted their fire.

"It was like somebody hit me with a ball bat. It knocked all the
breath and everything out of me. I think I was conscious. I realized
I was hit, and I thought my stomach had been blowed out. You
know what people hate to think about is a belly wound. And I
thought perhaps I had a belly wound because I couldn't feel anything, couldn't breathe. Then I began to get little short breaths and,
as it eased up a little, I had the guts to look at my toes, to see if I
could still move my toes. It was a daring thing to do, because there
might not be anything there. But I was able to move my feet around,
and I looked and they were functional and, to my amazement, there
wasn't blood everywhere.

"If there was a reason I survived, I think it was the good Lord. I
was praying like hell. I was praying like hell when I got blowed in

there. I couldn't make my legs work to come out of there. I don't mean physically. I mean, they didn't want to come out of that hole. I was just praying that God would give me the courage to get everything functioning—because I didn't want to. You know, you don't want to let fear suppress you. So I started praying. God, this looks like the end of this shit, but don't let me die like this. Let me go out there. Let me die like a man. And when I come out of that hole, I come out, not like John Wayne, but I damn sure was ready to do battle. And I went out there, and nothing went wrong again. I was able to stay with it.

"The stupid sonsabitches tried to charge us once, and I was down in one of their positions, so I shot the shit out of them. I had somebody else's M-16. Mine had been shot up.

"The action started that day when they suckered us in. We had gone in to assist this armor unit, the First Cav. We were not a full company [144] but we were a company. We helicoptered in and then rode on the tanks and half-tracks into a valley where these other troops had been hit. I believe it was Bravo Troop. They had suffered a lot of casualties.

"It was a big hilly area west of Tam Ky. I called them plateaus, farm rows with hedges that went up like pyramids. Every one had a hedgerow on the end and around it, and inside was the field. Every one of them was camouflaged. The enemy were dug in while we were all out in the open. They had every damn thing; they had rockets, they had RPGs [rocket propelled grenades], they had machine guns camouflaged and riflemen in each of these plateau areas. They had one 55 mm there, a big gun, and that's the one I knocked out with grenades later on.

"They were sniping at us as we were going in, and so everyone wanted to get off the armor and tracks and get down, get moving. We did that, and we got to the first hedge area. The tanks had to back off because they were getting hit by RPGs. We asked them [the artillery in the rear] to fire over us but because of the angle they couldn't fire at our level. They were able to fire at the next areas but they were just shooting wildly. They didn't know who they were firing at.

"We were spread out horizontally. I have one squad at this time, on the far right, moving with the platoon. The platoon leader gets forward with one of the squads, and he gets wounded. Some other people go down also. We received a lot of fire as we went to assist him, and we got pinned. That's when I was able to knock out one machine-gun position. The lieutenant is wounded and we have a couple of others dropped, but I can't get these people out yet.

"That's when I was able to knock this machine gun out with hand grenades. I just charged across and got into the hedgerow, stayed very low and threw a hand grenade and wiped them out. Just two people, but the bunker was full of RPGs. You ought to have seen the explosion. The whole fucking thing went up. They were standing on RPGs. So was the other one I took out. They were all fixed to bring in the tanks and hit them with the RPGs. They didn't expect us. They probably would have suckered the tanks and, as they moved up, the enemy would have stayed down and then they would have had 'em on all four sides. That's what they intended to do. It turned out to be a reinforced regiment of NVA, North Vietnamese army regulars, hundreds of them, in uniform. We were only a company. Odds like that you can have.

"The company commander, Treadwell, is pinned down over on the left. He was isolated. I got to him once and I was glad to get the fuck away from Treadwell and his element because they were catching shit. How they survived I don't know. I'd rather be on the move than sitting there pinned down like that.

"Back at our position on the right, another lieutenant came over to assist us. He tries to flank over and I holler at him, 'Don't do it!' because I tried that already. He gets zapped. I tell his men to stay back. Then this other guy does the same thing, but there wasn't going to be any flanking because the enemy were well fortified and they can protect each other. But that's how I ended up with all three platoons.

"There was another enemy position. This guy, I could see him, he had a different kind of hole, like an old machine-gun position that the Germans used. He had cut a hole, but he had left a pillar in the center. He would fire from the front, you'd throw a grenade and he'd run back around behind the pillar. Then he'd come right back around and start firing again. That SOB would put shit on us. I think he killed both the lieutenants. He was a brave little son of a bitch. I must have killed one of them because his was the only helmet I could still see in the foxhole. He was a sneaky son of a bitch, the hardest son of a bitch you ever saw to try to kill. I could see him moving and every time you'd get to where you were close enough to get at him, they would start wasting your ass from the flanks. I bounced rounds off his freaking helmet for an hour.

"I was lucky they didn't catch me the first time when I hit the bunker. So when I got back in the second time, I already knew I could get there. It's blown up and there ain't nothing there. I jumped in that hole and waited and I finally was able to crawl down the hedgerow and get close enough that I could blow his ass off. I got him with two grenades.

"The problem now was getting the platoon leader and the wounded people out of here. I told the tanks we had to have help and they finally got one tank up to us. I pulled him by this tree and I got up on the tank, and I would tell him where I thought these positions were, and what I wanted him to do was pull around, expose himself, dangerous as it was, and return fire so we could get to the wounded. We'd rehearse it: I'd say, 'At the bottom of that tree, about fifty yards right of there, fire your shotgun round and keep your .50 caliber machine guns plastered on them and back out while you're firing.' Then I would jump off the tank. I had guys that would run up there, and we would pull out a body or two. We'd carry as many as we could, but you didn't last long. This is all happening in seconds. The tank is taking rounds, shit is bouncing off him, and he's taking hits on purpose. He comes out and then we go on the other side of the tree and do the same thing, try to take out other targets. We still got other wounded to get out.

"We did this to get the wounded out so we could separate ourselves from the enemy and get some damn bombers in. I wanted to waste them with napalm, and they knew that. That's why they were trying to stay in close contact with us. There was a recoilless, a 55 mm antitank weapon that was causing a lot of damage. We had knocked out some of these positions and we had a hole up in there. The guys on the gun were easy to get to because we had knocked out these other two positions. When I say easy to get to, well, they were firing at my ass but nothing like it was before. It was set up on the ground. It had a big tripod that sat on the ground. I think they were moving it and firing it and moving it and firing it. All I know is they all had ahold of the weapon. I was firing on them when I went in there. I charged across there, bullets blazing, grenades ready. It was the dumb way to do it, but it seemed like the only one way, and we had to get those guys because they had the range on the tanks.

"After we got our wounded out far enough to where we could get jets in, we brought jets right down on their ass. We brought the F-100s in and everything else that would fly, anything that had napalm. They came in, I mean, right on top. You know how smooth they look coming in. You don't hear nothing. They're just moving. You look up and the eggs look like they're dropping in your pockets. They just go right over you, and you've got to get down because they were smoking them right on top of us. I was looking right up their exhaust when they would charge out, hit that afterburner and pull out. I swear I saw people blown in the air with napalm that day. I saw them go higher than napalm fire, and the planes just kept putting it on them. When the jets got through we were getting more organized, and we got our gunships in and we counterattacked what was left. But the only thing that was left was either smoking or running. If they were running, we were shooting.

"So we killed everybody we saw. I don't know how anybody ever counted them because we had to move out that night. We stacked weapons; there were weapons everywhere. It was getting dark and we had to pull out. We couldn't stay there that night. We had to set up somewhere else that we could secure. We had to get the tanks and tracks out of there and set up a perimeter. This was their turf. You can't trust those guys. Don't never bivouac in their area.

"I still don't know how many bodies we left there. There were bodies everywhere. They say we killed seven hundred and sixty of them by the end of the day with the artillery and the air and everything. I don't know. I heard rumors there were five hundred and fifty.

"As for our casualties, you always get the words *heavy*, *moderate*, or *light*. Now, normally, if you're a platoon and you get "heavy" casualties, the company you're part of gets "moderate" casualties. If you're a company and you get hit pretty bad, the battalion gets "moderate" casualties. You can soak it up with numbers. We suffered a lot of casualties but thank God for the helicopters. A lot of those guys are alive because of them. We have on that Wall [the Vietnam Veterans Memorial in Washington, D.C.] fifty-eight thousand people dead, killed as a result of Vietnam. Three hundred thousand wounded. Just think how big that Wall would be if we hadn't had the helicopter and medical technology.

"I don't know how many wounded we had. We had a track set up. That thing was loaded and reloaded I don't know how many times. It was loaded when I came back to put the lieutenant in there.

"That's a story in itself, because he's alive today. He was named Griffith, but I didn't know who he was. I always called him LT. Well, about two years ago this general called; he was the deputy commander of the Health Service Command in San Antonio. He wanted to have lunch with me.

"He told my secretary he used to be my platoon leader. Well, I knew my platoon leaders from my first tour. One was killed. I knew where the other one was at. And I had one lieutenant on my second tour who went over with me. I know I put him on a track and he can't be alive because he was shot right through the fuckin' neck and he was bleeding so bad I couldn't even stop it. I told him he was going to be fine. His eyes were that big around. And there were a lot of wounded in there. That damn track was getting shot up as well.

"So I said, 'Who is this lying son of a bitch?' I told my secretary, 'You bring him over. I want to have lunch with him. I'm going to find out who this lying general is, or even if he's really even a general.'

"Well, sure enough, he had survived. They had throwed him in a dead pile at one of the two hospitals. And two medics came out—this is the general's story—smoking cigarettes. And I think he said he could bat his eyes, or move his finger, I can't remember which. But one of those medics saw it, said, 'Hell, we got a live one here,' and they hauled him back in, were able to stabilize him, then sent him to Japan. He was there for ages. His spine had been almost completely severed and they had miraculously been able to tend it, and it grew back, however this was done.

"When he got discharged from the hospital, they made him a captain and sent him to Fort Benning, Georgia. Obviously he didn't want no more infantry, so he put in for medical school, never expecting to get it. But the army approved it, and he became a doctor. Then a surgeon. Then a frigging general. I thought he was dead all these years. Then one day he was speaking to a class of medics, a new class, a graduating class, and he told them he owed everything in his life to two people.

"One was his father, and he talked about how his father had brought him up, and everything. The other was this young staff sergeant that pulled him off the battlefield in Vietnam. He told them who it was, and said he must have got killed, or got out of the service and went somewhere. He thought he was from Arkansas.

"And somebody pipes up and says, 'Well, I know where he's at. Nick Bacon's the director of Veterans Affairs here.'

"And that's how the general found me. He came and had lunch with me, two years ago, or three. Normally, when I used to tell this story, I'd say he was killed and the other two were killed. But he's not dead. His name is Griffith. So, you see, God has a purpose for everybody. If he leaves you alive, that means he's still got something for you to do.

"I received the Medal of Honor in the White House from President Nixon on November twenty-fourth, nineteen sixty-nine, with my family there. My father came to Washington. He was very very ill by this time, and he was just overwhelmed by everything, actually. The whole family was. They sure didn't understand a great deal about it at the time. Country people, you know, but Dad was very proud, Mom was very proud, and so were my brothers and sisters. We were given the total VIP treatment, wined and dined, the nicest hotel, chauffeured limousine. It was big stuff. Decidedly big stuff.

"I missed Vietnam, but not exactly right after I left. A while later I really missed it. You know, playing fucking war games really gets to be a bore, with guys who have never been there. You have officers that are playing conventional games, and you're still fighting in Vietnam. They're probably right because, you know, we were looking at the Soviet Union then. There's China, there's Korea, and everything else. But you get all pissed off because the real war's over there, and that's where everybody's getting killed. And you're training conventional war. It used to piss me off bad."

Bacon got married a few days before he went to Washington to receive the Medal. He and his wife had two children and divorced after eight years. Sometime afterward he met his second wife, Tamera, who was in the military in Germany, and they wed in 1981. "We have three boys; one's in college. He's also in the National Guard. He'll be twenty in January. The others are fifteen and nine.

"I went into the Military Police after Vietnam. The infantry was boring." Later on, Bacon went into the recruiting command.

"There's good things and bad things happen to the Medal of Honor in the military. There's a lot of professional jealousy, especially with young officers. You know, you go out with a general's party tonight, and the lieutenant and the captain weren't invited, and tomorrow you got to live with them. There's a lot of things like that."

"I retired from the Army in 1984, after twenty-one years. I was promoted to sergeant major. I had got my GED, my high-school general equivalency diploma, in Germany when I was with the Eighth Division. They forced you to get the GED. Every time I had a chance I'd take a college course. That's how I ended up getting a formal education. You don't stay in the Army and make E-7, -8 and -9 unless you have all the skills. You have to have top-notch efficiency reports. There is no such thing as a mediocre efficiency report for officers in the senior enlisted."

Following retirement, Bacon worked as a Veterans Administration counselor in Arizona for a year and a half, then resigned to help John McCain run for the Senate. Later he was a city manager in Surprise, Arizona, for three years, then moved back to Arkansas. When Bill Clinton was elected President in 1992, he took the state director of Veterans Affairs to Washington, and Bacon was appointed in his place. He has held the position ever since.

"If you don't want to die of boredom, you got to stay creative. Don't let the grass grow under your feet. When you get to sixty, you figure you got ten or fifteen good years left. That's what I think now. If you're not having fun, if you're not doing what you wanna do, you're backing up. 'Cause you're running out of time.

"What do Medal of Honor recipients have in common? Integrity is one thing. They are a different breed, I will say that. Most of us are very humble. I like to think of myself as humble. I wouldn't want to be anything else. You'll find most of them have humility, which is an ingredient of greatness, I think. But there's some things you can't explain in words: There's a nobleness you see about them. You see it some in the military, and in professional areas. You know it when you see it. You don't always detect it, at first.

"There is a certain something that sets them apart, even if they are a country boy with little or no formal education. It's not that they're eloquent speakers; that's not it. Something comes out in them when they do things. They would probably be willing to die for certain things and to save others. And it's not because they wanted to be known as real brave or anything. It's something that they just do. You do it, and sometimes you think that it's over. There's nothing that's gonna change that, and so you're gonna do the best you can and, as you say *adiós* to this old world, you're gonna do it with as much honor as you can. I imagine there's a lot of POWs we'll never know about who died that way."

SEVENTEEN

Thomas Kelley

Lieutenant, Mobile Riverine Force, U.S. Navy
Mekong Delta, Vietnam
June 15, 1969

"I kept hearing them saying, 'He's dead, he's dead,'
and I'm saying, 'I'm not! I'm not!'"

Photo by Kristian Kozlowski

Thomas Kelley, commissioner of
Veterans' Services for the Commonwealth of Massachusetts, at
the age of sixty-three in fall 2002 at
his office in downtown Boston.

Lieutenant Thomas Kelley of the Mobile Riverine Force receives the Medal of Honor from
President Richard M. Nixon in May 1970,
nearly a year after he narrowly escaped death in
the Mekong Delta of South Vietnam.

272

THE DAY AFTER three Army Green Berets had been killed by an errant American bomb in Afghanistan, I met with Thomas Kelley in his office in downtown Boston, early on the morning of December 6, 2001. As commissioner of Veterans' Services for the Commonwealth of Massachusetts, Kelley was concerned about making contact with the family of one of the three slain soldiers, Sergeant 1st Class Daniel Henry Petihory of Cheshire, Massachusetts. "The main responsibility in taking care of him rightly belongs to the Army but we have some state programs to help his family, so we're trying to put that together for them this morning without intruding on them. You know what I mean?"

Kelley wasn't dead, but he should have been. His right eye was hanging from its socket, and a chunk of his skull was crushed. He had wounds in his upper body, hands, and arm and he had been knocked off his coxswain's seat down onto the floor of his boat. He was bleeding so profusely his crewmen thought he was gone. Instead he got up and started giving orders.

Ten months earlier, in 1968, Kelley had volunteered to go to Vietnam "because it seemed the right thing to do." He grew up in Boston, where he attended a Jesuit high school. After majoring in economics at Holy Cross in Worcester, Massachusetts, he joined the Navy, following two college pals, "basically on a whim," he said. "It was nothing patriotic, nothing noble. It was just something to do." He went to OCS in Newport, Rhode Island. It took four months to get through and then for the next eight years or so he served on a series of ships, rising from ensign to second lieutenant and then to lieutenant. "I volunteered to go to Vietnam because it was a cause which kind of grabbed my attention. I thought it was a pretty good cause. I wanted to go over there and do my business for my country. By that time I had noble plans and I wasn't just doing it on a whim. It seemed like the right thing to do.

"I went over because I firmly believed that country over there was fighting for democracy and we were there to help them maintain democracy, and I went over there with that in mind, and while I was there you just go day to day and you try to stay alive for that day. You do your job and get yourself and your men home safely and at the end of the year you go home, and you don't start to think about the big picture or whether it was a noble cause or whether we should have been there or not.

"Since then I have done an awful lot of reading, and I learned a lot of the background about why we were there and why we were there so long, but this was many years after the fact. While we were there I never had any questions about that. When you're fighting a war, you don't stop to think about that.

"I was there with the joint Army-Navy Mobile Riverine Force, which operated from nineteen sixty-seven through nineteen seventy on the Mekong Delta in the China Sea about forty-five miles from Saigon, and my job was to move Army troops basically up and down rivers and canals for their missions of seeking out and engaging the enemy. They used to ride on our boats because it was the Recon Delta area of Vietnam, very marshy and watery living. And going by boat was the most expedient way to get in there and get out of there. You remember the old boats they used to take troops ashore at Normandy? LCM, launching craft mechanized or something? They had bow ramps that would go down so troops could jump off into the water and wade ashore. Their capacity was roughly thirty men.

"We'd load up a company of soldiers or a platoon and take them up and down the rivers, drop them off, pick them up, provide fire support for them while they were ashore—that type of thing. They actually lived on a barracks ship which was anchored out in one of the rivers. We lived there with them. Alongside the barracks ship were these pontoons where our boats tied up, and so the soldiers would just climb over these pontoons and onto the boats and we'd take off. They were from the U.S. Ninth Infantry Division.

"There were probably three or four barracks ships, not all in the same place. They'd split up and go wherever the action was. There were about three hundred on a ship. They'd sleep, eat, and shower there, but they'd go out for three or four days at time. Then they'd come back, stay on the ship a few days, and rest up. I eventually commanded a group of about twenty-five of these LCMs, all run by the Navy. Each boat had a crew of four or five. The *Monitor* had the most firepower. [It carried a 40 mm cannon, two 20 mm cannons, a .50 caliber machine gun and grenade launcher, plus small arms.] It was there to provide the necessary fire support, whereas some of the other boats were strictly troop carriers so they had less firepower."

Kelley was in-country about ten months before he was injured. He calculates that his unit went on about thirty missions, ranging from one day to a week, encountering firefights maybe 10 percent of the time. "We had to be very careful. The rules of engagement were such that we were not allowed to return fire if there was any chance of civilian casualties. Somebody would pop up from a fox-hole or a spider hole or the treeline or something and let loose some rounds. They were usually concealed, but sometimes you'd see somebody up in a tree or something."

Kelley was commanding eight landing craft taking a company of soldiers off a South Vietnamese riverbank on June 15, 1969, when a landing ramp got stuck. About the same time a substantial force of Vietcong opened fire from the jungle on the opposite bank less than one hundred yards away. Kelley ordered his command ship, the *Monitor*, into midstream, fronting the enemy while he had the other craft flank him in order to surround the disabled boat. Crew-men climbed into the water to hand-crank the jammed ramp so they could get out of there.

Kelley was perched up high inside the *Monitor*, giving orders on a handheld radio. "The outside of the LCM was armor, inside it was lined with Styrofoam. If a round came in, it would detonate on the armor and the shrapnel would get absorbed in the Styrofoam unless somebody got lucky with a round that came in and detonated on a pipe. That's what happened to me: I got careless and a round came and detonated about six inches from my head, and it just blasted me away with shrapnel." That was when he found himself on the deck, and, as he told it, "I kept hearing them saying, 'He's dead, he's dead,' and I'm saying, 'I'm not! I'm not!'"

Blinded from the flowing blood, knocked to the deck, he continued to issue orders. "I was holding on to the radio, a handset fortunately, so I was able to keep talking into it to get us out of there. I was in charge of the group, so I had to tell the guys to keep shooting, all that sort of thing you do while you're in a firefight. A lot of rounds were being fired on both sides. I could not see anything. I was down in the bottom of the boat and guys were telling me what was going on, and so I was saying, 'Okay, you gotta do this, you gotta do that.' I was in kind of a state of shock, but I was able to keep our boats fighting, shooting long enough to suppress the enemy fire for as long as it took to get that ramp up."

"We were blasting the other shore to drive those guys out. They were probably VC; I never saw them. All I knew was they were shooting at us, and no Americans were killed that day." A few others were wounded, none so seriously as Kelley. "A corpsman named Doc Nelson [Richard Nelson of Hawkinsville, Georgia] who was on a different boat brought his boat alongside mine out in midstream, even while we were taking fire. He jumped onto my boat and gave me first aid, stabilized me, kept me going, saved my life. He's down in Georgia; we stay in touch."

The medic, Richard Nelson, seventy-one, later told me more about what had happened that day. He was forty at the time, ten years older than Kelley.

"We were like McHale's Navy, only crazier," Nelson recalled. "It was the first time since 1865 that the Army and Navy had worked together. The soldiers were the River Raiders, and we were the River Rats. We had four or five different types of boat. One threw a two-hundred-foot flame of napalm. We said, 'We are the makers of Crispy Critters.' One boat had two pythons, George and Agnes, that slept at your feet. George was ten feet long. There were no bugs because of these snakes. We had monkeys, somebody had a mongoose. They killed cobras. This mongoose had a black-and-white coat. He was constantly growing. He'd scare the hell out of you. They said, 'Doc, look what we got.' I said, 'That's got to go.' They took the mongoose out and shot him. We operated up the Mekong near the Parrot's Beak by Cambodia, an area that once grew ninety percent of the world's rice. It was so hot everyone wore shorts, no shirt, as little as you could. It rained for weeks at a time.

"One boat was always designated as the medical boat. We tried to use *W*s to designate names because the Vietnamese could not pronounce *W*. So the boat was *Whiskey 2*, and my name was Witch Doctor. They'd call the Witch Doc to come over to so-and-so boat, somebody is hurt. The coxswain would tie up and I would jump over. I'd be exposed in jumping. I have three Purple Hearts."

Tom Kelley was "an enlisted man's officer, a terrific person, very Boston, what you see is what you get. We all respected and loved him as our leader.

"The place where he was hit was called Rocket Alley. A V-42 rocket went off six inches from his helmet, and shrapnel was embedded in parts of his body. He was up in the cockpit. The concussion alone could have killed him. Any time you take a blow in the forehead above the nose from ear to ear, you are very likely to die from the force of the explosion and shrapnel. The men were a little panicky because they thought he had been killed, he looked that bad. But he continued to direct his boat to make sure they could free the ramp so they could get out of there. When we came alongside, I tried to get him to lay down, but he wouldn't. He stepped onto the medical boat with his eye hanging out on his cheek with some of his flesh holding it. It was pretty bloody.

"I got him onto my boat and laid him down. The eye was hanging down, and I flipped it back in and put a triple compress, a bandage like a big Kotex pad, two and half inches thick and six by nine in size with mini-tails, in very tight. You've got to have pressure. He didn't like it. He said, 'You're choking me.' I said, 'If you want to live, be quiet.' I was so scared he was going to go from the shock. We requested a dustoff [helicopter] right away. We thought of the rescue helicopters as Angels of Mercy. They were really something.

"Shrapnel had severed the nerves of the eye, and you couldn't save it. That is a very tender area. If he contracted secondary shock, he could easily have died. But he didn't. He's a tough man, and he was worried about his men. It was a combination of Boston, his training, and his constitution. That's how he made it."

Kelley remembers the first thirty minutes, "and after that I have no idea what happened. I don't know how they got back. We got out of the firefight, got out into safe waters, and they took me off by helicopter and that was the last thing I knew for about a month and a half. I never did see the after-action report." The helicopter took him to a nearby field hospital where he was further stabilized, then he went to an evacuation hospital. "I know I ended up back in Hawaii about two weeks later. The first surgery was to get me well enough to travel, then I had reconstructive surgery to make me look pretty again. They worked on my eye and my skull." Touching the right side of his head, Kelley adds, "This is all plastic, everything on this side, because a whole bunch of my skull was knocked away.

"I was very lucky. I lost an eye and a fair amount of skull, but I have really no bad effects, I have had a happy and safe life. This is a fake eye, my right eye—there's people who do this for a living, and they do a damn good job. I mean, they even paint the . . . you know how everybody has little red lines in their eyes, like if you had too much to drink? Well, they actually put little red threads in there. It takes them a long time to do it. I've gone through thirty years with one eye. It's not difficult, not really. You adjust to it. Catching a baseball coming right at me is a little difficult because of little depth perception problems, but you compensate for that. I can hit a golf ball, for example—not very well, but I can't blame my eye for that."

Kelley received the Medal of Honor at the White House from Richard Nixon in May of 1970. "There was a ceremony, a dozen of us, we got it all together in some room in the White House. It was the first time I had ever been there. Most of those recipients are still around, some have passed away. Senator Bob Kerrey of Nebraska, he was one of them."

In retrospect, would he have done anything different, knowing what he knows now? "I wouldn't have done anything differently. I was in the Navy, I was a professional warrior and I was sent to Vietnam, and I never did anything that I am ashamed of today or embarrassed about today when I was over there or at any other time in my Navy career."

Asked what he thought about a report that emerged in the summer of 2000 implicating Kerrey in the deaths of a group of Vietnamese women and children during a night action when Kerrey (see chapter 23) was a Navy SEAL, Kelley spoke carefully: "It showed that serving in combat is a very very difficult thing. When you come under fire, you instinctively react and do what you're trained to do, and I think that's what he did. He did what he was trained to do, and I don't know anything about any friendly fire or casualties. I really didn't follow the story. I know I talked to him about it, told him that he was my pal, and that was it. I'm not going to second-guess anybody in combat. I feel worse about what happened yesterday over in Afghanistan."

The repair work on Kelley's skull and eye socket was completed in Hawaii, where he went on limited duty for about a year and half, working ashore until he was finally declared fit for full duty. "I went back to sea and resumed my career as a naval officer in 1972 and went here and there for the next twenty years. I was an executive officer on a destroyer, I commanded another destroyer, did shore duty in Washington, D.C." He also was sent to Japan and Korea. He retired in 1990 and worked for the Department of Defense as a civilian in Washington, D.C., where he became a golfing buddy of Marine Colonel Harvey Barnum Jr., also a Medal recipient (see chapter 18). Kelley became commissioner of Veterans' Services in Massachusetts following Thomas Hudner.

Kelley is particularly proud of Massachusetts' concern for its veterans. "The primary function of my job is to be advocate for five hundred and fifty thousand veterans of the commonwealth, to administer the state benefits program, which is the best in the country. We do things here that no other state does for its vets. We are the only state with a veterans' service office in every single community. We have three hundred and fifty-one cities and towns, and every one has a vets' service office. I pretty much set policy on what programs are available, and they carry out our programs. Our commonwealth spends sixty million dollars a year in state taxpayer dollars on its vets. About ten million goes to annuities for Gold Star

Parents, Gold Star Wives, and one-hundred-percent-disabled vets. They each get fifteen hundred dollars tax free a year from the state. We are the only state that does that. Any vet who falls on hard times and needs money to pay the rent or basic necessities of life can walk into his or her city or town hall, see the veterans' office, and receive actual money for the necessities of life. We reimburse the town seventy-five cents on the dollar; the only state that does that also.

"There's a tradition in Massachusetts, starting with the North Bridge in Concord, with U.S. history starting here, a history of service. We take care of our own. When you think of John Adams, people like that who just embody service. Abe Lincoln's family was from here, right out near where Tom Hudner lives in Concord. There's a tradition here. The first Vietnam veterans' memorial in the U.S. was built in South Boston in 1982. The towns here seem to have paid more than their proportion in sending sons off to war.

"I've found in this job something I never stopped to think about before: Someone who serves in the military has no control over whether there's a war or no, so this state and all states treat their wartime vets different from how they treat their peacetime vets, which I think is fundamentally unfair. I'm trying to get that changed, so that anybody who serves is treated the same way when it comes to benefits. The Cold War was won by men and women who were not considered wartime veterans, tracking their subs, doing sonar, playing cat-and-mouse type of games."

Until his knees went bad, Kelley liked to run six miles a day. Now he does in-line skating instead. He and his wife had three daughters.

"I downplayed the fact that I was a Medal recipient until recently. I was too busy being a naval officer, and I certainly did not want to let having the Medal of Honor give me any special advantage when it came to accomplishing certain things, okay? I bent over backward to avoid that, so I ended up downplaying the Medal completely. But now I found that it does permit me to have doors opened here in the state of Massachusetts to help veterans, and for that reason alone I am probably more active than I used to be.

"I don't consider the Medal my personal property. As a recipient, I feel I am wearing it to represent all the men and women who have served over the years with the same dedication and courage. Having said all that, it did make me very aware of my responsibilities as a recipient, talking to kids, trying to instill the values of service, courage, honor, and duty, so it's been a very good part of my life. Personally and professionally it added a dimension. I certainly don't dwell on events of thirty-one years ago. That was thirty minutes out of my life and it came and went and life goes on. I've led a wonderful life since then."

About September 11: "We agreed earlier that this was a wakeup call, but I think the pain is being felt by other people. The American public is not going to have a sense that they're at war. We still have an all-volunteer force fighting our wars, so different from the way it was during World War II when every block had sons and daughters overseas. I'd love to see not necessarily a return to the draft as much as some sort of national service involving everybody. I think that would give us all a sense of sharing and belonging to the crisis we're in right now. I mean, it's almost business as usual: People are inconvenienced, the airlines, revenues are down because of dot-com companies going out of business, but nobody is really feeling the pain yet except those who lost loved ones in the events of September eleventh and now overseas in Afghanistan."

How would a national service work? "A couple of years right after high school is a good time, and it should be mandatory. In the Vietnam era there were so many ways to avoid service, college deferments, this, that, and the other thing, so that the notion of service fell on the shoulders of those who were less advantaged and were unable to do college and things like that. I just don't think that's the way it should be. I like to think back to the way it was when this country was formed. When people like John Adams and George Washington led the way, men of substance, means, and intellect. Yet they were the ones who sacrificed the most to make this country what it is today."

EIGHTEEN

Harvey Barnum Jr.

Forward Observer
Vietnam
December 18, 1965

*"The first thing I did was hit the deck. It was the first time
I'd ever been shot at! If anybody says, 'Were you scared?' you're
God damn right I was scared. I mean the whole world opened up, rockets,
mortars, machine guns, small arms fire. I hit the deck, and when I looked up
from underneath my helmet, all these young Marines were looking at me.
You could see it in their eyes: 'Okay, Lieutenant, we're in
a shit sandwich. What're we gonna do?''*

Harvey Barnum Jr. and his wife,
Martha Hill, at the inauguration
of George W. Bush.

by Robert M. Bush, CMOHS photographer

This photo of Marine Lieutenant Harvey Barnum Jr. was
taken on December 20, 1965, two days after the battle
for which he was to receive the Medal of Honor. Barnum
had just arrived back at his original battery position
south of Da Nang. He kneels, holding an M-14, in a
pose very similar to a photo he knew from home. That
picture portrayed a cousin, Fred Tyler, kneeling similarly
with an M-1 rifle. Tyler served with the Marines in the
occupation in Japan after World War II. The picture
stood on Barnum's uncle's table and young Harvey, or
Barney as he was to be known, saw it every time he visited his uncle while growing up.

282

HARVEY C. BARNUM JR. was still president of the Medal of Honor Society when we met at his home in Reston, Virginia, to discuss recipients who might be willing to sit for interviews for this book. He knew them all, of course, and of them all, he said, he displayed in his home the photo of only one, John Finn.

It was career day at Cheshire High School in Connecticut in the spring of 1958. Harvey Curtiss Barnum Jr. was class president, a scout leader who had lettered in football and starred in baseball. "I remember that day well. They brought in the military to speak to all the junior and senior boys. We came into the auditorium and the Air Force guy got up and started to speak, and there were catcalls and whistles. Then the Army guy. There were comments, you know, and giggles. Then the Navy guy, same thing. And this gunnery sergeant, a Marine gunnery sergeant, got up there. And he says, 'You know, there's no one in this room that I even want in my Marine Corps. This is the most unorganized, undisciplined group of young men I've ever seen. And the faculty, in the back of the room, I want to tell you, you all ought to be fired. If I was the principal, I'd throw you all out. Your job is to maintain discipline and set the example, and you're back there jawjacking and scratching your butts. No wonder these kids are undisciplined!' He says, 'I'm wasting my time.' And he walks off the stage.

"They break, and they had their tables all set up. And he's there, he's starting to put his stuff together to leave. Well, there must have been thirty guys standing there wanting to talk to him. And I was one of them. I'm sure the uniform had something to do with it, but I think it was just the discipline, the orderliness, the take-charge manner of that gunnery sergeant. If that's what the Marine Corps was about, you know, that's the way I think."

Young Harvey, or Barney, as he was known, signed up that day for the Platoon Leadership Training Program, the Marine Corps version of college ROTC, and did two six-week summer stints at the Marine Corps training center in Quantico, Virginia, while attending St. Anselm College in Manchester, New Hampshire. "It was like boot camp. They see if you want the Marine Corps; now they want to see if the Marine Corps wants you. It was very physical, everything that goes on in boot camp—the physical training, the rifle range, the obstacle course. And of course Quantico has a lot of what they call the hill trails. You get a lot of that, drill and parade. I was commissioned a second lieutenant when I graduated from college in June of sixty-two. I majored in economics."

The Cuban Missile Crisis came that fall and Barnum's time in basic school was compressed so that he graduated before Christmas of 1962, and then went to artillery school for a month before being sent to join the Third Marine Division in Okinawa. "That was my first tour, thirteen months. I was a forward observer, a second lieutenant. The forward observer from each battery goes out with each company of the infantry battalion, out in front. He's called an FO, and he has to pick out targets and then call them in to support the infantry's scheme of maneuver.

"The way it's designed, an artillery battery of six guns, say 105 mm howitzers, supports an infantry battalion. The artillery unit is positioned so it can support the infantry, and the infantry never outruns the artillery fan. Because it would be detrimental to their health. The only thing you have to remember is when you have a weapons system, an artillery battery, and ammunition, it goes where you send it. So it's very important that you know exactly where you are when you're out as a forward observer so you give them the right coordinates because, if you give them the wrong coordinates, those howitzer shells are gonna go where you send them. There's a mathematical procedure where you transform the coordinates from the ground site to where the gun is; it's all mathematics, a ground positioning system, a predecessor to GPS today. That's how you figure out the charge, then adjust it to the target, so the shell lands where you want it to go. The artillery is very important for the infantry." Barnum pauses, then recites: "*The infantry is the queen of battle; the artillery is the king of battle. We add dignity to what otherwise would be a vulgar brawl.*

"The other thing is, when you're getting in close with ammunition, there is a variance, a tolerance, if the powder doesn't burn totally right, or something. That's the danger when you bring it in tight—they call it *danger close*. It can be a little erratic. Like the action I was in, when we got ambushed, we were at the outer fringe of the artillery fan. I was calling it in from the maximum range, and they were firing over my head. I had a couple of people get injured by my own shell fragments, and that's the reason I stopped calling it in.

"My first tour really agreed with me. First I was a forward observer, and then I was the battery motor transport officer, and then I moved up to battalion staff; and other positions and ended up running four observation posts. So I got increased levels of responsibility that agreed with me, so I augmented, I put in the papers, went before the board and became a regular officer, which meant I could stay for a career," which he did, for twenty-seven years.

After Okinawa, Barnum was one of twelve artillery men sent back to the States, to Cherry Point, North Carolina, where they were attached to the Second Marine Air Wing. "They called it 'cross training' but, between you and I, it was to free a pilot to fly. They had all these shitty little jobs for us, although I had a good one: I had the career advisory center, and I was the assistant wing adjutant and top secret control officer, and in that role I went on Operation Steel Pike to Spain and controlled all the classified material. It was a big landing in Spain in 1964, a big exercise: infantry assault, air assault. And then from there, to my benefit, I got orders to the Marine Barracks in Pearl Harbor. And from there I went on temporary duty to Vietnam." By March of 1965, he was, at twenty-four, a first lieutenant, serving as a guard officer in the Marine Barracks in Oahu.

"There was a war going on in Vietnam and the Marines had landed, and the Marines back in the barracks in Oahu are security guys, you know? They're guarding gates and secure areas and saluting admirals and generals and doing protocol stuff. An officer came up with a program to send company-grade and senior staff noncommissioned officers to Vietnam in their MOS [military occupational specialty] for a couple of months to participate in combat operations, see what's going on, then come back to the security forces and teach some courses and keep the troops interested.

"The general thought it was a pretty good idea, and the first time was over the Christmas holidays of nineteen sixty-five. There were twenty-three officers in the Marine Barracks at Pearl Harbor, and I was the only bachelor. So I went to the commanding officer, a father of nine children, and I said, 'You know, boss, all the company officers are going to go, and they want to go, and they're all gonna get their chance but, it's the holidays, why don't you send me? I'm a bachelor.' So I got to go first. And of course my buddies, the other guys, were all pissed off at me, you know. So myself and a first sergeant from one of the companies were the first ones on this whole program to go, December nineteen sixty-five."

Wasn't it dangerous to volunteer as a forward observer?

"Well, being a Marine is dangerous. When I first got to Vietnam, I checked into the artillery regiment, then down to the artillery battalion and then down to Echo Battery, south of Da Nang. I was in Echo Battery for a couple of days and then I was assigned as an FO with Hotel Company, 2d Battalion, Ninth Marines. I was with them maybe two days, out on a mixed patrol with ARVNS when we were recalled and assigned to be a replacement company for Fox Company 2/7, which was in Operation Harvest Moon. The company had been shot up pretty bad, had a lot of immersion foot, a very painful foot condition caused by prolonged exposure of the feet in water. So we got in helicopters and flew off, landed up in the Que Son Mountains and joined the 2d Battalion, 7th Marines, commanded by Lieutenant Colonel Leon Utter." The battalion was on a prolonged search for the enemy and had slogged over twenty miles of terrain, ranging from flooded rice paddies to hills covered with jungle. The operation was winding down when Barnum's Hotel Company was assigned to the battalion rear unit.

"Now I've been in-country two weeks and I've been with this company one week. The people in the company don't even know my name except the headquarters element, the folks at headquarters. I'm a newbie; and not only that, I'm a newbie on temporary duty. So, anyway, we landed with the battalion. For the first couple of days I remember hearing some gunfire in one of the other areas. When I got assigned to Hotel Company, of course, I checked in with Captain Paul Gormley, the company commander. In fact, I stayed in his hooch for a couple of days and got to know him a little bit. There had been major engagements prior to our being landed. We were all expecting action. That's why we were out. We were looking for them." Was Barnum apprehensive? "Hell, no. I was looking forward to it. That's what I was trained for.

"I remember the night of the seventeenth of December, it rained like a son of a bitch, and my radio operator, Corporal Iacunato, and I were under a poncho trying to keep warm and dry. We had moved out so quickly we didn't have shelter halves. I don't know what the temperature was, but we were colder than a son of a gun. I remember that night, he and I, trying to keep the radios dry and keep dry ourselves, huddling just for body warmth.

"The next day we were moving. We were near the end of the operation. In fact, if we hadn't been ambushed on the eighteenth, we'd have made it to Route 1 and the operation would have terminated. So we were in a column, a battalion column, companies in line one behind the other but, you know, with flank security out."

The Marine battalion was traipsing along a narrow road winding through rice paddies bordered by hedgerows. Lying in wait was the 80th Vietcong Battalion. The Marines were completely surprised. How could that be with flankers well out on both sides?

"Well, there should have been. I can't see how we got into that ambush without knowing about it. They were dug in, they were concealed in spider holes and trench lines, but I can't believe that three companies went by them. I'm sure that everyone said, 'Oh, four more hours and we're out of this shit.' They'd been in combat, they're tired, they're wet, they'd been out a couple of weeks. We were terminating, so I'm sure the thought was that seeking out and finding the enemy, we'd done that, and it was time to return to base.

"I can't second-guess, but they were a well-disciplined unit. They were dug in around this village called Ky Phu, and they had let the first company go through, and the second company, and the headquarters company was in the village. Of course, we were the rear element. And they triggered the ambush all [in all directions] at the same time—both sides of the column, both sides of the village and both ends beyond the village.

"I heard some shooting up forward—and then all hell broke loose. They picked out Captain Gormley, I mean they picked him out. He's walking along, he's got a .45 on his hip, a map in his hand, the radio operator is behind with that big whip antenna. And you know Soviet doctrine: You take out the leadership, the troops will flounder. They were pretty God damn smart. They figured they'd wipe him out, everyone else would flounder, and they'd wipe us all out. At that point we had enemy on three sides of us, coming from the rear and the left and the right. The ones on our right flank were well entrenched. Those were the ones I took on with the counterattack.

"The first thing I did was hit the deck. It was the first time I'd ever been shot at. If anybody says, 'Were you scared?' you're God damn right I was scared. I mean the whole world opened up, rockets, mortars, machine guns, small-arms fire. I hit the deck, and when I looked up from underneath my helmet all these young Marines were looking at me. You could see it in their eyes: 'Okay, Lieutenant, we're in a shit sandwich. What're we gonna do?'

"The next thing I did was contact the artillery. I started doing my mission. I didn't know the company commander was down. I was probably thirty yards from him. I got my radio operator, and we crawled into a defiladed area and started calling in a fire mission. And with that I hear someone holler, 'The skipper's down!' and I see Doc Wes [Wesley Berrard, a corpsman from Chicago] run out, and he got shot three times by the time he got to Gormley. And then my scout sergeant, McLain, jumps out of the hole and runs out to protect Doc Wes, and he gets shot a couple of times. I don't know how much time has transpired now, but I finally ran out because the corpsman's still out there, and I notice that the radio operator's dead. I picked up

Captain Gormley and carried him back. And he's mortally wounded. He died in my arms. He was just, there was nothing left to him.

"Somebody was going out to help McLain back. I went out and helped Doc Wes back, and then I ran out a third time to get the radio off the dead operator. I brought it back, it was called a PRC 25, and strapped it to myself, took over the company and started giving orders. The first thing I did with the radio was call the battalion commander, Utter, and told him what had happened—Gormley was dead and I had assumed command of the company. I said, 'I've got one platoon preparing a counterattack, I've got this, I got that,' and he says, 'Well,' he says, 'young man, it sounds like you have things well in hand. Make sure everybody knows you're in charge. Spread the word you're the company commander.'

"Because, you know, I wasn't the next senior officer. And I didn't know where he was; still don't. Anyway, then I got the three platoon commanders back to my position, because they're all fighting their own little war, and I decided who needed to run the counterattack to our right. And that went well. We got troops on line to fire and maneuver right up to the trench line. There was a knoll up on the left, and I went up on that knoll with a 3.5 rocket launcher, Korean War vintage, and we had willy peter, white phosphorous rounds. I fired it on the trench line to mark it, and that's when I called in the Hueys, the helicopter gunships. We had fixed-wing aircraft overhead, but they couldn't come down because of the weather.

"The command net was on that PRC radio—the battalion commander, the battalion operation officer, all the company commanders, and General Jonas Platt, the task force commander, who was up overhead in a Huey. He was monitoring. He wasn't talking. The benefit was that by listening you knew what everybody else was doing and when you figured you were in worse trouble than the guy talking, you could cut in, and they were smart enough to realize it and back off. So I remember, after we ran the counterattack on my end, it was just intense, everywhere. They were closing in on us.

"I couldn't use the artillery battery because the enemy were so close to us on the right and I was firing over our heads. I tried it once, and it didn't work. We had six 60mm mortars, and they fired on the trench line. That was our organic artillery. So I was up on this knoll, and when I ran out of willy peter, I stood there and just pointed with my arms, and the gunships flew down my arms toward the trenches. I said, 'Use my arms as an axis.' I remember two gunships. My pack was shot up and I'm told by some of the troops that shit was landing all around me, gunfire, mortars, but you know, you're so damned busy you don't think about it. And the gunships were just great. Even when they ran out of ammunition they kept flying until the enemy realized, oh shit, that's the fourth time they've flown over and they haven't been shooting.

"So then they started to shoot at the gunships, and I called them off. And then I told them I was gonna need resupply, ammunition, and I had wounded men who had to be evacuated. They said, 'Do you have an area where we can land?' So I got the engineers on the back side of this hill, we blew some trees down, and that's when I brought in the H34 to take out the dead and wounded.

"I remember the first guy coming in, he says, 'We can't land! We can't land! It's a hot zone!' And I didn't know this until a couple of weeks ago, I read where some colonel quoted me as saying over the air, I said, 'Well, you son of a bitch, I'm standing right in the middle of it. If I can stand out here, you can land.' So he landed. And Doc Wes, you know, getting back to his story, here he'd been shot six times, and he continued to give aid to wounded and give advice. And when the helicopter came in, he was one of the worst wounded, and I tried to get him out, but he wouldn't let me put him on a helicopter until all the dead and wounded were accounted for. Then he let us put him on and, as we were putting him on, he got shot a seventh time. He survived.

"After we got them all out, this was well into the afternoon, the battalion CO says, 'You've got to come out.' He's up in the village. He says, 'You got to join up with us because we can't come back for you. Everyone's involved in a fight.' Of course, the weather is hazy, and it's getting late in the afternoon, and I know that if we're there that night we've had it. So I directed the platoon commanders to pile up all the unusable equipment and have the engineers blow it up. And then I had everybody take off their packs, throw them in a pile, and we burned them. That was so we would be light, so that if someone got shot, you could pick him up. You couldn't be carrying all that gear and evacuate. I wasn't going to get any helicopters back, so anybody that got shot from this time on, we had to carry out. So when I got word that all the equipment had been blown up and the packs had all been burned, they set up a base of fire for us in the village, directed against our right flank. The left flank had died down.

"We had about a two-hundred-meter run. There was a major trail right down through the middle of the rice paddy; it was a two-cart path. When we started, I reminded everybody: You don't leave anybody. So, if someone goes down, you pick him up. You know, that's what we're all about. That was my big thrust to these guys: Marines don't leave people on the battlefield. And at this point we'd been pretty successful. These young men said later, 'You know, you saved our lives. We were ready to do anything for you. Because what you said and told us to do worked.' When I told them to do something, they did it. That was the most phenomenal thing—they did it without hesitation. And if I told them something, and someone got shot, and I told someone else to do it, they didn't hesitate. That's what pulled us together as a team, because we never hesitated, and I have to tell you these guys were pretty fired up, pissed off because some of their buddies had been, you know . . . So when we started to hi diddle diddle, if someone went down, there were two guys there picking him up. We were running down the dikes with the enemy on the diagonal. Our people in the village sent that base of fire back at the enemy, to keep their heads down, and they were very effective.

"We coordinated. I would say, 'Okay, first squad, ready to go. Village, you ready? Commence the suppressing fire.' And my guys would take off. We had a few people shot coming out, but everybody made it. Nobody was killed. And I'll never forget when I got there, Leon Utter, Colonel Utter, was there and he said, 'I want to talk to you, Lieutenant.' And I said, 'Excuse me, sir, I'm busy. I don't have all my people accounted for yet.' In other words, I didn't have time to talk to the battalion commander because I hadn't got them all in. And I was standing there when I got to safety until every one of my guys came in. Then I got a count, then I went to the battalion commander and said, 'Everyone is accounted for.' They set us in position, we were in for the night, and I briefed him on all that went on, about the battle. I remember that night we got mortared and probed.

"And I remember the tough part. I was in a little shelter, sat with a gunny, going over the dog tags, who got shot, who got killed. I got a little emotional about that. [Marine Corps records say the enemy left 104 bodies on the battlefield, seventy-six killed by artillery fire. Eleven Marines were killed, including Captain Gormley and his radioman, and seventy-one were wounded.] And I'll never forget the next day when we moved out, we only had a few hours to go to reach Route 1. I noticed there were five Marines around me. I said to the gunny, 'What's all this?' They said, 'You saved our ass yesterday; we don't want anything to happen to you today.'

"So we got down to Route 1, not three hours away, and there were a lot of trucks there, and all the people from 2/7 got on these trucks to go south to Chu Lai, and they had trucks for my company, Hotel Company, to go north to Da Nang, where we'd started from. While we were loading the trucks we got sniped at from this village, and of course a lot of people hit the deck. Some were so tired they didn't even move. I ran up to the front because they were shooting at my guys. There was an Ontos [a small tracked vehicle armed with six 106 mm recoilless rifles] there, a tank killer; it was protection for the convoy. So I grabbed hold of the sergeant running that thing and I said, 'Level that fuckin' village!' And he turned those six guns on, and the next thing I know three huts just disappeared.

"The sniper rounds stop, and we get on our trucks and the battalion commander runs up. What's going on? What's going on? He's looking over at the dust of the village. I told him we were taking sniper fire, and I eliminated it. He says, 'Good job!' And he gets on the trucks and goes to Chu Lai, and we go north to a logistics area halfway to Da Nang. We get in after dark and we circle the wagons and my people are in position and I'm underneath a six-by [a ten-wheel truck used to drag artillery and haul troops and supplies] and someone wakes me up. He says, 'I'm Major So and So, and I'm running the investigation. Lieutenant So and So has reported that you used excessive force.' I said, 'What?' 'Well, you took an Ontos and you leveled a village.' I said, 'Yeah, we were getting shot at.' Well, this lieutenant, it was the first convoy he'd ever been on, and he thought I used excessive force because I, you know, I probably killed some civilians. And about that point, I'd had it. I was a little verbally abusive with this major, I'm told. And I go back to sleep.

"About one o'clock in the morning, someone's tugging on my legs again, and this time it's a colonel. And I say, 'Colonel, I got to tell you I ain't in the mood for discussing this any longer.' He says, 'No, you gotta come with me.' He says, 'I think you're going to get a Sunday school medal out of this battle you were just in. There's two colonels back here want to interview you. General Walt sent them down here.' So I go down to this tent, and there's a colonel and a lieutenant colonel, and they said, 'Can you generally describe the battle in Ky Phu because we got the word that you're going to be decorated out of that, at what level we don't know. But you're going to get a Sunday school medal out of it.' I remember them saying that. I guess I spent about forty-five minutes with them and finally, I said, 'Gents, I got to tell you, I can hardly keep my eyes open.' I mean I hadn't slept in a couple of days, and there's no adrenaline left. And they said, 'Okay, well, go back to sleep.'

"I got up in the morning, got all the troops together, and we're going to load them on the trucks. Turns out they've sent a captain down from Da Nang to take over the company, which pissed me off a little bit. Why couldn't they have waited until I got them back to Da Nang? But I said, 'Skipper, it's all yours.' Back in Da Nang, Iacunato, my radio operator, and I found our artillery battery, got our gear off, and got cleaned up. I immediately went to bed. I mean, we were just exhausted.

"When I woke up I went into the mess tent for a cup of coffee and the battery commander came in and said, 'We just got word that General Walt's putting you in for the Medal of Honor.'

"I dropped my coffee cup. At that point they were taking me to the hospital to get treatment for my feet, which were in bad shape. When you're in water three or four days in a row, your feet crinkle up and then they start to crack and then they bleed. They get infected. I mean, it's dangerous. So I went to the hospital and they worked on that, and then I came back and had to go see General Lew Walt [commanding general of the Third Marine Amphibious Force]. Then they started taking statements, and I wrote up a lot of people but my problem was, I didn't know anybody's name. Certain people I saw do heroic things but I didn't know who the hell they were.

"Christmas came and Cardinal Spellman, the military vicar, was there. I have pictures of me shaking his hand, because the word is out I've been recommended for the Medal of Honor, and I'm a celebrity now.

"And, you know, I'm twenty-five years old, a gun-slingin' wild-ass bachelor, and I've never taken myself seriously. Besides, some people had been killed. That was the hard part. I had to write all these statements, and I continued to work in the battery area. They didn't let me go out on any patrols, but I worked with the different battery units for a month, moved with them a couple of times. I had plenty to talk about, including combat, when I got back to Pearl Harbor.

"I talk to the young lieutenants about this because they all worry about it: How do you know what to do when the shit hits the fan? Am I gonna be prepared, am I gonna be ready? I think I was well prepared because, you know, every officer is an infantry officer first, every Marine is a rifleman. Then you train to be a tanker or artillery or whatever. Every lieutenant is trained at basic school to be an infantry officer first. Tactics, I learned all that, what to do in a given situation. It's like riding a bike. You just know how to do it, once you've learned. We trained hard at Quantico, and we paid attention. And in boot camp, enlisted men are taught that officers give directions, and they follow directions. So when I started giving orders, these young Marines did what I told 'em to do. Not because I was Barney Barnum but because I had a [lieutenant's] bar. They didn't even know my name.

"I think I was the motivator to get 'em going. The squad leaders knew what to do, fire team leaders knew what to do. When they first got pinned down, they were scared. And, you know, survival becomes a strong motivator. So what I did was get them in motion. I got them moving, and I did it by getting out in front of them. Then they knew what to do, and they took over. I was the quarterback calling the plays. I called the plays, and they executed them. We pulled together as a team."

After returning to Hawaii following his first visit to Vietnam in February of 1966, he was assigned to the armed services police. "On Valentine's Day, nineteen sixty-seven, a year later, I got the call from Washington saying the President was going to present me with the award on the twenty-seventh of February. Lyndon Johnson was in the White House. And then, after it was approved, the White House wouldn't decorate me. It was a bad time politically. Finally, I'm told, General Greene [General Wallace M. Greene, Commandant of the Marine Corps] said, 'He earned it, it's been approved. Either the White House presents it, or I'm presenting it.'"

The Marine Barracks at 8th and I Streets in Washington was selected for the ceremony. Barnum was the fourth Marine to receive the Medal of Honor for service in Vietnam. "It was so damn cold that day they had to hold the ceremony inside, in the band hall. They didn't have a parade. And that was great, because it was just a Marine ceremony. And Paul Nitze, the Secretary of the Navy, presented me with the award." Barnum's parents were there, his brother, aunts and uncles, some college buddies, along with Brigadier General Jonas M. Platt, who commanded Harvest Moon, and Lieutenant Colonel Leon Utter, who commanded the battalion.

Later that year Barnum went to New Orleans to receive the Military Man of the Year award from General Walt. "That's when he said, Do you want to be my traveling aide? I said, 'Well, sir, I have orders to the 2d Division.' And he said, 'Now, wait a minute. Just answer my question: Do you want to be my traveling aide?' And I said I'd love to. He said, 'Well, go back to Kansas City, get your car and drive home on leave, and then don't go to Camp Lejeune. Report to Marine headquarters at the Navy Annex at the Pentagon.' So I reported here, and became his aide.

"At that point, he said, 'You know, if you can last a year with me, you can go any place in this Marine Corps you want, but you got to last a year.' So when thirteen months were up, I reminded him of that. He said, 'Where do you want to go?' I said, 'Vietnam.' He said, 'Oh, you can't go back.' And I said, 'Sir. You told me.' So he pulled strings, and I went back to Vietnam in November of nineteen sixty-eight and became the commanding officer of Echo Battery [the same battery he was assigned to the first time], saw a lot of combat. I built seventeen firebases in Vietnam. We'd blow mountaintops off and go in and build gun positions and fly the guns in with helicopters. The infantry never got outside the artillery fan. If the infantry got near the end of the fan, we built another firebase. A firebase contains a battery with half a dozen guns, sometimes more than one battery.

"Senator Strom Thurmond gave me an American flag that had flown over the Capitol in Washington, D.C. I flew it over my firebases. Of course it was illegal, because the only place on foreign soil you can fly an American flag is at an embassy. I had many senior officers remind me of that when they came to my firebase, but none of them ever directed that I take it down. My mother had made a flag that flew under it, with the battery's sign on it: Thundering Guns of Death. She wasn't very happy about making that flag, but she made it anyway. That was our motto, Thundering Guns of Death. But that American flag became an aiming point for the enemy, and many times it took a lot of shrap metal and rounds. I remember asking my troops, 'Should I take that down?' And they said, 'Hell no.' My battery was attacked a couple of times. I had six 105 mm howitzers. We got attacked on Firebase Cunningham. I lost one gun. I got wounded, got hit with a mortar. Purple Heart. I left the country in September of sixty-nine when Nixon started a pullout.

"I guess, as I look back, if there's things you could change in life, one of them would have been contacting the widow of the Hotel Company commander, Captain Paul Gormley, when I got back from that first trip to Vietnam. But, see, I wasn't back. I was still in Hawaii, and I hadn't known him that long. She's remarried, I heard, and I've known people who knew her. I always felt a little guilty but I just never, you know, what do I say? I didn't know him. And I didn't want to get into the gory details of what he looked like when he died. They named the Marine Corps League after him in New Hampshire, and I sent them a lot of documents on him, and stuff. Someone has since contacted me and said he had a phone number for her, but I just never, you know, what do I say?

"I can remember when all this happened, and I came back to my hometown and they had a big parade. I could take just about so much being number one and being the guy out front but . . . just leave me alone. I guess the only time I ever talk about this battle is either with guys I was with, or with reporters, because I don't look back. I look ahead. I saw too many people who all they talked about was Vietnam this and Vietnam that. But I'll tell you right now, life is too short. I can't change what happened. It was an experience in my life that I was prepared for, and the good Lord was my guiding light. You know, why I didn't go [get killed], I have no idea. People can spout off on who was with them doing this and doing that in Vietnam, and I can't. I think the reason is I don't look back. I want to get on with life and do something that can affect tomorrow, you know what I mean? I believed in what we did in Vietnam. I was ready to go back. I stayed in the military for a career. That was my chosen way of life.

"The more I read about Vietnam now, the more pissed off I get. But I gotta tell you, those of us at my level in Vietnam did what we were told to do when we went there, okay? And we did a good job. We never lost a battle. We got our nose bloodied a few times, but we did what the national command authorities said to do. It's a shame, though, that we had to operate with one arm tied behind our back.

"Now, that having been said, people say, You know, we lost the war in Vietnam. We didn't lose the war in Vietnam. The war in Vietnam was lost across the river here [from the Pentagon] by these gutless politicians who were running the country. You never send in military unless you're going to send in enough to get the job done. And then you have to have an exit strategy. Because on the battlefield the best prepared wins; the second best prepared loses. If we're going to be ready to go any place at any time to fight in defense of freedom and win, by God, we gotta have the balls to do it right. Another thing is you don't chase them to the border and then not go after them. We weren't allowed to go into Laos and Cambodia. There's stories about Lyndon Johnson sitting on the commode in the White House, picking out targets in Vietnam from a list. What you could do, and what you couldn't do. If we'd done it right, put the right amount of troops in, let the military run it, we wouldn't have drug it out.

"That's where it was lost. But you know every false step is a learning experience. And think of this: Communism, as we know it today, I think, started coming apart because of the defeat [of the United States] in Vietnam, because of the battles in Vietnam. And when the Berlin Wall came down, I felt good because, I said, we were a part of that. Those of us who fought in Vietnam are part of that. Maybe I want to feel that way in my heart, I don't know. But I really do. I believe that."

Barnum, who today is Deputy Assistant Secretary of the Navy, Reserve Affairs, also served two years as president of the Medal of Honor Society, and over the years has grown well acquainted with the approximately one hundred and forty recipients still living. Like others who hold the Medal of Honor, he feels strongly about their being referred to as recipients, rather than winners. "You know, you're a winner in life, but you don't 'win' the Medal. You practice sports to go win a ball game; you work out for the Olympics to win a gold medal. But you don't go out to win a medal in combat. I mean, awards are in recognition of performance of duty, whether it's meritorious or for bravery, and should not be looked at any other way. Some guys did just individual acts, jumped on a grenade or did something that wasn't part of a team effort, but I think we all realized that we did what had to be done at the right time. We did it not out of personal aggrandizement but for love of our fellow Marine, or soldier or sailor or airman.

"I wear that medal for the guys who served with me. I think most of the guys feel that way. We're really a caretaker of that medal, for those who served with us. Because if it wasn't for the guy on your left and the guy on your right, we wouldn't be here now."

NINETEEN

Jay R. Vargas

Major, Company G, Fourth Marines
Dai Do Village, Vietnam
April 30–May 2, 1968

*"I went back and I found Smitty. I got him on my shoulder,
and he was a pretty stocky kid. Geez, I was dead at that point, I was
bleeding, I was weak. I get him on my shoulder, I turned around, we're
taking off, and he says, 'Skipper, skipper, I want my fuckin' arm.' I said, 'Jesus
Christ, Smitty.' But I turn around and I say, 'Where in the hell is it?'
I went back another fifteen yards, and I grabbed his arm
and said, 'Here, you asshole.' So he grabs his arm,
and we got back, and he got heli-lifted out."*

by Robert M. Bush, CMOHS photographer

Jay Vargas greets well-wishers along
the Medal of Honor parade route in
Boston during the Medal of Honor
Society convention held there in
October 2001.

Marine Corps Major Jay Vargas, "Teresa's boy,"
as the Arizona Navajos called him, in the official
photo taken about five years after he received the
Medal of Honor on May 16, 1970. President
Richard M. Nixon saw to it that Teresa's name
was engraved, at her son's request, on the back
of his Medal.

I MET WITH Vargas in his sparsely furnished office on the fourth floor of the Department of Veterans' Affairs Building in San Diego. His current title was Regional Veterans' Service Organization Liaison for the Department of Veterans' Affairs, which meant he was in charge of veterans' affairs in six states in the Southwest and Hawaii. He had a couple of hours before he had to depart on a flight to Oklahoma. He was direct and forthcoming with details of his personal life.

Jay Vargas was born on the kitchen table in his family's home in Winslow, Arizona, in 1937. There were twenty people at the house, and his mother was cooking when Jay arrived so abruptly there wasn't time to go to the hospital. His two older brothers, Angelo and Frank, fought in World War II; a third, Joseph, went to the Korean War. All were Marines. Heart problems run in the family—Joe died at thirty-six from a massive coronary, while Frank and the parents, Teresa and Emanuele, also died of heart problems. Jay, who was sixty-five in July of 2002, is fit. He blew out a knee jogging a couple of years ago so now he walks every day, two or three miles.

An outstanding high-school athlete, Vargas graduated from Winslow High in 1955. His teams won state championships in baseball and football. He briefly attended Arizona State, then came home to Northern Arizona University in Winslow on a full scholarship, athletic and academic. He graduated in 1961 with a degree in secondary education. He played baseball all four years. His batting average was an outstanding .310. "I had a very quick wrist. I played third base. I loved every minute of it. In fact, there's a stadium named after me in Winslow, called Vargas Field. One of the few punky little kids who did okay in baseball."

His life's dream was to play big-league ball, so after graduation he signed with the Los Angeles Dodgers organization and went to play for a Triple-A farm team in Portland, Oregon. "Now they're the Albuquerque Dukes. I went up for a while, stayed for a little while and . . . couldn't hit the slider. Well, I was broken-hearted. I think my eyes were going, and I didn't realize it. My Dad was a great guy. He said, 'How many kids get that far?' But the eyes were going, and then I joined the Marine Corps."

Vargas' mother, Teresa Sandini, came to the United States from Caltrano, Italy, around 1917. Among the passengers on the ship was Joseph Bonnano, destined to become a leading mafia boss in the States. "After he [Bonnano] retired, one of the few godfathers that really retired and never got bumped off, he settled in Tucson. I know we went there for a wedding, and she said, 'While I'm here, I'm gonna say hello.' I don't know how the friendship started other than they were all on that one boat." The Sandinis ended up in an Italian enclave in Rockford, Illinois, changing the family name to Sandona because of implications [of Mafia connections] reaching back to the Old Country, Jay said. "They didn't speak English, ever. It was all Italian."

Jay's father, Emanuele, came to the States from Madrid via Mexico. He became the back-shop foreman of a weekly newspaper in Gallup, New Mexico. He met Jay's mother in Gallup. "I don't know if you've ever heard of this, but she was one of the Fred Harvey girls. They were like waitresses, and they worked the La Posadas, the train station hotels and restaurants along the Santa Fe Railroad. They wore long brown dresses with white aprons, stiff collars, and a cap. The trains would stop overnight. You'd go in the cafes, and you'd be treated very well. First-class food, and the hotels were nice. And then the people would jump back on those old trains again, and take off next day. There was a hotel in Gallup, there was one in Winslow. They were both beautiful."

Teresa acquired a store, "actually a boot and saddle repair shop," Vargas recalled. "Then she started bringing in the Levi's and the shirts, stuff she figured the Indians, and the cowboys, would buy." She called it Angelo's, after her second son [who runs the business today]. "When she opened up that store, the Navajos and the Hopis were her biggest clients. Navajo was an unwritten language in those days. But she mastered their languages, learned them fluently. The reason they fell in love with her was that in those days it was Prohibition. Indians couldn't drink. So when they came into town on Fridays, the bootleggers would sell 'em whisky, wine, and take their government checks. And when they got done taking all their money, they would tell the Native American Indian to go to his 'squaw' or his wife or his girlfriend, and take their turquoise necklaces off and bring them, and they'd give them more wine in exchange.

"Well, my mother learned of that and she got pissed off. So she told the Indian ladies when they came into town on a Friday to turn in all their jewelry. We had a safe as big as a wall in our shop. They'd turn in their jewelry to her, she'd put their names on it, hang it up. And on Mondays, when they'd head back to the reservation, they'd come into the store, and she'd give it all back to them. So they all fell in love with her. They would hardly go to any other store to buy anything. I mean, she was a smart business lady.

"When she died, the first four rows of the left side of the church were all full of Indian women, Indian wives. They had come from miles and miles in their wagons just to go to the funeral. I escorted the casket and, well, I turned and looked, they all nodded at me, all at the same time. I was never called Jay by the Navajos. 'How do you do' is pronounced Ya ta hey. So they'd say, 'Ya ta hey, Teresa's boy.' I was never called Jay. It was always, 'Ya ta hey, Teresa's boy.'"

After giving up on baseball in the fall of '61, Vargas said to his father, "You know, Dad, I'm either gonna teach or maybe get my military obligation out of the way. And of course my brothers all said the Corps, the Corps, the Corps." Jay went to Officers Candidates School for three months, and came out a second lieutenant. In 1963, his battalion went to Okinawa for thirteen months. After the Gulf of Tonkin incident, his outfit sailed off the coast of Vietnam for 101 days. "We sent a few helicopters in, but that was about it. We went in, looked around, but there was nothing going on at that time."

It was about then that Vargas passed a grueling exam and became a regular officer in the Marines. "A lot of these young officers I had around me, if a kid had a dirty rifle, they would give the kid a special punishment for it. My philosophy was, If anybody had a dirty rifle, it wasn't the kid's fault. It was his damn leaders, the squad leader or his platoon sergeant or his gunny. That's who I'd blame. And if they ever marched into my office with that kind of charge, I'd say, 'Well, whose fault is this?' The room would go silent. Then I'd say, 'You know whose damn fault this is? It comes all the way up to me.'

"But I enjoyed commands. There were three things I wanted to do in the Corps, and I'm one of those that always liked to set objectives: One was to be able to lead Marines both in peacetime and combat. And I proved that I could do that. Another was I wanted to be called a colonel of Marines, a full colonel. And the third one was I always wanted to lead a regiment of Marines, five thousand Marines. And I got to accomplish all that.

"I had very few problems. I was always down at the grass roots with the enlisted people. I wanted to lead them. I wanted them to know that I cared for them, you know, I was gonna take care of them. And I still get calls, guys saying, 'God, Colonel, I wish to hell we could all get together again.' And a couple of times we have. We've had reunions, you know."

Following two years of training with the 1st Battalion, 28th Marines, Vargas got sent back to Vietnam in 1967. "And what happened? We all got individual orders. They said they're sending us over as a unit they had trained for war for almost two years, and they broke us all up and sent us individually to different organizations, which was stupid. I mean, we could have done wonderful things. But we ended up going into a bastard unit. Hate to say that, the 2d Battalion, Fourth Marines, but that's what they're called, the Magnificent Bastards. I picked them up in Subic Bay in the Philippines, then we got back aboard ships and went right back along the DMZ [demilitarized zone]. Our responsibility was from the Cua Viet River all the way to Khe San. I was a company commander, a captain, at that time."

He went into combat soon after. The following spring, late in April 1968, Vargas was relieved from command of his company after being wounded for a second time. Then the relief commander got hurt, "and there were no other guys to go up and take the com-

pany back, so I jumped in what they call a river boat, a little motorboat, and I went up during the night and took my company back.
Colonel Weise is saying, 'Where the hell is Jay?' He called me on
the radio and said, 'What the hell are you doing up there?' I said,
'I'm back up with my company.' And he says, 'Well, I was gonna
make that decision, but God damn it you already made it.' "

Vargas and a couple of men had crossed the river late that April
of '68 to recover three mortars. "Then they brought in some helicopters to lift us out of there, but we couldn't get out because the
first chopper took too many hits. And enemy artillery was coming
in also, so we aborted. I got one platoon and the mortars on that
one flight, and they flew back to the base camp, about two or three
miles. And I decided I'd had enough. We fought as long as we
could, and then I decided to do a night retrograde [retreat]. So I
took two companies and headquarters and we marched for hours,
under heavy artillery. One of our platoons got lost and went out in
the middle of the desert. I went and found them, brought them
back in, and we made it to base camp. They claimed there must
have been six hundred rounds dropped on us as we were retro-
grading down to this area, heavy artillery and missiles. But we only
lost, I think, two Marines. Everyone got wounded with shrapnel.
You couldn't help it. The only thing that saved us was that the sand
was so soft and mushy so when the rounds came in, a lot of the
explosions took place in the ground. But I was hit that night. My
leg was torn up, but I told the corpsman, 'Don't you dare report it.'
Because that was my third Purple Heart.

"In the meantime, these other companies were getting the shit
kicked out of them in a village called Dai Do, in Quang Tri
Province. Two boats picked us up the next morning, and each had
a tank in it. So we're going downriver, and Colonel Weise comes up
in a speedboat, gives me my five-paragraph order. My mission was
to come down and continue the attack into Dai Do. And none of
us have slept in twenty-four, thirty-some hours. Because when we
got back to base camp earlier, we had to clean, lock up, and get our
wounds taken care of. The sun was coming up when we took off

down the river, landed, and went across over seven hundred meters of rice paddies." Their aim was to gain a foothold in hedge groves on the enemy perimeter. "We were told it was a reinforced company, but it turned out it was a regiment of two thousand or three thousand of the 320th Division."

Vargas had two companies. His own and "the company over here," he said, pointing to a hand-drawn map. "It had lost all its officers, and the second lieutenant went into panicsville, and I got him settled down. There was another river that came down, and the Arvin, the South Vietnamese Army unit, was supposed to have this side. But after the firefight started, they went this way, and the adviser was calling me on the tack net saying he wanted to apologize but he couldn't stop these guys. They didn't want to fight. So that exposed my left flank. And before the hedgerows, there were machine-gun positions all along the front."

"One of my platoons got pinned down, so I went forward with two platoons up, one in reserve. I was right in the middle here, and I brought this reserve element through, right into the jaws of hell, almost like the Civil War. We were a line. And I've got mortar. I've got artillery. I've got naval gunfire. I've got air strikes going. And we just kept going and going until I got into the bunkers with grenades, threw them into the openings. I opened up the back side of one bunker and just sprayed; I think I killed eight of those people in there." Vargas had an M-16, a .45 handgun and, strapped to his leg, a sawed-off .12 gauge pump shotgun he had picked up on the field one day.

"I took three bunkers. So there must have been four in one and four in another. They were pretty much locked in, so they could cross-fire. I crawled from one to the other, shot a lot of smoke. I just said, 'Shit, where am I gonna go?' I wasn't gonna just lay there. So once the troopers saw me doing it, they got up, too, came right behind me. We were all bleeding. My kneecaps were pretty well bummed up. Then I got hit again there, shrapnel. They started calling artillery on top of them.

"And once we got into Dai Do, I'm thinking, 'Hey shit, I've got

time to get my wounded out,' so I had those tanks put a lot of our
wounded on them. But these guys, the bad guys, decided to counterattack at this stage, and they pushed us into the corner of the
village, into a cemetery, and then surrounded us. We're down to
about seventy-six guys. We'd probably started out with two hundred and sixteen.

"Anyway, they came around us, and everybody wrote us off.
General Westmoreland was on the net [Air Command Radio Net-
work], talked to us. Of course my battalion commander, division
commander, everybody, according to several I met later on, wrote
us off—because they just didn't think we were gonna make it.

"But what I did is I rained fire around us all night, calling in
artillery across from Dong Ha, and they just put a steel ring around
me, and I brought it within fifty yards of where we were, One five
fives [155 mm howitzers] and the One oh fives [105 mm howitzers].
And the river boats were shooting for us. They had mortars. And
Sloopy, the big gunships, the C-130s, they flew in here all night. We
didn't have much of a perimeter because these guys were coming in
during the night and throwing grenades like they were delivering
newspapers. But they didn't know where we were. There were some
fresh graves in the cemetery, NVAs that had been killed earlier, I
guess. They weren't that deep. The water table was there, too. And I
told the men to dig down till they found a body, throw it out, and get
in the grave. That's what we did. And we just formed a circle. I told
everybody, anybody that's dumb enough to get up, he's dead. The
smell? We didn't give a shit. So I had three bodies sitting by me when
I was in this hole, you know? What the hell. What are you gonna do?

"And what saved us again was the soft sand and the marsh, sucking up the shells. But when the sun came up, and this was amazing,
truly amazing, there were at least three hundred, maybe four hundred bodies around us that had been killed by our artillery, just all
over the place. And they're saying today there were two thousand
of them in the village there.

"After the sun came up, Echo Company, under Captain Jim Livingston, who also received a Medal of Honor, came over and took

a lot of pressure off us. And then the two of us went from here into the next village, which was called Dinh To. We went forward, about eighty of us in my unit and—because of the heavy artillery that we brought in and the air strikes—hundreds of these guys started running across these rice paddies. Our fixed-wing guys and the helicopter guys were having a field day. You could hear them on the air net saying, 'Jesus Christ, keep pushing 'em out because we're just flushing 'em down here.' After three days, what did they say, there were eighteen hundred bodies, almost two thousand in that battle. And we lost seventy-eight in the battalion. I lost seven, I think, in my company. And everybody was wounded.

"So we got into Dinh To, and then the enemy realized they could not go back out because of the air strikes, so they turned around and counterattacked, came right through us again. A lot of them didn't have ammo. They just wanted to get closer to us because they knew they'd have a chance to live. Then they started to come around from the side because our left flank was open. That's when we really started having hell.

"Livingston had already been wounded and his company was pulled back. And this other company was supposed to come up and help us, but because of the heavy volume of fire from the left flank, they couldn't make it. So what I did is start a retrograde, pulled my people back. And I brought in artillery on myself, which was perfect because the maps were wrong, and about forty of these guys stood up to charge us one more time and . . . I think it was an act of God . . . the artillery rounds landed right among those guys and just blew 'em to shit. But we had 'em running around us. They were just as confused as we were—as far as they were out of ammo, we were out of ammo. We were in hand-to-hand combat at this stage, bayonets, everything. Helmets. Rifle stocks. I saw Marines breaking stocks over guys' heads."

The North Vietnamese Army soldiers were smaller than the Americans, Vargas acknowledged, but this was not much of a factor in the hand-to-hand fighting "because, you know, I got down from one hundred and eighty pounds to one hundred and twenty-one. We had lost that much weight over there. We didn't hardly eat anymore, and everyone was skin and bones.

"It kind of reminded me of handing the football off, and all of a sudden the linemen are breaking through, and there's confusion, and everybody is eager to hit each other, tackle each other. I remember cutting a man's throat open very easily. I remember sticking my knife in the side of a guy's neck. It was either he or me. I can remember, being out of ammunition, hitting a couple with a rifle butt, you know, swinging it like a baseball bat. I remember taking another guy down and grabbing his Adam's apple and squeezing the hell out of it until I heard it crunch. What gave me the strength? Probably fear.

"They were doing the same thing to us. And these were well trained NVA, the 320th, in uniform, just like we were. They were knocking the hell out of us, too. And everybody was out of ammo. It was mass confusion, and strictly survival. Everybody was taking care of himself at this stage. And it was amazing how . . . I don't know, it kind of reminded me of a good-ass, hard-core scrimmage. It really did. For some reason, I have no idea why, I really felt that I was not gonna die. I really had that feeling. I just felt comfortable. I didn't feel I was gonna get it.

"The only thing I didn't want to happen to me was to be shot in the head. I mean, some guys say, if I get killed, I want the shot right in the forehead. I didn't. There were two things I was worried about. One was rats and snakes. The other was being shot in the head. A lot of people say you're scared all the time. I didn't have the time, I think. I had Marines to maneuver. I had artillery to bring in, air strikes to bring in, coordinating all that. I was always on the radio, moving with my troops. I didn't have time to really think about . . . The only time I got scared was when the rockets and the artillery came in, because you can't do anything about that. And you don't know where they're gonna hit. You can hear them coming in. But geez, you're down on the ground. I felt helpless during those times. I just didn't like to stay in one spot. One thing I did learn in moving my company down from that night retrograde is that you can walk through artillery. You can actually do that. I proved it to myself. You don't want to, because it's vicious stuff. I got everybody back. But they were scared shitless."

Besides his knee injury and assorted shrapnel wounds, Vargas was hit in the mouth. "When I got hit here," he said, "it split my lips apart. My teeth went in. Luckily, I had a great corpsman. He just kind of reached in and grabbed my teeth and pulled them back out. I couldn't talk on the radio because I was flapping. Weise still teases me about that also. He says, 'I couldn't understand what the hell Jay was saying.' I couldn't talk.

"This is the battalion commander who retired as a brigadier general. We used to call him Wild Bill. Wild Bill Weise. Great man. He was always up front with us, always in the thick of the fights. The last time he came up, I don't think he expected it to be that bad up there, and he just couldn't believe it. I mean, the NVA were running around already. They were just confused. They didn't want to crawl back into the village.

"Then I got hit again. Weise came up with a sergeant major. I'll never forget them jumping into a trench with us. The colonel said, 'What the hell are you doing?' I said, 'I just called artillery on myself, so I recommend you get the hell out of here.' And just as he turned Colonel Weise got shot three times in the back, in his lower spine. Sergeant major took an RPG rocket right in the chest. It didn't even go off. Just went right into his body."

With the sergeant major dead, Vargas picked up his wounded colonel and hauled him back to some corpsmen. "And on the way back, the NVA were coming from the left flank, and I was shooting. This guy comes out of a riverbank, he had us right in his sights, we were gone. I said, 'Oh shit.' Just then I stumbled, and my pistol went off. And they still tease me about this: The round hit the ground but ricocheted up and hit this sucker right in his stomach, blew his belt apart. I'll never forget his expression. He just stood there and looked at me, like, 'How the fuck did you do that?' And then he was gone. And Weise has always teased me about this: 'Vargas can't shoot a .45 worth a shit. You might as well give him a bunch of grenades.'

"So I got him back and then realized I had seven or eight

Marines back there. I went back in, carried out seven Marines. And I still get Christmas cards. I brought 'em all back. They were wounded and in shock. I had one kid who artillery had taken his arm off and burned him so bad it wasn't even bleeding. But he was sitting there in shock, and his arm was lying over there. And when I was dragging Weise out, I told him, 'Hey, Smitty, I'll come back and get you. I promise you I'll come back and get you.' He was in la-la land."

Two other Marines were helping Vargas pull men to safety. "I went back, and I found Smitty. I got him on my shoulder, and he was a pretty stocky kid. Geez, I was dead at the point, I was bleeding, I was weak. I get him on my shoulder, I turned around, we're taking off, and he says, 'Skipper, Skipper, I want my fuckin' arm.' I said, 'Jesus Christ, Smitty.' But I turn around and I say, 'Where the hell is it?' And I went back another fifteen yards, and I grabbed his arm and said, 'Here, you asshole.' So he grabs his arm, and we got back, and he got heli-lifted out.

"We had two medical ships out there, the *Sanctuary* and the *Repose*, [with] professional doctors from all over the world. They could do anything, right there. And that's what saved a lot of the Marines and soldiers. Anyway, I get heli-lifted out to the ship, and they take me into the operating room, and I was kind of weak and all I could hear was, 'Well, we're gonna have to take it off.' I thought they were talking about my leg, but it was the kid next to me. I screamed at the nurse, 'Hey, I don't want you to take my leg away.' She said, 'Oh no, we're not talking about you. We can repair your knee. We can fix that.' I said, 'Whew!' That's when I found out I weighed one hundred and twenty-one. For two or three days we never slept, never ate. I don't know how the hell we did it. It was just continuous fighting."

The Marine death toll was seventy-eight. "Hundreds and hundreds were wounded, of course. When they did the sweep, a friend of mine who became the operations officer said they had staked anywhere from eighteen hundred to two thousand bodies for burning—they had to do that because you couldn't bury that many people. We didn't have the heavy equipment to dig the trenches. What the NVA did, they had come across the DMZ between us and the Arvins, through a desert, traveling at night. I don't know how in the hell they did it, to get that many people in one position, and their main mission was to attack the Third Marine Division headquarters. They had got that close. So we spoiled their attack by hitting them head-on, right in the nose. I remember we were told it was a reinforced rifle company. It turned out to be the famous 320th Division, one of the best the NVA had."

"What we're all scared of right now is cancer, this Agent Orange, because four, maybe five of the fourteen officers we had in our outfit have died of cancer. We're starting to see a lot more of this, not just in our battalion. But we ate and slept and fought in that stuff when they sprayed along the DMZ. We didn't know any different. My ticket hasn't come up, yet, but recently we lost two others to cancer. Anyway, they've taken this battle of Dai Do as an example, and that book, *The Magnificent Bastards*, is now a text at the officers' candidate schools in both the Army and the Marine Corps."

His men had pressed for his nomination for the Medal of Honor, Vargas said. When he finally got home, he wasn't allowed to tell his wife, Dottie, other than to let her know he was being recommended for a "high award."

"She didn't know what the hell it was. After we had lost Mom in 1969, I called the White House. I learned this from my grandfather: It was customary in his lifetime that whenever a Spaniard met another Spaniard or a Latino for the first time, you always exchanged a gift or dedicated something to him. Well, I was like that throughout my life. When I would win an award in school for academics, I would always dedicate it to my mom. When I was in sports, I always dedicated it to my dad. Well, this time I said I'm gonna dedicate this to my mother. So I called the White House. I got some guy on the phone and said, 'This is Jay Vargas. Is Matt Caulfield or Sheehan or any of those guys, marines, around?' 'Nope,' he said. 'What can I do for you?' I said, 'I understand I'm coming back now to receive the Medal of Honor, and I'd like to have my mother's name put on the back.' The voice says, 'I can take care of that.' I said, 'Oh yeah, well, you make sure that that gets approved, because that's what I really want.'

"He says, 'I can do that.' And I kept thinking, 'Who the fuck am I talking to?' So I said, 'Who am I talking to, sir?' He said, 'This is Dick.' I said, 'Oh, well, would you let Matt and some of those guys know that I really want this?' He said, 'I told you I could take care of this.' I said, 'That easily?' He said, 'Yeah, this is Dick Nixon.' There was a long pause and then a little chuckle. And he said, 'Jay, I know you're coming back here. Is that what you really want to do?' I said, 'Yes, sir, I would really want to do that.' Then I said, 'Why are you answering the phone, sir?' He says, 'I was just coming down here to find my senior Marine aide, and the phone was ringing, so I picked it up.'

"So I get back to Washington, and he did a beautiful job. There were eight us, I think. It was Armed Forces Day, May sixteenth, nineteen seventy. And the President did a wonderful thing. He turned to the press and said, 'Jay is dedicating the presentation of this medal to his mother, Maria Sandona Vargas.' It was engraved on the back. He showed them the medal. Some of the press guys thought that was my name, and it's taken years to clear it up.

"But Nixon did his homework. He melted my dad, my brothers. He turned to my dad and said, 'How's the newspaper going?' And my dad was just petrified, he said, 'How did you know about that?' Nixon said, 'I know you're the foreman of the shop back there. And Angelo, how's everything with the stores, the western attire stores? And Frank, how's the Santa Fe Railroad?' Damn, he was good. What a politician. What a statesman." Vargas went on to relate how two of his girls, in little white dresses, grew bored and went to sit on the floor, and Nixon joined them there, charming them, their mother, and, of course, the assembled press. Indeed, the photo made the front pages next day. Jay's father was given a tour of the monuments and he even had lunch with the President.

"He was in heaven. He goes back to Winslow and he's telling people, 'You know, I had lunch with the President.' They said, 'Yeah, right, you're smoking dope again.' They didn't believe him.

He said, 'No, I have photographs.' So he laid this all out. He became the most famous man in Winslow. For a guy who'd never flown, never left a little town, he had a good time.

"From then on, for me, it was just busy times with the Medal, but I had good teachers. A lot of the generals told me, 'Don't blow it. Watch your drinking. Don't cause any trouble because you've earned the highest medal. You're always gonna be showtime. You can't get a parking ticket.' And that's the hardest part, you can't . . . [live it up] like the old college days. Of course, I don't do it any more anyway. But you've really got to watch yourself. And I think they knew that I've always been a "we" man, "us." I don't think I'll ever change. That Medal could have gone to sixty-eight other guys that day, really could. So when I wear it, I wear it for everyone who's ever served. That's the way I look at the Medal."

Among the traits that he finds his fellow recipients to have in common is, unsurprisingly, courage. "They're very confident people. It's amazing. We all came from little bitty towns. A lot of us came from very poor families. They're down-to-earth people. They're not braggers. They just seem like they were put into a position for a very short period and whatever came out of them came out ten times stronger than you would ever expect your body or person to do in a particular situation. What drove me was I cared so much for my Marines. That was my family, and my responsibility was to lead them. I would have gone into the jaws of hell for them. That's a strong loyalty that comes from every Medal recipient I've met, and they're very patriotic. It's like those country-and-western songs I grew up with. You know, they love kids, dogs, and all women."

After retiring at the age of fifty-four in June of 1992, Vargas was out fishing in the middle of some lake when a ranger pulled up in a motorboat and handed him a telephone. It was Pete Wilson, the governor of California, wanting him to direct the state conservation corps. That didn't work out, but Vargas eventually became director of veterans' affairs, for the next six and a half years, "My budget was three-point-six billion dollars. We had three-point-one million veterans in the state of California, number one in the nation, followed by Florida and then Texas."

Then, in July of 2001, he was named one of six Regional Veterans' Service Organization Liaisons by Anthony J. Principi, George W. Bush's secretary of Veterans Affairs. "We kind of troubleshoot, work with the directors of the regional offices, the CEOs of all the hospitals, the veterans' organizations. I'm dealing with the outreach programs, touching the hands of veterans that don't belong to the organizations. I think we're doing very good. I think the six of us have dug up some bones that need to be corrected, and the secretary is doing that. It's a big operation. We're getting older, we veterans. The VA health-care system is the best in the world, but now they're starting to come in the front doors. They're hurting, you know? And the hospitals are going through ugly, ugly budget cuts."

"I had thirty great years in the Marine Corps. I accomplished my goals. If they would have let me stay till a hundred years old, I would have stayed. I loved it that much. I was basically very lucky to command everything from a platoon to a company to a regiment of five thousand Marines. I was always in command, and I loved leading and setting an example and taking care of marines. It was in my blood."

"After [Vargas had commanded] the regiment, General P. X. Kelly and General Barrows, General Wilson, they all were saying, You need to come back to Washington. And I don't know if we want to talk about this but, basically, one of my daughters got into drugs, pretty heavily. So I had a choice of either going through drydock with her, or continuing on, to put my [general's] star on, because they were all saying, You're an automatic star, boy. But I chose her. I elected not to go for the star." Vargas and his wife, Dottie, had married on September 28, 1963. They had three daughters.

Vargas wept as he told the story. "When I had the regiment, we moved up to this area, and the high school was a rich kids' high school, and the ones who used to come over, I thought, were clean-cut kids. You couldn't prove to me they were druggies. Half of one of the athletic teams finally got busted. They were all on cocaine.

And she said she went to a party and it all started there. That stuff was all over the place, that white stuff. And she tried marijuana, cocaine, you name it. And then she disappeared for a while, and we found her down on Broadway at some hotel with a bunch of other druggies. And we just went in there until I could find her. Found her under a blanket, and we took her home. I was very thankful but, I tell you what, it was a tough go.

"Drydock was tough. Boy, I didn't like that. It was in El Coronado, up on the hillside up here there's a hospital. We had to go every day, for about six months. Spend the evenings there. It was about three months there, when she went through all the counseling, cleaned her body up and it was three more months going down every night just for counseling sessions and talking with other parents. That was a tough one.

"And it was tough giving up the Corps. When you have two commandants and a future commandant telling you that you're in line . . . because I got selected early twice, what they call deep-selected. So I was on a fast track, but I chose her. You have to go with what's inside you. And I did. I feel great about it now." His daughter, he said, is doing fine today.

TWENTY

Clarence Sasser

Army Medic
Mekong Delta, Vietnam
January 10, 1968

*"I'm trying to be gentle about it, but it
probably was a raw fuck-up."*

Clarence Sasser, fifty-two, at the
November 1999 convention of the
Medal of Honor Society in
Riverside, California.

by Robert M. Bush, CMOHS photographer

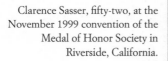

Copyright © 1969, Houston Chronicle Publishing Company. Reprinted with permission, all rights reserved.

Army medic Clarence Sasser, twenty-one years old, addresses a student assembly at Angleton High School near his hometown of Rosharon, Texas, in May 1969, two months after receiving the Medal of Honor from President Richard M. Nixon in the White House. Sasser graduated from Marshall High School in Angleton in 1965, only months before the school district was integrated.

CLARENCE SASSER has lived his whole life in the Rosharon area, south of Houston. Despite his work with the Veterans Administration, he avoids publicity as much as he can and he does not like to recall the day of the action for which he received the Medal of Honor. It is too painful. He lives alone in a comfortable home and has many friends in the area.

"Ethel Morant and I were married in nineteen seventy-one. We raised three boys. She was killed in a car wreck in ninety-six, a month short of twenty-five years of marriage. It happened I guess maybe seven, eight miles up this road here, a drunk driver caused it. It was five-thirty in the evening. She was on her way to school. The driver is in the state pen now.

"I'm well acquainted with grief, to say the least, but it still doesn't make it any easier or anything. Probably the fortunate thing for me was that the boys were grown. Billy had just graduated from high school and was in his first semester at college. That made it somewhat easier. I didn't have any small babies on my hands. But on the other hand it made it even harder, I guess, because I'm here by myself. Probably the hardest thing about it has been, and it seems so superficial, is, you know, eating alone, the care and maintenance of yourself. It's just overall having somebody to take care of you. I tell everybody, whenever the subject comes up, give your woman a kiss or a pat on the butt, and tell her you appreciate her because if you lose her, it becomes quite a problem, you know, dealing with it. Life is fragile, full of surprises but we wouldn't have it any other way—probably."

Clarence Sasser was born September 2, 1947, in Rosharon, Texas, about thirty-five miles south of Houston, not far from his current home. "We had a truck farm, you know; we raised pigs and vegetables. We were on twenty-five acres. I have four sisters and two brothers. They're all alive and well. I'm number two. My father died but my mom is still alive. She's seventy-seven. She moans and groans, you know how they do. I tell her, 'Well, Mom, you're still able to hold a car between those lines, so it can't be too bad.'

"Anyway, back in the middle fifties everybody had a milk cow and raised a calf for beef. My father ran the farm and was caretaker of a recreational area for a company out of Houston. We had spring and summer vegetables, the beans, the peas, the mustard, meaning the greens, corn, cucumbers. It was quite a lot of work. We didn't use horses. We had tractors. We bought grain shorts, basically wheat hulls, and we had a contract with a milk company up in Houston and we'd go get outdated milk and mix that with the ground-up hulls and feed that to the pigs.

"We sold the hogs live, but we'd butcher our own for meat. When the cold weather came in the fall—we call them northers down here—usually a Saturday, would be hog-killing morning. We used one of the old-fashioned fifty-five-gallon drums, and after you killed one, you would drop the whole hog right down in the boiling water in the drum and then lift him out and roll him over onto a sheet of plywood, and then you'd go to work scraping the hair off. It was hard work. You'd have the whole hog hanging up, probably one hundred and seventy pounds dressed out. My mom made head-cheese. And we had sausage and then hams in the smokehouse.

"You didn't dare let the fire come up in the smokehouse. That would ruin the meat. And then it ruined you. Daddy didn't play that. You'd get a licking. So you watched it pretty close. My father's name was Will Sasser, and he'd give you a licking when you earned it. He had served in World War II, as a truck driver. He and my mom divorced—there were me and my brother and my oldest sister. Then she remarried, to Jerome Brown, and there were four other kids, so I was actually raised by a stepfather.

"I graduated from Marshall High School in 1965, in Angleton, Texas. You have to appreciate the scenario back then. It was an all-black high school. The school district integrated at the start of the nineteen sixty-six–sixty-seven school year, long after Little Rock." Growing up in a segregated society was terrible, Sasser acknowledged, "but you have to put it in perspective. I'm sure it was even worse for my parents. We kids had minimal contact with whites other than maybe at the store or the gas station. There were no overt incidents, no harassment that I remember, but it was there. Whites didn't prey on blacks. It was a little bit better than that in this part of the country. Rosharon was a very small town. You had to go in the back door of the local cafe if you wanted a hamburger. I guess it was a case of, as kids, knowing your place, which may be a bad or terrible thing to say, but it was a fact. It was a way of life. Going in the back door, the people that were doing the cooking were black. You knew them. That's just the way it was, good, bad, or indifferent."

Sasser described himself as knowledgeable about the successes of black soldiers in World War II despite the discrimination that was widespread throughout the American military. "I know about the Red Ball Express and the Montfort Point Marines, and of course everybody knew about the Tuskegee airmen.

"The very nature of what was going on was insidious and self-perpetuating. I think it's correct that the bigotry grew out of an American military dominated by white southerners, and it included the service academies. Most of the bases were in the South, and in the spirit of cooperation, certain things were done to appease the local populace. I agree with Vernon Baker [see chapter 5] that it was horrible, and I agree there was a backlash and the military appeared to just forget all the black participation in the Spanish-American War, the Indian wars, the Civil War. For instance a lot of people don't know now that Theodore Roosevelt's victory at San Juan Hill was dominated by black troops.

"Almost all of this country west of here, almost to the California line, was controlled by blacks—the Buffalo Soldiers of the 9th and 10th Cavalry. I think it's human nature to forget, especially with the insidious nature of racism, which is meant to demoralize and keep down people who are different from yourself. Some people feel they got to put others down in order to feel good about themselves.

"But it's hard to oppress people. It costs a lot, and I think that may have been a guiding factor. It was awfully damned expensive to keep those separate units and that, combined with the perform-ance of the 92d Division, the Red Ball Express, and the Tuskegee airmen—each and every time they were given an opportunity and an objective, they accomplished it—that was what spurred Mr. Truman to order the integration of the services in 1947. At some point it no longer becomes economically feasible, particularly when you have a growing cluster of people you can use.

"And Vietnam accelerated that. The rich white kids weren't going because of deferments and Canada and all that, so to accomplish what the military felt was an end, you had to have the means, and that was the pool of black kids. Everything opened up. I think Vietnam spurred it, and of course it was assisted by, if I can be so bold as to say, our performance."

Weighing a hefty 190 pounds at five feet eight in high school, Sasser hurled the shot and discus in track and played guard and tackle in football. "I like to think I was a fair student. Out of sixty-three in my graduating class, I was number four. I went to the University of Houston the following fall. There were not many blacks, but I had no trouble from that perspective. My trouble was having to work and go to school, paying my way. I was drafted in April, in my second year, because I had dropped down to half-time and was working. I went down and told them I was still in school part-time and they let me stay until June, so I got a year and half of credits. After I got out of the Army, I did go back to college and got some more credits and then, I ended up getting married and then, you know, family comes first."

He went through basic training at Fort Polk, Louisiana, from June 15 to the end of July. "Everyone's finishing basic and they publish who's going to what MOS—Military Occupational Specialty. I was assigned to be a medic. I would like to think it had something to do with the battery of tests they gave us at the reception station. I think that's the purpose of those tests, to sort you out."

Medical training was at Fort Sam Houston in San Antonio. "Essentially it was learning to administer first aid, stabilizing a trauma situation [bullet or shrapnel wound] to where the subject can be taken to competent medical help. You were fundamentally an EMT, an emergency medical technician. I think in fact the current EMTs are based on what came out of Vietnam, particularly today's ambulance helicopters, which grew out of the dustoffs [medical rescue helicopters] in Vietnam.

"Our focus in Vietnam was ninety percent combat trauma, but where I was down in the Mekong Delta, we did do preventive medicine, what with the water and the fungus and the rashes. And of course we had the old pecker checker, for VD and rashes. Down in the Delta, there were rashes and crotch rot that would extend even to the penis. Very painful. Once it gets to that point you have iodine and that's a trauma in itself. Jungle rot was the problem we had with the feet."

Sasser came home for a week's leave at the end of the summer of 1967, and then flew to Oakland and from there to Vietnam, to a replacement station at Long Binh. "I arrived right after my twentieth birthday. I was thinking, probably like everybody else, I hope I don't get messed up. I didn't think about death too much because I firmly believed I would be back. I guess with somebody that young, young and dumb, you don't think about death. It was always getting maimed or losing an arm or a leg."

Sasser was assigned to Alpha Company, 3d Battalion, 9th Infantry Division. Morale was good in the company. There were plenty of blacks and Hispanics along with white soldiers, black officers, black noncoms, he recalled. "I've always been a person to get along with other people. Over there, everybody depended on everybody. It hadn't got bad, the way it did after the assassination of Martin Luther King in the spring of 1968.

"My unit was part of what they called the Mobile Riverine Force, where Tom Kelley was [see chapter 17]. They used armored troop carriers to ferry us up the rivers for missions. We lived on ships near the mouth of the Mekong Delta. Our patrols were fairly short—they would never leave us out longer than four or five days because of the effect of water on the skin. It was really destructive. We usually traveled in company force, one medic per platoon, which would be thirty-six guys if you were at full strength, which you seldom were."

Sasser went on several patrols between his arrival in the Delta in late September and January ten, the day he performed the actions that led to his receiving the Medal of Honor. "We would go out and stay three, four days at a time and you were constantly wet." He saw men die from combat injuries while he was treating them. "That's quite . . . quite a . . . quite a situation. It's hard to imagine anything more difficult."

When he was sent to the line company, Sasser was issued an M-16 rifle, but he didn't carry it on patrol. "I carried a .45 on my hip. You had a backpack with medical supplies, and a medical bag, like a big fat briefcase. Most of the stuff was fairly light, bandages, stuff like that. And you carried your own food. And I'd always carry a couple of bandoliers of M-60 machine-gun ammo, also, just to help. We had learned to suture cuts, and instead of plasma we used what we called ringers, a solution that builds volume in the blood, administered intravenously, just like plasma."

On the morning of January 10, 1968, Alpha Company was assigned to take part in a battalion-size search-and-destroy mission. "Third Battalion, 60th Infantry. We went in by helicopter that day. We had gone out by boat, then put ashore, then loaded on the Huey transport helicopters, which held twelve or fourteen, including a crew of four. My company of one hundred and six was set to be backup. We were going to have an easy time of it that day. At least that was what we thought. Then the sergeant told us that choppers were on the way, we had to go investigate an area that was pretty heavily occupied. Actually it was a base-camp buildup for the coming Tet Offensive [a series of coordinated attacks by the North Vietnamese on cities throughout the country], NVA cadre [leaders] but primarily Vietcong soldiers, about thirteen hundred of them." The target area was in Cai Be District, in the western part of a province called Dinh Tuong.

"We got loaded onto fifteen or twenty choppers and headed to this area to check it out. I guess from that point we called it a separate search-and-destroy or reconnaissance in force, but it got bad pretty quick. We rode about fifteen, twenty minutes in the choppers and somebody picked out an LZ, a landing zone, in a rice paddy full of water, maybe a big ten-acre rectangle surrounded on three sides by woods. I was on the fourth chopper that went in that morning, probably about ten-thirty. We started coming in and the door gunners started discharging their weapons and then, Get ready, and then you see a chopper hit and it drops down into the water, and there's twelve to fifteen guys on it, there's no doubt then. Now you got to go in. So that was it.

"The choppers come down, they hover and you jump off into the rice paddy, mud and water nearly waist deep. It was difficult moving in it. As I said, the door gunners were firing and the order comes: Everybody off! Everybody off! I got to the door and I jumped, and that's when a bullet hit the back part of my leg, just a grazing type wound, but it probably would have killed me if I hadn't jumped. But essentially I was all right. So everybody jumps in to try to rescue the downed helicopter.

"I think that's all the enemy was waiting for. They had us surrounded on three sides and all their mortars—that's primarily what they had, mortars—were zeroed in on the rice paddy. And they had .30 caliber machine guns and, of course, the AK47s. The distance across the paddy was three hundred to four hundred yards. They started chopping us up immediately"—Sasser's voice breaks— "and guys were dropping like flies, and now they're hollering 'Medic! Medic! Doc! Doc!' All that kind of stuff." The other three medics in the company apparently were killed in a very short time.

"The immediate thing was to get to some kind of protection— except in a rice paddy there isn't any, except for the levees, which really weren't that much protection. You knew the general direction the gunfire and mortars were coming from, mostly both flanks. The first guy I got to was badly hurt. He had been shot through the chest, a sucking chest wound. Our bandages were pretty ingenious. You take the wrapper off and put that next to the wound and then put the bandage, the field dressing, on over that. They had strings on them to tie with and you'd draw it down tight as you could. After

I bandaged him, I told him to try to keep his head above water, except this guy was half in and half out of consciousness.

"But that's all you can do, and go on to the next one. Bullets were flying, mortars were coming in. You can't run in that water. And it didn't take long to figure out that if you raised [yourself] up, you were dead. They had snipers all around. It was a setup. I learned pretty quickly that it was easier to drag yourself over the water and mud by gripping a handful of rice and pulling yourself along. I went from one guy to the next for the next two or three hours and then would go back to check on them, when things died down a little bit, but the VC were still lobbing mortars every place. We could barely even return fire, and there was no way you could set a machine gun up, but a couple of guys I patched up, I gave their weapons back to them, and said, 'Come on, man, let's get back to firing so we can get out of here.'

"The levees, the dikes, crossed, and the best protection was to get in a corner. Guys tried to get in the corners and fight back from there. The enemy never rushed us, which was understandable because they would have had to come into the paddy, and we were still able to return fire, so it was more of a whittling-down approach they took. All we could do was spray the wood lines. We had mortars with us, but the crew had no way of setting them up. The snipers were working, too, and as far as I know, all the officers were gone and the sergeants were understandably keeping their heads down.

"They sent a company to help us, but they got jumped, so they couldn't get to us. All we got was air support from the Phantoms. My respect for the Phantoms went up immediately. Man, they were dropping napalm on the wood lines, laying it in there so close that a lot of times you'd think the pilot was going to get his tail caught in it when he pulled up, it was that close. But they had to do something or we were going to be killed. We were out there more than twelve hours, and only twelve or fourteen men out of one hundred and six came out without being wounded or killed. I was the oniliest medic that lived."

An after-action report issued on January 12 said there were twenty-four killed and fifty-nine injured, but Sasser called that "shaded," adding that he remained convinced that at least thirty-five Americans died in the rice paddy that day. "We were just chopped up. It was probably not a prudent decision to send us into a rice paddy that close to the woods after you saw the enemy. I mean, you ought to presume that if you saw them, they saw you, and you ought to presume that they would be expecting you. I'm trying to be gentle about it, but it probably was a raw fuck-up.

"It didn't take a rocket scientist to know they could figure out you were going to investigate them. As it turned out it was a buildup for Tet, and they were there in force, and Alpha Company walked right into the middle of it. We Americans sometimes do. In retrospect, I would equate it to arrogance. We were a very good fighting force, I believed then and I still believe, but some of the decisions were not prudent, I thought.

"A lot of field-grade officers, the lieutenant colonels and the colonels, made, in my opinion, grievous errors in fighting the war, in the Ia Drang, Ashau Valley. Such as in this case, sending men into an area where you have been seen. I mean, we were *Army*. We were used to the humpin', the walkin'. Put us off and let us go there. Don't just send us into the middle of a bull's-eye.

"The decisions were the result of gung-ho officers that were weaned working on tactics, guys getting their tickets punched. You know, with half a million guys over there, the thing we used to say before this incident occurred was, 'What the hell goin' on?' You can take us and arm us and put us down here at the bottom of the country, start at one end and walk the length of it, and be through with it. I know that's ridiculously simple and everything, but I still think to this day that could have been a valid strategy."

Sasser was wounded for the second time about three hours after the drop into the rice paddy. "I had been moving around treating guys, and if you've been there, you could always tell when the mortars were coming in, where they were going to land in proximity to where you were. So I heard it. I heard it comin', so I was trying to get to one of those corners. I knew it was coming from thataway and I was coming from thataway, and I was trying to roll over the top of the dike to get to a corner when it hit. A couple of them hit, probably about fifteen feet from me, and I'm on top of the dike, trying to roll over on the other side and the shrapnel just sprayed all of my left side, my shoulder, my back, my hip, and my leg.

"The hurting was something because, when mortar shells explode, that shit's hot, I mean real hot, and ragged, those fragments tearing and burning. But I knew it wasn't life threatening. It hurt like hell and I was bleeding, but unless shell fragments hit an artery or a nerve, it's more aggravation and pain than life threatening.

"I rolled over the dike and lay there a while. A guy who was a friend called, 'Hey, Doc, did that getcha?' I hollered, 'Yeah, I'm all right. I'm a little bit hurt, but I'm all right.' I went back over to where he was lying stretched out in the water with his head up on the dike. I lay there with him for a while, rested, rested, just rested, and then a while later went to see about another guy who was hollering Doc. I went to see about him, and when I came back another mortar had killed the guy who had called to see if I was all right. I came back, and he's a mess, been mortared. He had already been shot. That's why he was lying up there. I had run out of dressings, but I guess as luck would have it, I found one of the other medics' bag and on top of that most of the guys carried a couple of field dressings with them. Of course I used up all the morphine and stuff and was able to start a couple of IVs. I carried two bottles of blood filler.

"A little while later, I moved and found another group of guys. Every once in a while somebody would raise up and let off a few rounds, and duck back down, and I was lying there with them. I fired my .45 a few times, just playing, between interludes, just playing, just playing, I say playing. Thinking about it later, that's probably when the enemy pulled out, or went and jumped on the other company coming to rescue us. But they left snipers and mortars around. It got quiet. The fighting would wax and wane, so I raised up to look, and that's when a sniper hit me right here, on top of the skull, and the bullet bounced off. I wasn't wearing a helmet. You couldn't keep up with a helmet in all of this. But I'd say the bullet bounced, just the right angle the way it hit, and glanced off. It left me with a hell of a headache. It knocked me out for a couple of hours, bled like crazy. I thought I was dead, you know, until I started coming to, a couple of hours later, and realized I'm still here, because of the sounds I was hearing, the sporadic firing, the mortars coming in and then I realized, 'Well, hell, I guess I'm not dead.' But it was very painful.

"I didn't do much from then on. After dark we did succeed in making it to the wood line, I would say probably about seven o'clock. You had no perception of time out there. The ones that could move were able to get there themselves. Some of the others who weren't injured were able to move those who were hurt bad. By now, my leg's swollen, my back's swollen, and I have one hell of a headache, but I got myself to the treeline. I was able to crawl in, using that technique I had, using the rice to drag me along.

"The Phantoms were working the wood line, Puff [the high-firing AC-47 helicopter gunship known as Puff the Magic Dragon] had come in and was spraying the wood lines and, like I say, that's what saved us. If they hadn't come in, I think at some time the enemy would have completely overrun us. About this time we had radio contact, because I remember Sergeant Peters asking for assistance, and I remember our artillery helping us out. They were whomping that stuff to us, man, they were walking it to us, and you just knew the next one was going to be right on top of you. They were walking it to us, and then they skipped us. They did it. It was sort of hair-raising: Are they going to miss us, or what? And you see it walking toward you. And then all of sudden it's behind you.

"In retrospect, I was really pretty lucky. The good Lord sort of looked out for me. I could have been really messed up getting off the chopper the first time; the second time I could have been messed up when the mortar hit; the third time when the sniper hit me in the head." Sasser did not include the fourth time, when the soldier he had been lying next to was killed by a mortar shortly after he had left to help another man. "I didn't count that, because no injury resulted.

"It was pretty terrible. You know what the hardest thing was? The hardest thing was laying down all night, listening to them beg for their mamas."

Forcing out these words, Clarence Sasser broke down. "Soldiers dying, calling for their mothers, the ones we couldn't get in. Some were still out in the rice paddy. That was the hardest part, laying there all night hearing them moan and groan, beg for help, beg for their mama, and you were so tired, exhausted, dehydrated. It's not very glamorous, no sir, it isn't. It is not a good story. But then I guess it's consistent with war.

"We were lying in the rice paddy that night, and the little group I was in, maybe six or seven guys, they told me I did a good job. They told me they were going to see that I get a medal. Well, you take that with a grain of salt. You were still alive even though all night you heard the guys hollering. You heard one scream, holler, beg for help, and then you would hear the moaning, and you knew he died. That was the perversity of it, them telling me I did a good job when all these men were dying.

"But I did what I did because it was my job, and if I didn't do it, none of us were going to get out. At least that's what I felt. I still stand with that. I have no idea at what point the other medics were killed. I did see another one working at the start, but later on I didn't see anybody.

"The first chopper that came in was a gunship. It was about three the next morning when they made the first test run. The gunship didn't get no fire, and then they started coming in to get us. Fifty-five wounded, fourteen unhurt, thirty-five or forty dead. I'm just guessing at the time.

"After the dustoff, we were taken to the Mobile Riverine Force base camp, also the 9th Infantry Division base camp, where they had an evacuation hospital, a trauma hospital. They dug out my shrapnel, and they had to debride the wound because shrapnel is so hot it cauterizes and I guess destroys tissue, so all that they cut out. They couldn't do much for my head. I was lucky the slug didn't go through.

"I definitely think I have a guardian angel. I definitely think that. I think that was His will: Go home, have three children and raise them right. Do that, and other things I do now, like helping people."

Sasser was kept at the base hospital until the end of January, until the start of the Tet Offensive. "They needed the bed space, so they evacked me out to a hospital in Japan. At this time, my leg is still pretty bad, but I can hobble along on crutches. The rest of that time, February to March, I was in the hospital, Camp Zama, in Japan, eighty-four days all told.

"What happened next is a story in itself. Being a medic, and I like to think I was a competent one, after I recovered, I got reassigned over there. They were going to send me back [to Vietman], but a good doctor needed medics at Zama. By now, Tet's well under way, and a lot of injuries are coming through, and they need assistance. Being a personable person, I was reassigned to work at the dispensary at Zama so I wouldn't have to go back. They kept me from going back. So I lucked out on that, because my year wouldn't have been up for four or five months.

"One morning several months afterward I came into the dispensary, and the captain, his name was Derrick, called me into his office and told me the general wanted to see me. I say, 'What?' He said, 'I don't know. You just need to go see him. A car will be here to pick you up.'

"So I went over, walked in, saluted. The general said, 'At ease.' I'm a Spec-4 by now. He told me he had orders to get me back to the States. 'For what?' He said, 'You're going to Washington. They're going to present you the Medal of Honor.' This was early January nineteen sixty-nine, almost a year since the battle."

Sasser flew to Oakland, spent the night with a stepsister, then flew down to Los Angeles, where he had a brother and an aunt, and a couple of days later he flew home to Houston. "They were all happy, of course, to see me, and I told them why I was back. They were happy. They took it, I guess probably like I now take it, that I did my job. I did a good job. My father was aware of the medal. He had been in World War II. He knew what it meant. My mom and sisters and brothers, all seven, went to Washington with me. My stepdad didn't go. Nor my daddy." Sasser laughs. "They would not get on a plane. They would not fly."

He received the Medal in the East Room of the White House, with Fred Zabitosky and Joe Hooper. "They're both dead now. We were Mr. Nixon's first presentations. He had just taken office in January sixty-nine and this was March. He didn't say much. He cracked a few jokes. He was quite comical when he unwound. His people showed my folks around Washington, D.C. It was probably the best time that a farm family from southeast Texas would ever get."

Sasser had been reassigned to nearby Fort Belvoir, Virginia. "My two years of duty is coming up in June, so I stayed around Belvoir with no particular job. I got a couple re-up [reenlistment] talks and all that. 'No.' I said, 'Nope. I signed on for two years, that's it. That's it. Nope. I made it through. I'm not signing up again for you to send me back,' although I don't know if that would have happened. There were guys who went back." [Military policy is to keep Medal of Honor recipients from harm's way, but Mitchell Paige from World War II, Lew Millett from Korea, and Jack Jacobs and Harvey Barnum from Vietnam were among recipients who returned to combat.] "A lot of guys were wacky, man," Sasser said.

He had met Ethel Morant on his return from Japan. "When I was released from the Army, I came back home, got me a job for the summer, and in September I went back to college, up to Texas A&M. But I didn't finish. As I said earlier, things happened. Ethel became pregnant in the spring of 1971, and we got married in November. Babies started coming. I went to work for Dow Chemical as a plant operator. In the spring of seventy-three I left Dow and went to work for Amoco, another chemical company, doing essentially the same work. I stayed there until June of nineteen seventy-seven, took a month off, then went to work for the Veterans Administration here in Houston. I started out as a contact representative, dealing with the public, the veterans, and I essentially have been doing that ever since. I'll be fifty-five, so I have a few more years to go to get my thirty in. I have done pretty well. I don't have any regrets."

Sasser said he was acquainted with most of the other living recipients of the Medal of Honor. "I don't think they have much in common, other than the medal. They're all from diverse backgrounds, and they had diverse services and jobs in the military. What they do have in common I would say is, they take charge in situations. They are people who felt that something needed doing at a particular time and somebody had to do it. Words like *bravery* and *courage* are words that come after the fact; they're retroactive, retrospective-type words. I think probably the biggest thing you find, particularly if you read the citations, is that there was a feeling that somebody had to do something."

Commenting on the fact that no Medals of Honor were awarded to blacks who served in World War II [until 1997; see chapter 5] and that twenty were awarded during the Vietnam War, Sasser said, "I think considerable progress has been made from the time of Mr. Truman's order to integrate the services in nineteen forty-seven. I think the color of your skin has very very little effect in the military today. In fact, I think the rest of society is lagging behind the military. The military usually lags behind society, but on this issue I think the military has transcended society. Now it's the best place to be, as evidenced by the number of black guys who rank in the upper echelons. Not only Colin Powell, who was head of the Joint Chiefs, but also J. Paul Reason, who is commander in chief of the Atlantic Fleet."

Sasser takes pride in his house. "I self-contracted it. We got a stock plan from an architect, and my wife and I had it built in nineteen eighty-six: four bedrooms, twenty-one hundred fifty-five square feet. "We didn't want one too big, knowing the boys would be gone and then we'd be stuck with a big old house. This is comfortable."

The boys, however, are his real pride. "Ross is a graduate of the University of Texas, and a teacher. Benjamin, an engineer, graduated from Southwest Texas State. Billy is a senior at Sam Houston State. He's in animal science, but says he wants to be a game warden. I told him to bring home all the fish he confiscates. I'm very proud of them. They were all boys, black males, and that was a special challenge. There's a stereotype of black males, and I'm proud my boys aren't like that. I'm really proud that my wife and I raised them the way we did. I'm talking from the point of young people who become adults with no direction, no focus, no nothing. No goals. The prisons here are filled with black kids.

"I make appearances, and I select what I do very carefully. I usually do active-duty situations, speaking at military reservations, posts or bases, and at high schools. I like to tell the schoolkids that the actions they take should be directed toward their benefit, meaning: Don't go out there and do something wrong. That's not to your benefit. Have goals, be disciplined, follow that discipline to that goal."

TWENTY-ONE

Joe Jackson

Lieutenant Colonel, U.S. Air Force
Kham Duc, Vietnam
May 12, 1968

*"I was three years old, maybe four, and one of my brothers
and I, we'd been fishing, and we were walking down the road when
this airplane flew over, and it started doing acrobatics in the sky, around the
clouds. I looked up and thought that it would be the greatest thing in
the whole world if I could do that. I remember that specifically.
That was the first thing I remember in my life."*

Joe Jackson was already a veteran of
World War II and Korea, where he
flew many missions over the Chosin
Reservoir, before he served in Vietnam.
The action for which he received the
Medal of Honor occurred on May 12,
1968, when Jackson was forty-five years
old. President Lyndon B. Johnson decorated him in the White House eight
months later, on January 16, 1969.

"The world's hottest fighter pilot," as Joe Jackson
humorously described himself, at Tyndall Field,
Florida, in 1944, where he flew P-40s, P-47s, and
P-63s. Eager and skilled though he was, Jackson
never got to fly in combat until he went to Korea
in the 1950s.

334

WHEN HE GAVE this account of his life, in August 2002, Joe Jackson was nearly blind in his left eye as a result of macular degeneration. For several years he owned a private plane, a Cessna Cutlass, but he'd sold it three years previously to his son David, a pilot for Delta in Dallas, "for ten bucks." Jackson added, "I think I miss that airplane more than anything else." Joe and his wife, Rose, appear comfortably settled on a couple of verdant acres in Kent, Washington. Rose is a master gardener and seems happy to be in one place, especially after having lived in twenty-nine different locations during Joe's thirty years in the military.

Joe Jackson was a Georgia farm boy, born on March 14, 1923. "My father died of a stroke when I was eleven. It was the middle of the Depression, and things were tough. We had lost the farm earlier in the Depression, so we were just church mice. We had practically nothing. We were very poor as far as material things were concerned, but we were rather rich in family life and spiritual things. My mother kept the family together. My older brothers worked in the mills around Newman and gave her money. I had six brothers, no sisters. I'm the seventh boy. My mother was a devout Christian, and we were brought up that way. We went to the Baptist church."

The family lived and worked on rented farms until Joe was thirteen, when his mother moved to Newman. "Things were tough financially. I wanted to drop out of high school and go to work at the Ford garage. They said, You can work full-time here, and I wanted to do that because I would make a huge sum, twelve bucks a week, but my mother said no. She said, 'We'll make out. We won't starve to death. I want you to get your education because, once you get your high-school education, nobody can take that away from you, and you'll come out ahead much better than if you didn't have it. If you'll do that,' she said, 'I'll support you in anything you want after you come out of high school.' So I went ahead and finished. Of course, college was out of the question, so after graduating in the spring of nineteen forty, I went away to a trade school, a Chris-

tian school established to train ministers, at Taquoa Falls, Georgia.
But I went there for skills training, not to become a minister. They
had carpentry, and they advertised having airplane mechanics, and
that's why I went. I wanted to become an airplane mechanic."

It was here that Jackson recounted an early memory: "I was three
years old, maybe four, and one of my brothers and I, we'd been fishing, and we were walking down the road when this airplane flew
over, and it started doing acrobatics in the sky, around the clouds. I
looked up and thought that it would be the greatest thing in the
whole world if I could do that. I remember that specifically. That
was the first thing I remember in my life." But he knew, coming out
of high school, that this was an impossible dream, so he chose the
next best thing—to fix planes if he could not fly them.

In the spring of '41, having finally completed the course he
needed, Jackson started job hunting. It was six months before Pearl
Harbor. "I finally went back to the guy who was running the school,
to ask him about a job, and he said, 'No, and you're not gonna get
one either. You don't have any experience. I'll tell you what you can
do. You can join the Army Air Corps, and get some experience, and
when you get out three years from now, you can get a job.' It was just
before my eighteenth birthday, and I had to get my mother to sign."

"On December seventh, I was at Orlando Army Air Field in the
barracks and some guy came in and says, 'Any of you guys want to
go to town, you better get out of here right now, because the Japs
have just attacked Pearl Harbor and they're going to close the
post.' I think everyone on the whole base put on their civvies and
headed for town. I didn't drink then, and I haven't drunk much
since. I had a girlfriend downtown, nothing serious. We usually
went to church on Sunday night together. I did not get to town
again for quite a while.

"In January we were transferred to Westover Field, Massachusetts. The B-25 bombers and air crews did antisub patrol in the
North Atlantic. I was a mechanic and got promoted to staff sergeant. I was working the night shift, and a buddy came to me one
morning and said he was supposed to go out as a flight engineer and

said he was sick and didn't feel like going, and would I take his flight? I said sure. We took off, and we were climbing up and the pilot turned to me and said, 'The right engine is on fire. What do I do?' I said, 'You feather it.'

"That means you turn the prop to the wind so the engine won't turn, and when he did that the fire went out, and we went back and landed. My thought process was this: That pilot is a captain, he's got a college education, and when an engine caught fire, he didn't know what to do. I know what to do, so I'm as smart as he is; if I'm as smart as he is, I can fly an airplane too. I always wanted to be a pilot anyway, so I went to the aviation cadet office and said I wanted to sign up. The guy says, 'Okay, where did you go to college?' I says, 'I didn't.' He says, 'I'm sorry, you can't be an aviation cadet with no college.' I said, 'Okay,' and I went back to work.

"A short time after, this guy called me up and said, 'Do you still want to go to aviation cadets?' I said, 'Yeah.' He said, 'Well, they got a new deal. They have an exam here, and if you can pass this exam and pass a physical, you can go. You don't have to have college anymore.' So I went over and took the exam and passed it and the physical, and in September I got orders to go to aviation cadet training."

Earlier that year, a friend had persuaded him to go on a blind date with Rose Parmentier of Chicopee, Massachusetts. "He said, 'My girlfriend's got a girlfriend, and we'll get together and go to the movies or whatever.' At this point, Rose, who was to marry Joe on September 7, 1944, interjected with a laugh, "We went roller-skating, and neither one of us could stand up." And Jackson added with a laugh of his own, "Yeah, we were skating on thin ice."

Jackson went to preflight training in Dothan, Alabama, with a group of enlisted men, sergeants who had passed the test. "Morse Code to me was the most difficult challenge I ever had. I never learned code. I could do five words a minute, but I made a lot of mistakes. It was used a lot then. Everything was by dead reckoning, or following railroad tracks and roads.

"Night navigation was easy because they had light lines all over the United States, twenty miles or so apart. You could look out ahead and see blink blink blink, these rotating beacons. Each one would flash a certain code, a certain sequence so you could figure out where you were. I started training in a PT-19, a little single-engine plane that was built by Fairchild. As time went on I flew a lot of planes and, primarily because I became a fighter pilot, I flew P-47s, P-51s, P-40s, P-63s, then F-82s and F-84s when they came along—that was Korea. I got my wings in April of forty-three and my commission as a second lieutenant."

Jackson was sent to Eglin Field in Florida to be a test pilot, but when he got there he found that twenty pilots had been sent for two openings. "So, to pick the two pilots, they chose scientifically—they drew straws. I drew a short straw and went and became a gunnery instructor and a tow pilot, towing targets so guys could shoot at them in the air. And I, Judas Priest, I thought, this is no place for the hottest fighter pilot in the whole world. But, you know, I enjoyed it, and I think at that field I really learned to fly. Before that, I could get in an airplane and go through all the procedures and do that very well, but learning an airplane by feel and knowledge of what it can do is different."

After nine months he transferred to another field where there was a training school for gunners in B-17s and B-24 bombers. "They learned how to fire at airplanes attacking them. My job was to go up and make attacks on these bombers so the gun crews could practice, following me with their guns, .30 calibers, and make training movies of it. Later on, we got an airplane, the P-63, which we called the Pinball Machine. It was painted orange, with armor plating on the leading edge of the wings and the tail and in the nose, and the gunners actually fired frangible bullets at us. The bullets were made of Bakelite and pressed lead powder and they were supposed to shatter. They didn't always shatter. They shot a few down, but nothing bad came of it."

The hottest fighter pilot in the world was dying to get to the war. "I couldn't wait. I wanted to go to Europe so bad, you couldn't believe it. But they kept saying, No, we need you here to supervise this group of fighter pilots. There were about twenty-five of us. They made me the squadron commander, first lieutenant. So I stayed and, just as the war was over, I got orders to go to Tennessee to learn to fly the B-24. Oh, I hated that. By that time, I was a really dedicated fighter pilot. I didn't want anything to do with bombers." He made captain by December 1944.

Once the war ended, Joe finally got sent to Germany, to be part of the Army of Occupation. Rose came too.

"We were very happy we went, mainly because we saw the devastation that had occurred. It brought home the lesson that we should never get involved in another war. It was ridiculous. Everything was destroyed. When they closed out our base at Nordholz in the latter part of forty-six, we got transferred down near Kassel, Germany, which was just a heap of rubble. All the streets were just covered with rubble. About every fourth street was open so that you could pass through. It still stank with dead and decaying bodies. I don't know whether they were animal bodies or people bodies, but it still smelled bad."

Returning home, Jackson discovered he could not get out of the military. "They were still discharging people who had served overseas during the war. They had first priority for getting out. When it came my turn, late in forty-seven or early forty-eight, I took leave and went looking for a job, but I couldn't find one because all of these guys ahead of me had taken all the jobs. So I went back and said to Rose, 'Hey, you know, maybe we'll stay a couple more years and things will settle down and then I'll get out.' " Then the Korean War came along.

Meanwhile, the Army Air Corps had become the United States Air Force. President Truman had signed the National Defense Reorganization Act on September 18, 1947, Jackson recalled, and one of its provisions made the Air Force a separate and equal service.

The hot fighter pilot finally got his chance in Korea except, "By that time I had grown up, and it wasn't what I expected, actually."

Rose remembered, "He did tell me when we first got married, he said, 'What am I gonna tell my kids some day when they ask me, "Dad, what did you do in the war?" ' And, he says, 'I didn't do anything but teach a bunch of kids to shoot at me.' He was not very happy then, but he grew up after that."

In fact, Jackson went on to fly 107 missions with the 27th Fighter Wing in Korea, in the F-84 jet. He received the Distinguished Flying Cross but doesn't remember why. "I really don't remember. I was in about eight aerial combats, and I got shot at enough but never got hit. I didn't down any. We did some escort missions where the MiG-15s were zooming right on through our formations, but they were so much faster that we just had no chance of catching them. They were a Mach 1 airplane. You couldn't catch them. I came home with an airplane with several holes in it from ground fire on many occasions.

"I got over there just as the Chinese were coming south in nineteen fifty. We did a lot of interdiction of supplies and stuff that was being sent down in oxcarts, trucks, and other ways to support the Chinese. There used to be a radio show quiz program at that time and, if you answered all the questions correctly, you became a Lemac. The program was sponsored by the Camel cigarette company—Lemac is Camel spelled backward. And we had one guy we called Lemac because he went out on a mission and here was this string of camels going down the road carrying enemy supplies and he shot one, and it blew up.

"He actually shot five, and they all five blew up, and that's how he got the name Lemac. We cut the little camels out of his cigarette pack and pasted them on his helmet.

"I have been up to the Chosin Reservoir many many times. We helped cover the Marine retreat out of the Chosin Reservoir area. The Korean War ended in 1953, and it was another year or so after that before I could get out, and I said to Rose, 'You know, if we stayed another seven years, I could retire with a pension. I'd have twenty years in.' She said, 'Okay.' " The Jacksons' daughter, Bonnie, had come along in 1949 and a son, David, was born in 1953. Joe had gone to Korea as a captain and in February of 1951 he was promoted to major, a rank he held for eleven years. In that time he also left the reserves and received a regular commission, which guaranteed job safety. Reserve officers could be released with no warning during periodic reductions in force.

"In nineteen sixty-one, my twenty years would have been up. I was assigned to Strategic Air Command headquarters, and I was going to the University of Omaha to get a degree in education. I was twenty years late getting a college education, and I was working on my degree. I figured to get out and become a schoolteacher. When I was getting near the end of my education at the University of Omaha, I got selected to attend the Air War College at Maxwell Air Force Base and, if you took some extra courses, you could get a master's degree in political science. I said, wow, I can get a master's degree, and I'd have a lot better chance getting a job teaching when I get out. But when I got through, because the government paid for my education, I had another three-year service obligation.

"I was assigned to Headquarters U.S. Air Forces in Europe in Wiesbaden. We went over there in sixty-four and, before my three-year commitment was up, I got a consecutive overseas tour assignment to Vietnam." Jackson was sent back to the States for training while Rose stayed in Wiesbaden. While he was gone, Rose said, "I had a daughter graduate from high school in Germany. We had tried to get out of the military. Enough was enough. He was going to retire when we came back from Wiesbaden. He was in his forties now. They told him, 'You can retire when you get back, but you have to go to Vietnam first.' "

Before he left for Vietnam, Jackson, by now a lieutenant colonel, recalled, "I was checking out in the C-123, a cargo plane that was designed and built as a glider. It was supposed to be used during the invasion of Europe, to land small tanks and artillery pieces behind German lines, or during the invasion of Normandy. But it came along too late and they didn't get enough people trained. It was just sitting out there. They had hundreds of them that had never been used. Then, after the war, the Air Force decided it needed light transport, so they put two high-powered reciprocating engines on it, and it was now a C-123 propeller plane. That's what I checked out in and what I was flying when I went to Vietnam.

"I went through the Air Force advanced survival school at Fairchild Air Force base in Spokane. They gave you all sorts of stuff, they'd torture you, want you to eat snakes, find your way in the dark and walk ten miles a day on no food for five days, hand-to-hand combat. I think I must have lost twenty-five pounds during those thirty days. I was forty-four years old now. I thought it was very inconsiderate of them to do this." He had two months of training in Florida with the C-123, Rose came home and he got her settled, then went to the Philippines where he went through another survival school. "We called it the Snake School. Actually it was jungle survival, about two weeks of it, miserable mainly because of rain rain rain."

Once there, he was assigned to the 311th Air Commando Squadron, which resupplied Special Forces camps, out-of-the-way airfields, and small military groups throughout the country. Initially he was stationed in the south near Cam Ranh Bay. Then he was transferred up to Da Nang, where he commanded a detachment of airplanes that resupplied the First Corps, reaching from the Demilitarized Zone down to Chun-Yon on the coast.

"That was my area of responsibility. I had six airplanes and about one hundred men plus the air crews.

"May twelfth, nineteen sixty-eight, was Mother's Day, Sunday. I was scheduled to go on a flight check with Jesse Campbell as a copilot. He was a major and the flight check officer too. It was a routine mission, just fly up and down the coast. We went up to Dong Ha, just south of the DMZ and to several bases both up and back. About noon I got back to Chu Lai, a Marine base about fifty miles southeast of Da Nang and got recalled. They said come back to Da Nang. As we were going back, they said they wanted to evacuate Kham Duc, a Special Forces camp about fifty miles southwest of Da Nang, right next to the Laotian border. The camp was being overrun by between four thousand and six thousand North Vietnamese regulars.

"So I flew over there and reported in. They had an airborne command post, a C-130, and a group of people on board with radios and stuff who were directing ground operations from the air. I checked in and they said, 'Go to the southwest of the field and orbit at nine thousand feet. We'll call ya.'

"Campbell meanwhile had said my flight check was over. You can fly the airplane okay, no problem. Let's not worry about that while we have this mission to contend with. We had a flight engineer, Technical Sergeant Edward Trejo. The loadmaster was Sergeant Manson Grubbs; he was supposed to take care of cargo and the pilots and look after passengers, if we had any. That was the crew. So there we are, orbiting at nine thousand feet.

"Kham Duc had a satellite base, Ngok Tavak, to the southwest that could look right across the border, just inside Laos, and they could spy on the men and supplies going up and down the trail, Route 14. They'd had a patrol out on the ninth of May, and they ran into a North Vietnamese patrol and had a little firefight, and they captured one of the soldiers and brought him back. During interrogation, he said they were going to overrun Kham Duc sometime in the next few days. The commander of Ngok Tavak decided to withdraw into the main camp at Kham Duc, which called for reinforcements. On the tenth they sent in a battalion of soldiers, around six hundred or so, under the command of a Lieutenant Colonel Nelson. When he got there, he put out seven outposts around the airfield and during the night on the tenth and the eleventh, all seven outposts were overrun. Some of the people got back, but most of them were either killed or captured.

"The fighting got so hot on the eleventh that during the evening it was decided that they would evacuate Kham Duc beginning the next day, the twelfth of May. The next morning one of my friends flying a C-123 went in, picked up a load, and got out. A C-130 went in, and he had one of his four main landing-gear tires shot out. His right wing was perforated with quite a bit of automatic-weapons fire, and it was leaking fuel like crazy. He had a load of cargo on board as well and, when he landed and picked up a load of evacuees, he couldn't get off the ground. The flat tire caused too much drag in the wheel well, and he had to unload everybody and try to chop the tire off.

"As the morning went on, a bunch of airplanes and two helicopters were shot down. One crashed and burned in the middle of the runway. Another helicopter was shot down. Its pilot bailed out, landed off base, and was picked up later by helicopter. An observation plane was shot down, and a couple of fighters were shot down. They crashed en route back to their home base and not in the immediate vicinity." In all, eight American aircraft, two big Army Chinook helicopters, two Marine Corps C-46s, two Air Force C-130s, the observation aircraft, and an A-1 jet, were shot down that day.

"In view of the heavy loss of aircraft, they called off the evacuation during the morning. Meanwhile the crew with Colonel Daryl Cole, the guy who had the flat tire, had chopped it off the rim with bayonets and fire axes. They had to cut through that heavy tough rubber and casing and got it off the wheel. I don't know whether they unloaded the cargo or not, but I think they took a few of the civilians who were dependents of the South Vietnamese soldiers (there were fifteen hundred Americans and South Vietnamese at the camp) out with them, along with the three-man combat control team that was supposed to control the operations on the ground.

"That plane has two main landing-gear tires on each side, and one of them was okay. So, after they chopped off the second one, they got off the ground and headed back for Cam Ranh Bay.

"Along about noon they decided to resume the evacuation, and that was when I was recalled to go in. The first plane in was a C-130 and it had all four engines shot out plus the hydraulic system, and it was lucky to be able to hit the runway. It ran through the remains of that helicopter that had crashed and burned. It rolled on and ran off the side of the runway and into a ditch and was destroyed. The next C-130 that went in picked up about one hundred and fifty evacuees, mostly South Viet dependents and some soldiers and, when it took off, it was shot down and all of them were lost. Every one of them was lost. [The pilot was Major Bernard Bucher, who was posthumously awarded the Air Force Cross.] The next C-130 was able to pick up a load of people, and it got out of there under heavy mortar and automatic-weapons fire. It got back to Cam Ranh Bay with over one thousand holes in it.

"A guy I didn't know then but later became friends with was a forward air controller just outside the perimeter of the base. He started coordinating fighter attacks with transports coming in. He'd put one airplane down on either side of the runway, laying down fire to keep the heads of the North Vietnamese down while the transport landed. After that they were able to get in and get out without too much problem, although I think all of them got some kind of damage.

"That went on for the rest of the afternoon." The combat control team had come out, to Cam Ranh Bay, but then, upon learning the evacuation had resumed, turned around and went back into Kham Duc. So when they got back, the airplane pilot left them off and picked up the last of the battalion. He came under real heavy mortar and automatic-weapons attack but he got off, and he left the three combat control guys there.

"He called in the airborne command post and said he had picked up the last of the survivors. And so the airborne command post called the fighter commander and said, 'Burn the camp to the ground.' But the C-130 pilot said, 'No, no, no. I just left the combat control team off. You still got three guys on the ground there.'

"It wasn't hard to understand how it happened. Everything is confusion. Everything is confusion. People have been fighting like crazy and shooting, and as soon as these three guys hit the ground, they knew they had to get under cover. The guys that were ready to go knew they had to get on that airplane right now and get out of there. So they swapped places and the three guys got left on the ground.

"They asked a couple of planes to go down and take a look and see if they could locate them. No luck. Then they asked a guy in a 123 that had been there long before us if he would go down and land to see if he could draw them out of hiding. He landed and he came under heavy automatic-weapons fire and applied the power to go around. I was watching all this in my orbit, I was over the airfield at that time, and I could see these tracers coming out of the jungle toward that airplane.

"Oh, I cringed. Just as he lifted off he saw the three guys coming out of the bunkers and heading for the runway and they dove into the ditch alongside. I couldn't see the guys but I saw his touchdown, and when he got off the ground you could still see the fire coming out of the jungle at him. Anyway, he's low on fuel by now and he can't make another approach, but he called in that he had seen the combat control team heading for the ditch just a little bit south and west of the wrecked helicopter that was on the runway. So I knew where he was talking about, and when the airborne command post asked if there would be anybody that would attempt to pick them up, I was the most logical person to do it.

"So we called, 'Roger, going in!' We were at nine thousand feet. I put the props in flat pitch, put the landing gear down, put the flaps down. We called it the assault position, where it was hanging just about straight down. The purpose was to create drag, slow the plane down. I pitched the nose over and was going down as steep as the airplane could go. It had a limit on it, one hundred and thirty-five knots in that configuration, and that's the speed I went down at. I don't know how fast it truly was. Anyway, in one two hundred and seventy-degree turn, a steep, steep spiral, I lost the nine thousand feet and was able to lay out about one thousand feet from the end of the runway, and to touch down in the first one hundred feet of runway, just corkscrew down, and land." Jackson had the C-123 diving at 4,000 feet per minute, eight times the normal rate of descent for a cargo plane, supposedly well beyond its capabilities.

"As I rolled down the runway, I briefed the crew that I was not gonna use reverse on the propellers to help me stop. I said I was only going to use the brakes because, if I reversed the propellers, it would shut down the two auxiliary jet engines. We had two engines installed on the C-123 over there to help us, because the performance out of those short Vietnamese airfields was really dangerous. We needed more power, so these two jets really were a lifesaver. I don't want to sit here long enough to start those engines again. It took more than a minute to start each one of them.

"As I hit the runway, they were shooting at us just like they had at that other airplane. I was able to stop directly opposite where those three guys were, almost as if I planned it. They started running for the airplane and, at about that time, the enemy fired a five-inch 122 mm rocket at the airplane. That rocket scooted down the runway and broke in half and stopped right in front of us. I mean right immediately in front of the airplane. And it didn't go off. I didn't see it coming, but Jesse Campbell called it out.

"I was looking in back to see when the three guys got on board. Then Grubbs called out, 'They're on board!' So I put the power on the recips [reciprocating engines, i.e., the propellers] and Campbell ran up the power on the jets, because they were operated by toggle switches. I had the throttles up and he was running up the jets as I taxied around that rocket and started rolling down the runway. And just as we left this place, where the plane was parked, the runway erupted with mortar fire. They had zeroed us in and blasted the spot just as we took off. Right behind me.

"Anyway, we got off the ground okay, taking fire as we went."

The combat control team consisted of Major John Gallagher, Technical Sergeant Mort Freedman, and Sergeant Jim Lundie. "The officer was not a regular member of the combat control team. I don't know why he was there. Freedman was the senior guy. I think Lundie was a staff sergeant. Combat control is all really tough guys: They go through SEAL training, and they go through the Green Beret training, and they go through parachute school at Fort Benning. Oh, they are tough.

"As I was flying back to Da Nang, one of them, Lundie, came up to the cockpit and said to me, I want to see you when you stand up. I said, 'Why is that?' He had his hands out like a basketball and he said, 'Because I bet you got balls that big around.'

"I said to him, 'No, they're about the size of a peanut right now, I'm so scared.'

"An artist named Keith Ferris, who painted the B-17 in the

Smithsonian Institution, *Little Willie Comes Home*, later painted a picture of what happened at Kham Duc and sent me a slide of it for a critique. He said he had to take some artistic liberties to get everything in. But anyway he named his portrait *The Miracle at Kham Duc.* He told me, he says, 'You know, really there were two miracles there.' He says, 'Number one, the fact you got in and got out, and number two, there was not one bullet hole in your airplane.'

"A unique thing about this was that this is the only mission, the only activity that resulted in an award of the Medal of Honor where a photograph was made of it while it was taking place. I have that photograph. It was shot from the air. I don't know who took it. But it shows my plane on the runway, the wrecked helicopter, and you can just make out two little dots showing two of the three guys as they were running for the plane.

"I mentioned this happened on Mother's Day? Well, I'm the only guy I know of that gets Mother's Day cards. I used to get them from guys that were in the Army that were in that battalion that went in to reinforce. Last year I got one from a newspaper editor down here in southwest Washington."

Jackson said he was surprised to learn he was to receive the Medal of Honor, which was presented to him at the White House by Lyndon B. Johnson on January 16, 1969, several days before he left office. "I don't know what he said. He was talking all the time."

Did Jackson feel that he deserved the Medal? "I never thought about it. I was sent there to participate, but they still wanted to know if there was anybody who would volunteer to pick these guys up. You know, people have asked me, 'Why did you do such a thing?' My answer is, 'It was the right thing to do. And I was the most logical person to do it.' By that time I was a military professional. My thoughts were: You should save your butt. The mission was to get the three guys, I got the three guys, and we got out of there okay, and I'm happy. That was the limit of my thinking.

"If you start thinking about medals, you're gonna lose your shirt. I've heard of several people who set out to win, not win, but be awarded the Medal of Honor and, to my knowledge, every one of them got killed."

Over the years since that day at Kham Duc, Jackson said, he had not heard from the major but he did hear from Freedman and Lundie occasionally. He had invited all three men to his Medal of Honor service but they were unable to attend, and they lost touch. Then, he recalled, "My son attended the Air Force Academy, graduating in 1976. While he was there Mort Freedman was a parachute instructor, and my son became acquainted with him. My wife and I went out there to visit our son, and he took us down to Mort's house. He lived on base and we met his family, spent a few hours together. His wife broke down in tears. I think she started crying before she said hello."

His son also was with him when he met Lundie again. In 1997, "we were invited to go to Charlotte, North Carolina, for the races and to help celebrate the fiftieth anniversary of the Air Force. I was one of four guys who were introduced to the crowd from a platform out in front of the grandstand. After a while I was told there was somebody who wanted to meet me. In a few minutes this guy comes through the door, and it's Jim Lundie. We had a very emotional reunion. My son was there, and he observed all this and told his mother. We were in a suite alongside the racetrack, and there must have been fifty people in there. Everybody broke down and was crying."

Joe Jackson finally managed to retire from the Air Force, on December 31, 1973, to take a job with the Boeing Company. "They wanted me to go to Iran and set up a training program for the Iranian Air Force. I went over with Rose for three years and got the program going. We came home in 1977. They offered me a job consulting back here in Seattle, so I took it and that's how we got out here. We bought this place in Kent in 1985, when I retired. Then I became a gardener's helper. My Rose can grow anything."

TWENTY-TWO

James Bond Stockdale

Hoa Lo Prison
Hanoi, North Vietnam
1965–1973

*"The test of character is not 'hanging in there' when the
light at the end of the tunnel is expected, but performance of duty
and persistence of example when the situation rules out
the possibility of the light ever coming."*

by Robert M. Bush, CMOHS photographer

Jim and Sybil at the Patriots Award
dinner of the Medal of Honor Society
in Pueblo, Colorado, on September
22, 2000. He is convinced that Sybil's
highly publicized actions on behalf of
him and the other prisoners of war in
Hanoi saved them from death at the
hands of the North Vietnamese.

A year after he was released from
captivity in Hanoi, James Bond
Stockdale, by now a rear admiral,
speaks into a reporter's microphone
with his wife, Sybil, at his side on
January 24, 1974. Stockdale had just
assumed command of the antisub-
marine warfare wing of the Pacific
Fleet in San Diego.

AP Wide World Photo

I MET WITH James Stockdale in the Coronado, California, home pur-
chased by his wife in 1963 while he was away on a naval tour of duty.
We had spoken before at length on the telephone and again, after we
met in Coronado. He was calm and matter-of-fact in recounting his
experiences as a prisoner of war for more than seven years. Brain-
washing, *Stockdale said, was a journalist's word. The principal means*
of persuasion in a prisoner-of-war camp was the inflicting of pain, and
his North Vietnamese captors were very good at this.

"I've had a crippled leg ever since I got shot down and then
mauled by a mob in the street in North Vietnam. I don't need canes.
I just limp along. I can't raise my left arm above the shoulder. I try
to swim a mile two or three times a week in my own homemade
stroke. It's a crippled man's crawl, I guess you'd call it. That's how
I stay healthy.

"I do quite a lot of writing. My wife, Sybil, and I coauthored a
big book about Vietnam, *In Love and War*. I did two other books
on Vietnam also. A couple years ago I went to all three service academies, attending colloquia on character development. I gave talks
and signed books at West Point, and then in November the Naval
Academy had a celebration in my honor. We went into this big
alumni hall and there were two fellow prisoners from the same
Naval Academy class I was in, nineteen forty-six. They got up and
said what it was like to be in prison with the Old Man.

"I was the only wing commander to survive an ejection, so I was
number one in managing in prison for seven and a half years. I got
handled roughly because they knew I was putting out instructions
on how to resist. I had altogether about four years in solitary. I was
tortured fifteen times. They had trained guards put you through it.
We called it 'the ropes.' No American ever beat the ropes. The main
thing was to shut off blood circulation in your upper body. They
didn't pull fingernails out, or any of those things. Instead they'd
weave manila ropes around your arms until you were smitten with
pain, your shoulders distended.

"In time they'd proceed to bend you double as they pulled the ropes up. You realized you wouldn't be able to tie your pajama strings for a month because of the nerve damage in your arms. There's the pain and the mental problem of knowing that, if you want to save the use of your arms, you have to give up at some point. And, finally, he puts his foot on the back of your head with your face down on the concrete so you have claustrophobia and you're puking. So somewhere you say, 'I submit.' Then you get your wits together and figure a way to trivialize whatever it is they're going to have you write, try to make it humorous or absurd in some way.

"I came to get a purchase on the thing because I never went downtown. They wanted to take me downtown in Hanoi and hold a press conference. There were a lot of threats. They'd say you'll regret it if you act up. I'd been through the ropes five times one week, a very bad one, and they said, 'Okay, you're going downtown tomorrow. Take a shower.' The guard took me across, put me in an old cell with a showerhead and handed me a razor. He flipped the peephole as I was cutting my head with the razor. I had blood running down my shoulders.

"He ran me naked back through this area where all the people, clerks, were working in the prison. These two officers were enraged because this had been set up by the commissar, the guy in charge. They were going to give me a hat and take me downtown that way. I had to come up with something, try to figure a way to disfigure myself. I looked at the toilet bucket. Then I took this big fifty-pound mahogany quiz stool and started beating my cheeks, thump thump thump, outside this ceremonial room. By the time they got there, my eyes were just about swollen shut and that was the end of the game for now because they couldn't get me ready, make me presentable. That was my salvation. Because to go downtown was humiliation."

Stockdale was born on December 23, 1923, in Abingdon, Illinois. He played junior varsity football at the Naval Academy in Annapolis with Tom Hudner (see chapter 7), and Jimmy Carter was a classmate. Following graduation in 1946, Stockdale said, "You had to go to sea in those days. I had nearly three years on destroyers, major cruisers out of Newport, Rhode Island. Unlike Hudner, I never got to Korea. I even wrote a letter once, saying I'd pay my way to San Diego if they'd send me to Korea, but they said no. I got my wings the summer of 1950, at the height of the Korean War, actually. We went to Pensacola for basic air training and then to Corpus Christi, Texas, for advanced. It took about two and half years altogether.

"From there I went to a squadron in Norfolk, went to school for a while, and then I had the good fortune to draw Test Pilot School, at Patuxent River, Maryland. That's a three-year tour. We had seventeen in my class, and the senior guy was John Glenn. We're really buddies. We'd known each other before. And he said he was going to leave his wife up in Ohio because he had to brush up on math. He'd got there early. He finished the math courses in college, but he said I had to help him with some of the problems, calculus and things like that. I said I could do that, but he had to keep me posted on the good things to do in flying. That didn't come to much, but I flew a couple of times with him. So we kind of traded off. We laugh about that now. We flew experimental aircraft.

"Glenn went into the astronaut program, and I went back and climbed the ladder. The dean wanted me to teach Airplane Performance and write a handbook. So I went right to work and wrote my own textbook, and I would give the first course in the morning. I copied the style of an old chemistry professor I knew at a little college I went to in Illinois before I went to Annapolis. The course was kind of competitive. I got so I really liked that course, and I went and got a blank pistol. And when a guy said a dumb thing, I would shoot at him.

"I fired at a doctor who was flight surgeon one time and he said, 'God, you see this necktie?' That wad from that blank went right through his necktie, burned a hole in it. And he said, 'I'm glad you didn't shoot me in the eye.' But he was good-natured about it.

"I flew every afternoon, and we probably had at Patuxent River forty-one different kinds of airplanes, and you got around to most of them. I specialized in the crown jewel of the time, which was the

Crusader. It was a carrier aircraft, the same plane I flew in Vietnam. The Vietnam War started August fourth, nineteen sixty-four. I made five carrier cruises. I led the strike that started the war. I had a skipper who had really taken a shine to me and he said, 'I'm gonna make sure you get to be air wing commander of the *Oriskany*.' There was one thing I hadn't racked up, and that was air wing commander.

"I 'owned' all the airplanes, and you got eighty or ninety airplanes on a big aircraft carrier like the *Oriskany*. We'd go to sea for two or three weeks at a time. I'd fly twice a day, Crusaders and the A-4, which was a fine little plane with a lot of different capabilities. All the flights I took, including the flight that started the war, I was flying a Crusader. I had eight Crusaders with me. We were bombing." He had flown almost two hundred missions.

"I was shot down on September ninth, nineteen sixty-five. I was in an A-4 when I was shot down, flying about one hundred and fifty feet, trying to get rid of bombs, throwing them into a rail yard. Then I heard this boom, boom, boom. And then I was on fire and I was coming down. It was a 57 mm gun on a truck. It hit all over my plane. I could see the bullets coming from it. I mean, I was pointing right at it. And I knew I was going to have to get out of there [bail out].

"I knew where I was going. I could see this little town, and I said, 'This is it.' I ejected two minutes after I knew the plane was fatally hit. I only had just a few minutes in the air, and I landed right on the main street of this town. Then I look up and here came the locals. They weren't in uniform. But this was the strong boys of the town defending its honor. So they just knocked me flat. It was the quarterback sack of the century. Next thing I know, they've got me down and there are about twenty-five or thirty of them hammering and twisting and bending and doing everything. After about five minutes of that, a guy with a pith helmet blew a whistle.

"He didn't speak a word of English. Nobody in that town did. He signaled for me to get up, but I couldn't because my leg was so badly damaged, badly broken right at the knee. It was later operated on three times in a Vietnamese hospital, just to get it under me. There was a myth out there, or maybe it wasn't, but the policy supposedly was they never released ex-prisoners if they had amputations."

"After my capture they hauled me in the back of a truck to prison. The guy in charge was pretty articulate, spoke good English, and when he saw my leg jutting out there, he knew they'd have to amputate, which meant they'd have to kill me—unless some miracle happened. They put me on a Ping-Pong table and finally a doctor came in the night and punched a needle into my knee and sucked out puss and blood and squirted it in a pan. He did it again the next night, and then they put me in the back of truck and took me blindfolded to a hospital on the waterfront. They took me around back and tapped on a window and put me through it on a stretcher, slipped me in the back door so the North Vietnamese wouldn't know they were treating an American prisoner."

Stockdale underwent an extremely scary operation. They had an operating table. "And here came the doctor, a little short guy. And he opened his case and took this . . . saw. Then it was a hammer. I said, 'No! No, no cut the leg!' It was still stuck way out there, and he was going to try to put it in. And when I woke up, the first thing I did was look to see where my leg was, and it was there, in a cast, and it was straight. He had said there was no sign of a knee, but he found a way to fuse the bones. I was on crutches for about a year." It would be four years before Stockdale could walk without pain.

In August of 1964, more than a year earlier, he had flown a mission over the Gulf of Tonkin when American destroyers supposedly were attacked by North Vietnamese PT boats, leading to the Tonkin Gulf Resolution, approved by the House and Senate August 7. The resolution opened the way for the United States entry into the Vietnam War. There was no actual declaration of war. But the problem was there had been no enemy attacks, and Stockdale was acutely aware of this. "We were about to launch a war under false pretenses," he said. That didn't bother him so much because he felt a war was coming anyway. But it seemed to him important that the grounds for entering the war be legitimate. And his great dread, upon capture, was that somehow the North Vietnamese would torture knowledge of the falsely reported attack from him and use it for propaganda purposes.

"They were just getting around to the rope treatment about that time. The first one to get the ropes was a guy named Lieutenant [junior grade] Rodney Knutson. He was right across the prison from me. I could look at him. We were always in solo cells, but we found a way to communicate. About the rope, he said, there's no way you can beat this thing. It's really bad. By the end of our stay in prison, we were pretty well sure that at least eight guys had died in the ropes. They were probably new guys and didn't know you had to be a good actor. You were either gonna die or you were gonna convince them you were at your end.

"Two people would come into your cell. One guy would carry in a big iron pole and as part of a dramatic exercise he would let it fall. Clang, clang. Then he'd get these lugs and you'd be attached to this pole. The lugs were on your ankles and they would plug into the bar. He would take the ropes and drape them around your shoulder so that eventually he would have the rope coming down under the pipe, and he would be pulling up on it, forcing you down and trying to get your arms bent back to where you could feel your breastbone on the verge of breaking. Then he would bend you over and stand on your back. He's barefooted, and he's pulling these ropes up to get you to disappear into a V shape. And when he got that done, he'd put his heel right behind your head and mash your face down into the cement.

"He wasn't going to break your nose necessarily. But you submit. I think a lot of our guys, the first time around, they . . . well, we'll never know what happened but we knew they disappeared. We didn't see any bodies around. Maybe they carried them out. I don't know. But by deduction, eight disappeared. And then we found out after we'd come home and the case had been reviewed, there had been eight more, guys we didn't even know were flying. Eventually it came to about sixteen guys.

"The purpose was to get you intimidated enough to recite anti-American propaganda on a stage in downtown Hanoi. So when you'd say, 'I submit,' they'd start unraveling the ropes and then you'd sit down with this English-speaking officer who would see what he could get out of you. And you'd play a game of wits with the interrogator. And that's when you really had to get tricky.

"I really got good at it. I never went downtown. I could beat myself up to where I couldn't open my eyes. They couldn't display me. They knew it was hopeless. I went through the ropes fifteen times. I was in solitary most of the time. I was careless one time and I was caught. I thought I was guarding myself, but I was careless and got caught. I was writing a message with a rat turd. You'd wet it with your tongue. We had paper towels or coarse toilet paper to write on.

"There are thirteen of us now, in the headquarters building of the Army. They only had one interrogator and he was kind of simple-minded. In this case, I was to put the message in a bottle under the sink of a privy right outside my cell. That's where I would dab my face with water and get ready for the day. I'd sent many notes, and we all knew how to handle them. I'd send jokes sometimes. If it was important—about an escape or something—you had to be pretty careful. But it was a kind of recreation, really."

Stockdale as senior man was in command of the prisoners, who looked to him for morale and direction. "My rules would not allow a prisoner to fake submission to the ropes," he said. "We all went through significant pain before we could submit." In addition to passing messages written with rat turds, he said, they worked out various methods of communication by tapping on walls, snapping towels, and other means.

"It was a homemade code. Nobody in America knew it. It was a five-by-five matrix. We had two smart guys, early shootdowns, and one of them had gone to a survival school and they had a code, this five-by-five matrix. It means *ABCD* off the top and then *AH*, whatever they are, going down the side, so two snaps would make one letter. Snap snap would be *A. B* would bomp bomp bomp and so on. You had to listen but we'd get so we had slang, quick, short . . . *R* . . . Just use the *R* . . . pause . . . *U* . . . and the *OK*. Yes or no. The Vietnamese knew what was going on, after a while."

One night in mid-1967, after he had been shackled and tied for
two weeks to an outdoor bath stall that was part of the wall surrounding a prison courtyard, Stockdale said, he was jerked out of
the stall by an angry guard and beaten severely in a dark courtyard.
The other three sides of the compound contained multitiered cells
holding American prisoners. The more than one hundred Americans in the cells could hear the blows and kicks being administered
to him. After he was dragged back to his stall, Stockdale said, an
American prisoner snapped out a message with a wet towel. "He
sent three letters," Stockdale said, "paused, then two more: *GBU*
(God Bless You), *JS* (Jim Stockdale).

"I was the people's choice for leadership. I was the highest-rank-
ing naval officer there. I didn't think the rest of them could handle
the torture as well as I did; and they were glad to have somebody
else take the heat. One day in September 1969, a little over four
years after I was shot down, the Vietnamese took me into a little
shed I had never seen before. They had caught me with that note
giving cell block captains fresh orders for strengthening resistance.
I named the hut Calcutta. The dark hole of Calcutta. There were
two kinds of leg irons, one set painful and the other just cumbersome. And the guard put on the cumbersome. Then he came back
and put on the painful ones. He was weeping.

"Next morning I was taken to the main torture room of Hoa
Lo prison, and the guards were weeping. I wondered what was
going on. Then I thought maybe Ho Chi Minh, the leader of
North Vietnam, was dying. He died the next day. That information was submitted to me by this little shit of an officer. He said,
'You must be very cautious about your actions because we are in
a crisis. Our president died this morning. Tomorrow is the day we
bring you down!'

"They put me in a straight chair with traveling irons on my legs
and had me sit up all night. I was depressed, and I thought of our
eight shipmates who had died by what I called torture overshoots.
It was largely my rules that had put them in torture. I thought
maybe I was part of the problem. I didn't know what to do. I knew

I had to do something. I decided I had to react because I had set myself up as leader of the American POW contingent in Hoa Lo Prison. I couldn't just sit there and be coerced. It doesn't seem like a very reasonable thing when I describe it this way, but I decided to cut my wrists, disfigure myself with the hope that might bring change."

The room had plate-glass windows and an exposed light switch. The guard came by every two hours. After the guard passed, Stockdale, in loose leg irons and loose arm straps, hobbled over to the light switch, turned it off, and then pulled the drapes back and cracked the glass with the heel of his hand. Taking the longest shards, he turned the light back on, waddled back to his chair, and began stabbing his wrists with shards of glass. As he recalled it, the blood was blue, then red, and as it began to run harder, he grew faint and sank to the floor.

"I finally passed out. The next thing I heard was this scream. And the guy came in and picked me up and laid me back. I was on my face in the blood. They picked me up and wiped off my face. A doctor came and stitched me up. The room was full of soldiers, and they were ashamed in some way. You'd think they would have been belligerent, but they were kind of like . . . this was a disgrace to the North Vietnamese army that they would do that even to an American. They scrubbed the floors with some kind of disinfectant and left.

"They brought in a bunk, put me to bed, and I went to sleep. They left a soldier at the foot of the bed with a rifle. He was silent all night. Next morning I heard the door open and it was the commissar, carrying two cups of tea. He was in charge of all the prison camps in North Vietnam. He was kind of a sensitive man. He gave instructions to the soldier to undo my leg irons and said, 'Would you like a cup of tea, Stawdale?' Then he said, 'You and I are fellow officers. We have sons that are grown. You know, what happened last night was a catastrophe.' He said, 'I may bear the consequences of this, and so might you.' He arranged for me to be taken out and put back in the shed. I sat out there about three months while my arms were healing.

"It was December when I got back into the regular prison system. I was there for two days, and I had enough savvy to know how
to communicate with people and I learned two things: One, that no
American had been in the ropes since I'd done that; and the second
thing was the commissar had been dismissed."

Stockdale did not get home for three more years, until the spring
of 1973. It was then that he discovered that his wife, Sybil, had led
a family group to Paris in the fall of 1969, about the time he was
cutting his wrists, to urge the North Vietnamese to grant better
treatment to American POWs. She became something of an international public figure and, Stockdale came to believe, she saved his
life because "the last thing they wanted on their hands was Sybil
Stockdale's dead husband."

"I had learned he was a prisoner eight months after he was shot
down," Sybil Stockdale said. "He was listed as missing initially.

"I was the initial board chairman of the National League of Families of Prisoners in Southeast Asia, started in October of 1966."
These were wives of POWs, primarily. "At our first meeting we
were briefed beforehand not to discuss, reveal that our husbands
were POWs because our government did not want to involve the
American people in the war emotionally. That was [Secretary of
Defense Robert S.] McNamara's grand plan to keep the people
emotionally separated. For example, they never called up the
reserves. They didn't do the things they normally would have." As
long as the war was kept on the fringe of public awareness, she said,
"then they would not have to fight it the way they should have."

But, as time went by and little was done, and the other wives
became outspoken activists on behalf of their husbands, Stockdale
was allowed to write her and she wrote back. They managed to set
up a code by which he was able to report on the number of prisoners and other information about what was occurring. "After
eight months, I got two letters from him in the mailbox," she said.
"The North Vietnamese let him do it because they were setting him
up for propaganda purposes. The last thing the North Vietnamese
wanted was for him to be dead."

Sybil Stockdale saw her husband for the first time in nearly eight years, on television, when he came off the plane at Clark Air Force Base in the Philippines the night of February 12, 1973. Stockdale was forty-nine years old. His hair had turned white, he weighed 140 pounds, and he could not raise his left arm. "It was pretty dramatic," she said. "I always thought it was significant that he was released on Lincoln's birthday. We had one telephone call and by chance one of our sons taped it, when Jim called from Clark. It was an overwhelming experience to talk to your husband when you haven't talked to him for seven and a half years. I said things about his leg being stiff because I'd seen him get off the airplane. I said, 'Is it your right leg?' He said, 'No, it's my left.' Then I said, 'And is it your right shoulder?' and he said, 'No, it's my left.' I mean, it was this rather inane conversation. And one point I said, 'I can't believe it, can you, Jim?' And he said, 'No, Syb, I can't.'

"I first saw him in person at Miramar Naval Air Station in San Diego on the fifteenth of February. There were twelve or fifteen of us wives in the waiting room as they came off the plane. You would think we were all excited, but you could have heard a pin drop in that room—it was just total silence. We were all very very frightened about what the future might hold. It was pretty scary. We didn't know what kind of shape they were in. We didn't know what was going to happen, how they would behave." The wives had been told the men would probably be sexually impotent, they might prove hostile toward loved ones.

"Jim and I were extremely fortunate. We had a very strong marriage. We had been married eighteen years before he was shot down. When he left, our sons were fourteen, ten, five, and three years old. When he came home, they were twenty-two, eighteen, thirteen, and eleven. I had bought our house in Coronado [San Diego] in 1963 when Jim was on a cruise, and it became our home during the time he was in prison. Each son went to him after he came home and said, 'You aren't going to sell our house, are you, Dad?' The two younger boys were not used to living with a father. They didn't know him as a father. But after a couple of years each went to him in his own way and said, 'You know, I know you now, and I'm glad you're my dad.'

"The first night the POWs stayed at Balboa Hospital, the naval hospital for San Diego, and that first night Jim kept saying to me in the hospital, 'You won't leave me, will you? You won't leave me, will you?' I said, 'No, of course, I won't.' He had a suite because he was senior personnel, so we had a bedroom and a small living room. We had supper served, they brought it to this living room table in the suite, and we sat down. Of course, this was the first time we had all sat down together for eight years, because he was gone awhile before he was captured.

"I said, 'Jim, do you want to say grace?' He bowed his head, and he started to kind of shake, and he said, 'Syb, I can't.' So I said, 'Well, let's just say our family grace.' And we did. We held hands and said, 'God is great, God is good, let us thank him for our food.' Then after dinner the boys went home and I stayed. I didn't know if I was supposed to or not, but I certainly wasn't going to leave him. There was a narrow high hospital bed, a single bed, in the bedroom and it didn't look too comfortable, so we just made a kind of love nest on the rugs with quilts and things on the floor. That was fine with him, of course. He was used to sleeping on a hard surface." And, she indicated, the briefings in regard to impotence turned out to be wrong, at least insofar as her husband was concerned.

"I think he came home the next afternoon, just to look around, and then went back to the hospital. I stayed with him all the time. Then I think he came home the next day. I remember the first night we were here. At one point, he jumped out of bed and said, 'I can't sleep on this soft stuff.' So he got down on the floor, and I lay down next to him."

When things settled down, Stockdale alarmed his wife by informing her he wanted command of an aircraft carrier, but luckily he got promoted to rear admiral, which placed him in a different bracket of command.

In April 1976, he was transferred to the Pentagon and later became president of the Naval War College in Newport, Rhode

Island. At the ceremony for her husband's retirement from the Navy, Sybil Stockdale was given the United States Navy's Distinguished Public Service Award from the Navy for her efforts on behalf of the POWs. At the time she was the only wife of an active-duty naval officer to receive the honor. Following retirement as a vice admiral, Stockdale served as president of the Citadel in Charleston, South Carolina, and went on from there to become a senior research fellow and lecturer at Stanford. In 1992, he ran for vice president with Ross Perot.

Sixteen years earlier, on March 4, 1976, James Bond Stockdale received the Medal of Honor from President Gerald Ford in the White House. Stockdale had once declared: "The test of character is not 'hanging in there' when the light at the end of the tunnel is expected, but performance of duty and persistence of example when the situation rules out the possibility of the light ever coming." Therefore, he said, he felt his Medal of Honor was "well earned," adding, "I figured I did a good job. I guess I won the battle. Because there was no light at the end of the tunnel."

TWENTY-THREE

Bob Kerrey

Navy SEAL
Vietnam
March 14, 1969

*"In general, all human beings have harsh experiences.
It's the great voyage of human life
to suffer losses."*

Bob Kerrey, fifty-nine, president of
New School University in New York
City, in his office during fall 2002.

Bob Kerrey in the U.S. Navy in 1967, two
years before he was sent to Vietnam.

364

AFTER SERVING two terms in the United States Senate from 1988 through 2000, Bob Kerrey became president of New School University in New York City in January 2001. I met with him twice in his office at the New School for this interview. Our conversation was unlike any other I had with a Medal of Honor recipient, focusing primarily on ethical matters, war, patriotism, guilt, and redemption. Kerrey has lived a life of extremes ranging from horror encountered in the depths of combat to great heights in personal, civic, and political achievement. He did not have to grant the interview for this book, yet he was willing to do so. I admired him for that.

In 1969, Lieutenant Bob Kerrey of Nebraska took part in two critical incidents of combat in Vietnam as a twenty-five-year-old Navy SEAL team commander. The first occurred on February 25, the second on March 14, a few weeks later. In the February incident, he led seven men into a hamlet called Thanh Phong in the eastern Mekong Delta on a mission to capture the village secretary, a senior Vietcong leader.

Accounts of exactly what took place vary, but it is undisputed that Kerrey and his men were responsible for killing at least thirteen unarmed women and children in the hamlet, assertedly to prevent them from alerting enemy soldiers who might cut off the SEALs' escape route. Kerrey today accepts full responsibility for the deaths.

In the second incident, on March 14, Kerrey landed in the dark with eight men off an island in Nha Trang Bay, north of Cam Ranh Bay, and climbed a relatively steep cliff without ropes. Dividing his men, he led four of them down toward the Vietcong camp. They began taking enemy fire and, as Kerrey dropped into firing position, an enemy grenade, possibly homemade, exploded at his feet, ripping away the heel and sole of his right foot and severely damaging his calf. He held himself and his men together, calling in fire support from his second element. They caught the Vietcong in a cross fire, capturing prisoners and securing and defending an extraction site, so that Kerrey could be taken off the island by a medevac helicopter. It was reported that the captured prisoners provided valuable information to the allied effort. None of his men was hurt.

Kerrey's foot, ankle, and calf were so badly damaged that the entire lower leg, from six inches below the knee, was amputated when he got to a veterans' hospital in Philadelphia some weeks afterward. He was there about ten months. Scar tissue at the site of the amputation and the hard wooden socket of the prosthesis caused him continuing pain and considerable difficulty for several years afterward. He had spent a little over fifty days in Vietnam.

The killings in Thanh Phong became public knowledge when they were reported by Gregory L. Vistica in a *New York Times Magazine* article, along with comments from Kerrey, in the spring of 2001. A year later, Kerrey described his life from the time he was born in 1942 to 1970 in a memoir entitled *When I Was a Young Man*, published by Harcourt. The intended subject of the book was his Uncle John, who had disappeared off the Philippines during World War II, but the book instead turned out to focus on Kerrey's Nebraska upbringing, military service, the atrocity in Thanh Phong, and the amputation—not only of his lower leg, but of the innocence that had characterized his life up until February 25, 1969.

He told of being wakened at 2 A.M. by "bloody nightmares" back at his parents' home in Lincoln, Nebraska, following his release from the hospital. "In the dream I saw the faces of the people I had killed and many more besides. They walked past me in an unending line. Their faces and bodies were mangled and rotting from their wounds. As they drew close every one of them asked the same question, 'Why? Why did you do this to me?' I could not answer and I could not move. . . . All I could do was listen to the cries and the identical, repeated question. Awake, I was too terrified to close my eyes again for fear I would fall asleep and the dream would return."

Describing his feelings earlier in the hospital in Cam Ranh in Vietnam shortly after being wounded, he said, "I didn't hate to be leaving the platoon, and I was happy to be going home even in the condition I was in. I had convinced myself that my injury was retribution, rather than a combat wound from heroic duty. My spirit was in darkness. Like Jonah, the whale had swallowed me; unlike him, I believed I would spend eternity in the belly of the beast."

But Kerrey was to find the strength he needed to come out of it, even to the point where he was willing to sit and talk with me about what had happened to him. Now, more than thirty years after that moment, asked if he had emerged from that notion, he answered, "I don't think I permanently have." But he added that he had gradually come to terms with his actions that February, and his nightmares disappeared about five years later. "You do it [come to terms] through people being kind to you, and learning to take love on board. You do it through prayer and you do it through evaluation of what it means to live. I have now had the opportunity to carry that memory into action, to do things with it. Because the truth is, if you believe it's retribution, and you carry that out, you bring it up on the table and say, 'Okay, it's retribution.' But what does that actually mean? It means I should suffer for the rest of my life, but I neither rationally nor with faith believe that's the right answer.

"When I was growing as a child, I had this picture of a pile of rocks 'up there.' Somebody in my Sunday school class must have told me that God keeps a big pile of rocks up there, and every time you do something bad, he throws another rock on the pile. It was a picture that I had. If you follow that out, it becomes self-destructive. It doesn't become something that's good; it becomes something that's bad. So, how do you live a good life?"

First, Kerrey acknowledged, he had to find a way to forgive himself, "although as I said, it's never permanent. This is not the only time I ever hurt somebody. That was a great line at the end of *Saving Private Ryan*, when Private Ryan turns to his wife and says, 'Tell me I've been a good man.' Because he had this survival guilt, and he wanted to be a good man because his life had been saved.

"The hardest thing to lose of all, and maybe the most important thing, is to lose your innocence and, now that I've lost my innocence, what do I do? Do I become a cynic, do I become embittered and hate the world? Do I hate myself and hate the world, or do I love myself and love the world? I think the right choice is to love yourself and love the world. It's something that evolves through thought and action, and it's never permanent. This [choice] is not a revelation. It's not a permanent acquisition of Zen enlightenment. It's a condition that can disappear in a second. You're constantly having to choose to figure it out."

Kerrey said that the only thing in life in which he truly believed was the power of human kindness. "The thing about kindness is, it's powerful to give it, and it's powerful to receive it." It was the expression of kindness to him from so many different areas, he said, that enabled him to turn his life around.

"Cynicism is poisonous to the person who feels it. It's actually less poisonous to the person who's on the receiving end. It's the person who becomes a cynic—and I would guess that's where I was in 1970—who says I doubt any human being has the capacity to do good. The thing that cynicism does is it closes you off to receipt, and you shrivel up in a hurry. Your heart becomes like a walnut. It's better to receive than to give. I don't think you can give unless you're able to receive and be able to say, 'You are a good person for giving that to me.' There are times when you're given something by somebody whom you don't like and you don't want to like. And it's inconvenient for you to like them.

"Skepticism is good. The skeptic merely comes and says I want you to prove it. I'm doubtful. But cynicism is poisonous. Also self-indulgence, which I think is the worst sin, in some ways the only sin worth worrying about. It's the sin that produces bad things. It's self-centeredness that causes you to say, 'I'm the most important thing on earth—*my* safety, *my* security, *my* health, *my* wealth—you become a slave to all these fears that you're going to lose something.

"Grief is part of life. In general, all human beings have harsh experiences. It's the great voyage of human life to suffer losses. You can't live life without losing your mom, losing your dad, losing your friends, losing your youth, losing something. The choice you have to make in the midst of that loss, especially afterwards, is, what do I do now? What do I make of this? Is it happening just to me? Is some terrible punishment being inflicted on me, or is it a symptom of living? If you conclude the latter, then it's possible to learn, to become excited about what's remaining.

"One of the things that's interesting about life is that paradoxes can be very cruel. And one of the cruelest of all is, if you're afraid of losing something, you give up your freedom. If you're afraid of dying, it's the worst of all because, when you're afraid of becoming old, afraid of death, you don't live. I talked with a guy the other day who was on one of these diets where you quit eating everything, and he thinks he's going to live to be one hundred and ten. So, okay, he's going to live to be one hundred and ten. What are you giving up? Well, my sexual drive is gone. My rear end has gotten so bony it's hard to sit down. I can't eat anything. I never get to drink any wine, I can't have any meat, I don't get any great sauces and, you know, I basically eat green things that aren't seasoned. What kind of living is that?

"Not a year goes by without my getting called by somebody who's got a friend or relative who suffered some loss or another. It's usually a loss of a body part. As a consequence of being a high-profile amputee, people will call me and say, I've got a friend who's going through something similar. Right at the top of the list of the things I advise is, Don't pretend it's not happening. Grieve it. It's okay to grieve it. Allowing yourself to grieve doesn't mean that you're weak, that you're not going to be in control of things, all those things you're afraid of when you're right at the edge of grief. You can pull back and deny yourself that experience, and if you do, it's exceptionally difficult to come out of it in the daylight."

Kerrey likes to say that human beings are a lot more than the worst things they've done in their lives. Still, he added, "I feel that I did it; it feels today like it was almost meant to be. You know, it's a constant check on my own arrogance, a constant check on my own tendency to believe I'm more superior than I am. It's a constant check on this idea that's embedded in all of us as human beings—that we're infallible. We can't make mistakes. And it's a constant reminder of something I need to teach my own children, which is that your integrity lies in your next decision.

"Second chances to correct mistakes are the stuff of movies, not life. I had spent my life preparing for easy decisions, and when the difficult one came I wasn't ready. Physical stamina and intellectual strength were not enough.

"It shouldn't cause you not to get in the ring, because sometimes you're going to make a terrible choice, you're going to hurt somebody, and you wish you hadn't and you go, oh my god, How do I get it back? But you don't get it back. You just have to try to make a better decision, a better choice the next time around, the next time you have a chance to choose. Part of it has come with the past couple of years, too. I don't know whether it's the time or what, but I've had lots of conversations with other veterans from the second battle of the Philippines all the way up through Vietnam, where people say, Let me tell you that you generally are better than the worst thing you ever did. So part of it is just coming to terms with that truth."

The right action that night in Thanh Phong would have been to simply leave the village, take his men and depart, even knowing they were at risk, Kerrey said. "That would have been the best course of action. I didn't have an interpreter that night, so we were flying blind. We didn't have medevac helicopters. We didn't have gunship support, we didn't have artillery. We had hard evidence, and we now know that there were armed people in that village that night. The *Washington Post* went back, as if it was Chillicothe, Ohio, and interviewed people in the community and found three guys who said, 'Yep, we were armed that night, but we were asleep.' This was an unlikely possibility but, yeah, I think if I was doing it again—if I had been more senior and with more experience and perhaps with a different crew of people—I think we'd have done it differently. That wasn't really my first action, but it was close to it."

He adds, "We were forty minutes from the boats. That's the problem in this kind of an operation. Sometimes your escape route can get cut off and the boat can't get to you. With no gunship, no medevac choppers, it was possible to get in pretty serious trouble. Let's say the guys that were interviewed afterwards were telling the truth and that all they had was a couple of carbines. Well, two carbines put two men on the ground dead, I got four that need to carry them out, and it doesn't take long before seven are gone. So the operating urgency is to make certain you're able to get out of there. With seven guys and two wounded, it's pretty tough to imagine you're going to be much of a fighting force going out.

"I say I would have done it differently, but again that's in the category of hindsight. I think it would have been better to do it differently. It also would have been better if I'd been twenty thousand feet up in an airplane and couldn't see what I was doing. That's another way of looking at it."

As for the island assault on March 14, "We saw it in daylight. We knew basically what we were going to have to do. We had some climbing. It's described as a cliff, but it wasn't. It was certainly a vertical ascent, but we didn't have to use ropes or anything. I guess we went in after midnight, probably hit the beach at one o'clock in the morning. We came in off the swift boats, lowered these inflatables, and paddled in, put the boats on the beach and then climbed the cliff. And my guys afterwards, they came right back down that and went back out on the boat.

"Our problem was once we got up there we couldn't find our second group of enemy. We found the first but couldn't find the second. I think they woke up. I think we got in there too late, and they were moving out. They could have heard us. We were above the first group of SEALs that dropped off to the first sleeping group. We were heading back down when we made contact—myself and three guys, all carrying M-16s. I could see movement, but I couldn't see much of anything. It was very reduced visibility that night.

"I was in a hurdler's position because I had just dropped down to go into a firing position, because I saw somebody in front of me. It was too rocky to flatten out." The grenade, "or whatever it was," came up against his foot. "Whatever it was, it was fairly dirty because they were pulling stuff out of it [his leg] for months afterward. The grenade could have been handmade, because there was wood in there and other crud. That's what these guys were doing on the island. They were making ordnance."

"The surgeons in Japan said they were going to try to save as much as they could, because the protocol then, especially with a dirty wound, was to leave it open and let it heal so you don't seal up infection inside. That was the thing they worried about more than anything else. They did a couple of debriding operations in Japan and basically left it all intact." They put a foot-shaped cast on that enabled the wound to drain.

The problem was there wasn't that much left to the foot. When Kerrey got to the hospital in Philadelphia, and doctors cracked the cast open, "I knew it was in bad shape when I saw the remaining two toes had darkened with gangrene. You could see the foot was gone, the ankle was gone and there was significant damage to both the tibia and the fibula and the calf was just spread out . . . like. Basically I just had the two bones going up to the toe so when it was casted it looked like a foot," except it wasn't.

Once the lower leg came off early in 1970, Kerrey encountered a whole new set of difficulties that dogged him for several years. "The last surgery I had was 1978; that was the key operation, this old guy with the VA, who removed this very wide serpentine scar that ran across my tibia. This all started in sixty-nine–seventy. The leg itself had lots of scarring that had to be revised and the pros-thesis was heavy, it was wood, it was hot, it was hard to hold the healing because there was a lot more pressure on it, heavier sus-pension that attached it to the body. What happens is the scar tis-sue breaks down. A little bit of bleeding is healthy, part of the healing process, but once you put the sock and leg back on, it's dark and it's almost anaerobic, so it's very difficult to heal. Then you take it off at night and you've got infection in there, and once you get infection you get swelling and once you get swelling it doesn't fit anymore so it becomes a vicious cycle that's very very hard to stop, very very difficult to keep you in business so you can walk. I didn't like crutches. It was a psychological thing."

The "old guy with the VA," whose memory Kerrey treasures,

repaired the stump of his leg so well that four years later, in 1981, in Lincoln, Nebraska, he was able to run a marathon, twenty-six-plus miles. "The only thing behind me was a cop car. I ran it very slow for the first half. Once I got about thirteen miles, I knew I could make it, then I stepped it up a bit. After I ran it, I didn't have any desire to do another one. All I wanted was to get through."

Kerrey accepted the Medal of Honor from President Richard M. Nixon on May 14, 1970. "I didn't feel like I was a hero when they presented me the medal. I didn't go to Vietnam for any other reason than it was my duty. I went over there, and I was there a relatively brief time. I didn't come back feeling that I was a hero. I don't today. I did my three years in the Navy, which was enormously beneficial to me. I loved the Navy, loved SEAL Team One, but I came back, hung up my uniform, put on my civilian clothes, and became a civilian again. And I received the Medal for people who got nothing. I don't say that with any false modesty. I say that genuinely and sincerely believing the action warranted no recognition beyond, you know, it's just another guy going over and doing what he's told to do."

Kerrey also felt that a lot of luck comes into play over the awarding of the Medal of Honor or any other major decoration. "I was the administrative officer for SEAL Team One, and wrote a few of them, so I know you have to have something beyond heroic action: It's got to be witnessed; it's got to be witnessed by somebody who can write; it's got to be written by somebody who likes you; and then it's got to make its way through the mysterious food chain. Sometimes it makes its way through; sometimes it doesn't."

Of the other Medal recipients, he said, "I think for the most part they're ordinary guys who did an extraordinary thing and most of us recognize that, you know, there but for the grace of God goes somebody else. And most of them feel that they received it for others and that their own actions were not especially heroic."

And even at the time he had deeply ambivalent feelings about both the war and President Nixon, who he felt had lied when he said in 1968 that he had a plan to end the war. "The war seemed like such a terrible mistake politically, morally, and militarily. I think

we were so caught up in the Cold War fears and the Cold War rhet-
oric that we made a terrible mistake in seeing communism as a
monolithic force. And it wasn't. And in Vietnam's case, missing that
there was a great nationalist movement, that their desire to get rid
of foreigners, their desire for an independent Vietnam was such a
powerful motivator that they had the capacity to sustain the effort
far greater than our anticipation. We ignored this great desire for
independence and freedom that was going on all over the world. So
there is no black-and-white judgment about Vietnam."

But while Kerrey's conviction about the war has not changed
over time, he added, "There is something good in there. That is to
say, if I'm sitting with a woman who says, 'My husband was killed
over there. Are you telling me he died in vain?' I say, 'No, I think
he went for a very good reason.' The idea of keeping a people free
is not a small idea. The willingness to put your life on the line for
somebody that has a different skin color, a different eye shape, different language, different rules and religions is about as good a
thing as a human being can do. So the war isn't completely bad. It's
not completely immoral by any stretch of the imagination."

Kerrey was able to find a second chance in his life, which he managed to revive as he went on to run his marathon, establish a chain
of restaurants and health clubs in Omaha, become governor of
Nebraska, and serve twelve years in the Senate, where he had the
opportunity to consider many of these questions about war and
peace from a very different perspective.

"The greatest moment that I had, the most moving moment that
I had when I was in politics, was the sixth of June 1994, the fiftieth
anniversary of D-Day, listening to old men talk about what it was
like to land on Omaha Beach. These were kids, men who were just
beyond being called boys, and selected because they were green.
No guarantee of veterans' benefits, no guarantee of anything. They
risked everything, not for the freedom of themselves but for the
freedom of Europeans. They liberated a continent, they liberated
human beings who are free today as a consequence, and it's not a
cliché. It's absolute hard truth, and they did it not only because they

were told to do it but because it was better than the alternative, remaining safely inside the continent of the United States and negotiating a peace with the National Socialist Party and allowing the Germans to retain control of France and the Lowland Countries and elsewhere. So it was a hard and bloody battle on behalf of somebody else."

The war in Vietnam, he noted, wasn't analogous to World War II. "The two big differences are that World War II united the country, and Vietnam divided it, although one thing I discovered in writing my own story was that Americans—like the parents of my dad and his brother, the Greatest Generation—were certainly divided about whether or not to go into World War II, and didn't enter it until we were attacked. The nineteen thirty-eight–thirty-nine debate over whether to enter the war was probably the most contentious debate in the twentieth century. But once America was attacked on the seventh of December nineteen forty-one, the nation was unified for the objective of unconditional surrender. That was all that was acceptable, by whatever means necessary, including bombing Hiroshima and Nagasaki.

"The second big difference was that, unlike World War II, Vietnam was a guerrilla war fought on terrain that was 'occupied' by the enemy. That's a huge difference and, although there were great set-piece battles with the Marines and some Army divisions and other units all the way down the Delta, there were significant numbers of people, ourselves included, that fought the war right in the villages and cities and, in our case, a nation that was being invaded by another nation from the north.

"It got very confusing because, at home, the people in the United States decided they didn't want to fight the war led by President Johnson anymore. The pivotal year was nineteen sixty-eight. I mean, can you imagine George Bush going on television today or, better still, Roosevelt going on TV in nineteen forty-four and saying, 'I'm not going to run for reelection. This war has drug on too long. I'm going to negotiate with the National Socialist Party and with Japan simultaneously and try to get a peace agreement'?"

Asked if, knowing what he knows now, would he still have gone to Vietnam, Kerrey replied, "I think it's an impossible question. I think the answer would likely be yes, but the trouble is I can't know then what I know today. I got into a discussion once with a guy named Bobby Howard, who was a Medal of Honor recipient. I think he did five or six full tours to Vietnam, and we were arguing in the early eighties about bringing back the draft, registration for the draft. I had participated in demonstrations against it at the post office before I ran for governor. I did so because I felt the draft was too selective and I felt there were too many ways to get out of it, and it was basically, Do you have the money, do you have the privilege, do you have the means to buy your way out?

"Anyway, I was part of this, and Bobby saw that in the newspaper, and he was arguing with me and he said, 'I think you're wrong.' And I said, 'Well, Bobby, my view is, if you really want to find out if your cause is just, you ought to draft men at thirty, not eighteen.' He said, 'You're wrong. It wouldn't work at thirty. From eighteen to twenty-five, if you give me control over when a man sleeps and how much sleep he's gonna get and when a man eats and how much food he's gonna eat, I can get him to do anything I want. Then, after twenty-five or twenty-six, they start to ask questions and they're no damn good anymore.' "

Consequently, Kerrey said, "The challenge isn't so much me answering whether I would go again. The challenge now is under what circumstances am I going to ask somebody else to go. Because that's my birthright and my responsibility as a citizen, trying to decide: Do I want men to go to Afghanistan, do I want them to go to Iraq?"

Kerrey left the Senate in 2000 to become president of New School University in New York City in January 2001. He had two children from a 1970s marriage that lasted four years and then remained single for twenty-one years—a period that included a relationship with the actress Debra Winger. He then married Sarah Paley of New York City, with whom, at fifty-eight, he had a son, Henry Emmet, born in September 2001.

Why did he leave the Senate? "Well, you just get one time to run around the track, and you know I'd been in the Senate for twelve years and I was governor of Nebraska for four. There are other ways to serve, and this is a terrific opportunity. I have a chance to build this university. I'm not out of politics. My view can still be heard, and I've got a wife and baby now, and a great new life. I try to contribute in other ways. I couldn't have written this book [his memoir, *When I Was a Young Man*] while I was still in the Senate. So there're other things a human being can do besides being in the Senate."

Rather than wearing him down, Kerrey said, twelve years on the political scene in Washington "restored my patriotism." He added, "I suspect most people wouldn't think you could become more patriotic serving in the Congress, but I did. I define my patriotism as loving my country, as a consequence of seeing the good that this nation can do. Being a witness to it in 1989, when the Berlin Wall came down. Being a witness to it when Kim Jung Il of South Korea stands before a joint session of Congress and thanks America for keeping his country free. Being a witness to it when I see the Congress appropriate money for people like myself who were injured in 1969 and didn't have any political power. Just seeing the goodness of the country." Patriotism, he added, "has got to be unselfish and fearless, as opposed to, I'm worried about my taxes going up, I'm worried about suffering a little bit here, I'm not willing to use cars that get better fuel economy because I don't want any inconvenience at all. There are, unfortunately, times when patriotism becomes a litmus test, when you're either with us or against us and in that environment, it's no longer patriotism. It's darker, it's not good. There're all kinds of patriotic acts that don't involve waving the flag, that don't involve 'learning how to be an American.' I think patriotism can be a really powerful and good force. But it can also be a force that excludes, that's us versus them, that we're superior and everyone else is inferior."

Kerrey went on to relate how, in 1989, the Supreme Court ruled that burning the American flag was free speech. "When I first heard that decision, I thought that was terrible, that we've got to change the Constitution so we can pass legislation protecting the American flag, so you can't burn an American flag. And then I read the opinion, and I found myself saying, 'You know, they're right.' I've got to be willing to allow somebody who's saying we're a free country the right to demonstrate by burning the American flag. I've got to allow that to be part of speech. As angry as I might be by it, as tormented as I may be when I see somebody burning the American flag, I've gotta tolerate that. It's part of allowing another man to have his free speech. It's the unpopular speech that needs to be protected. I mean, burning the flag is in no way dangerous. It in no way incites people to riot and hurt other people. It doesn't violate, in other words, the doctrine of relative rights. All it does, it says something that I don't like. So, over the next ten years, I led the effort against that flag-burning amendment, against my friends in the American Legion, the VFW, who wanted to make the change, because I believe that's part of being an American, saying we embrace that freedom."

Kerrey strongly believes that history should be taught differently than it is now, and that doing so would affect the actions of young people in times of crisis. "I don't think we prepare young people very well to make the tough decisions. "The thing we do with children—and it was done when I was raised—is we remove them from the adults when the adults are making decisions, and so we don't show them that adults make bad decisions. And that's what you have to figure out in life. You have to figure out how to make good decisions. You're going to make good ones, and you're going to make bad ones, and they get tough. The toughest ones are the ones that come very quick and that are connected to ethics."

"When I was, say, fifteen years old in 1958, I could have gone and talked to a veteran of World War I or World War II and said, 'Tell me your story.' They could have taught us with these men who had experience in war, instead of giving us a dry history book. I think that to understand history, to be excited by history, a human being needs something. You need the capacity to feel sympathy for the people you're reading about in the story.

"I read *War and Peace* from cover to cover last summer, and what I found remarkable was how Tolstoy was able to bring his own philosophy of life into the story without distracting you from it. His big theme was that history was not the sum of actions of 'great men.' It was the sum of actions of lots of individuals. It is true that your actions get hemmed in by contingency but there is no 'great master plan' up there. There is no inevitability. You choose. The moment comes. You choose."

CITATIONS

*Note: The citations do not always coincide
with the recollections of the recipients.*

BACON, NICKY DANIEL

Rank and organization: Staff Sergeant, U.S. Army, Company B, 4th Battalion, 21st Infantry, 11th Infantry Brigade, Americal Division.
Place and date: West of Tam Ky, Republic of Vietnam, 26 August 1968.
Entered service at: Phoenix, Arizona.
Born: 25 November 1945, Caraway, Arkansas.

Citation: For conspicuous gallantry and intrepidity in action at the risk of his life above and beyond the call of duty. S/Sgt. Bacon distinguished himself while serving as a squad leader with the 1st Platoon, Company B, during an operation west of Tam Ky. When Company B came under fire from an enemy bunker line to the front, S/Sgt. Bacon quickly organized his men and led them forward in an assault. He advanced on a hostile bunker and destroyed it with grenades. As he did so, several fellow soldiers including the 1st Platoon leader, were struck by machine-gun fire and fell wounded in an exposed position forward of the rest of the platoon. S/Sgt. Bacon immediately assumed command of the platoon and assaulted the hostile gun position, finally killing the enemy gun crew in a single-handed effort. When the 3d Platoon moved to S/Sgt. Bacon's location, its leader was also wounded. Without hesitation S/Sgt. Bacon took charge of the additional platoon and continued the fight. In the ensuing action he personally killed four more enemy soldiers and silenced an antitank weapon. Under his leadership and example, the members of both platoons accepted his authority without question. Continuing to ignore the intense hostile fire, he climbed up on the exposed deck of a tank and directed fire into the enemy position while several wounded men were evacuated. As a result of S/Sgt. Bacon's extraordinary efforts, his company was able to move forward, eliminate the enemy positions, and rescue the men trapped to the front. S/Sgt. Bacon's bravery at the risk of his life was in the highest traditions of the military service and reflects great credit upon himself, his unit, and the U.S. Army.

BAKER, VERNON J.

Rank and organization: First Lieutenant, Infantry, U.S. Army Company
    C, 370th Regiment, 92nd Infantry Division.
Place and date: Near Viareggio, Italy, 5–6 April 1945.
Birth: 17 December 1919, Cheyenne, Wyoming.

Citation: For conspicuous gallantry and intrepidity at the risk of his own life above and beyond the call of duty in action on 5 and 6 April 1945, Lieutenant Baker advanced at the head of his weapons platoon, along with Company C's three rifle platoons, toward their objective: Castle Aghinolfi—a German mountain strong point on the high ground just east of the coastal highway and about two miles from the 370th Infantry Regiment's line of departure. Moving more rapidly than the rest of the company, Lieutenant Baker and about twenty-five men reached the south side of a draw some 250 yards from the castle within two hours. In reconnoitering for a suitable position to set up a machine gun, Lieutenant Baker observed two cylindrical objects pointing out of a slit in a mount at the edge of a hill. Crawling up and under the opening, he stuck his M-1 into the slit and emptied the clip, killing the observation post's two occupants. Moving to another position in the same area, Lieutenant Baker stumbled upon a well-camouflaged machine-gun nest, the crew of which was eating breakfast. He shot and killed both enemy soldiers. After Captain John F. Runyon, Company C's Commander, joined the group, a German soldier appeared from the draw and hurled a grenade which failed to explode. Lieutenant Baker shot the enemy soldier twice as he tried to flee. Lieutenant Baker then went down into the draw alone. There he blasted open the concealed entrance to another dugout with a hand grenade, shot one German soldier who emerged after the explosion, tossed another grenade into the dugout, and entered firing his submachine gun, killing two more Germans. As Lieutenant Baker climbed back out of the draw, enemy machine-gun and mortar fire began to inflict heavy casualties among the group of twenty-five soldiers, killing or wounding about two-thirds of them. When expected reinforcements did not arrive, Capt. Runyon ordered a withdrawal in two groups. Lieutenant Baker volunteered to cover the withdrawal of the first group, which consisted of mostly walking wounded, and to remain to assist in the evacuation of the more seriously wounded. During the second group's withdrawal, Lieutenant Baker, supported by covering fire from one of his platoon members, destroyed two machine-gun positions (previously bypassed during the assault) with hand grenades. In all, Lieutenant Baker accounted for nine dead enemy soldiers, elimination of three machine-gun positions, an observation post, and a dugout. On the following night, Lieutenant Baker voluntarily led a battalion advance through enemy mine fields and heavy fire toward the division objective. Lieutenant Baker's fighting spirit and daring leadership were an inspiration to his men and exemplify the highest traditions of the military service.

BARBER, WILLIAM E.

Rank and organization: Captain, U.S. Marine Corps, commanding officer, Company F, 2d Battalion, 7th Marines, 1st Marine Division (Rein.).

Place and date: Chosin Reservoir area, Korea, 28 November to 2 December 1950.

Entered service at: West Liberty, Kentucky.

Born: 30 November 1919, Dehart, Kentucky.

Citation: For conspicuous gallantry and intrepidity at the risk of his life above and beyond the call of duty as commanding officer of Company F in action against enemy aggressor forces. Assigned to defend a three-mile mountain pass along the division's main supply line and commanding the only route of approach in the march from Yudam-ni to Hagaru-ri, Capt. Barber took position with his battle-weary troops and, before nightfall, had dug in and set up a defense along the frozen, snow-covered hillside. When a force of estimated regimental strength savagely attacked during the night, inflicting heavy casualties and finally surrounding his position following a bitterly fought seven-hour conflict, Capt. Barber, after repulsing the enemy, gave assurance that he could hold if supplied by airdrops and requested permission to stand fast when orders were received by radio to fight his way back to a relieving force after two reinforcing units had been driven back under fierce resistance in their attempts to reach the isolated troops. Aware that leaving the position would sever contact with the eight thousand marines trapped at Yudam-ni and jeopardize their chances of joining the three thousand more awaiting their arrival in Hagaru-ri for the continued drive to the sea, he chose to risk loss of his command rather than sacrifice more men if the enemy seized control and forced a renewed battle to regain the position, or abandon his many wounded who were unable to walk. Although severely wounded in the leg in the early morning of the 29th, Capt. Barber continued to maintain personal control, often moving up and down the lines on a stretcher to direct the defense and consistently encouraging and inspiring his men to supreme efforts despite the staggering opposition. Waging desperate battle throughout five days and six nights of repeated onslaughts launched by the fanatical aggressors, he and his heroic command accounted for approximately one thousand enemy dead in this epic stand in bitter subzero weather, and when the company was relieved only 82 of his original 220 men were able to walk away from the position so valiantly defended against insuperable odds. His profound faith and courage, great personal valor, and unwavering fortitude were decisive factors in the successful withdrawal of the division from the death trap in the Chosin Reservoir sector and reflect the highest credit upon Capt. Barber, his intrepid officers and men, and the U.S. Naval Service.

BARNUM, HARVEY C., JR.

Rank and organization: Captain (then Lt.), U.S. Marine Corps, Company H, 2d Battalion, 9th Marines, 3d Marine Division (Rein).

Place and date: Ky Phu in Quang Tin Province, Republic of Vietnam, 18 December 1965.

Entered service at: Cheshire, Connecticut.

Born: 21 July 1940, Cheshire, Connecticut.

Citation: For conspicuous gallantry and intrepidity at the risk of his life above and beyond the call of duty. When the company was suddenly pinned down by a hail of extremely accurate enemy fire and was quickly separated from the remainder of the battalion by over five hundred meters of open and fire-swept ground, and casualties mounted rapidly. Lt. Barnum quickly made a hazardous reconnaissance of the area, seeking targets for his artillery. Finding the rifle company commander mortally wounded and the radio operator killed, he, with complete disregard for his safety, gave aid to the dying commander, then removed the radio from the dead operator and strapped it to himself. He immediately assumed command of the rifle company, and moving at once into the midst of the heavy fire, rallying and giving encouragement to all units, reorganized them to replace the loss of key personnel and led their attack on enemy positions from which deadly fire continued to come. His sound and swift decisions and his obvious calm served to stabilize the badly decimated units, and his gallant example as he stood exposed repeatedly to point out targets served as an inspiration to all. Provided with two armed helicopters, he moved fearlessly through enemy fire to control the air attack against the firmly entrenched enemy while skillfully directing one platoon in a successful counterattack on the key enemy positions. Having thus cleared a small area, he requested and directed the landing of two transport helicopters for the evacuation of the dead and wounded. He then assisted in the mopping up and final seizure of the battalion's objective. His gallant initiative and heroic conduct reflected great credit upon himself and were in keeping with the highest traditions of the Marine Corps and the U.S. Naval Service.

BUCHA, PAUL W.

Rank and organization: Captain, U.S. Army, Company D, 3d Battalion, 187th Infantry, 3d Brigade, 101st Airborne Division.

Place and date: Near Phuoc Vinh, Binh Duong Province, Republic of Vietnam, 16–19 March 1968.

Entered service at: U.S. Military Academy, West Point, New York.

Born: 1 August 1943, Washington, D.C.

Citation: For conspicuous gallantry and intrepidity in action at the risk of his life above and beyond the call of duty. Capt. Bucha distinguished himself while serving as commanding officer, Company D, on a reconnaissance-in-force mission against enemy forces near Phuoc Vinh. The company was inserted by helicopter into the suspected enemy stronghold to locate and destroy the enemy. During this period Capt. Bucha aggressively and courageously led his men in the destruction of enemy fortifications and base areas and eliminated scattered resistance impeding the advance of the company. On 18 March while advancing to contact, the lead elements of the company became engaged by the heavy automatic-weapon, heavy machine-gun, rocket-propelled-grenade, claymore-mine, and small-arms fire of an estimated battalion-size force. Capt. Bucha, with complete disregard for his safety, moved to the threatened area to direct the defense and ordered reinforcements to the aid of the lead element. Seeing that his men were pinned down by heavy machine-gun fire from a concealed bunker located some forty meters to the front of the positions, Capt. Bucha crawled through the hail of fire to single-handedly destroy the bunker with grenades. During this heroic action Capt. Bucha received a painful shrapnel wound. Returning to the perimeter, he observed that his unit could not hold its positions and repel the human-wave assaults launched by the determined enemy. Capt. Bucha ordered the withdrawal of the unit elements and covered the withdrawal to positions of a company perimeter from which he could direct fire upon the charging enemy. When one friendly element retrieving casualties was ambushed and cut off from the perimeter, Capt. Bucha ordered them to feign death and he directed artillery fire around them. During the night Capt. Bucha moved throughout the position, distributing ammunition, providing encouragement, and ensuring the integrity of the defense. He directed artillery, helicopter-gunship, and Air Force–gunship fire on the enemy strong points and attacking forces, marking the positions with smoke grenades. Using flashlights in complete view of enemy snipers, he directed the medical evacuation of three air-ambulance loads of seriously wounded personnel and the helicopter supply of his company. At daybreak Capt. Bucha led a rescue party to recover the dead and wounded members of the ambushed element. During the period of intensive combat, Capt. Bucha, by his extraordinary heroism, inspirational example, outstanding leadership, and professional competence, led his company in the decimation of a superior enemy force which left 156 dead on the battlefield. His bravery and gallantry at the risk of his life are in the highest traditions of the military service. Capt. Bucha has reflected great credit on himself, his unit, and the U.S. Army.

CAFFERATA, HECTOR A., JR.

Rank and organization: Private, U.S. Marine Corps Reserve, Company F,
    2d Battalion, 7th Marines, 1st Marine Division (Rein.).
Place and date: Korea, 28 November 1950.
Entered service at: Dover, New Jersey.
Born: 4 November 1929, New York, New York.

Citation: For conspicuous gallantry and intrepidity at the risk of his life
above and beyond the call of duty while serving as a rifleman with Company F, in action against enemy aggressor forces. When all the other members of his fire team became casualties, creating a gap in the lines, during
the initial phase of a vicious attack launched by a fanatical enemy of regimental strength against his company's hill position, Pvt. Cafferata waged
a lone battle with grenades and rifle fire as the attack gained momentum
and the enemy threatened penetration through the gap and endangered
the integrity of the entire defensive perimeter. Making a target of himself
under the devastating fire from automatic weapons, rifles, grenades, and
mortars, he maneuvered up and down the line and delivered accurate and
effective fire against the onrushing force, killing fifteen, wounding many
more, and forcing the others to withdraw so that reinforcements could
move up and consolidate the position. Again fighting desperately against
a renewed onslaught later that same morning when a hostile grenade
landed in a shallow entrenchment occupied by wounded marines, Pvt.
Cafferata rushed into the gully under heavy fire, seized the deadly missile
in his right hand and hurled it free of his comrades before it detonated,
severing part of one finger and seriously wounding him in the right hand
and arm. Courageously ignoring the intense pain, he staunchly fought on
until he was struck by a sniper's bullet and forced to submit to evacuation
for medical treatment. Stouthearted and indomitable, Pvt. Cafferata, by
his fortitude, great personal valor, and dauntless perseverance in the face
of almost certain death, saved the lives of several of his fellow marines and
contributed essentially to the success achieved by his company in main-
taining its defensive position against tremendous odds. His extraordinary
heroism throughout was in keeping with the highest traditions of the U.S.
Naval Service.

DOSS, DESMOND T.

Rank and organization: Private First Class, U.S. Army, Medical Detachment, 307th Infantry, 77th Infantry Division.
Place and date: Near Urasoe Mura, Okinawa, Ryukyu Islands, 29 April–21 May 1945.
Entered service at: Lynchburg, Virginia.
Birth: Lynchburg, Virginia. 1 November 1945.

Citation: He was a company aid man when the 1st Battalion assaulted a jagged escarpment 400 feet high. As our troops gained the summit, a heavy concentration of artillery, mortar, and machine-gun fire crashed into them, inflicting approximately seventy-five casualties and driving the others back. Pfc. Doss refused to seek cover and remained in the fire-swept area with the many stricken, carrying them one by one to the edge of the escarpment and there lowering them on a rope-supported litter down the face of a cliff to friendly hands. On 2 May, he exposed himself to heavy rifle and mortar fire in rescuing a wounded man two hundred yards forward of the lines on the same escarpment; and two days later he treated four men who had been cut down while assaulting a strongly defended cave, advancing through a shower of grenades to within eight yards of enemy forces in a cave's mouth, where he dressed his comrades' wounds before making four separate trips under fire to evacuate them to safety. On 5 May, he unhesitatingly braved enemy shelling and small-arms fire to assist an artillery officer. He applied bandages, moved his patient to a spot that offered protection from small-arms fire, and, while artillery and mortar shells fell close by, painstakingly administered plasma. Later that day, when an American was severely wounded by fire from a cave, Pfc. Doss crawled to him where he had fallen twenty-five feet from the enemy position, rendered aid, and carried him one hundred yards to safety while continually exposed to enemy fire. On 21 May, in a night attack on high ground near Shuri, he remained in exposed territory while the rest of his company took cover, fearlessly risking the chance that he would be mistaken for an infiltrating Japanese and giving aid to the injured until he was himself seriously wounded in the legs by the explosion of a grenade. Rather than call another aid man from cover, he cared for his own injuries and waited five hours before litter bearers reached him and started carrying him to cover. The trio was caught in an enemy tank attack and Pfc. Doss, seeing a more critically wounded man nearby, crawled off the litter and directed the bearers to give their first attention to the other man. Awaiting the litter bearers' return, he was again struck, this time suffering a compound fracture of one arm. With magnificent fortitude he bound a rifle stock to his shattered arm as a splint and then crawled three hundred yards over rough terrain to the aid station. Through his outstanding bravery and unflinching determination in the face of desperately dangerous conditions Pfc. Doss saved the lives of many soldiers. His name became a symbol throughout the 77th Infantry Division for outstanding gallantry far above and beyond the call of duty.

EHLERS, WALTER D.

Rank and organization: Staff Sergeant, U.S. Army, 18th Infantry, 1st Infantry Division.
Place and date: Near Goville, France, 9–10 June 1944.
Entered service at: Manhattan, Kansas.
Birth: Junction City, Kansas. 19 December 1944.

Citation: For conspicuous gallantry and intrepidity at the risk of his life above and beyond the call of duty on 9–10 June 1944, near Goville, France. S/Sgt. Ehlers, always acting as the spearhead of the attack, repeatedly led his men against heavily defended enemy strong points exposing himself to deadly hostile fire whenever the situation required heroic and courageous leadership. Without waiting for an order, S/Sgt. Ehlers far ahead of his men, led his squad against a strongly defended enemy strong point, personally killing four of an enemy patrol who attacked him en route. Then crawling forward under withering machine-gun fire, he pounced upon the gun crew and put it out of action. Turning his attention to two mortars protected by the cross fire of two machine guns, S/Sgt. Ehlers led his men through this hail of bullets to kill or put to flight the enemy of the mortar section, killing three men himself. After mopping up the mortar positions, he again advanced on a machine gun, his progress effectively covered by his squad. When he was almost on top of the gun he leaped to his feet and, although greatly outnumbered, he knocked out the position single-handedly. The next day, having advanced deep into enemy territory, the platoon of which S/Sgt. Ehlers was a member, finding itself in an untenable position as the enemy brought increased mortar, machine-gun, and small-arms fire to bear on it, was ordered to withdraw. S/Sgt. Ehlers, after his squad had covered the withdrawal of the remainder of the platoon, stood up and by continuous fire at the semicircle of enemy placements, diverted the bulk of the heavy hostile fire on himself, thus permitting the members of his own squad to withdraw. At this point, though wounded himself, he carried his wounded automatic rifleman to safety and then returned fearlessly over the shell-swept field to retrieve the automatic rifle which he was unable to carry previously. After having his wound treated, he refused to be evacuated, and returned to lead his squad. The intrepid leadership, indomitable courage, and fearless aggressiveness displayed by S/Sgt. Ehlers in the face of overwhelming enemy forces serve as an inspiration to others.

FINN, JOHN WILLIAM

Rank and organization: Lieutenant, U.S. Navy.
Place and date: Naval Air Station, Kaneohe Bay, Territory of Hawaii, 7 December 1941.
Entered service at: California.
Born: 23 July 1909, Los Angeles, California.

Citation: For extraordinary heroism, distinguished service, and devotion above and beyond the call of duty. During the first attack by Japanese airplanes on the Naval Air Station, Kaneohe Bay, on 7 December 1941, Lt. Finn promptly secured and manned a .50 caliber machine gun mounted on an instruction stand in a completely exposed section of the parking ramp, which was under heavy enemy machine-gun strafing fire. Although painfully wounded many times, he continued to man this gun and to return the enemy's fire vigorously and with telling effect throughout the enemy strafing and bombing attacks and with complete disregard for his own personal safety. It was only by specific orders that he was persuaded to leave his post to seek medical attention. Following first-aid treatment, although obviously suffering much pain and moving with great difficulty, he returned to the squadron area and actively supervised the rearming of returning planes. His extraordinary heroism and conduct in this action were in keeping with the highest traditions of the U.S. Naval Service.

HERNANDEZ, RODOLFO P.

Rank and organization: Corporal, U.S. Army, Company G, 187th Airborne Regimental Combat Team.
Place and date: Near Wontong-ni, Korea, 31 May 1951.
Entered service at: Fowler, California.
Born: 14 April 1931, Colton, California.

Citation: Cpl. Hernandez, a member of Company G, distinguished himself by conspicuous gallantry and intrepidity above and beyond the call of duty in action against the enemy. His platoon, in defensive positions on Hill 420, came under ruthless attack by a numerically superior and fanatical hostile force, accompanied by heavy artillery, mortar, and machinegun fire which inflicted numerous casualties on the platoon. His comrades were forced to withdraw due to lack of ammunition but Cpl. Hernandez, although wounded in an exchange of grenades, continued to deliver deadly fire into the ranks of the onrushing assailants until a ruptured cartridge rendered his rifle inoperative. Immediately leaving his position, Cpl. Hernandez rushed the enemy armed only with rifle and bayonet. Fearlessly engaging the foe, he killed six of the enemy before falling unconscious from grenade, bayonet, and bullet wounds; but his heroic action momentarily halted the enemy advance and enabled his unit to counterattack and retake the lost ground. The indomitable fighting spirit, outstanding courage, and tenacious devotion to duty clearly demonstrated by Cpl. Hernandez reflect the highest credit upon himself, the infantry, and the U.S. Army.

HUDNER, THOMAS JEROME, JR.

Rank and organization: Lieutenant (jg) U.S. Navy, pilot in Fighter Squadron 32, attached to USS *Leyte*.
Place and date: Chosin Reservoir area of Korea, 4 December 1950.
Entered service at: Fall River, Massachusetts.
Born: 31 August 1924, Fall River, Massachusetts.

Citation: For conspicuous gallantry and intrepidity at the risk of his life above and beyond the call of duty as a pilot in Fighter Squadron 32, while attempting to rescue a squadron mate whose plane, struck by antiaircraft fire and trailing smoke, was forced down behind enemy lines. Quickly maneuvering to circle the downed pilot and protect him from enemy troops infesting the area, Lt. (jg) Hudner risked his life to save the injured flier who was trapped alive in the burning wreckage. Fully aware of the extreme danger in landing on the rough mountainous terrain and the scant hope of escape or survival in subzero temperature, he put his plane down skillfully in a deliberate wheels-up landing in the presence of enemy troops. With his bare hands, he packed the fuselage with snow to keep the flames away from the pilot and struggled to pull him free. Unsuccessful in this, he returned to his crashed aircraft and radioed other airborne planes, requesting that a helicopter be dispatched with an ax and fire extinguisher. He then remained on the spot despite the continuing danger from enemy action and, with the assistance of the rescue pilot, renewed a desperate but unavailing battle against time, cold, and flames. Lt. (jg) Hudner's exceptionally valiant action and selfless devotion to a shipmate sustain and enhance the highest traditions of the U.S. Naval Service.

INOUYE, DANIEL K.

Rank and organization: Second Lieutenant, U.S. Army, Company E, 442nd RCT.

Place and date: Near San Terenzo, Italy, 21 April 1945.

Entered service at: Honolulu, Hawaii.

Born: 7 February 1924, Honolulu, Hawaii.

Citation: For conspicuous gallantry and intrepidity at the risk of his life above and beyond the call of duty. First Lieutenant Daniel K. Inouye distinguished himself by extraordinary heroism in action on 21 April 1945, in the vicinity of San Terenzo, Italy. While attacking a defended ridge guarding an important road junction, First Lieutenant Inouye (then Second Lieutenant) skillfully directed his platoon through a hail of automatic-weapons and small-arms fire in a swift enveloping movement that resulted in the capture of an artillery and mortar post and brought his men to within forty yards of the hostile force. Emplaced in bunkers and rock formations, the enemy halted the advance with cross fire from three machine guns. With complete disregard for personal safety, First Lieutenant Inouye boldly crawled up the treacherous slope to within five yards of the nearest machine gun and hurled two grenades, destroying the emplacement. Before the enemy could retaliate, he stood up and neutralized a second machine-gun nest with a burst from his submachine gun. Although wounded by a sniper's bullet, he continued to engage other hostile positions at close range until an exploding grenade shattered his right arm. Despite the intense pain, he refused evacuation and continued to direct his platoon until enemy resistance was broken and his men were again deployed in defensive positions. In the attack, twenty-five enemy soldiers were killed and eight others captured. By his gallant, aggressive tactics and by his indomitable leadership, he enabled his platoon to advance through formidable resistance, and was instrumental in the capture of the ridge. First Lieutenant Inouye's extraordinary heroism and devotion to duty are in keeping with the highest traditions of military service and reflect great credit on him, his unit, and the U.S. Army.

JACKSON, JOE M.

Rank and organization: Lieutenant Colonel, U.S. Air Force, 311th Air Commando Squadron, Da Nang, Republic of Vietnam.
Place and date: Kham Duc, Republic of Vietnam, 12 May 1968.
Entered service at: Newman, Georgia.
Born: 14 March 1923, Newman, Georgia.

Citation: For conspicuous gallantry and intrepidity in action at the risk of his life above and beyond the call of duty. Lt. Col. Jackson distinguished himself as pilot of a C-123 aircraft. Lt. Col. Jackson volunteered to attempt the rescue of a three-man USAF Combat Control Team from the Special Forces camp at Kham Duc. Hostile forces had overrun the forward outpost and established gun positions on the airstrip. They were raking the camp with small arms, mortars, light and heavy automatic weapons, and recoilless rifle fire. The camp was engulfed in flames and ammunition dumps were continuously exploding and littering the runway with debris. In addition, eight aircraft had been destroyed by the intense enemy fire and one aircraft remained on the runway reducing its usable length to only 2,200 feet. To further complicate the landing, the weather was deteriorating rapidly, thereby permitting only one air strike prior to his landing. Although fully aware of the extreme danger and likely failure of such an attempt. Lt. Col. Jackson elected to land his aircraft and attempt a rescue. Displaying superb airmanship and extraordinary heroism, he landed his aircraft near the point where the combat control team was reported to be hiding. While on the ground, his aircraft was the target of intense hostile fire. A rocket landed in front of the nose of the aircraft but failed to explode. Once the combat control team was aboard, Lt. Col. Jackson succeeded in getting airborne despite the hostile fire directed across the runway in front of his aircraft. Lt. Col. Jackson's profound concern for his fellowmen, at the risk of his life above and beyond the call of duty, is in keeping with the highest traditions of the U.S. Air Force and reflects great credit upon himself and the Armed Forces of his country.

JACOBS, JACK H.

Rank and organization: Captain, U.S. Army, U.S. Army Element, U.S. Military Assistance Command, Republic of Vietnam.

Place and date: Kien Phong Province, Republic of Vietnam, 9 March 1968.

Entered service at: Trenton, New Jersey.

Born: 2 August 1945, Brooklyn, New York.

Citation: For conspicuous gallantry and intrepidity in action at the risk of his life above and beyond the call of duty. Capt. Jacobs (then 1st Lt.) distinguished himself while serving as assistant battalion advisor, 2d Battalion, 16th Infantry, 9th Infantry Division, Army of the Republic of Vietnam. The 2d Battalion was advancing to contact when it came under intense heavy machine-gun and mortar fire from a Vietcong battalion positioned in well-fortified bunkers. As the 2d Battalion deployed into attack formation its advance was halted by devastating fire. Capt. Jacobs, with the command element of the lead company, called for and directed air strikes on the enemy positions to facilitate a renewed attack. Due to the intensity of the enemy fire and heavy casualties to the command group, including the company commander, the attack stopped and the friendly troops became disorganized. Although wounded by mortar fragments, Capt. Jacobs assumed command of the allied company, ordered a withdrawal from the exposed position, and established a defensive perimeter. Despite profuse bleeding from head wounds which impaired his vision, Capt. Jacobs, with complete disregard for his safety, returned under intense fire to evacuate a seriously wounded advisor to the safety of a wooded area where he administered lifesaving first aid. He then returned through heavy automatic-weapons fire to evacuate the wounded company commander. Capt. Jacobs made repeated trips across the fire-swept open rice paddies evacuating wounded and their weapons. On three separate occasions, Capt. Jacobs contacted and drove off Vietcong squads who were searching for allied wounded and weapons, single-handedly killing three and wounding several others. His gallant actions and extraordinary heroism saved the lives of one U.S. advisor and thirteen allied soldiers. Through his effort the allied company was restored to an effective fighting unit and prevented defeat of the friendly forces by a strong and determined enemy. Capt. Jacobs, by his gallantry and bravery in action in the highest traditions of the military service, has reflected great credit upon himself, his unit, and the U.S. Army.

KELLEY, THOMAS G.

Rank and organization: Lieutenant Commander, U.S. Navy, River Assault Division 152.

Place and date: Ong Muong Canal, Kien Hoa province, Republic of Vietnam, 15 June 1969.

Entered service at: Boston, Massachusetts.

Born: 13 May 1939, Boston, Massachusetts.

Citation: For conspicuous gallantry and intrepidity at the risk of his life above and beyond the call of duty in the afternoon while serving as commander of River Assault Division 152 during combat operations against enemy aggressor forces. Lt. Comdr. (then Lt.) Kelley was in charge of a column of eight river assault craft which were extracting one company of U.S. Army infantry troops on the east bank of the Ong Muong Canal in Kien Hoa province, when one of the armored troop carriers reported a mechanical failure of a loading ramp. At approximately the same time, Vietcong forces opened fire from the opposite bank of the canal. After issuing orders for the crippled troop carrier to raise its ramp manually, and for the remaining boats to form a protective cordon around the disabled craft, Lt. Comdr. Kelley, realizing the extreme danger to his column and its inability to clear the ambush site until the crippled unit was repaired, boldly maneuvered the monitor in which he was embarked to the exposed side of the protective cordon fire, and ordered the monitor to commence firing. Suddenly, an enemy rocket scored a direct hit on the coxswain's flat, the shell penetrating the thick armor plate, and the explosion spraying shrapnel in all directions. Sustaining serious head wounds from the blast, which hurled him to the deck of the monitor, Lt. Cmdr. Kelley disregarded his severe injuries and attempted to continue directing the other boats. Although unable to move from the deck or to speak clearly into the radio, he succeeded in relaying his commands through one of his men until the enemy attack was silenced and the boats were able to move to an area of safety. Lt. Comdr. Kelley's brilliant leadership, bold initiative, and resolute determination served to inspire his men and provide the impetus needed to carry out the mission after he was medically evacuated by helicopter. His extraordinary courage under fire and his selfless devotion to duty sustain and enhance the finest traditions of the U.S. Naval Service.

KERREY, JOSEPH ROBERT

Rank and organization: Lieutenant, Junior Grade, U.S. Naval Reserve, Sea, Air, and Land Team (SEAL).

Place and date: Near Nha Trang Bay, Republic of Vietnam, 14 March 1969.

Entered service at: Omaha, Nebraska.

Born: 27 August 1943, Lincoln, Nebraska.

Citation: For conspicuous gallantry and intrepidity at the risk of his life above and beyond the call of duty while serving as a SEAL team leader during action against enemy aggressor (Vietcong) forces. Acting in response to reliable intelligence, Lt. (jg) Kerrey led his SEAL team on a mission to capture important members of the enemy's area political cadre known to be located on an island in the bay of Nha Trang. In order to surprise the enemy, he and his team scaled a 350-foot sheer cliff to place themselves above the ledge on which the enemy was located. Splitting his team in two elements and coordinating both, Lt.(jg) Kerrey led his men in the treacherous downward descent to the enemy's camp. Just as they neared the end of their descent, intense enemy fire was directed at them, and Lt. (jg) Kerrey received massive injuries from a grenade which exploded at his feet and threw him backward onto the jagged rocks. Although bleeding profusely and suffering great pain, he displayed outstanding courage and presence of mind in immediately directing his element's fire into the heart of the enemy camp. Utilizing his radioman, Lt.

(jg) Kerrey called in the second element's fire support which caught the confused Vietcong in a devastating cross fire. After successfully suppressing the enemy's fire, and although immobilized by his multiple wounds, he continued to maintain calm, superlative control as he ordered his team to secure and defend an extraction site. Lt. (jg) Kerrey resolutely directed his men, despite his near unconscious state, until he was eventually evacuated by helicopter. The havoc brought to the enemy by this very successful mission cannot be overestimated. The enemy soldiers who were captured provided critical intelligence to the allied effort. Lt. (jg) Kerrey's courageous and inspiring leadership, valiant fighting spirit, and tenacious devotion to duty in the face of almost overwhelming opposition sustain and enhance the finest traditions of the U.S. Naval Service.

MILLETT, LEWIS L.

Rank and organization: Captain, U.S. Army, Company E, 27th Infantry Regiment.

Place and date: Vicinity of Soam-Ni, Korea, 7 February 1951.

Entered service at: Mechanic Falls, Maine.

Born: 15 December 1920, Mechanic Falls, Maine.

Citation: Capt. Millett, Company E, distinguished himself by conspicuous gallantry and intrepidity above and beyond the call of duty in action. While personally leading his company in an attack against a strongly held position he noted that the 1st Platoon was pinned down by small-arms, automatic, and antitank fire. Capt. Millett ordered the 3d Platoon forward, placed himself at the head of the two platoons, and, with fixed bayonet, led the assault up the fire-swept hill. In the fierce charge Capt. Millett bayoneted two enemy soldiers and boldly continued on, throwing grenades, clubbing and bayoneting the enemy, while urging his men forward by shouting encouragement. Despite vicious opposing fire, the whirlwind hand-to-hand assault carried to the crest of the hill. His dauntless leadership and personal courage so inspired his men that they stormed into the hostile position and used their bayonets with such lethal effect that the enemy fled in wild disorder. During this fierce onslaught Capt. Millett was wounded by grenade fragments but refused evacuation until the objective was taken and firmly secured. The superb leadership, conspicuous courage, and consummate devotion to duty demonstrated by

Capt. Millett were directly responsible for the successful accomplishment of a hazardous mission and reflect the highest credit on himself and the heroic traditions of the military service.

MIYAMURA, HIROSHI H.

Rank and organization: Corporal, U.S. Army, Company H, 7th Infantry Regiment, 3rd Infantry Division.
Place and date: Near Taejon-ni, Korea, 24 and 25 April 1951.
Entered service at: Gallup, New Mexico.
Birth: Gallup, New Mexico.

Citation: Cpl. Miyamura, a member of Company H, distinguished himself by conspicuous gallantry and intrepidity above and beyond the call of duty in action against the enemy. On the night of 24 April, Company H was occupying a defensive position when the enemy fanatically attacked, threatening to overrun the position. Cpl. Miyamura, a machine-gun squad leader, aware of the imminent danger to his men, unhesitatingly jumped from his shelter wielding his bayonet in close hand-to-hand combat killing approximately ten of the enemy. Returning to his position, he administered first aid to the wounded and directed their evacuation. As another savage assault hit the line, he manned his machine gun and delivered withering fire until his ammunition was expended. He ordered the squad to withdraw while he stayed behind to render the gun inoperative. He then bayoneted his way through infiltrated enemy soldiers to a second gun emplacement and assisted in its operation. When the intensity of the attack necessitated the withdrawal of the company, Cpl. Miyamura ordered his men to fall back while he remained to cover their movement. He killed more than fifty of the enemy before his ammunition was depleted and he was severely wounded. He maintained his magnificent stand despite his painful wounds, continuing to repel the attack until his position was overrun. When last seen he was fighting ferociously against an overwhelming number of enemy soldiers. Cpl. Miyamura's indomitable heroism and consummate devotion to duty reflect the utmost glory on himself and uphold the illustrious traditions of the military service.

MURPHY, RAYMOND G.

Rank and organization: Second Lieutenant, U.S. Marine Corps Reserve,
    Company A, 1st Battalion, 5th Marines, 1st Marine Division (Rein.).
Place and date: Korea, 3 February 1953.
Entered service at: Pueblo, Colorado.
Born: 14 January 1930, Pueblo, Colorado.

Citation: For conspicuous gallantry and intrepidity at the risk of his life above and beyond the call of duty as a platoon commander of Company A, in action against enemy aggressor forces. Although painfully wounded by fragments from an enemy mortar shell while leading his evacuation platoon in support of assault units attacking a cleverly concealed and well-entrenched hostile force occupying commanding ground, 2d Lt. Murphy steadfastly refused medical aid and continued to lead his men up a hill through a withering barrage of hostile mortar and small-arms fire, skillfully maneuvering his force from one position to the next and shouting words of encouragement. Undeterred by the increasing intense enemy fire, he immediately located casualties as they fell and made several trips up and down the fire-swept hill to direct evacuation teams to the wounded, personally carrying many of the stricken marines to safety. When reinforcements were needed by the assaulting elements, 2d Lt. Murphy employed part of his unit as support and, during the ensuing battle, personally killed two of the enemy with his pistol. With all the wounded evacuated and the assaulting units beginning to disengage, he remained behind with a carbine to cover the movement of friendly forces off the hill and, though suffering intense pain from his previous wounds, seized an automatic rifle to provide more firepower when the enemy reappeared in the trenches. After reaching the base of the hill, he organized a search party and again ascended the slope for a final check on missing marines, locating and carrying the bodies of a machine-gun crew back down the hill. Wounded a second time while conducting the entire force to the line of departure through a continuing barrage of enemy small-arms, artillery, and mortar fire, he again refused medical assistance until assured that every one of his men, including all casualties, had preceded him to the main lines. His resolute and inspiring leadership, exceptional fortitude, and great personal valor reflect the highest credit upon 2d Lt. Murphy and enhance the finest traditions of the U.S. Naval Service.

PAIGE, MITCHELL

Rank and organization: Platoon Sergeant, U.S. Marine Corps.
Place and date: Solomon Islands, 26 October 1942.
Entered service at: Pennsylvania.
Born: 31 August 1918, Charleroi, Pennsylvania.

Citation: For extraordinary heroism and conspicuous gallantry in action above and beyond the call of duty while serving with a company of marines in combat against enemy Japanese forces in the Solomon Islands on 26 October 1942. When the enemy broke through the line Sergeant Paige, commanding a machine-gun section with fearless determination, continued to direct the fire of his gunners until all his men were either killed or wounded. Alone, against the deadly hail of Japanese shells, and wounded himself, he manned his gun and when it was destroyed, took over another, moving from gun to gun, never ceasing his withering fire against the advancing hordes until reinforcements finally arrived. Then, forming a new line, he dauntlessly and aggressively led a bayonet charge, driving the enemy back and preventing a breakthrough in our lines. His great personal valor and unyielding devotion to duty were in keeping with the highest traditions of the U.S. Naval Service.

RASCON, ALFRED V.

Rank and organization: Specialist Fourth Class, U.S. Army, Reconnaissance Platoon, Headquarters Company, 1st Battalion (Airborne), 503rd Infantry, 173d Airborne Brigade (Separate).
Place and date: Republic of Vietnam, 16 March 1966.
Born: 1945, Chihuahua, Mexico.

Citation: Specialist Four Alfred Rascon distinguished himself by a series of extraordinarily courageous acts on 16 March 1966, while assigned as a medic to the Reconnaissance Platoon, Headquarters Company, 1st Battalion (Airborne), 503rd Infantry, 173d Airborne Brigade (Separate). While moving to reinforce its sister battalion under intense enemy attack, the Reconnaissance Platoon came under heavy fire from a numerically superior enemy force. The intense enemy fire from crew-served weapons and grenades severely wounded several point squad soldiers. Specialist Rascon, ignoring directions to stay behind shelter until covering fire could be provided, made his way forward. He repeatedly tried to reach the severely wounded point machine gunner lying on an open enemy trail, but was driven back each time by the withering fire. Disregarding his personal safety, he jumped to his feet, ignoring flying bullets and exploding grenades to reach his comrade. To protect him from further wounds, he intentionally placed his body between the soldier and enemy machine guns, sustaining numerous shrapnel injuries and a serious wound to the hip. Disregarding his serious wounds he dragged the larger soldier from the fire-raked trail. Hearing the second machine gunner yell that he was running out of ammunition, Specialist Rascon, under heavy enemy fire, crawled back to the wounded machine gunner, stripping him of his bandoliers of ammunition, giving them to the machine gunner who continued his suppressive fire. Specialist Rascon, fearing the abandoned machine gun, its ammunition, and spare barrel could fall into enemy hands, made his way to retrieve them. On the way, he was wounded in the face and torso by grenade fragments, but disregarded these wounds to recover the abandoned machine gun, ammunition, and spare barrel items, enabling another soldier to provide added suppressive fire to the pinned-down squad. In searching for the wounded, he saw the point grenadier being wounded by small-arms fire and grenades being thrown at him. Disregarding his own life and his numerous wounds, Specialist Rascon reached and covered him with his body, absorbing the blasts from the exploding grenades, and saving the soldier's life, but sustaining additional wounds to his body. While making his way to the wounded point squad leader, grenades were hurled at the sergeant. Again, in complete disregard for his own life, he reached and covered the sergeant with his body, absorbing the full force of the grenade explosions. Once more Specialist Rascon was critically wounded by shrapnel, but disregarded his own wounds to continue to search for and aid the wounded. Severely wounded, he remained on the battlefield, inspiring his fellow soldiers to continue the battle. After the enemy broke contact, he disregarded aid for himself, instead treating the wounded and directing their evacuation. Only after being placed on the evacuation helicopter did he allow aid to be given to him. Specialist Rascon's extraordinary valor in the face of deadly enemy fire, his heroism in rescuing the wounded, and his gallantry by repeatedly risking his own life for his fellow soldiers are in keeping with the highest traditions of military service and reflect great credit upon himself, his unit, and the U.S. Army.

SASSER, CLARENCE EUGENE

Rank and organization: Specialist Fifth Class (then Pfc.), U.S. Army, Headquarters Company, 3d Battalion, 60th Infantry, 9th Infantry Division.

Place and date: Ding Tuong Province, Republic of Vietnam, 10 January 1968.

Entered service at: Houston, Texas.

Born: 12 September 1947, Chenango, Texas.

Citation: For conspicuous gallantry and intrepidity in action at the risk of his life above and beyond the call of duty. Sp5c. Sasser distinguished himself while assigned to Headquarters and Headquarters Company, 3d Battalion. He was serving as a medical aidman with Company A, 3d Battalion, on a reconnaissance in force operation. His company was making an air assault when suddenly it was taken under heavy small-arms, recoilless-rifle, machine-gun, and rocket fire from well-fortified enemy positions on three sides of the landing zone. During the first few minutes, over thirty casualties were sustained. Without hesitation, Sp5c. Sasser ran across an open rice paddy through a hail of fire to assist the wounded. After helping one man to safety, he was painfully wounded in the left shoulder by fragments of an exploding rocket. Refusing medical attention, he ran through a barrage of rocket and automatic-weapons fire to aid casualties of the initial attack and, after giving them urgently needed treatment, continued to search for other wounded. Despite two additional wounds immobilizing his legs, he dragged himself through the mud toward another soldier one hundred meters away. Although in agonizing pain and faint from loss of blood, Sp5c. Sasser reached the man, treated him, and proceeded on to encourage another group of soldiers to crawl two hundred meters to relative safety. There he attended their wounds for five hours until they were evacuated. Sp5c. Sasser's extraordinary heroism is in keeping with the highest traditions of the military service and reflects great credit upon himself, his unit, and the U.S. Army.

STOCKDALE, JAMES B.

Rank and organization: Rear Admiral (then Captain), U.S. Navy.

Place and date: Hoa Lo prison, Hanoi, North Vietnam, 4 September 1969.

Entered service at: Abingdon, Illinois.

Born: 23 December 1923, Abingdon, Illinois.

Citation: For conspicuous gallantry and intrepidity at the risk of his life above and beyond the call of duty while senior naval officer in the prisoner-of-war camps of North Vietnam. Recognized by his captors as the leader in the prisoners'-of-war resistance to interrogation and in their refusal to participate in propaganda exploitation, Rear Adm. Stockdale was singled out for interrogation and attendant torture after he was detected in a covert communications attempt. Sensing the start of another purge, and aware that his earlier efforts at self-disfiguration to dissuade his captors from exploiting him for propaganda purposes had resulted in cruel and agonizing punishment, Rear Adm. Stockdale resolved to make himself a symbol of resistance regardless of personal sacrifice. He deliberately inflicted a near-mortal wound to his person in order to convince his captors of his willingness to give up his life rather than capitulate. He was subsequently discovered and revived by the North Vietnamese who, convinced of his indomitable spirit, abated in their employment of excessive harassment and torture toward all the prisoners of war. By his heroic action, at great peril to himself, he earned the everlasting gratitude of his fellow prisoners and of his country. Rear Adm. Stockdale's valiant leadership and extraordinary courage in a hostile environment sustain and enhance the finest traditions of the U.S. Naval Service.

VARGAS, JAY R.

Rank and organization: Major (then Capt.), U.S. Marine Corps, Company G, 2d Battalion, 4th Marines, 9th Marine Amphibious Brigade.

Place and date: Dai Do, Republic of Vietnam, 30 April to 2 May 1968.

Entered service at: Winslow, Arizona.

Born: 29 July 1940, Winslow, Arizona.

Citation: For conspicuous gallantry and intrepidity at the risk of his life above and beyond the call of duty while serving as commanding officer, Company G, in action against enemy forces from 30 April to 2 May 1968.

On 1 May 1968, though suffering from wounds he had incurred while relocating his unit under heavy enemy fire the preceding day, Maj. Vargas combined Company G with two other companies and led his men in an attack on the fortified village of Dai Do. Exercising expert leadership, he maneuvered his Marines across seven hundred meters of open rice paddy while under intense enemy mortar, rocket, and artillery fire and obtained a foothold in two hedgerows on the enemy perimeter, only to have elements of his company become pinned down by the intense enemy fire. Leading his reserve platoon to the aid of his beleaguered men, Maj. Vargas inspired his men to renew their relentless advance, while destroying a number of enemy bunkers. Again wounded by grenade fragments, he refused aid as he moved about the hazardous area reorganizing his unit into a strong defense perimeter at the edge of the village. Shortly after the objective was secured, the enemy commenced a series of counterattacks and probes which lasted throughout the night but were unsuccessful as the gallant defenders of Company G stood firm in their hard-won enclave. Reinforced the following morning, the marines launched a renewed assault through Dai Do on the village of Dinh To, to which the enemy retaliated with a massive counterattack resulting in hand-to-hand combat. Maj. Vargas remained in the open, encouraging and rendering assistance to his Marines when he was hit for the third time in the three-day battle. Observing his battalion commander sustain a serious wound, he disregarded his excruciating pain, crossed the fire-swept area, and carried his commander to a covered position, then resumed supervising and encouraging his men while simultaneously assisting in organizing the battalion's perimeter defense. His gallant actions uphold the highest traditions of the Marine Corps and the U.S. Naval Service.

ABOUT THE AUTHOR

A veteran newspaper and magazine writer-editor, Larry Smith has written on military matters for *Parade* magazine. He also is the author of a novel, *The Original*. He is a 1962 graduate of the University of Michigan. Smith, who grew up on a Michigan farm, worked on newspapers in Wyoming; California; Westchester County, New York; and with the *New York Daily News* and the *New York Times* prior to serving nineteen years as the managing editor of *Parade*. He is a former president of the Overseas Press Club of America and a member of the Explorers Club. While he never attempted basic training in a military unit, he has run four New York City marathons and climbed Mount McKinley in Alaska and Mont Blanc in France. He and his wife, Dorothea, have three children.